The
Time
of
AIDS

Gilbert Herdt ■ Shirley Lindenbaum

The
Time
of
AIDS

Social Analysis, Theory, and Method

SAGE PUBLICATIONS
International Educational and Professional Publisher
Newbury Park   London   New Delhi

Permission to use a panel from *Night Fears* (1985-86, a glaze terra cotta 19½" × 58½" × 6½") for the cover art has been granted by the artist, Steve Rogers.

For information address:

 SAGE Publications, Inc.
2455 Teller Road
Newbury Park, California 91320

SAGE Publications Ltd.
6 Bonhill Street
London EC2A 4PU
United Kingdom

SAGE Publications India Pvt. Ltd.
M-32 Market
Greater Kailash I
New Delhi 110 048 India

Printed in the United States of America

Library of Congress Cataloging-in-Publication Data

Main entry under title:

The Time of AIDS: social analysis, theory, and method / edited by
    Gilbert Herdt, Shirley Lindenbaum.
        p.   cm.
    Based on a conference held June 25 to July 1, 1990 in Estes Park,
Colorado, sponsored by the Wenner-Gren Foundation for
Anthropological Research, Inc.
    Includes bibliographical references.
    ISBN 0-8039-4372-5 (cl).—ISBN 0-8039-4373-3 (pb)
    1. AIDS (Disease)—Social aspects—Congresses. I. Herdt, Gilbert
H., 1949-   . II. Lindenbaum, Shirley. III. Wenner-Gren Foundation
for Anthropological Research.
    [DNLM: 1. Acquired Immunodeficiency Syndrome—congresses.
2. Social Sciences—congresses.   WD 308 T583 1990]
RC607.A26T56   1992
362.1'969792—dc20
DNLM/DLC   91-42005

92 93 94 95 10 9 8 7 6 5 4 3 2

Sage Production Editor: Astrid Virding

Contents

Preface   vii
  Gilbert Herdt

PART I. Social History and Representation

1. Introduction   3
      Gilbert Herdt

2. Epidemics and Researchers: AIDS and the   27
    Practice of Social Studies
      John H. Gagnon

3. AIDS: History and Contemporary History   41
      Virginia Berridge

4. AIDS, HIV, and the Cultural Construction of Reality   65
      Paula A. Treichler

PART II. Method and Theory in Western Society

5. Sex, Lies, and Ethnography   101
      Paul R. Abramson

6. Mapping Terra Incognita: Sex Research for AIDS   124
    Prevention—An Urgent Agenda for the 1990s
      Ralph Bolton

7. Anthropological Witnessing for African Americans: 159
    Power, Responsibility, and Choice in the
    Age of AIDS
      Ernest Quimby

8. The Implications of Constructionist Theory for   185
    Social Research on the AIDS Epidemic Among Gay Men
        Martin P. Levine

9. "IV Drug Users" and "Sex Partners":   199
    The Limits of Epidemiological Categories and the
    Ethnography of Risk
        Stephanie Kane and *Theresa Mason*

PART III. Cross-Cultural Studies

10. Sexual Diversity, Cultural Analysis, and   225
    AIDS Education in Brazil
        Richard G. Parker

11. Use of Ethnosexual Data on Men of Mexican   243
    Origin for HIV/AIDS Prevention Programs
        Joseph M. Carrier and *J. Raúl Magaña*

12. Women at Risk: Case Studies from Zaire   259
        Brooke Grundfest Schoepf

13. New Disorder, Old Dilemmas: 287
    AIDS and Anthropology in Haiti
        Paul Farmer

14. Knowledge and Action in the Shadow of AIDS   319
        Shirley Lindenbaum

    Acknowledgments   335
    About the Authors   337

Preface

The plan of this book arose from a simple idea several years ago: The AIDS epidemic is forcing us to change the way we think about and study culture. Especially in anthropology and the social sciences, we have begun to see how AIDS has challenged approaches and assumptions about culture and society, cultural groups and practices, especially those that involve stigma and the forbidden—what is illegal, immoral, or illicit in the representation of persons and groups. My own interest especially concerns the understanding of how AIDS has changed culture theory and ethnography.

These interests had grown out of issues that stemmed in part from discussions of the American Anthropological Association Task Force on AIDS, of which I was a member, along with Shirley Lindenbaum and several other contributors to this book. However, our concerns were also with how the AIDS epidemic is changing the approach to social analysis in other fields as well, including history, sociology, and psychology. What we were looking for was an interdisciplinary social science forum, reflective of the roles of culture, epidemiology, and medicine in the epidemic, that would enable us to look more closely at these issues.

The opportunity to convene such a conference came from a generous invitation of the Wenner-Gren Foundation for Anthropological Research, Inc., which has for decades funded much fine research and most of the significant conferences in the field. Our conference was held June 25 to July 1, 1990, in Estes Park, Colorado. In all, nine anthropologists, three sociologists, one linguist, one psychologist, and two social historians took part.

The meetings were cochaired by myself and Shirley Lindenbaum. Papers were prepared in advance and then discussed, with significant commentaries, throughout the meeting. Significant periods of the conference were devoted to theory, method, and practice, with the final session concerned with critical theory and the ethics of social science work on AIDS and applied social research. A review and discussion of these proceedings, by Richard K. Herrell, conference monitor, has recently been published in the article "HIV/AIDS Research and the Social Sciences" in *Current Anthropology* (Volume 32, number 2, pp. 199-203, 1991). The results of the conference are presented herein as chapters in this book.

The conference was extraordinary in many ways, intellectually and personally, for one would have to search a long time to find a group of brighter, livelier, and more cordial scholars. Moreover, the AIDS epidemic is for many of these contributors a personal, as well as professional, matter, having affected the lives of their lovers, friends, and family members.

The conference had this personal side for me too. In 1987, I gave one of the first plenary addresses on anthropology and AIDS at the annual meetings of the American Anthropological Association in Chicago. At the time, I didn't know very much about AIDS. But I was in the midst of conducting a study of the culture and development of gay and lesbian youth in Chicago, which was completed in 1989, and I was learning very quickly about the centrality and meanings of AIDS in the lives of these young people. My personal experience of the epidemic was limited. Since that time, however, some friends and colleagues have been diagnosed with AIDS, and several have died from the disease. And, in May 1990, my youngest brother, Tom Herdt, a lawyer and poet aged 32, was taken by AIDS. The lives of my family will never be the same because of this, and AIDS has for me now a much more personal meaning than before. I mention this because science is never apart from human values and the problems of everyday life. The AIDS epidemic has both angered and inspired many persons in their work on the social dimension of the disease, on the education and prevention of it, and on the delivery of services to those who are suffering from it. For those of us in whom the anthropological imagination is a way of life, these emotions can be the source of new insights and a deeper understanding of how culture must adapt to AIDS. And this is helpful to us, this transformation of our grief and anguish into a common discourse, the better to live with and in society under the sign of AIDS.

We wish to thank the Wenner-Gren Foundation for its generosity in hosting the conference and, in particular, we are grateful to its president, Dr. Sydel Silverman, for her vision of and commitment to this project on the cultural dimensions of AIDS. We would also like to thank Laurie Obbink and Ann Berg of the Wenner-Gren Foundation, who were such wonderful conference hosts and organizers. Richard Herrell deserves a special thanks for his fine work as conference reporter and colleague. For special assistance in thinking about and editing this volume, I am grateful to my friends Paul Abramson, Joe Carrier, John Gagnon, and Martin Levine. I am particularly indebted to my friend and colleague Shirley Lindenbaum for her help and good spirit in working with me from the conception of the conference idea to the completion of this book.

Finally, thoughts of my brother and his death were very close to me during this conference. This book is a commemoration of his loss to me and, for others, the loss of their own loved ones to the pandemic.

—Gilbert Herdt

PART I

Social History and Representation

1

Introduction

GILBERT HERDT

The disease of AIDS is changing social reality. It is not only affecting how we live and organize society but how we in anthropology and the social sciences must analyze that reality. Some may feel it is too strong to claim that a virus can transform society and culture. However, more than other diseases, AIDS/HIV has exposed the "hidden vulnerabilities in the human condition" (Fineberg, 1988, p. 128). It has become a global epidemic, and even its metaphors are lethal, some have said (Sontag, 1988). By May 1983, for example, it was already widely reported: "People now said that so-and-so was 'diagnosed' and you didn't have to ask what with; for gay men, it had become a verb that needed no object" (Shilts, 1987, p. 285). When the mass media encountered the worlds of those identified with the disease, first in America and then abroad, their life ways were often felt to be shocking and were represented as "kinky" or "marginal subcultures"—illegal, illicit, and immoral. AIDS has changed much in our lives since then, not only in society but in public health, the university, and government policy. It is transforming social science, but only recently have we begun to study these effects on social analysis—on how we think about culture and behavior in anthropology, sociology, social history, and psychology.

The history of the AIDS epidemic, now into its second decade, shows the progressive impact of the disease on science and society. Beginning from its first reported instances in 1979-1980, AIDS has spread throughout the globe and is now reported in 130 countries. Millions now carry the virus (Carballo, Cleland, Carael, & Albrecht, 1989). Surely this will be among the most devastating epidemics since the black plague of the Middle Ages, the cholera epidemics of the 1800s, and the great influenza pandemic of 1918-1919. Much human effort and scientific ink have already been spent on the tragedy. Now, with the war of 1991 behind us, we search for ways in which to confront the burdens of the disease, ever mindful of the other problems that face our society. Gradually, the epidemic is being strategically mapped in the effort to educate people and prevent the spread of the disease, to care for clinical patients, and their families and loved ones. Today, those affected by the disease demand that health care and scientific specialists no longer exclude their social needs and identities from their response to the epidemic. But this is problematic, Brandt (1985, p. 195) has said, because it challenges two sets of values "highly prized by our culture": the fundamental civil liberties of the individual and the role of the state in assuring public welfare. The provision of the necessary knowledge from social science is no easy matter, and the reasons this is so are also of concern in this book.

Culture and Knowledge of AIDS

That the disease is changing social consciousness is now clear. What AIDS is doing, with an ever-quickening pace, is to challenge basic assumptions about the relationships between culture and deviance, sexuality, drug inject-ing, HIV transmission, and unsuspected forms of disease spread. AIDS, as we are learning from these links, is so strongly associated with social stigma that it has become the very face of contagion in our time (Brandt, 1985, p. 194). And because AIDS is overrepresented in "minority" populations, it raises complex questions about how a "subgroup" is organized and repre-sented in a mass society such as ours (see, e.g., Mays & Cochran, 1988; Quimby & Friedman, 1989; Rist, 1989). For instance, in what sense is homosexuality a "minority" or a "subculture," with gays and lesbians its citizens (Bolton, this volume; Herdt, 1989; Murray & Payne, 1988; Weeks, 1985)? Is it right to speak of a "drug culture" or a "subculture of prostitu-tion"? And, again, what constitutes "risk" and risky social practices (Doug-las, 1986)? Furthermore, who gets to represent disease knowledge to what publics, and under what circumstances do these images reveal biases as well as blind spots (Gilman, 1988; Treichler, this volume)? Are the images of science and medicine also representations of culture as much as our myths and rituals? And just how does one go about the task of employing social science methods, such as interviewing and ethnography, to uncover the epidemiology of the disease (Abramson & Herdt, 1990; Parker, Herdt, &

Carballo, 1991)? Are the methods of epidemiology up to the task (Anderson & May, 1990)?

There is, in fact, widespread disagreement among specialists regarding these questions, as we shall see. And yet the discoveries resulting from attempts to tackle these problems are commanding attention and new demands for behavioral research (Turner et al., 1989). As Ralph Bolton (in press) shows in a recent bibliography on AIDS and anthropology, many contributions have emerged from field-workers already.

AIDS is refiguring social reality as much as AIDS representations are reshaping knowledge of the disease both at home and abroad. So great are these effects, and so rapidly have they taken shape in popular discourse, that some suggest we remain largely unconscious of them. Treichler (1987, p. 31) refers to this consequence as an "epidemic of signification," by which she means that "the name AIDS in part *constructs* the disease and helps make it intelligible." The perspective of social constructionists (Farmer, this volume; Levine, this volume) suggests that AIDS is a double metaphor in the cultures that we would study: It is not only a model *of* the reality of those afflicted by the disease, but it provides a model *for* responding to and representing its risk and contagion for others.[1] Culture shapes our responses to the disease, many of us in the social sciences believe, but, increasingly, the disease is a common denominator of our social life and ontological reality (Gagnon, 1989, this volume). It does this, for example, by advising how we should engage in sexual intercourse—that is, by cues regarding what is felt to be "safe" and "risky" (Koop, 1986; and see Abramson, 1988; Reiss & Leik, 1989). Further, it forcibly redesigns our cultural life course (Boxer & Cohler, 1989), introducing death and suffering prematurely, altering our expectations about living a short or long life and whether we are surrounded by family and loved ones or not throughout its course. In this view, AIDS not only becomes a Grim Reaper but, in the sense of Randy Shilts's comments cited above, it has a social force and is a player in many arenas of life (see Carrier & Magaña, this volume).

Throughout recent work on AIDS, one is impressed by how much the concept of culture has become central to the relevant studies. As Bolton (1989, p. 6) has written elsewhere: "To know AIDS is to know much about human societies and cultures as well, for AIDS is a phenomenon that afflicts societies while HIV undermines the health of individuals" (Abramson & Herdt, 1990; Farmer & Kleinman, 1989; Feldman & Johnson, 1986; Gorman, 1986; Parker, 1987). Let our discussion here be aided by three long-standing perspectives of social and cultural inquiry.

First, then, is the question of how the culture concept is relevant to the study of AIDS. Shall we, to illustrate, represent America as but one culture or tradition, symbolically represented in its values and policies as the White Anglo-Saxon/Northern European hegemony? Or does it represent many and diverse cultural communities? Increasingly, we tend to the latter view (Herdt & Boxer, in press). When public authorities, whether the president or arch-bishops, advocate sexual abstinence as the "proper" moral response to the sexual risk of AIDS, their advice not only reveals their own cultural beliefs and standards but presumes that their countrymen share in them completely (Farmer & Kleinman, 1989). Obviously, this sweeping social ideology no longer applies in all cases; neither is its political rhetoric entirely convincing on all public issues even to the presumed political mainstream in the polity (Gagnon, 1989; Lang, 1991; Shilts, 1987). At issue is an objectification of our cultural boundaries, a struggle for the symbolic definition of "margin" and political "mainstream" (see, this volume, Lindenbaum's discussion; reviewed in Herdt, Leap, & Sovine, 1991; Schoepf et al., 1988). Do we consider groups beyond the "mainstream" to be in our culture or to have "subcultures" of their own? Are prostitutes, for instance, such a subculture (de Zalduondo, 1991)? And homosexuals or gays/lesbians (see Herdt, in press)? One can at least imagine them as such, given the notoriety of the gay movement in the press (Herdt, in press). But what of the so-elusive "bisex-ual" and that particularly rare and seldom seen species, the "married bisexual man" (Gagnon, 1989; Klein & Wolf, 1985)? Are these different sexualities to be represented as "groups"? The problem is how we are to think of a "group" in the purely epidemiological and not sociocultural sense.

The social and sexual activities of any one of these populations are largely defined, in the cultural reality of the larger society, as illicit, illegal, or at the very least immoral. AIDS does not care that this cultural construction of each of these categories as an Other has long been with us (Bolton, this volume; Brandt, 1985; Treichler, this volume). Traditionally, the peripherality of such groups was reflected in the absence of study of them by anthropology (Bolton, 1989; Herdt, 1987). It is not simply the cultural role or practices of these marginals but *their very nature* that defies the normal canons of humanity and moral being necessary to membership in "mainstream" society (Sontag, 1988). What we are learning from AIDS research is the need to identify multiple cultural voices and cultures in the context of the epidemic, each of which faces the common threat of disease but responds in culturally distinct ways to it (Pollak, 1988; Shorter, 1990).

Second, how do we in anthropology and the social sciences *access* the cultural groups most vulnerable and "at risk" in the effort to prevent AIDS

(Gorman & Mallon, 1989)? What methods do we employ and, in turn, what problems do they pose for the scientific[2] study of culture (reviewed in Abramson 1990; Abramson & Herdt, 1990; Herdt & Boxer, 1991; Marshall & Bennett, 1990; Nelkin, 1987). The situated knowledge of the anthropologist is valuable in studying the risks and behaviors of these cultural groups. Yet, our ethnographic knowledge is problematic: Anthropologists are also cultural actors, prone to the blind spots and folk theories of their own society (see Bolton, and Farmer, this volume). If it is true that the illness of AIDS "moves along the fault lines of a society," as Bateson and Gatsby (1988) suggest, then it is equally true that anthropologists have no special protection from its social "earthquakes" or political fallout. AIDS exacts its own human costs from those who would do participant observation and fieldwork (Quimby, this volume). It is not easy for American (White or African-American? Male or female? Old or young? Gay or straight? there is, you see, no homogeneous "American") field-workers to penetrate the world of the prostitute or drug injector, as Kane and Mason (this volume) show. The investigation of the sexual is sensitive in this regard (Herdt & Stoller, 1990). The ethical dilemmas of such work are immediately suggested, for example, by the controversial approach of Ralph Bolton on the participant observation of sexual behavior. You learn about hidden sexuality in this way, Bolton suggests. (Yet, even within the conference in which he presented his work, there was strong disagreement among the participants about whether this was the best and proper means of ethnographic method.) Clearly, the shape of the ethnographic or social science account of AIDS knowledge and disease must grapple with such long-standing problems in methodology, for which there are no easy or ethically transparent answers.

Third, what is this social science knowledge good for? How, that is, shall we deploy what we learn from these investigations to solve the problems the epidemic poses for society? It is not enough, as Levine (this volume) reminds us, that we conduct an AIDS study. We must also provide the means to translate the knowledge into education and prevention measures (Gamson, 1990; Parker, this volume). Some social scientists advocate going further by social action and applied anthropology (see Schoepf, and Farmer, this volume) to address basic inequities and social ills that create the fault lines of risk for AIDS. I am reminded here of a basic point made early in the epidemic by Carballo et al. (1989): that AIDS is a disease associated with minorities, persons of color, gays, and Haitians—that is, underprivileged and marginal people. Without a concept of culture provided by social science analysis, persons on the margins remain cut off not only from medical science and clinical treatment but also from the education, prevention, and care that should be addressed to their particular needs (Chuang et al., 1989; Herdt & Boxer, 1991; Turner et al., 1989). Thus knowledge of cultures is linked directly to empowerment.

We have an opportunity not only to stop the spread of the epidemic and alleviate the suffering caused by it. Through the use of AIDS research, then, we are led to utopian prospects of positive change in the basic conditions of stigmatized and marginal persons in their own land (reviewed, in part, in Lindenbaum's chapter).

A Culture of AIDS?

The notion of a "global culture"—one thinks of the media broadcasters' seductive oxymoron "global village"—crept into the "language" of AIDS early in the pandemic. It is certainly true that AIDS is a global problem, present in most countries, and of concern to all of humanity (Mann, 1988). However, this AIDS metaphor, while it might have bolstered the scientific need for the global culture study by anthropology, also has another effect (see, e.g., Parker, 1990; Parker et al., 1991). That is, the "global culture" implicitly suggests that the cultural practices and beliefs of countries are *not all that different*. Indeed, just about anyone (anthropologists or not) could study them. It hinted that the peril posed by AIDS was so powerful in leveling cultural differences that our responses would be identical. What matters in studying these trends is the recognition that AIDS is carving out a sort of social geography of its own, the signs and symbols of which can be identified and measured from this place to that, and with more or less the same lens (see the critiques of Farmer, Levine, and Treichler, respectively, in this volume). Certainly this raises the issue of our scientific paradigms and their cross-cultural sensitivity to, or clumsiness in, handling group differences (see Lindenbaum, and Abramson, this volume; Parker et al., 1991).

Perhaps the pandemic has confronted us with an anthropological never-never land, so to speak: a continuing "evolution" of cultural construction regarding the nature of cultural groups (Treichler, this volume). Culture no longer seems to be such a "steady state" phenomenon (Bateson, 1972). The once so singular voice, the "mainstream" homogeneity of U.S. society, is being differentiated. Multiple cultural publics with somewhat competing voices and social needs have emerged (Bellah et al., 1985).

Here, especially, the notion of culture margin enters again. AIDS presents, for instance, a sort of social X ray of who is classified as mainstream and peripheral, deviant and normal (Carrier & Magaña, this volume; Gagnon, 1989). The scientific use and abuse of the "promiscuities" paradigm and the accusation of responsibility for AIDS to homosexuals is a case in point (Levine & Troiden, 1988; Murray & Payne, 1988). Notice how the representation of drug culture and drug injectors automatically registers in the audience a sense that such persons must be "junkies" or "freaks" who could not possibly be middle-class friends, family, or neighbors—and yet they sometimes are (Kane, 1990; Quimby, this volume; Shilts, 1987). The same bias of the hidden and invisible emerges in sexual study, where the representation of the sexuality of heterosexuals and homosexuals is compared (Abramson & Herdt, 1990). It does not occur to many women to think that their friends and family members participate in the practice of anal receptive intercourse with their lovers or husbands, because vaginal heterosexual intercourse is the cultural norm. Yet the evidence suggests that female receptive anal intercourse is more common than once believed and is increasing in incidence (Bolling & Voeller, 1987, and Wyatt et al., 1988, reviewed in Abramson & Herdt, 1990, pp. 226-227).

Culture can be used to stigmatize groups as well. The hidden preconception—that there is a culture of AIDS—is nicely illustrated by the hoary problems associated with the current use of the old notion of "subculture." A language of margin/mainstream is invoked in the imagery itself, with undertones of primary and secondary claims to social authenticity (Treichler, 1987). "Subculture" is a way of legitimizing a group or practice, or of repudiating them or it, simultaneously. A "subculture" implies (among other things) that its people or their reality lie below, beneath, or encapsulated within the cultural world of the "mainstream." The *drug subculture* is a pejorative label largely because of the illegality. Thus the prefix *sub* indexes a subterranean world, previously hidden or closed, such as the poor street prostitute's scene—with its shifting cultural players—in urban Brazil (Parker, Chapter 10) or Africa (Schoepf, Chapter 12). Often this social reality is sufficiently removed from normative social analysis that it is ignored in behavioral education and prevention efforts (see, for example, Gagnon, 1989, on bisexuality and social networks). It takes gay-sensitive investigators to determine, for instance, the motives of gay men in taking the HIV test (Siegel, Levine, Brooks, & Kern, 1989). The subculture may indeed be removed as well from clinical practice, whether for the doctors (Shilts, 1987, is particularly negative here) or the nurses, only some of whom are sensitive to the specialized patient needs suggested by the concept of the "culture of caring" (Fox et al., 1991).

The cultural domains or "scenes" of these groups are felt to be beyond the purview and boundaries of what is normal, ordinary, and economically sanguine.[3] In social science lingo, it translates into what is "predictable" in an experimental design (Coates et al., 1988) or even "knowable" in an ethnographic study (Herdt & Boxer, 1991). We can decipher the cognitions and emotions of actors who are strange to us by seeing them as links in a chain—as a sequence of behavioral acts ("sexual risk behaviors") with objects ("sex workers") rather than full-blooded cultural actors. Obviously, such a framework and such a language are dehumanizing.

The culture of AIDS in this image is one whose constituency would hardly be claimed by any country. Such people are not only marginal and without political power, their everyday practices and beliefs are consistently represented as illegal, immoral, and illicit (Herdt, 1987). The worldview of these Others is being discovered and described, but not necessarily socially accepted: gays, sex workers, IV drug users, hemophiliacs, bisexuals, heterosexuals with multiple partners, and others occupy cultural worlds very difficult to legitimize by conventional standards. Much of these "life-styles" is imagined to stem from "irrational" behavior. Why, for instance, can't the drug injectors simply "kick the habit" or the sex workers "find a decent job"? Much of it is imagined to be objective fact, without influence of our cultural biases. It is obvious that bigotry influences such preconceptions. What were the facts of AIDS prior to the emergence of such cultural images of the margins, prior, for example, to current expressions of homophobia (Treichler, 1987)? We might imagine that such margins or subcultures, like gays or IV drug injectors, are populations with their own rules that determine who is or is not a member and how they accrue social power in their own local scene (Turner et al., 1989).

Here is the dilemma of AIDS policies regarding those in the margins of culture. Whenever "culture" is politically and officially stamped upon a subgroup, that group's needs must be addressed by the state (Pollak, 1988). When a risk behavior, such as drug injecting, is identified with the norms of a culture, as in the notion of "drug culture/subculture," it is given the seal of medical and scientific legitimacy. As leaders of the gay and lesbian movement have also discovered, such a political process leads to new claims as well—asking their fair share of rights and entitlement in health care and the compassion of the changing public sentiment (Lang, 1991; Quam & Ford, 1990).

Perhaps the centrality of medical science in the definition of normality— and, therefore, of culture, as these examples imply—suggests why it has been a battleground since the 19th century for the social definition of public policy over issues such as AIDS (Brandt, 1985; Foucault, 1973; Misztal & Moss, 1990). But this poses a paradox for science. How can science—the ultimate in rational understanding—accept as legitimate practices that its own culture defines as illegal, immoral, or illicit? One might argue that science is outside of the conventions of society, but this ignores how much science is a part of our culture (Gagnon, this volume). Do we not thereby legitimize the desires on which such a life is lived (Gagnon, 1989; Herdt & Stoller, 1990)? Yet we cannot legitimize drug injecting, for example, because we know that it is addictive and injurious to health. Such practices destabilize our own commonsense standards (Geertz, 1984) of what is healthy, good, and worthy of desire (Sontag, 1988).

A parallel problem has beset many Second and Third World countries in their struggle to define public health policies that are both acceptable politically and economically and medically competent in tackling AIDS (Misztal & Moss, 1990). A fundamental disparity may exist between the standards of those afflicted with the disease and the standards or morals of the government (Murray & Payne, 1988; Shilts, 1987). Worse, a double standard may be applied either to certain categories of people (men versus women) or with regard to certain culture ideals versus pragmatic actions (e.g., an ideal standard that sex occurs only in marriage, precluding adultery; Abramson & Herdt, 1990; Parker et al., 1991). As Farmer's analysis of Haiti demonstrates, rational choice, planning, and politics all joined with prejudice in the AIDS-related policies of Haiti and its neighbors, especially the powerful United States, which has had a difficult history of handling Haitian immigrants.

These national AIDS policies are, in short, more a patchwork of complex political and social compromise, public health negotiations, and received stereotypes and prejudices than merely the product of rational scientific design (Berridge, this volume). There is no guarantee that the lessons of history from prior epidemics, or the lessons of culture from present-day anthropology, will enable us to predict or control the AIDS epidemic.

AIDS has changed from being an acute to a chronic disease that poses so many uncertainties in the lives of persons with AIDS (Weitz, 1989). People associated with AIDS and patients suffering its effects attempt to exert as much control as possible over the disease. By extension, those who study the disease may also attempt to express control, even in ways that seem irrational. Indeed, one almost senses the magical thought process that is involved here, as if, in desperation, people would try anything to control an uncontrollable world (see Luhrmann, 1989).

The Categories of Epidemiology

It is well known, though not yet documented sufficiently, that the chief complaint of cross-cultural researchers studying AIDS is the rigidity and insensitivity of the major categories in epidemiology that have been applied to the description and explanation of HIV patterns across countries (Abramson & Herdt, 1990; Bolton, 1989; Carrier, 1989; Gorman, 1986; Parker, 1987; Parker et al., 1991). As a participant in many AIDS symposia, one senses a defensiveness on the part of social scientists. Certainly this has not prevented anthropologists from working with epidemiological colleagues (see, e.g., Stall, Coates, & Hoff, 1988; and see the bibliography by Bolton, in press). The paradigm of science is a factor here, but it is not simply a matter of the current debate within anthropology on what is science (Geertz, 1984; Spiro, 1986) or within the behavioral sciences on "hard" versus "soft" science, to take the observations of Abramson as a cue (this volume).

The more critical point concerns the debate over the role of the lone individual in the AIDS epidemic. A continuing debate concerns the unit of analysis for an investigation of AIDS—should it be the individual, a population, or a society? The entire discussion of the "health belief model" and its failure in the context of the pandemic follows from this issue (Montgomery et al., 1989). Epidemiologists often fail to understand how social and cultural processes influence and even predict disease spread (Berridge, this volume). Frankenberg points out that the emphasis upon individuals and not groups aggregates characteristics of the disease with the suffering of the person. This approach loses sight of the cultural context that determines individual responses to the disease and support for those who suffer from it.

Here, the conventional distinction between disease and illness is of help (Kleinman, 1988), and it suggests that an exclusive concern with the medical signs and symptoms at the expense of understanding their social and psychological status and perception in the society is crucial. "Society" and "culture," in the more "egocentric" agenda, is reduced to the 2×2 table, to probabilities, or to behavioral frequencies for a "group" estimate by inference from the sample. Gagnon's work (1989, and this volume) has reviewed these issues, appreciating the enormity of the AIDS challenge to science while simultaneously understanding the need for human tolerance and humanistic values in the conduct of analysis.

Perhaps no problem of the epidemic received more scrutiny with regard to anthropology and epidemiology than the definition of AIDS "risk." The metaphors of contagion abound in this discourse (Sontag, 1988). The well-known problem of assessing risk in the epidemic has brought a chorus of criticisms about who or what is at "risk"—groups and categories, "risky" behaviors and practices. Indeed, it was the debate over the difference between a risk "group" and a risk "practice" (such as anal intercourse) that signified to the players at an earlier stage what kind of science would apply to this epidemic and who was and was not culturally sensitive and conceptually naive regarding its social context (Bolton, 1989, this volume; Coates et al., 1988; Gagnon, 1989; Levine, this volume; Murray & Payne, 1988; Treichler, this volume). One might have thought, a few years ago, that a risk is a risk, and if "you have seen one you have seen them all."[4] And yet risk is, as Mary Douglas has said (1986), obviously culturally defined and, under certain circumstances and with certain categories or groups, a matter of no small concern in terms of its social control. The parallel notion of a "risk milieu" arises (Zenilman, 1988), while others have spoken of subjective/objective risk perceptions, and "exposure milieus" to AIDS risk, mediated, for instance, by type of sexual partner and place of sexual interaction (reviewed in Herdt & Boxer, in press; Voeller et al., 1990). According to Mary Douglas, again, risk means "danger," especially of corruption of persons and boundaries; whereas, for the World Health Organization, risk has meant a calculated exposure to disease exposure or infection.

The definition of risk reveals examples of how culture is implicitly "hidden" in the categories and assumptions of epidemiology. Consider, for example, the seemingly simple question: Who is the subject's sexual partner (Parker et al., 1991)? Though the notion of sexual partner may seem obvious, it varies across cultures and is probably the source of significant error in research design. Whether a partnership is sexual and/or social, culturally approved or disapproved (hetero-/homosexual, marital/adulterous), voluntary or coercive, is of real import in survey and fieldwork studies (Abramson & Herdt, 1990). If a community places a value on marriage and monogamy, respondents may be unwilling to discuss adultery, especially with an outsider unknown to them. In Africa, for instance, this issue of extramarital relations is a key to understanding the transmission of HIV (Obbo, 1990). Cultures vary enormously in how they approve of sexuality outside of the context of marriage and reproduction; indeed, within the same society, such as the United States, changes within its own ideology—from an emphasis upon reproduction to one of pleasure—vary across time (D'Emilio & Freedman, 1988; Voeller et al., 1990). When sex is exchanged for money, gifts, or other favors, it is necessary as well to understand how the definition of sexual partner may support or violate normative community standards in order to sample the range of sexual practice within that population (de Zalduondo, 1991; Schoepf, this volume). These variations suggest the difficulty of applying a single standard of "sex" and sexual partners across societies. Thus such criticisms reveal the weakness of measures that depend exclusively upon questionnaires or instruments whose questions are not culturally attuned to the community in question (Abramson & Herdt, 1990; Parker, this volume).

The Lessons of Culture

The anthropological approach has spelled out significant areas of study and problems for investigation that have sometimes responded to these problems in epidemiology. Many have called for an application of anthropological concepts and methods to disease study and prevention (Parket et al., 1991).

All of this is a matter of consternation to the global study of AIDS. What is needed, AIDS doctors and epidemiologists have felt, is a cross-cultural "survey" approach that would, in the manner of the so-called KABP (knowledge, attitudes, beliefs, and practices) studies, reveal the critical missing data. The WHO's global program was meant in part to do this (Carballo et al., 1989). Important strides have been made, given the problematic nature of the categories of epidemiology reviewed above. But who is to know (especially in advance) what the critical "data chunks" are? So, do such studies not require a contextual knowledge, and deeper language and culture study, from which to understand the "missing" links in the chain of transmission and the response to the suffering? Thus perhaps nowhere have the criticisms of anthropologists directed toward the epidemiological approach been more severe than those that concern the "quick-and-dirty" ethnographic "surveys" insinuated by Bolton (Chapter 6) and Kane and Mason (Chapter 9), among others. What is at stake here? Many have called for a much more cultural approach.

We might think of such a call as a kind of "lessons of culture" approach, taking the hint of Virginia Berridge (this volume) that the historical record of the past will best indicate how this AIDS epidemic will go. The historian's early conception was that a study of past epidemics would tell us how this one would go. The cultural analogy is clear. It is a view that suggests: If only we could learn the lessons of cultural beliefs and practices, we could save lives by stopping the spread of the epidemic and thereby alleviate much human suffering. By analogy, if only we could utilize understanding of culture to predict the transmission, we would be able to predict the course of the spread of the disease.[5] The lessons of culture approach would proceed something like this.

But if epidemiology has been wont to identify the necessary research strategies for a cross-cultural investigation of AIDS, then anthropology has by no means had an easier time of doing it. The "lessons of culture" approach is problematic because it rests upon two questionable premises. One is that the ethnological record holds insights for stopping the epidemic, if only we would access them (Conant, 1988; Reining, Bongaarts, Way, & Conant, 1989); while the other suggests that anthropologists are better suited to do basic AIDS research, especially in projects necessitating the analysis of sociocultural factors. Let us examine each of these.

The first premise raises a major problem. Generally, the cross-cultural archives have proven inadequate to the task of studying HIV transmission. But, then, the ethnographic record has been difficult to tap in the face of other kinds of social problems as well (see, for example, the review in Bolton, 1989). Anthropology's difficulty arises from an incomplete and inconsistent base of information and its application due, in part, to the old antipathy to "applied" anthropology (see, e.g., Foster, 1969). In part too this antipathy resulted from a large reliance upon the study of exotic rather than urbanized Western communities, where the problems of health and cultural policy differ so radically (Turner et al., 1989). Because the two sources of AIDS/HIV transmission—sex and drug injecting—are not well studied or represented in anthropology, either historically or today, the basic material for AIDS education/prevention is limited (see, e.g., Herdt et al., 1991; Parker et al., 1991; Voeller et al., 1990). One source of the deficit is the HRAF (Human Relations Area Files, established at Yale) cross-cultural archive. Many of these anthropological reports were collected decades ago. Not only are they outdated (and in some cases impossible to update, given culture change), but they are loaded with the (often hidden or implicit) biases of the time.[6] Thus the HRAF tells us virtually nothing of drug injecting as a cross-cultural pattern.

To take, for example, sexuality: The anthropological record is also very incomplete (reviewed in Herdt & Stoller, 1990; Parker et al., 1991). Only of late have anthropologists recognized the problems attendant upon sexual behavior study (Carrier, 1989; Carrier & Magaña, this volume). So too is the record in contemporary society less than adequate to the task, Gagnon (1989) tells us. We have as of yet an incomplete picture of cross-cultural variation in sexual development and practices (Herdt, 1990), and this is a difficulty because the exposure to AIDS/HIV may occur at different points in the life course development of persons. Furthermore, since the time of Mead's (1961) important review, it has been noted that sexuality is, in many cultures, private and privileged knowledge. Abramson (this volume) introduces the problems of memory bias and cultural ideals as distortions of accounts of remembered sexual experience (Abramson & Herdt, 1990). We rarely can observe sexuality directly, so that its study continues to rely upon verbal and memory accounts of sexual behavior and histories, and herein lies the potential bias of cultural stereotypes (sexism, homophobia) and their representation in institutions, discourse, and media. (See Bolton's discussion of the issue in this volume.) The record on homosexual behavior cross-culturally and in our own society is filled with gaps, not to mention an incomplete understanding of how this sexuality is related to others in development and adult functioning (reviewed in Herdt, 1984, 1987, 1989, 1990, in press). Thus we must be cautious, as Margaret Mead (1961) once warned, when statements of reported incidence or absence of practices, such as adultery or homosexual behavior, are made for a culture, especially an entire culture, and especially when no quantitative data are used to back up the claim.

The second premise is more complex and contentious to discuss: Is the anthropologist better equipped than other social scientists to study the culture of AIDS? Leaving aside, for the moment, the problem of cross-disciplinary study, to which we shall return, is it true, as some have argued, that anthropology can tackle the problems of AIDS better? The field-worker is, by historical definition, both insider and outsider, stranger and friend. We are usually known at the grass-roots level and our work reflects a deeper understanding of issues such as what is risk, how do PWAs live their lives, and what are their needs (Gorman & Mallon, 1989; Lang, 1991). But where, as noted above, many would claim that the cross-cultural record is disappointing, the second premise is more difficult both to justify and to critique. Nevertheless, the number of African anthropologists and social scientists who are contributing to the AIDS prevention/education effort is increasing and may represent an important indication of a new trend (see, e.g., Obbo, 1990). Being an anthropologist is helpful but does not automatically provide the necessary qualifications for either being accepted as an "insider" in the local scene or having the expertise and interest to study it if one were.

A fundamental sign of the problem concerns how we in anthropology and the social sciences have dealt with variation in beliefs and behavior within a culture. The notion of uniform standards of behavior within a culture has come under increasing criticism (Farmer, this volume). The postmodernists refer to this under the rubric of plural voices omitted or included in the text (see, e.g., Clifford & Marcus, 1985; Farmer, this volume; Treichler, this volume). This "lumping" into a broad "middle" rather than "splitting" into multiple cultural realities is in part the carryover of functionalism and the male-centered anthropology of the past (reviewed in Strathern, 1988). Anthropology has sometimes been too reliant upon verbal as opposed to nonverbal observation, and this may exaggerate "ideology" in the representations of the "culture." How often, for instance, have women's attitudes been replaced by men's, or men's activities and ideals substituted for the women's, not only by Margaret Mead (who preferred to work with men rather than women) but today as well. Class, racial, and age differences are ignored or glossed together in the study of group standards (Stack, 1989) as, for instance, in the development of sexuality (Herdt, 1990). It is impossible at times to understand in what situations or with what language sexuality has been studied, and this is why the work of those such as Carrier and Magaña (this volume) and Bolton (this volume) is so welcome.

In short, intracultural variation continues to be ignored; both its causes and effects are laced into the study of AIDS (Dalton, 1989) and social analyses more broadly (Levine, this volume). We wonder now whether that which was illegal, immoral, or illicit within the margins and "nonmiddles" of culture was hidden or ignored by the ethnographers of the past (but see Edgerton, 1986). Hence the assumptions of the "lessons of culture" are somewhat flawed and pose a challenge to the cultural study of AIDS and how it is creating culture change before our eyes.

To assess cultural variation, we must recognize the critical difference between ethnography and cross-country research. An ethnography—the results of direct participant observation in the method of anthropology—is fundamentally concerned with a description of behavior in terms of the language and culture of its insiders. The salience of local categories and meanings is above all crucial in understanding the context of human behavior and experience (reviewed recently in Herdt & Stoller, 1990, chap. 1). A cross-country study, on the other hand, is less concerned with local categories and meanings than with the application of a uniform measure or protocol from another culture to individuals within the locale of study (see, e.g., Offer et al., 1988, on adolescence, and the critique of Triandis, 1988). Key questions of validity and reliability are thus lodged in such work (see Abramson, this volume; Turner et al., 1989).

The so-called rapid ethnographic assessment raises all of these problems ferociously, as I suggested above. In defense of the approach, however, it must be said that the year or two years of study needed for an authentic culture study is nearly impossible in the context of the epidemic. For instance, focus groups as a method are of value and have been put to good use in AIDS research (Parker et al., 1991). Furthermore, anthropologists in established academic settings are sometimes unwilling to do such research or unable to get the time off for the necessarily urgent design of the study.

Finally, we would be remiss not to observe that anthropologists seemed initially so shy of this epidemic, unwilling, in the case of African studies, to enter into the urgent fray of the disease or its impacts.

Another issue concerns the involvement of "indigenous" workers. If one lacked the time to launch even a brief ethnographic study prior to the larger survey, or if it was felt that such surveys were inadequate or a waste of time, another approach was to tap the community by appointing an "indigenous" investigator as a part of the team. The identification of "indigenous," beginning about three years or so ago in the RFPs of funding agencies, remained vague, sometimes, one suspects, intentionally ambiguous, because the investigator was unsure how to define the role. "Indigenous," it turns out, does not mean "trained in anthropology" or even necessarily acquainted with the local culture or "language"[7] (especially local meanings and idioms of speech) of the community. It might mean a "member of the community" in the sense of someone who resides in or is identified with local people. It may mean, however, someone whose social traits, such as speaking a language or being a person of color, would be identified by *outsiders* with the insider's networks. Sometimes this ploy works, sometimes not, depending upon several factors, including the intelligence and skills of the person in question. It is clearly an advantage of sorts for a Spanish-speaking woman to work with other Spanish-speaking women; but does it not matter that she is of Mexican origin and the others are from Puerto Rico (see Herdt & Boxer, 1991)? And, again, it surely is an advantage for a gay man to study and work with other gay men (Bolton, this volume); but what if the outsider is middle class and White and the others are lower-class African American (see Herdt et al., 1991; Quimby, this volume)?

Simply being a member of a community does not guarantee the kind of deeper insider knowledge or participation that Malinowski showed would be required: being both stranger and friend, capable of living life with the natives to render their point of view (see Farmer, this volume). An appreciation of the context is thus of real import to the success of the AIDS study and the validity of its measures, while the issues continue to vex anthropology.[8] We are learning that how we represent ourselves, and how we are represented in the media, is decisive in education and prevention efforts. Researchers have discovered that "credibility" in the community—or association with "credible" authorities—can make all the difference in the response rate to protocols and the quality of those responses (Parker et al., 1991). A culturally sensitive AIDS project implies the ability to speak the same "language" and work within the same culture as the target population

(Kane & Mason, this volume). Gaining community support for intervention measures and the delivery of services to those most in need are clearly enhanced by such qualities of cultural rapport (see Siegel et al., 1989, as well as Herdt & Boxer, 1991; Levine, this volume).

The lessons of culture imply not only that the knowledge of sociocultural factors is crucial in fighting the disease but that anthropologists are better than other social scientists in grappling with the social issues posed by the epidemic. Most of us believe that society and culture are critical dimensions of the epidemic and the effort to prevent its spread. But where do we go from here?

To be a credible ethnographer of AIDS in a particular community is no small task—indeed, many of the chapters in this book are testimonies to this point—but certain rare qualities are required. One must be schooled in the lessons of culture though not necessarily an anthropologist. And one must be willing to brave the association of stigma with the disease and controversy that the study is likely to create in the community. For example, it requires researchers of the caliber of Joe Carrier, studying sexual behavior in Mexico and Mexican Americans for 20 years. Working together with Raul Magaña, an anthropologist of Mexican descent, Carrier has facilitated path-breaking analyses of sexual transmission of AIDS and HIV prevention and education now so critical to the cultural insights they are applying in their work within public health settings in Southern California.

There are insiders and insiders, as Treichler shows in her remarkable account of the last international AIDS conference held in San Francisco. Who is "knowledgeable" and an "expert" is changing; indeed, it is a matter of considerable political dispute. This is being redefined constantly by what people know and *who* they know. Biomedical knowledge and discourse is ever so adapted to this game of experts and "breakthroughs," and one implication of the epidemic in general is that, perhaps, never again will the public and government be so passive concerning the role that medical research plays in public health (see Brandt, 1985). Where the doctors are privileged in this game, anthropologist are at a disadvantage; rare is the M.D./Ph.D., such as Paul Farmer, who is willing to undertake long-term research in a place such as Haiti. We will soon have to face the fact that training must be interdisciplinary, otherwise our analyses will be limited in understanding the interaction between "high-tech" culture and cultural studies (see Gagnon, this volume). A critical examination of these problems will again raise the reason for seeing that the most thoughtful analysis is going to require cross-disciplinary work of an unprecedented nature.

Beyond Stigma:
The Ethics of Applied Practice

Anthropologists, like professionals in other fields, at first shunned the epidemic and its research impact on their field (Bolton, this volume). Why this happened is a source of debate (Herdt et al., 1991). Was it because we had no relevant data? Or expertise with diseases (not true of medical anthropologists, who generally came forth earlier)? Or was it opposition to doing "applied anthropology," or was it, again, a disinterest in or even fear of studying the illegal, immoral, or illicit in cultures? The practices of drug injecting or prostitution, for example, *were by their nature* excluded from the normative design of culture study in the past. One senses that, in AIDS grant applications, the use of an anthropologist is justifiable in a funded application the farther removed in social reality one becomes from the broad middle-class norms of U.S. and Northern Europeans cultures. But among sex workers or drug users, and in gay culture too, it is easier to make the argument for an insider anthropologist to gain insights and access hidden information for prevention and education (Bolton, this volume; Levine, this volume).

It is one thing to struggle with the abstract ideas of separating cultural ideal from pragmatic behavior, or with pluralizing the "voice" that appears in our ethnographic accounts' of the way that social networks create links of risk for HIV transmission. It is quite another matter, however, to deal with the illegal, immoral, and illicit, and not because anthropologists are unfamiliar with such but because we are unused to dealing with that which would challenge the cultural norm to the extent of illegal activities (Kane, 1990). Neither did we expect that, by studying the marginal or illicit, we too would become marginalized in our own field.

This marginalization imposes a burden upon the field-worker. To bring "home" an account of illegal, illicit, or immoral practices is to implicitly violate the norms of our own society. We are not supposed to know of such things; or, if we do, we are not supposed to participate in them, as the Malinowskian ideology of participant observation effectively requires (Herdt & Stoller, 1990). As Frankenberg suggests in his conference paper, one must be wicked or ignorant, morally flawed, or cognitively deficient to engage in the practices associated with an epidemic. These actors are not only out of reach of society: They remain cultural renegades, disparaged and delegitimized by those authorities or power groups unwilling to acknowledge their existence and share the resources necessary to protect it. How is the anthropologist to avoid the stigmatizing association of the forbidden and illegal?

Take as a problematic issue what some have called the cultural notion of "condom awareness." New attitudes and relations now characterize the way condoms are used and the decisions and choices made regarding partnership relations. As the discussion of partnership above illustrates, with variations in partnerships, people use condoms with some but not with other partners. Among sex workers, it may be common practice to use condoms with clients but not with their lovers of choice (Kane, 1990; Schoepf, this volume). Issues relating to the sexual history of the Other, expectations of the relationships, gender, age, ethnicity, and degree of knowledge appear to influence these decisions. Issues of power and subordination enter in, as women of color, for instance, may feel unable to refuse their lovers for fear of loss of support (Kane, and Schoepf, this volume; Mays & Cochran, 1988). Much has been written about the issues in the field of family planning and contraceptives, and, as Martha Ward (1991) has said, this foretells the prospects and problems of the future of "safe sex" campaigns. The lessons of culture are difficult to implement.

The chapters in this book are testimonies to discoveries being made in how culture and society are affected by the epidemic and how we must think about these problems in new ways. The epidemic is making us recognize now more than ever that we are in need of new means to bridge the social sciences and to blend and access each others' methodologies and insights. Just as the global events of the Great Depression, and of World War II, fundamentally altered the ways in which a whole generation of social scientists considered how to do their work, so too, I believe, we shall be transformed by the impact of AIDS. How we carry on this work is as much a matter of innovation and opportunism as it is of foresight and planning. We bear the burdens of AIDS better by knowing that we are contributing, in however small ways, to its ultimate defeat.

Notes

1. See Geertz (1966) for this somewhat overused metaphor.

2. Though *science* is a bad word to some and a sign of prepostmodern mentality to others—and, indeed, though I regard anthropology as a science, I feel that ethnography is an art (Herdt & Stoller, 1990) and so I am squeamish about scientism too—nonetheless, we must agree that we strive for some of the tenets of science, of which rigorous demonstration of the conditions of observation and the description of the material so derived are to me critical to anthropology as to the other social sciences.

3. We are dealing, of course, with health care as well, and the reimbursement schemes of overloaded hospitals, that discipline treatment of the poor or marginal.

4. Critics, such as members of ACT UP—the AIDS activist organization—have rightly pointed out that certain agents, such as archbishops of the church, in emphasizing "celibacy" or "abstinence" as a response to the epidemic, and in refusing to support the use of condoms for sexual intercourse, generally ignore or play down not only the contextual risks involved but the different kinds of risks that are involved.

5. We shall ignore for the moment that this is an extremely "hardy" and "intelligent" virus that continues to adapt to new niches and challenges and is, indeed, now more than one virus.

6. For instance, there is a bias that homosexual behavior does not occur in a particular culture or culture area (reviewed in Herdt, 1984; Read, 1980), which may not be explicated but remain a subtext in an account. In cases, such as those of Melanesia and Africa, where change has abolished traditional culture, it is no longer possible to "test" statements of absence or presence, and the student is, therefore, hindered in making valid cross-cultural correlations.

7. Even linguists puzzle the language of AIDS; Leap (1991) discusses this.

8. Nearly 20 years ago, Robert Levine (1973/1982) first argued for a "bicultural" research team, a Western anthropologist working with an indigenous social scientist, such as in Africa or India, to undertake the problem of deeper language and culture study. Hardly anyone has tackled the suggestion or succeeded in implementing it, but the implications continue to plague anthropology's search for cross-cultural truth (see Herdt & Stoller, 1990; Stigler et al., 1989; and see the significant review on AIDS research in Turner et al., 1989).

References

Abramson, P. R. (1984). *Sarah: A sexual biography*. Albany: State University of New York Press.

Abramson, P. R. (1988). Sexual assessment and the epidemiology of AIDS. *Journal of Sexual Research, 25,* 323-346.

Abramson, P. R. (1990). Sexual science: Emerging discipline or oxymoron. *Journal of Sex Research, 27,* 147-165.

Abramson, P. R., & Herdt, G. (1990). The assessment of sexual practices relevant to the transmission of AIDS: A global perspective. *Journal of Sex Research, 27,* 215-232.

Anderson, R. M., & May, R. M. (1990). *Infectious diseases of humans: Dynamics and control.* Oxford: Oxford University Press.

Bateson, C., & Gatsby, R. (1988). *Thinking AIDS: The social response to the biological threat.* Reading, MA: Addison-Wesley.

Bateson, G. (1972). *Steps to an ecology of mind.* New York: Ballentine.

Bellah, R., et al. (1985). *Habits of the heart.* Berkeley: University of California.

Bolton, R. (1987). *AIDS and culture: The case of Norway.* Paper presented at annual meeting of the American Anthropological Association, Chicago.

Bolton, R. (1989). (Ed.). *The AIDS pandemic: A global emergency.* New York: Gordon and Breach.

Bolton, R. (in press). AIDS literature for anthropologists: A working bibliography. *Journal of Sex Research.*

Boxer, A., & Cohler, B. J. (1989). The life course of gay and lesbian youth: An immodest proposal for the study of lives. In G. Herdt (Ed.), *Gay and lesbian youth* (pp. 315-355). New York: Harrington Park.

Brandt, A. M. (1985). *No magic bullet.* New York: Oxford University Press.

Carballo, M., Cleland, J., Carael, M., & Albrecht, G. (1989). A cross national study of patterns of sexual behavior. *Journal of Sex Research, 26,* 287-299.

Carrier, J. (1989). Sexual behavior and the spread of AIDS in Mexico. In *The AIDS pandeuric: A global emergency.* New York: Gordon and Breach.

Chuang, H. T., et al. (1989). Psychosocial distress and well-being among gay and bisexual men with human immunodeficiency virus infection. *American Journal of Psychiatry, 146,* 7.

Clifford, J., & Marcus, G. E. (Eds.). (1985). *Writing culture.* Berkeley: University of California Press.

Coates, T. J., et al. (1988). Behavioral risk reduction for HIV infection among gay and bisexual men. *American Psychological Association, 43*(11), 878-885.

Cochran, S. D., et al. (1988). Ethnic minorities and AIDS. In A. Lewis (Ed.), *Nursing care of the person with AIDS/ARC.* Rockville, MD: Aspen.

Conant, F. P. (1988). Evaluating social science data relating to AIDS in Africa. In N. Miller & R. C. Rockwell (Eds.), *AIDS in Africa: The social and policy impact* (pp. 197-209). Lewiston, NY: Edwin Mellen.

Dalton, H. L. (1989). AIDS in blackface. *Daedalus, 118,* 205-227.

Defoe, D. (1665). *A journal of the plague year.* London: Routledge.

D'Emilio, J., & Freedman, G. (1988). *Intimate matters.* New York: Harper & Row.

de Zaluondo, B. O. (1991). Prostitution viewed cross-culturally: Toward recontextualizing sex work in intervention research. [Special issue, Sex, AIDS and Anthropology; G. Herdt, W. Leap, & M. Sovine, Eds.]. *Journal of Sex Research, 28,* 223-248.

Douglas, M. (1986). *Culture and risk.* New York: Russell Sage.

Edgerton, R. (1986). *Rules, exceptions, and social order.* Berkeley: University of California Press.

Farmer, P. (1990). Sending sickness: Sorcery, politics, and changing concepts of AIDS in rural Haiti. *Medical Anthropology Quarterly, 4,* 6-27.

Farmer, P., & Kleinman, A. (1989). AIDS as human suffering. *Daedalus, 118*(2), 135-162.

Feldman, D. A., & Johnson, T. M. (Eds.). (1986). Introduction. In *The social dimension of AIDS: Methods and theory* (pp. 1-12). New York: Praeger.

Fine, M. (1988). Sexuality, schooling, and adolescent females: The missing discourse of desire. *Harvard Educational Review, 58,* 29-53.

Fineberg, H. V. (1988, October). The social dimensions of AIDS. *Scientific American,* pp. 128-134.

Foster, G. M. (1969). *Applied anthropology.* Boston: Little, Brown.

Foucault, M. (1973). *The birth of the clinic* (A. M. S. Smith, Trans.). New York: Pantheon.

Fox, R. C., et al. (1991). The culture of caring: AIDS and the nursing profession. In D. Nelkin et al. (Eds.), *A disease of society* (pp. 119-149). New York: Cambridge University Press.

Gagnon, J. H. (1989). Disease and desire. *Daedalus, 118,* 47-77.

Gamson, J. (1990). Rubber wars: Struggles over the condom in the United States. *Journal of the History of Sexuality, 1,* 262-282.

Gebbie, K. M. (1989). The President's Commission on AIDS: What did it do? *American Journal of Public Health, 79,* 868-870.

Geertz, C. (1966). Religion as a cultural system. In M. Banton (Ed.), *Anthropological approaches to the study of religion* (pp. 1-46). London: Tavistock.

Geertz, C. (1984). Common sense as a cultural system. In *Local knowledge* (pp. 73-93). New York: Basic Books.

Gilman, S. L. (1988). AIDS and syphilis: The ichnography of disease. In D. Crimp (Ed.), *AIDS: Cultural analysis/cultural activism* (pp. 87-107). Cambridge: MIT Press.

Gorman, M. E. (1986). The AIDS epidemic in San Francisco: Epidemiological and anthropological perspectives. In C. R. Janes, R. Stall, & S. M. Gifford (Eds.), *Anthropology and epidemiology: Interdisciplinary approaches to the study of health and disease* (pp. 157-172). Dordrecht, the Netherlands: D. Reidel.

Gorman, M. E., & Mallon, D. (1989). The role of a community-based health education program in the prevention of AIDS. In R. Bolton (Ed.), *The AIDS pandemic: A global emergency* (pp. 67-74). New York: Gordon and Breach.

Hays, R. B., Kegeles, S. M., & Coates, T. J. (1990). High HIV risk-taking among young gay men. *AIDS, 4,* 901-906.

Herdt, G. (1981). *Guardians of the flutes: Idioms of masculinity.* New York: McGraw-Hill.

Herdt, G. (Ed.). (1984). *Ritualized homosexuality in Melanesia.* Berkeley: University of California Press.

Herdt, G. (1987). AIDS and anthropology. *Anthropology Today, 3,* 1-3.

Herdt, G. (1989). Introduction: Gay and lesbian youth, emergent identities, and cultural scenes at home and abroad. *Journal of Homosexuality, 17,* 1-42.

Herdt, G. (1990). Developmental continuity as a dimension of sexual orientation across cultures. In D. McWhirter (Ed.), *Homosexuality and heterosexuality: The Kinsey scale and current research.* New York: Oxford University Press.

Herdt, G. (Ed.). (in press). *Gay culture in America.* Boston: Beacon.

Herdt, G., & Boxer, A. (1991). Ethnographic issues in the study of AIDS. *Journal of Sex Research, 28*(2), 171-188.

Herdt, G., & Boxer, A. (in press). Sexual identity and risk for AIDS among gay youth in Chicago. In T. Dyson (Ed.), *Anthroplocial demography and AIDS.* Liege, Belgium: International Union for the Scientific Study of Population.

Herdt, G., Leap, W., & Sovine, M. (Eds.). (1991). Sex, AIDS, and anthropology [Special issue]. *Journal of Sex Research.*

Herdt, G., & Stoller, R. J. (1990). *Intimate communications.* New York: Columbia University Press.

Kane, S. (1990). AIDS, addiction and condom use: Sources of sexual risk for heterosexual women. *Journal of Sex Research, 27,* 427-444.

Klein, F., & Wolf, T. J. (Eds.). (1985). *Bisexualities: Theory and practice* [Special issue]. *Journal of Homosexuality, 11*(1/2).

Kleinman, A. (1988). *The illness narratives.* New York: Basic Books.

Koop, C. E. (1986). *Surgeon general's report on acquired immune deficiency syndrome.* Washington, DC: U.S. Department of Health.

Lang, N. (1991). Difficult decisions: Ethics and AIDS. [Special issue, Sex, AIDS and Anthropology; G. Herdt, W. Leap, & M. Sovine, Eds.]. *Journal of Sex Research, 28,* 249-262.

Leap, W. L. (1991). AIDS, linguistics, and the study of non-neutral discourse. *Journal of Sex Research, 28,* 275-288.

Levine, M. P., & Troiden, R. R. (1988). The myth of sexual compulsivity. *Journal of Sex Research, 25,* 347-363.

Levine, R. A. (1982). *Culture, behavior, and personality* (2nd ed.). Chicago: Aldine. (Original work published 1973)

Luhrmann, T. (1989). *The witch's craft.* Cambridge: Cambridge University Press.

Mann, J. (1988). *Global AIDS: Epidemiology, impact, projection and the global strategy.* London: World Summit of Ministers of Health on Programmes for AIDS Prevention.

Marshall, P. A., & Bennett, L. A. (Eds.). (1990). Culture and behavior in the AIDS epidemic. *Medical Anthropological Quarterly, 4.*

Martin, J. L., et al. (1989). Sexual behavior changes and HIV antibody in a cohort of New York City gay men. *AJPH, 79*(4), 269-294.

Mays, V., & Cochran, S. D. (1988). Issues in the perception of AIDS risk and risk reduction activities by Black and Hispanic/Latina women. *American Psychologist, 43*(11), 949-957.

Mead, M. (1961). Cultural determinants of sexual behavior. In *Sex and internal secretions* (pp. 1433-1479). Baltimore: Williams and Wilkins.

Misztal, D., & Moss, B. A. (1990). *Action on AIDS.* New York: Greenwood.

Montgomery, S. B., et al. (1989). The health belief model in understanding compliance with preventive recommendations for AIDS: How useful? *AIDS Education and Prevention, 4,* 303-323.

Murray, S. O., & Payne, K. W. (1988). Medical policy without scientific evidence: The promiscuity paradigm and AIDS. *California Sociologist, 11*(1-2), 13-54.

Nelkin, D. (1987). AIDS and the social sciences: Review of useful knowledge and research needs. *Reviews of Infectious Diseases, 9*(5), 980-986.

Nelkin, D., Willis, D. P., & Parris, S. V. (Eds.). (1991). *A disease of society: Cultural and institutional responses to AIDS.* New York: Cambridge University Press.

Obbo, C. (1990). *Sexual relations before AIDS.* Presented at the conference on Anthropological Studies Relevant to the Sexual Transmission of HIV, Sanderborg, Denmark.

Offer, D., et al. (1988). *The teenage world.* New York: Plenum.

Ostow, D. G. (1989). AIDS prevention through effective education. *Daedalus, 118,* 229-254.

Parker, R. (1987). Acquired immunodeficiency syndrome in urban Brazil. *Medical Anthropology Quarterly, 1,* 155-175.

Parker, R. G. (1990). *Male prostitution, bisexual behavior, and HIV transmission in urban Brazil.* Presented at the conference on Anthropological Studies Relevant to the Sexual Transmission of HIV, Sanderborg, Denmark.

Parker, R. G., Herdt, G., & Carballo, M. (1991). Sexual culture, HIV transmission, and AIDS research. *Journal of Sex Research, 28,* 75-96..

Pollak, M. (1988). *Les Homosexuals et le Sida.* Paris: A. M. Metáilié).

Quam, M., & Ford, N. (1990). AIDS policies and practices in the United States. In B. A. Misztal & D. Moss (Eds.), *Action on AIDS.* New York: Greenwood.

Quimby, E., & Friedman, J. R. (1989). Dynamics of Black mobilization against AIDS in New York City. *Social Problems, 36,* 403-415.

Read, K. E. (1980). *Other voices.* Novato, CA: Chandler & Sharpe.

Reining, P., Bongaarts, J., Way, P., & Conant, F. (1989). *The relationship between male circumcision and HIV infection in African populations.* Presented at TAP 86, Fifth International Conference on AIDS, Montreal.

Reiss, I. L., & Leik, R. K. (1989). Evaluating strategies to avoid AIDS: Number of partners versus use of condoms. *Journal of Sex Research, 26,* 411-433.

Rist, D. Y. (1989). AIDS as apocalypse. *Christopher Street, 132,* 11-14.

Schoepf, B. G., et al. (1988). AIDS, women and society in Central Africa. In R. Kulstand (Ed.), *AIDS, 1988: AAAS symposium papers* (pp. 175-181). Washington, DC: American Association for the Advancement of Science.

Shilts, R. (1987). *And the band played on.* New York: St. Martin's.

Shorter, E. (1990). *What can two historical examples of sexually-transmitted diseases teach us about AIDS?* Presented at the conference on Anthropological Studies Relevant to the Sexual Transmission of HIV, Sanderborg, Denmark.

Siegel, K., LeVine, M. P., Brooks, C., & Kern, R. (1989). The motives of gay men for taking or not taking the HIV antibody test. *Social Problems, 36,* 368-383.

Sonenstein, F. L., Pleck, J. H., & Ku, L. C. (1989). Sexual activity, condom use and AIDS awareness among adolescent males. *Family Planning Perspectives, 21,* 152-158.

Sontag, S. (1988). *AIDS and its metaphors.* New York: Farrar, Straus and Giroux.

Spiro, M. (1986). Cultural relativism and the future of anthropology. *Cultural Anthropology, 1,* 259-286.

Stack, K. B. (1989). Toward a unified theory of class, race, and gender. *American Ethnologist, 16,* 534-550.

Stall, R. D., Coates, T. J., & Hoff, C. (1988). Behavioral risk reduction for HIV infection among gay and bisexual men. *American Psychologist, 43*(11), 878-885.

Stigler, J. W., et al. (1989). *Cultural psychology.* Cambridge: Cambridge University Press.

Strathern, M. (1988). *The gender of the gift.* Berkeley: University of California Press.

Swenson, R. M. (1988, Spring). Plagues, history, and AIDS. *The American Scholar,* pp. 183-200.

Treichler, P. A. (1987). AIDS, homophobia, and biomedical discourse: An epidemic of signification. *Cultural Studies, 1,* 32-70.

Triandis, H. (1988). Commentary. In D. Offer et al., *The teenage world* (pp. 127-128). New York: Plenum.

Turner, F., et al. (1989). *AIDS: Sexual behavior and intravenous drug use.* Washington, DC: National Academy Press.

Voeller, B., et al. (Eds.). (1990). *AIDS and sex: An integrated biomedical and biobehavioral approach.* New York: Oxford University Press.

Ward, M. (1991). Cupid's touch: The lessons of the family planning movement for the AIDS epidemic. *Journal of Sex Research, 28,* 289-306.

Weeks, J. (1985). *Sexuality and its discontents.* London: Routledge & Kegan Paul.

Weitz, R. (1989). Uncertainty and the lives of persons with AIDS. *Journal of Health and Social Behavior, 30,* 270-281.

Wyatt, G., et al. (1988). Kinsey revisited Part I: Comparisons of the sexual socialization and sexual behavior of white women over 33 years. *Archives of Sexual Behavior, 17,* 201-240.

Zenilman, J. (1988). Sexually transmitted diseases in homosexual adolescents. *Journal of Adolescent Medicine, 9,* 129-138.

2

Epidemics and Researchers:
AIDS and the Practice of Social Studies

JOHN H. GAGNON

Doing Science and Doing Authority

If the AIDS epidemics[1] have done nothing else, they have emphasized the interpenetration of science and power in all of its forms, including the politics of reality, and in this emphasis have demonstrated that the authority claims of the sciences rest in large measure upon their *appearance* as objective, detached, and pure of purpose. This is not a new recognition, but it takes on a greater salience at the current moment because Science as constituted in certain research communities has become identified as the lead agency in providing solutions for the epidemics. The biomedical sciences are charged with understanding the virus and its impacts on the immune system and discovering both a vaccine to prevent further spread and treatments for opportunistic infections as well as the direct effects of the virus. The social and behavioral sciences are to produce recipes for behavior change that will prevent transmission as well as produce compliance with healthy life-styles (until the "magic bullet" comes along). These tasks are to be accomplished in the face of rapidly changing epidemics that are cross cultural in scope and interdisciplinary in their methodological and theoretical demands on the scientific community. An adequate *technical* response to HIV disease demands that scientists quickly acquire reliable knowledge that can be turned into applied programs that work. However, beyond the technical requirements of such a task, there is the matter of implementing these programs in actual cultural and social contexts, implementations that will have impacts on far more aspects of social life than HIV/AIDS treatment or prevention. Behavior change is required not only of those at risk but of the widest range of both direct and indirect participants in the epidemics in all of the affected cultures.

The medical profession, which is the conduit for the delivery of the work of biomedical scientists, provides a relatively complete apparatus of legitimation that produces the ability of the individual physician to tell people what to do to reduce illness. This moment of assured superordination in the doctor-patient encounter is the result of an entire system of symbols and institutions of healing that bulk large in the structure of Western societies. As a result, physicians and their surrogates have been willing to give advice or make rules with a confidence that occurs less often among social or behavioral scientists. Yet, by taking on a similar role in the epidemics, the behavioral and social sciences are running the risk of having to take on a similar mantel of authority. They are expected to produce results in the form of tried and tested interventions that will reduce the rate of infection or increase compliance with drug regimes. They are to gather precise data usable in regression equations that model the epidemic, or they are to conduct randomized trials of educational programs that mimic the drug trials of their medical betters. *In the context of the epidemics, social scientists are expected to tell people what to do under conditions of uncertainty.*

Epidemics and Accidents

One of the images that comes to mind during reflections on the course of the HIV/AIDS epidemics is the behavior of the operators in the control room of the nuclear power plant at Three Mile Island in the first moments of the accident. Untoward and unexpected events were occurring with incredible rapidity in the bowels of the reactor vessel and lights were flashing in the control room that were believed (within some limits) to provide information to the operators about what was going on inside the great machine. The operators had a "theory of the machine," which had been constituted in their training and in the everyday practice of running the plant, and that theory of the machine was the basis on which they formulated their beliefs about what could and could not happen in the machine, chose which control board lights to believe and which to ignore, and decided what actions to take next. Everyone knows the results (for a description of this process, see Perrow, 1984).

The application of this metaphor to the HIV/AIDS epidemic is not exact, but there were many features in common during the first years of the epidemics. In the early 1980s, a dangerous and unknown disease suddenly appeared in the United States that required a rapid response by agencies and individuals responsible for the nation's health, a response that would necessarily be based on inadequate knowledge. The designated operators of the affected parts of the social machine needed to react and to do something. In the opening stages of the epidemics, when they had a multiplicity of theories and a paucity of data, they nevertheless conducted research guided by these theories and they gave advice to their masters as well as those who were ill. In addition to these directly illness-related activities, the designated operators worried about their own careers and protected their institutional interests, they took notice of the interests of others in the system, and they took for granted "how the system works." These responses of the designated operators of the system were part of the ecology of the epidemics and central to shaping the character of the epidemic/accident (see Shilts, 1987, for one representation of the opening years of the epidemic and Crimp, 1987, for one of many counterrepresentations).

There are some differences both in fact and in the application of the accident metaphor. Perhaps the most important substantive difference is that Three Mile Island was a far more transient event than the HIV/AIDS epidemics. In moments, the critical events in the reactor vessel were over, and perhaps a week passed before the major events in the machine were concluded. It was the work of the next decade to assign the blame, sanitize the rubble, amortize the costs, and hopefully learn the lessons that would prevent similar untoward events in the future. The costs to the nuclear power industry were profound, but the damage to those living near the plant as well as to the social order at large was limited.

One major difference between TMI and HIV/AIDS is that the epidemics will continue to evolve over time (we are now in their second decade in the United States and there will assuredly be a third) with their character constantly being reshaped by attempts to deal with them. Another difference is that, unlike the great but passive and dedicated machine that is a nuclear power plant, the HIV/AIDS epidemics are embodied in an active set of human collectivities. In the case of the epidemics, the designated operators were and are part of the social machine that they wish to manage. While management of the epidemics has become more stabilized in their second decade, there is a continuing stream of potential operators who press into the control room offering new advice, point to ignored lights on the control board, and attempt to pull levers to make things happen.

The Lines of Cleavage

As the epidemics move into their second decade, the coalitions formed in the opening days of the epidemics are eroding. In 1985, the activists and the biomedical researchers covertly combined against the Reagan administration; now that these researchers are better funded and have taken traditional stances about what is good science, the activists attack them. A few years ago, nearly everyone was against contact tracing; now, with new modes of treatment available, old opponents of contact tracing believe it has a new usefulness. New alliances are forming based on ethnic interests, and struggles between drug activists and traditional community leaders opposed to needle exchange have continued in the African American community. The temporary nature of factional and ideological alliances that constitute all social relations in modern life have become accentuated by the dynamic character of the epidemics.

Notes from a Meeting: Day 1

The opening addresses at the Sixth International Conference on AIDS in San Francisco focused on a common theme: that every person who was in the great exposition hall of the Moscone Convention Center (perhaps excluding the police, the janitors, and the service personnel but including the journalists), as well as those who boycotted or could not come to the meeting because of immigration restrictions on those with HIV/AIDS, shared a common cause and a common enemy: the AIDS virus. Everyone, it was said, was engaged in a great crusade—persons living with HIV and AIDS, social workers, activists, virologists, pharmaceutical houses, the GPA of the WHO, community workers, sociologists, direct care physicians, the CDC, the NIAID, Genentech, grant reviewers at NIH, and on and on. The ubiquitous inclusionary phrase was "physicians and scientists and activists."

If persons with HIV/AIDS or those at risk for infection had any enemies other than the "diabolical virus" that insinuates itself into the cell, they were surely not among us. Everybody mentioned how they opposed the Immigration and Naturalization Service restrictions on travel, which had no scientific basis, especially to scientific meetings where the free interchange of ideas was the only goal. A few speakers mentioned the abstractions of racism and sexism and poverty without mentioning the names of the guilty. The mayor of San Francisco said that AIDS was a disaster similar to the recent earthquake that had shattered parts of his community and that it should be addressed with the same levels of outpouring of moral and fiscal support. The mayor, a Democrat, mentioned that the Republicans in the executive branch of the national government might be part of the problem.

Only the speaker from ACT UP offered a more political analysis by remarking that he was losing his faith in the whole enterprise represented by AIDS International, Inc. In a rhetorical move artfully posed to raise the anxieties of the audience, he suggested that he was considering Larry Kramer's advice that he become an AIDS terrorist. He named the names of those who, from the ACT UP perspective, made life difficult for PLWH/As: these included members of the doctors group at the NIH that approved clinical trials, Burroughs Welcome, George Bush, and Jessie Helms. He invited the audience, many of whom had voted for George Bush, to shout in common chorus with the activists (who had gathered in front of the hall) anti-Bush slogans. In the end, he too called for unity; we were, by our presence at the meeting, honorary members of ACT UP.

And after these many speeches, the plenary speaker, a Kenyan woman dressed in modernized traditional dress, spoke in a quiet and dignified but quite predictable way, naming no names, about HIV/AIDS and the situation of women and children in Africa. As she spoke, a quarter, perhaps a third, of the audience drifted out of the hall toward the wine and cheese and fruit heaped on tables around the exhibits set up by the great international medical-pharmaceutical institutions.

A postmodernist pendant: Earlier in the evening, the San Francisco Symphony played, the San Francisco Gay Chorus sang, and we could all watch the speakers and ourselves and little video statements by a rainbow coalition of persons living with HIV and AIDS on giant video screens spread across the hall.

*   *   *

What the plenary speakers at the International AIDS Conference wanted to deny, even though some knew it to be true, is that the AIDS epidemics and the individual and collective response to them are part of a struggle between contending factions over how to define what the epidemics are and, in consequence, how to allocate resources to deal with them (or not deal with them). Everybody in that great hall was *not* on the same side. Even those persons living with HIV/AIDS differed on what to do (will it be ACT UP or GMHC or Queer Nation or some combination of the three?), and their concerns with staying alive in a quality way were related only to the work of a very small proportion of the scientists and physicians who were present. The cleavages and the potential for cleavage ran through the hall, the pharmaceutical houses versus the third party payers and the patients, one virology laboratory pitted against another in a race for publication, the sociologist who wanted a grant versus the physician who had the grant, those in on the ground floor versus the new contenders, the women and African Americans and Latino Americans against "white-middle class gay men," the Third World against the First, the sick against the well.[2]

Consider simply the problem of usage. Acronyms have disappeared: *GRID, ARC, HTLV3*. More "correct" usages appear: *AIDS victims* gave way to *persons with AIDS* and that gives way to *persons living with HIV/AIDS*. Usages clash across group boundaries: African American and Hispanic American, and Asian American, are proposed as parallels to European American as alliances based on color words ("people of color"; *black, white, brown, yellow,* which had already disappeared) may be in decline. Multicultural speak contests with race speak as the appropriate language for distinguishing between groups. Each step in this process of renaming involves both the embracing of fictions as well as the articulation of truths. What cultures does the *Asian American* label disguise and what new cultures and constituencies will its usage create? Is this a temporary "necessary fiction" in much the same way that *Hispanic* was before *Latino* and *Latina*?

Each of these contentious moments of naming are minicrises of meaning for both the practice and the ideology of social studies as science. Such minicrises, if taken seriously, should have (but rarely do have) consequences for the actual doing of science. If one is serious about issues of gender, then the stubs of tables need to contain the words *woman/women* or *man/men* rather than the biological *female* and *male*. Consider what this does to data series such as the census in which reports on females and males over 100 years assumed that biological continuity is a surrogate for cultural continuity. Or the shift in emphasis that would be required to take adequate notice that women and men in West Africa are not the same cultural creatures as women and men in Sweden, to take seriously the contention that persons *are* differently gendered in different cultures. Similarly, if one thinks about the new names for ethnic groups, should one ask the question: "Do you consider yourself Black, White, . . ." or "African American, Hispanic American, European American . . ." and how should the stub at the end of the table read?

The Distribution of Doubt

The willingness to dress in the cloak of authority demanded by the practical considerations of epidemics varies among students of cultural and social life; indeed, there are a fair number who wonder about the label "science" when it is applied to social and cultural studies, not because they share the doubts of the hard sciences about the soft sciences but because they have doubts about positivist science, hard or soft (Fleck, 1935/1979; Kuhn, 1970, 1977). The relativist historians and anthropologists of science, feminist scholars as well as the older traditions of the sociology of knowledge with its roots in Freud and Marx, have been deeply influential in producing a serious crisis of confidence in social and cultural studies, a crisis characterized by an increased prevalence of "epistemological doubters." This kind of doubt goes well beyond the issues raised by even serious "methodological doubters," among whom it is recognized that theories are limited, techniques are imperfect, and data are often error laden. However, such methodological doubters believe that theories may be refined, techniques improved, error reduced, bias accounted for, and that there are some true parameters in nature that human efforts at discovery may approximate. "Nature does not lie," the physical scientist says, "it must only be asked the right question." It is methodological doubt that characterizes the majority of mainline social science professionals who have strong personal and professional commitments to participation in programs of behavior monitoring and change and whose career lines have been defined by giving programmatic advice to policymakers about what to do when faced with various social problems.

Those whose doubt is epistemological go further than those whose doubts extend only to issues of method. For the epistemological doubters, the problem is not in the method or the technique, it is in the practice of doing social science. Put succinctly, it is argued that social researchers do not discover social facts, they participate in their production and reproduction (Geertz, 1973, 1983). This view is at the core of Foucault, the strong theories of social constructionism and symbolic interactionism, relativist theories of the production of scientific knowledge as well as the pragmatist tradition from Pierce to Dewey to Mead to Rorty (1979). The actions of knowledge producers in the social world are part of the production and reproduction of that world: Knowledge is what is good to think, and beliefs are deployed in systems of power and authority. It is not that truth displaces error but that current ideology and practice are replaced by new ideologies and new practices.

The argument is made that the right to explain social phenomenon is not neutral and that who explains a phenomena and how it is explained is central to the control—or, more strongly, the construction—of that phenomenon (Foucault, 1978, 1979; Peckham, 1969, 1979). The analytic distinction between control in the weak sense of participating in the social management of a phenomenon and control in the strong sense that involves the social construction of a phenomenon is one of emphasis. Clearly, one merges into the other; medical doctors, when diagnosing and treating "homosexuals and bisexuals with AIDS," participate in both the management of the behavior of the patient and the maintenance of the "culturally approved" social category, the "homosexual." In both of these senses of control—management and construction—scientists and their explanations are part and parcel of the production of the phenomenon that they study.

Both methodological and epistemological doubt are problematic in the changing contexts of the epidemics, though the effects of the latter are far more extensive than the former. Methodological doubt can be solved by better methods, though there are methodological doubters who believe that the problems of method cannot be solved with sufficient promptness to offer proper guidance either to individuals or to institutions that wish to take pathways that will reduce the risks associated with HIV/AIDS. Epistemological doubters worry whether the information produced in the research process may be so tainted by ideology and by the potential for affirming oppressive social and cultural practices that it will do more harm than good.

Stances and Standing

Many of the students of social and cultural life were attracted to the epidemics for personal reasons or because their prior work was of special relevance to the populations who were infected with HIV. In the United States, the marginality of the populations infected was reflected in the marginality to the professions of many of the social scientists who were first engaged by the epidemics. Persons in social and cultural studies who have research interests in sexuality, drug use, poverty, ethnicity, or women are often as marginal to their professions as the persons studied are to the societies in which they live. Some researchers are members of the groups they studied. This is particularly true of women (many of whom are feminists, some of whom are lesbians), gay men, members of cultural minorities, and the formerly poor. There are, however, only a few currently poor, intravenous drug users, or current members of the "underclass" to be found in the cadres of HIV/AIDS researchers (yet they are found among community "representatives" and "contacts," though they may differ from the natives in the same way that informants differ from those on whom they inform). Many of these researchers, though not all, came to the HIV/AIDS epidemics with more than medicalized visions of what needed to be done.

Indeed, it was among this group of social and cultural researchers that "epistemological doubt" was most common, in part because either they or the persons they had studied had been the targets of "scientific objectivism." At first- or secondhand, they knew that science had been an important element in both the system of social control as well as the construction of social reality. Women researchers knew about sexism, ethnic minority researchers about racism, gay male and lesbian researchers about homophobia, and the formerly poor about poverty.

It was clear to many that the traditional medical approaches to HIV/AIDS and persons living with HIV/AIDS were deeply inadequate and in many cases harmful. Doctors still believed that there were *homosexuals* in the sense of the late 19th-century version of that word and had to be disabused at nearly every turn about gay life. Medical professionals still need to be disabused of the notion that intravenous drug users are universally sneaky, unreliable, weak willed, and treacherous in addition to being noncompliant with medical regimes. If the medical profession's gaze rarely rises above the level of the symptom in normal times, in HIV/AIDS times, it often focuses on the level of the cell, the molecule, or the gene. As persons living with HIV/AIDS struggle to be persons (and not an acronym: *PLWH/A*), scientists are interested in arcane measures of biological functions in the immune system. It is true that the attention given to this level of the organism is what will make people well in the magic bullet sense—AZT does extend life somewhat, aerosolized pentamidine does prevent and treat PCP for a time, the hoped-for vaccine will prevent transmission—however, in the view from the laboratory, the patient may appear to be more and more like the genetically similar white rats that can be ordered from some breeding colony.

At least some of the social scientists who were called to the cause felt uneasy about their new collaboration with the biomedical sciences because they had been at the forefront of criticizing the medical model in health care as well as the medicalization of all social problems. It is hard to tell what has happened to this uneasiness as the traditional medical establishment has successfully occupied the terrain of AIDS and HIV disease. There is (or ought to be) an exquisite tension created for the gay scientist who opposes the essentialist psychiatric vision of "homosexuality" while working in a research unit that tests for and diagnoses "AIDS dementia" or studies the psychiatric natural history of AIDS among "homosexual and bisexuals." Similarly, a certain anguish should be felt by the woman researcher who studies the social networks of women patients in hospitals where the same women do not participate in drug trials. Perhaps in the daily struggle of "doing" the work, the anomalies are ignored or swallowed or reduced in significance because of the larger goals.

The capture of the high ground of epidemic by biomedical science is expressed in more ways than by the fact that they receive three quarters of the money allocated for HIV/AIDS research by the federal government or that the studies that the social scientists do usually mimic the studies that the doctors do. Consider the roles that social scientists play at the interface between the biomedical profession and the "community" or their role as "prevention scientists." The interface role is often played by social scientists who are members of "the afflicted communities" when they use their community membership to explain the culture of their community to biomedical scientists and when they aid biomedical scientists in securing the cooperation of the community in the production of serums, data, and behavioral compliance. The representation of this relationship in all of its individual and collective complexity is very difficult. The job of the "prevention scientist" is to find ways to reduce transmission at the individual and community levels, and this involves attempts to create "behavioral interventions" that can be proven to "work." Here again, membership in either afflicted or potentially afflicted communities is an important source of authority in intervention design even if measurement strategies are quite conventional. These roles can be experienced as either being required by the epidemic (as a natural force) or as the result of the structures of domination that exist between the biomedical establishment and their social and behavioral science coworkers/subordinates.

The Decline of Scientific Sanctity

The participation of social and behavioral scientists who are members of the "afflicted communities" and others who are marginal to the larger scientific enterprise in the epidemic is made more complex by the social mobilization of cultural groups to resist "scientific" queries and methods and answers. The most obvious of these forms of resistance has been participation in randomized placebo-control drug trials by persons living with HIV/AIDS. It is easy to forget how normal such trials, or approximations to them, have become in biomedical science since the 1950s. There have been many trials in which persons with fatal illnesses have passively allowed themselves to be allocated by the luck of the draw to no-treatment conditions in which the physician could be sure that the patient was not being helped in ways that were better than normal practice. The willingness to resist medical authority has not always been very strong even in extremis (though there is considerable evidence of noncompliance in many other drug trials).

This recent challenge to medical authority has been abetted by an accumulating list of medical catastrophes. Thalidomide babies, the increased incidence of vaginal cancer among those treated with DES, the deaths of patients as a result of the Cutter vaccine, the resistance of surgeons to lumpectomies (versus radical mastectomies) are constant reminders of the fragility of medical knowledge and practice. Such disasters are, of course, swords with two edges—biomedical researchers use them to argue for increased care and control in the production of new treatments, critics of biomedical research use them to point out the scientific and ideological failures of medicine as well as, in some cases, the venality of the scientists. Outside of medicine, the failed promises of science (perhaps only defined as such by the "risk averse") that are manifested in Three Mile Island and Chernobyl, Love Canal, and Rocky Flats—and lest social scientists forget, the War on Poverty and public housing projects—have increased the level of collective mistrust in the scientific/technological enterprise, even among scientists.

The increased vulnerability of science to external criticism rests on more than its mistakes. Accusations of "materialism" and greed and politicking for the Nobel prize have become increasingly common. Arrowsmith and Madame Curie seem to have made a deal with Genentech or Burroughs Welcome and, in making a deal, they have given up even the appearance of virtue. In this scramble for the material rewards, can fraud be far behind? Here the crucial point is that extrascientific groups become more central in deciding on what the scientific standards are and how they should be applied. From the right, there is a new breed of religious critics who are intervening in science both in a larger arena (e.g., creationism and evolution) but more particularly in the management of HIV/AIDS itself. Religious groups have had an impact on government funding of intervention programs that are "too sexually explicit," have killed condom education programs, have prevented surveys of sexual conduct, and have engaged in television campaigns against the reports of scientific bodies. Finally, political groups both in local areas and at the national level have resisted programs of needle exchange on the grounds that this would result in "sending the wrong message about drugs."

In each of these examples of external intervention in scientific affairs, there is evidence of a larger agenda (the problem of fraud in science, the struggle between science and religion, and the "war on drugs") in which the

HIV/AIDS epidemics have supplied an additional opportunity for conflict. In this set of conflicts, the social scientist is particularly vulnerable, for in the above list it is only the problem of fraud and profiteering that is aimed at the biomedical sciences. It is the behavioral intervention programs and the data gathering efforts of the social scientists that are most likely to be attacked by traditional religious and political groups. It is perhaps an irony that many social and behavioral scientists who are pleased by the interventions of the "community" in the scientific process are themselves the target of intervention by other communities.

Doubt and Participation

The demands of the HIV/AIDS epidemics have been and will be practical and immediate. Many students of social and cultural life, even those with deep "epistemological doubts," have and will participate as *social scientists* in goal-oriented research, do surveys that they know are flawed, and compare statistical results even though they know the limits of statistics. They will conduct applied ethnographies that focus on the part and not the whole, prepare and score psychological tests even though they do not believe in traits, engage in thin description, and, all in all, submit themselves to the rigors of positivist science. The goal of such activities will surely be worthy—saving lives. At the same time, the speed at which the epidemic and its representations are moving means that today's facts and today's advice might be tomorrow's falsehoods. Many social scientists have been and will be caught between their impulse to doubt (either methodologically or epistemologically) and the consequent pressures to disengage and criticize and the pressures of the epidemics to participate, to engage in research that has the primary goal of managing and changing the lives of those who are its subjects/victims rather than the social and cultural order in which they live.

Researchers in social and cultural social studies have a peculiar place in the history of the epidemics, because some of these researchers understand the particular tension between the practical necessity of research participation that may be of some use and the understanding that such participation may result in the reproduction of oppression. The experience of this tension should be understood as a trouble, not a pain. The ultimate pain of the epidemics is inflicted on those who are living with and dying of HIV/AIDS; other pains, even those experienced by those most intimate with those who are living and dying with the disease, usually recede, albeit slowly, with forgetfulness.

Notes from a Conference: Day 5

The closing speeches of the conference were directed at unity. There will be no meeting in Boston if U.S. immigration rules against the entry of persons living with HIV/AIDS are maintained, said an important speaker. Applause. Cheers. But there was a profound uneasiness in the hall. There was a rumor that ACT UP had a copy of the remarks that were to be made by Louis Sullivan, Secretary of the Department of Health and Human Services, and there would be a ZAP. It was clear that those on the podium were anxiously aware of the movement in the audience as activists handed out flyers to physicians and researchers. Anthony Fauci condemned ACT UP for condemning members of the clinical trials group, particularly for naming names, while holding out the kind of olive branch that would continue the symbiosis between the ill and the physicians and researchers. The place of Louis Sullivan on the program was changed to the end. As he rose to speak, the activists gathered around the front of the room began to shout so loudly that Sullivan, when he spoke, could not be heard. Many in the audience who were not shouting stood and turned their backs to the speaker. Others drifted out the door, some deafened, others angry, many wondering what this had to do with their epidemic.

Notes

1. The plural form of *epidemic* is a deliberate usage. The epidemics do not have some "natural course" even as the disease HIV/AIDS does not have a "natural history." HIV/AIDS is a different epidemic among the inner-city poor than it is among various groups of men who have sex with men, and the epidemic is not the same in the Soviet Union, Zaire, or Thailand. The social and cultural ecology of the epidemics creates the response to disease that creates the course of the epidemics in any given society or sector of a society. Similarly, the presence or absence of specific cultures of illness and health and available technologies of health care will create the sociomedical history of HIV/AIDS.

2. The HIV/AIDS epidemics can best be understood theoretically as an "ecology of games" (Long, 1958). As Long pointed out, even bounded communities are a complex of individuals who play many roles and have many personal and organizational allegiances (which constitute groups and institutions). In such communities, individuals and groups contend both directly and indirectly with each other, often not even realizing that they are in opposition. Even individuals have divided interests such that, when they play the role of parent, it may conflict with their role as worker, not only in private and psychologically, where most role conflict is thought to occur, but in the public arena as well. Parent wants better schools, taxpayer wants lower taxes, worker wants to get to work faster, mother wants more stop signs, and so on. In situations of recognized community conflict, the calls of community leaders for individuals to subordinate their interests to the higher interests of the community are not simply appeals for community. Such situations

are more often those in which the "higher interest" of the community coincides with the interests of those who make the calls for the community. Such a perspective that points out that social life is the outcome of contending groups is particularly appropriate to the inchoate and ad hoc aggregate of groups and individuals that make up the AIDS epidemics and their constituencies.

References

Crimp, D. (1987). How to have promiscuity in an epidemic. *October, 43*, 237-268.

Fleck, L. (1979). *The genesis of a scientific fact*. Chicago: University of Chicago Press. (Original work published 1935)

Foucault, M. (1978). *The history of sexuality: Vol. 1. An introduction*. New York: Pantheon.

Foucault, M. (1979). *Discipline and punish: The birth of the prison*. New York: Pantheon.

Geertz, C. (1973). *The interpretation of cultures*. New York: Basic Books.

Geertz, C. (1983). *Local knowledge*. New York: Basic Books.

Kuhn, T. S. (1970). *The structure of scientific revolutions* (2nd ed.). Chicago: University of Chicago Press.

Kuhn, T. S. (1977). *The essential tension*. Chicago: University of Chicago Press.

Long, N. (1958). The local community as an ecology of games. *American Journal of Sociology, 64*(3), 251-261.

Peckham, M. (1969). *Art and pornography: An experiment in explanation*. New York: Basic Books.

Peckham, M. (1979). *Explanation and power: The control of human behavior*. New York: Seabury.

Perrow, C. (1984) *Normal accidents*. New York: Basic Books.

Rorty, R. (1979). *Philosophy and the mirror of nature*. Princeton, NJ: Princeton University Press.

Shilts, R. (1987). *And the band played on*. New York: St. Martin's.

3

AIDS: History and
Contemporary History

VIRGINIA BERRIDGE

History and historians have had a significant role in interpreting the AIDS epidemic. This chapter aims to analyze what that role has been and how it has changed over time. History, in some national responses to AIDS, became a directly policy-relevant science. There have been later "uses of history" too, among them a more sophisticated use of "history as background" and the development of the "contemporary history" of AIDS itself, historians chronicling the very recent past. The recent policy history of AIDS in the United Kingdom provides an example and has implications for the concept of "relevant history" and the relation of history to policy. These functions for history cannot be exercised in isolation; AIDS has served to underline the reciprocities between the perceptions of that discipline and those of other social sciences and has stimulated a greater awareness of the nature of the boundaries.

The primary focus in this chapter is the role played by history in the British AIDS story. In policy terms, that story may be briefly outlined; in Britain, the policy reaction has passed through three stages (Berridge & Strong, 1991a). The years from 1981 to 1986 were a time when AIDS was seen as a new and potentially epidemic disease, when AIDS was an open policy area.

AUTHOR'S NOTE. I am grateful to the Nuffield Provincial Hospitals Trust for financial support and to Ingrid James for secretarial assistance. This chapter derives from work done jointly with Philip Strong, a medical sociologist, on the history of the social impact of AIDS in the United Kingdom.

This period saw the outbreak of the disease in several widely differing groups, the development of public alarm and social stigmatization, and a lack of scientific certainty about the nature of the disease. On the policy side, there was relatively little official action but, behind the scenes, considerable openness to new policy actors and the establishment of a new policy community around AIDS. This was a period of policy development from below. It was succeeded in 1986-1987 by a brief stage of quasi-wartime emergency, in which national politicians and senior nonmedical civil servants intervened. A high-level consensual political response emerged. From 1987 on, these two phases have been followed by a third, the current period of slow "normalization" of the disease, in which the rate of growth of the epidemic has slowed and public interest and panic markedly decreased. Official institutions have been established and formal procedures adopted and reviewed; paid professionals have replaced the earlier volunteers. The high-level political response has gone; the problem now is to maintain the salience of AIDS on the policy agenda. How far this particular national model of policy development can be generally applied is open to further research. A cross-national comparison of the United States, Britain, and Sweden suggests broadly similar stages of development, although with significant national differences in detailed areas of response (Fox, Day, & Klein, 1989). In France and in the Netherlands too, the overall stages of development have been similar, although with national divergences both in time scale and in reactions to particular issues (Berridge, 1990; Steffen, 1990). The three-stage model of policy change over time seems applicable at least to most western European countries.

AIDS and the "Lesson of History"

In the early phase, history had its own special role in relation to AIDS. The novelty and shock of a life-threatening infectious disease of potentially epidemic proportions in the late 20th century rapidly led to a search for explanatory models with some degree of predictive power. How had society reacted to and dealt with past epidemics? Could the past give a clue to the end of this particular disease story? What forms of reaction were appropriate? The input from historical experience was actively sought. Historical consciousness was not confined to historians. Many nonhistorical books on AIDS made reasoned obeisance to the historical record. Historians of cholera and other epidemics found themselves catapulted into a round of AIDS conferences that actively sought to hear the "lesson of history." The annual international AIDS conference, a jamboree of mammoth proportions, developed a history strand amid a primarily clinical, scientific, and epidemiological focus. In Britain, the preexisting historical interests of two key actors, Professor Michael Adler at the Middlesex Hospital and Sir Donald Acheson, chief medical officer at the Department of Health, ensured that the historical record was brought into the policy debates. The reports of the chief medical officer in the early AIDS years were consciously historical. The *Annual Report* was, it was stated, a historical record of current issues; AIDS also needed to be assessed in the context of past disease. The fight against it was akin to the work of Sir John Simon and the 19th-century public health pioneers.

This historical input also has its own historiography, which can tell us at one and the same time something about the stages of social and policy reaction to AIDS but also something about the nature of historical involvement in current policy events, about the whole notion of "relevant history." That discussion will be left to the concluding section. For the moment, the chapter will focus on how historical input mirrored the stages of social and policy reaction. This can be divided into two quite distinct stages—first, the "panic" period of policy reaction that drew historical parallels with examples of epidemic disease in past societies, and, second, as AIDS has become encapsulated within a normal or chronic model of disease, the role of historians in writing "contemporary history" has come to the fore.

Of what did the initial historical input consist? It focused on three broad areas: the role of epidemic disease in past societies, in particular, the association between disease and "moral panic" or disease and stigmatized minorities; the tradition of voluntarism in the area of sexually transmitted diseases and, in particular, the case of the Contagious Diseases Acts in Britain in the 19th century; and more general questions of public health policy and the means of carrying them out, such as quarantine or notification, thus contributing to the classic debate between the common good and individual rights. Take, for example, the book *AIDS: The Burdens of History* edited by Elizabeth Fee and Daniel Fox (1989a). Articles in the Fee and Fox volume exemplify the range of this early historical interest. The collection derives in part from a 1986 *Millbank Quarterly* supplement that gave a range of historical responses to the epidemic. Charles Rosenberg provided a historiographic discussion of social historians' views of disease, ranging from the historians' acceptance of medical categories and optimistic faith in the powers of science and medicine in the 1930s and 1940s to the radical skepticism of the 1960s and 1970s. AIDS, he argued, would blunt the assault of the more fervent social constructionists. Guenter Risse looked at the social context of epidemic disease and the ways in which political and health organizations had responded. Two chapters specifically examined the public health issues involved. David Musto analyzed quarantine in relation to AIDS. Dorothy and Roy Porter explored the history of public health in Britain to examine the conflicts arising—through compulsory vaccination, for example—between individual freedom and the public good, a debate that they expanded further in a later article (Porter & Porter, 1988). Here they concluded—from a discussion of the lunacy laws, compulsory vaccination, the Contagious Diseases Acts, and the 1889 and 1899 Notification of Diseases Acts—that securing public health depended as much on the balance of power between preventive and curative medicine as anything else. Other chapters in the Fee-Fox collection deal specifically with the question of reactions toward sexually transmitted diseases. Elizabeth Fee, in a paper on venereal disease in 20th-century Baltimore, discussed how the Black community there was held largely responsible for syphilis, which was perceived as a disease of the guilty. Allan Brandt's study of social responses to venereal disease showed how these have expressed cultural anxieties about contagion, contamination, and sexuality. He urges policymakers to pay attention to the history of STDs before deciding on health and social policies for dealing with AIDS (Brandt, 1987).

Discussion of such historical examples as the struggles over compulsory vaccination in the 19th century seemed appropriate when talk of quarantine and the isolation of AIDS sufferers was in the air and public fear was at its height. The range of historical material brought to bear was great. One article can stand as an example. In December 1986 (when the panic reaction to AIDS was at its peak), the historian Roy Porter wrote an editorial in the *British Medical Journal.* Headed "History Says No to the Policeman's Response to AIDS," it argued strongly, using the historical precedent of the Contagious Diseases Acts, against adding AIDS to the list of notifiable diseases (Porter, 1986, pp. 1589-1590).

> Historical precedent says "no." For unlike casually contagious diseases, sexually transmitted diseases constitute a special case in which the direct methods of the law have been tried, found wanting, and abandoned. . . . Desperate diseases may require desperate remedies. Faced with the enormity of the suffering AIDS will inflict, humanity demands that we at least consider draconian measures such as compulsory screening for suspected virus carriers and further steps to protect others. Experience suggests, however, that this would be unwise.

This editorial, unlike many based on historical perspectives, attracted considerable interest. For arguments such as these were not, at that stage, simply academic. These forms of historical perspective were not simply the usual icing on the cake. In the British context at least, the historical arguments appear to have had some degree of policy impact. Porter's type of argument, drawing on analogies from the history of public health in relation to civil liberties and on historical examples of the control of sexually transmitted diseases, also entered into the policy area. In particular, the traditions of voluntary and nonpunitive control in the area of sexually transmitted disease were central to the debate. Sir Donald Acheson, in his evidence to the House of Commons Social Services Committee inquiry into AIDS in 1987, cited the historical record as a prime reason for avoiding a punitive response to AIDS. The "lesson of history" in that area also entered into the arguments in 1985 around whether AIDS should be made a notifiable disease. Extension in that year of the Public Health (Notification of Disease) Regulations of 1984 to cover AIDS did allow draconian precautions—for instance, the compulsory removal of a dangerously infected AIDS sufferer to hospital. But this regulation was used only once, and the demand for notification was thereby deflected. The historical arguments and analogies thus seem to have been of some importance in initial British policy formation. In the United States, the "lesson of history" was also used to support the liberal policy line. But opponents of the liberal approach also pointed to historical precedent. The particular "lesson of history" was not a consensual one. The historical response was mediated by the nature of the particular political system through which it filtered.

Drugs and the "Lesson of History"

At times of policy flux, the "lesson of history" takes on a vivid life. AIDS in the 1980s is not the only example. Others can be cited; for example, the relationship between historical analysis and policies in the mental health area, in particular, in the 1960s and 1970s (Scull, 1989). The historical input into drug control policy over time has also been significant. It provides instructive contrasts that are of relevance for the relation of history to policy. In the 1960s and 1970s, at a time of policy change, the historical record was brought into play. The focus was U.S. drug policy. Attempts to liberalize U.S. drug policy and to introduce methadone maintenance, outpatient treatment, and a role for doctors turned to the contrast between British and U.S. experience for justification. How this came about needs a brief explanation

(Berridge, 1984; Musto, 1973). The United States in the 1920s adopted a penal system of narcotic control. Legal decisions under the 1914 Harrison Narcotics Act established that maintenance prescribing was not legitimate. Addicts were thrown on the resources of the black market operated by the criminal underworld, and doctors who prescribed to them were liable to end up in prison. In the 1950s and 1960s, moves were made to substitute disease views of addiction and medical treatment for criminal prosecution. Marie Nyswander's *The Drug Addict as a Patient* (1956) and the report of the joint committee of the American Bar Association and the American Medical Association (1958) argued for a medical approach. The "British System," which offered the possibility of medical maintenance prescribing, was seen as a shining example of the possibilities of medical control. The Rolleston Report of 1926, which had confirmed the legitimacy of such prescribing options, was, it was argued, the cause of Britain's small addict population. Reformers like Troy Duster and Edwin Schur looked to the British system as an ideal and cited the history of its origins in contrast to the "wrong turning" taken by the United States. Interest was such that, at one stage, two U.S. funding agencies, the Drug Abuse Council and the National Institute on Drug Abuse, were supporting major studies of the history of British drug policy. The implications for U.S. drug policy in the 1960s and 1970s appeared to be clear. The history of British drug policy in the 1920s and after emerged as a powerful rhetorical symbol in the minds of policy reformers.

Rolleston and the 1920s provided the type of "lesson of history" for drug policy in the 1960s that the Contagious Diseases Acts provided for AIDS in the 1980s. In Britain, when debate again began around drug policy in the late 1970s, the traditional "liberal" interpretations of Rolleston were revived. But there have been few attempts to draw out the "lesson of history" so far as AIDS and drug policy in the 1980s are concerned. Unlike the initial historical input into AIDS, the impact of AIDS on drug policy, in Britain at least, has not brought forth the historical debates that marked the earlier period of policy flux. The emphasis has tended to be on the essential newness of the impact of AIDS on mechanisms of drug control. As I have argued elsewhere, AIDS did not usher in totally new directions in drug policy but enhanced and made possible the achievement of preexisting policy objectives (Berridge, 1991). But the achievement of those preexisting objectives, their attainment of political and practical feasibility, was better achieved in those circumstances by an emphasis on the essential newness of developments, as a response to potentially epidemic and unusual circumstances. In such a situation, it suited no policy interest to call on the historical record. The "lesson of history" could bring no practical policy advantage, by contrast with AIDS.

The Later Uses of History

History as Background

The form of historical input for AIDS policies has also changed over time. The early period has passed and with it the role for epidemic history. AIDS is no longer in many senses an open policy area. The difference is conceptualized in the contrast between the *Millbank* collection in 1986, full of historical parallels, and a special issue of *Daedalus* in 1989 ("Living with AIDS," 1989). There, only one article, by Charles Rosenberg, makes direct reference to the historical perspective. Rosenberg's piece too is distinctly postheroic in tone. It notes the range of policy choices in an epidemic; TB, far more widespread in the 19th century, did not elicit the moral and political pressure for immediate action evoked by yellow fever or cholera. The historical reaction to AIDS is clearly less apocalyptic. Comments Rosenberg, "Epidemics ordinarily end with a whimper, not a bang." The historical input mirrors the normalization of AIDS itself. Chronic, not epidemic disease, is the focus.

But this is not the end of the matter for AIDS and history. For AIDS, in its later stages, has opened up the possibility of different types of input and different forms of historical relevance. The uses of history are developing, and can develop, in a more sophisticated way than in the early stages of the epidemic. Three forms of historical input can be outlined—broadly, history as background, or the way in which particular social, political, and national relations mediate the impact of disease; the "prehistory" of AIDS, the history of areas with which AIDS has intersected; and, finally, AIDS itself as history, the chronicling of policy development around the disease and its social impact, the "contemporary history" of a current issue in health policy. This chapter focuses on the latter two of these three forms of input, but the potential role of history as background should not be forgotten. The issue is not a blanket application of the history of reactions to past epidemics to the present. But, as Shirley Lindenbaum has argued, historians should analyze why AIDS is both like and unlike past epidemics and should be aware of the ways in which reactions to disease have been mediated by historically specific social and political relations.[1] Reactions to disease cannot be generalized; there is some value in looking at different ideological approaches to different diseases, for example, the different ways in which pellagra and hookworm were interpreted in the U.S. cotton economy in the 1920s. The way in which stigma in relation to disease has been historically situated is also of importance. Leprosy, for example, reappeared as a stigmatized disease in western European perceptions in the 19th century when it was discovered in nations being colonized; this was not a continuous history of stigma but a retainting. The contemporary dichotomy between individual and public rights in health matters is also historically specific, medical expertise mediating and serving to define the boundaries between the individual and the public. Particular national and colonial histories also mediate responses to disease. There is in general a need to move from the early "epidemics of history" approach to an understanding of the historically specific social and political relations of disease.

AIDS as History: The Prehistory of AIDS

Part of the more specific historical response to the relationship between disease and history has been the concept of AIDS itself as a historical occurrence. Many of the early protagonists in the "epidemic" phases of the disease were conscious that they were living through historic events. Now the notion of AIDS itself as history has come to the fore and with it the potential role of the "contemporary history" of health policy. Among the protagonists of this development have been the historians Elizabeth Fee and Daniel Fox. At a conference, AIDS and the Historian, in 1988, they argued that history, through AIDS, was refining itself and resuming its role as a policy science. They suggested the concept of combat historians as useful in elucidating the historians' role and argued for reciprocity with studies in other disciplines and the policy professions (Fee & Fox, 1989a, 1989b). The group of historians around Guenter Risse in San Francisco have also been important in researching both the early history of AIDS and its scientific and clinical medical contexts.[2]

The contemporary history of AIDS is focusing on two areas. The first arises from the historians' sense of continuity with the past and has looked for precedents and at the "prehistory" of areas with which AIDS has intersected. The second has sought to write the history of the disease itself either in national or in cross-national contexts. The notion of the "prehistory" of AIDS fits with the historical sense of continuity and of change in policy development. AIDS itself might be new—and many interpretations have rightly stressed the novelty and shock of a new and potentially epidemic disease. But the agendas into which it was fit were not. For example, in the U.S. context, Martin Levine has analyzed the preexisting "background noise" in the coherent middle-class gay communities in New York and San Francisco. Issues such as the demedicalization of homosexuality (and its potential remedicalization via AIDS) and opposition to safe sex were important because of the previous gay rights agenda.[3] The initial reaction to AIDS cannot be understood without this prehistory. Likewise, the scientific and clinical reaction to AIDS needs to be set into the context of shifts in clinical medicine and in scientific research after World War II. The historical context of the relationship between research and commercial interests, for example, has been explored through a study of wartime pharmaceutical research and the development of penicillin (Adams, 1989). The policy issues surrounding hepatitis B have been analyzed as, in some senses, the precursor of AIDS—although with important differences in reaction (Muraskin, 1988). Some of this material has recently been discussed at a working conference.[4] Drug policy and the impact of AIDS provides a specific illustration of the importance of prehistory. Ernest Quimby's chapter in this volume analyzes how the impact of AIDS on U.S. drug policy should be interpreted in the light of preexisting tensions, in particular, the launch of a new "war on drugs" and the debates around the issue of the relationship of ethnic minorities to drugs. In the British context, AIDS has been seen as bringing a radical change in drug policy with a focus on a public health-oriented and harm minimization policy rather than the "war on drugs" approach. Seen in the light of the prehistory of policy, AIDS appears more realistically as a catalyst, bringing about changes already inherent in the existing directions and alliances within policy (Berridge, 1991). In this as in other areas, the impact of the disease is impossible to assess without a sense of prehistory.

The "Contemporary History" of AIDS

So far as the history of AIDS itself is concerned, work has emerged from a combination of historians and policy scientists. The Americans, with their earlier experience of the disease, have taken the lead. Some of the papers in the Fee-Fox volume go into some analytic detail. Gerald Oppenheimer contrasts the roles played by epidemiologists and virologists in the scientific construction of AIDS. Epidemiologists played a prominent part in defining and ordering the disease—and first named it "AIDS." The isolation of the virus, however, redefined AIDS as a set of biomedical problems open to chemical resolution in the form of drugs and vaccines. Daniel Fox, in a paper titled "AIDS and the American Health Polity," uses the response to AIDS as prism through which to view the structure of the U.S. health care system and the health policy process. This U.S. domination of the AIDS history story is only in part remedied by a paper "AIDS: The Intellectual Agenda" by Jeffrey Weeks (1988). This assigns a periodization to the U.K. AIDS story and discusses a number of historical, social science, political, and social policy issues. Weeks perceptively comments on the way in which AIDS has laid bare the complexities of policy formation in pluralist societies. But he draws relatively little on his previous work on the history of gay politics. Activism tends to predominate rather than a historian's appreciation of where AIDS has fitted in and what it has done for that culture and political scene. Other analyses come from a mixture of historians and policy scientists—for example, the cross-national comparison by Fox, Day, and Klein (1989). This article refutes the standard line in most analyses of Anglo-American AIDS policy that AIDS was a heaven-sent opportunity for the populist New Right governments of the 1980s. Government action was scandalously slow because government simply did not care so long as merely gay men were affected. High-level political intervention occurred only when the threat to the heterosexual population became clear. Fox, Day, and Klein take a different line. In their account, neither right-wing ideology nor public opinion had much effect. A lot of noise was made, but policy, as in almost all health arenas, was still dominated by the traditional, liberal, biomedical elite. This analysis underestimates the openness and fluidity of AIDS policymaking, at least in the early stages, as is argued below. But it, nonetheless, serves as a powerful and skeptical corrective to widely disseminated analysis.

Contemporary historians are active in Britain, the United States, and elsewhere—with studies of the early clinical and scientific response to the disease, of the CDC's response to AIDS, of the development of AIDS policies in the United Kingdom and in France, for example. Such work must be produced in alliance with the concepts and methodologies of other disciplines. It draws on "journalistic history" such as Shilt's *And the Band Played On* (1988) and Robin McKie's British version, *Panic: The Story of AIDS* (1986). The contribution from journalistic accounts and the relationship between journalism and contemporary history has been discussed elsewhere, as has the conceptual and pragmatic contribution of academic sociology (Berridge & Strong, 1991b; Strong & Berridge, 1990). The input from policy studies is also important—and perhaps, for historians, the most novel approach. British political science has a well-developed analysis of general policy formation, and there is a strong school of social policy/social administration analysis with a particular focus on welfare policy (including historical case studies; Hall, Land, Parker, & Webb, 1975). But there is less systematic work on health problems. Nonetheless, what is available provides important conceptual additions to the historian's baggage. A further piece by Day and Klein (1989) sees the development of major government interest in AIDS in the United Kingdom in 1986-1987 as an example of government signaling to the public that the issue was to be dealt with as one of consensus. John Street (1988), another political scientist, has also focused on that political "emergency" reaction, stressing how the public health lobby, in attracting political support, at the same time lost its early power and influence. And Pettigrew and Ferlie's (1989) analysis of AIDS policy development in a particular health district has focused on how structures and organizations accommodate to rapid and radical change. Most important, those studies have underlined the need to expand the range of theoretical input into contemporary history. We need to know about theories of policy systems; about the stages of policy formation, implementation, and impact; about agenda setting and hidden agendas; about the policy process and the location of power and interest. Anthropological perspectives too, as the conference on which this book is based demonstrated, can fruitfully intersect with the contemporary history of AIDS, in particular, through shared interests in the formation and transformation of culture over time and concepts of the social construction of scientific ideas, as the next section will indicate.

AIDS Policies in the United Kingdom: The Early Years 1981-1986

This is not to argue that such concepts or methodologies should dominate contemporary history—of AIDS or of other areas of health policy. But the particular sensitivities of historians can enhance the impact of methods and concepts derived from other disciplines. Traditional historical methodology, with its faithfulness to documents and its assessment of sources, must, so historians have argued, be central. This chapter will now turn to illustrate briefly from the AIDS Social History Programme's own work on AIDS policies in the United Kingdom. In particular, it will examine the early period of the reaction to the disease from 1981 to 1986, prior to the years of political emergency reaction. It will argue that AIDS was a new and open policy area at that stage. There were no established departmental, local, or health authority mechanisms in which it could be encompassed. There were no established expert advisory mechanisms that could deal with it; in fact, there were no experts. There was no preexisting "policy community" around

AIDS. This period, therefore, illustrates clearly how a policy community developed around the disease, how gay activists, clinicians, and scientists coalesced and consorted, sometimes uneasily around the issue, and how links were established with the Department of Health and, in particular, the public health interests within that department. Most current interpretations of policy reactions to the epidemic have focused on AIDS policymaking as a top-down process, whereby government reacted in traditionally consensual ways, sending signals about appropriate reactions into the public domain. But, in the earlier period of reaction, policy was formed in rather a different way—in a bottom-up rather than a top-down way, with a volunteer rather than an official ethos. The policy line—of the danger of a heterosexual epidemic, of the danger to the general population rather than to particular "risk groups"—which was later adopted and expanded at the political level, was first laid down by the group of "new entrants" to the policymaking scene.

Take, for example, the early gay response and how it developed. Some gay men in the United States in the early 1980s began to hear of people dying of strange cancers. A member of a student gay group in Cambridge recalled how their gay help line began to get calls after a BBC *Horizon* program, "Killer in the Village," in 1983. They began to look around for information and to hold weekly meetings on AIDS and health issues. "We were groping in the dark. There was no sense of there being anyone other than us to turn to." Some immediately saw the potential seriousness of the disease.

> My first encounter with AIDS was a tiny little one sentence in the *Guardian* in 1981 about two deaths in the States. A friend of mine pointed to it and said it was going to be the biggest issue in our lives.[5]

But this was far from being a general reaction. A man, who was later among the first to be diagnosed seropositive, recalled:

> My reaction at that time insofar as I considered it a personal threat—my reaction was to distance myself from it—there were small numbers and so it was unlikely to affect one personally. . . . I didn't take much notice, it seemed so remote . . . that was a general reaction.[6]

But in May 1983, that reaction began to change. The *Horizon* program "Killer in the Village" appears to have had a key impact on the gay response. Volunteers at the Gay and Lesbian Switchboard in London arranged to open up a special line after the program and volunteers were specifically briefed. "For a number of days after, a lot of very worried people were ringing. . . . The "Killer in the Village" programme was absolutely crucial."[7]

The Gay and Lesbian Switchboard was of central importance in the initial response. In May 1983, more than 200 attended the country's first public conference on AIDS organized by the Switchboard. Mel Rosen, director of the New York-based Gay Men's Health Crisis, spoke. Some present at the conference remembered his words: "There's a train coming down the track and it's heading at you." A member of the audience recalled, "I was struck by the potential gravity of what was happening and the absolute silence on what was happening—there was very little in the mainstream press."[8] The *Horizon* program also led to the refounding (also in 1983) of the Terrence Higgins Trust. The trust had originally been established the previous year (as the Terry Higgins Trust) by friends of Terrence Higgins, who had died of AIDS in abject circumstances in a London hospital. In its initial incarnation, it had a working-class ethos ("they were East End wide boys really") and was associated with the Motor Sports Club, a group of gay bikers.[9] But, in 1983, it changed into a very different organization. After the Switchboard conference, the trust developed under the aegis of middle-class gay men with organizational and political experience and some with specific health education expertise. These "alternative professionals," as one put it, dropped the earlier emphasis on fund-raising for research and moved toward a focus on health education and an input into policy. A key figure in this process was Tony Whitehead, formerly a Switchboard volunteer and later chairman of the Trust Steering Committee. By the end of 1983, the trust was producing its first leaflets on AIDS and, early in 1984, it opened its own AIDS help line. Articles in the gay press—for example, by Julian Meldrum, who was the trust's press officer and also a *Capital Gay* correspondent—forced discussion of issues like safe sex and the role of promiscuity within the gay community. One gay man recalled, "Safe sex really hit London at the end of 1984."

Also involved in the initial gay response at a medical level was the Gay Medical Association, which produced a leaflet early on directed at doctors dealing with AIDS. Its response was to stress the potential and actual heterosexual nature of the disease. In April 1983, a letter in the *British Medical Journal* made this point strongly. An AIDS review article by Professor Waterson had compared the syndrome to diseases of overcrowded poultry, relating it, as was common at that time, to the use of nitrates and the high number of sexual contacts among some gay men. Gay Medical Association representatives commented,

> Of course, promiscuity is an important factor in the spread of communicable diseases, but promiscuity is not the prerogative of homosexuals. . . . The homosexual community has demonstrated its awareness of its own health problems. We are confident that it will respond to health education programmes which are not underwritten by any prejudice or moralising. (Farrell et al., 1983, p. 1143)

The correspondents pointed out that this was a condition that could potentially affect the whole of society—already around 25% of cases to date had not been in homosexual males.

The voluntaristic, self-helping ethos of the initial response is clear—for example, in Body Positive, a group for seropositive people that was set up at the end of 1984:

> After our eight weeks course (organized by the Terrence Higgins Trust) came to an end, six of us decided we didn't want it to end . . . we decided to continue to meet; one of the six had a flat in Earl's Court and met every week and decided we had something quite important . . . we organized a disco . . . it was a way of re-creating a familiar social setting but with HTLV III out in the open.[10]

There were levels of volunteer expertise—in Body Positive, people were there because of the virus not because of organizational and movement experience.

The "gay freemasonry," already existing networks of gay men, operated to spread advice and information and to develop reactions to the disease. By 1983-1984, organized sections of the gay community had developed specifically around the AIDS issue. AIDS had provided a common focus for a number of diverse strands of gay organization building, arising out of the gay health-based organizations of the 1970s, like Switchboard and Friend; it had also filled the organizational vacuum left after the virtual demise of gay political organizations in the early 1980s. The new policy aims were threefold: to convey the message of the dangers of AIDS to gay men; to develop a more public role (but without thereby sacrificing credibility among gays) by raising public and political awareness of the dangers of an AIDS epidemic; and to prevent the danger of an antigay backlash by stressing—as the Gay Medical Association had done—the idea the AIDS was potentially and actually a heterosexual disease. This was not just pressure group politics. Because AIDS was such a "new" policy area, there was a chance for effective policy input.

> I was involved in a meeting with the CMO [chief medical officer], the Editor of *Capital Gay* and Tony Whitehead towards the end of 1984. . . . He'd heard about

us from X, who'd been prominent as a gay activist in the early 1970s. People from the Department of Health had been running around asking who to talk to.[11]

Gay men became part of the emergent policy lobby around AIDS.

Another part of that policy lobby was also forming at around the same time. Clinical and scientific expertise on AIDS was also in the process of being established. The human immunodeficiency virus was first identified in 1983. Up to and for some time after that date, there was an absence of the kind of scientific knowledge and the type of scientific certainty that had come to be an expected concomitant of any normal fight against disease. Professor Waterson's (1983) summary demonstrated the uncertainty: "The most sinister feature of this acquired immune deficiency is that it appears to be communicable, perhaps principally by intimate physical contact." This scientific vacuum led to explanations couched in terms of morality rather than of science, for example, the "hot bed theory" that

> the traffic in human material in certain quarters by abnormal routes has reached such a level that, combined with the effects of drug abuse of various kinds, the sheer weight of chemical and microbial insult to the body in general, and to T-lymphocytes in particular, goes beyond the tolerable limit. (Waterson, 1983, pp. 43-46)

The *Annual Report of the Chief Medical Officer for 1983* (1984) did not moralize but was no less tentative.

> Expert opinion suggests that there is no risk of contracting AIDS as a result of casual or social contact with AIDS patients e.g., on public transport, in restaurants, or in private dwellings. The spread of AIDS appears to require intimate contact.

The range of explanations being advanced in the scientific and medical press—links with African swine fever, the virus emerging from Africa or Haiti—show scientific orthodoxy in the process of being constructed.

The construction of AIDS as scientific reality, a process analyzed by Paula Treichler, was legitimated by the establishment of clinical and scientific expertise. AIDS experts came initially from a range of areas such as immunology and virology, and from cancer research, where work on retroviruses had been undertaken for the previous 20 years and where the change from studying chicken viruses to human retroviruses had already been made because of new directions in leukemia research. Significantly too, AIDS brought the area of sexually transmitted diseases and genitourinary medicine in from the cold. One participant commented:

It was a "Cinderella specialty" with poor facilities and second rate people working on it. . . . You could go into genito-urinary medicine without a higher medical qualification. . . . It was a pretty poor service in terms of the quality of physicians and facilities, . . . AIDS has helped—it's made genito-urinary medicine a primary career option.[12]

AIDS meant too that a specialty not normally close to the center of policy formation in the health arena was drawn very directly into a policy advisory role. It also meant that "new men," scientists and clinicians without much previous experience or a track record in policy advice, found themselves in a position of direct influence. One commented, in relation to the AIDS role in the Medical Research Council,

There may have been some jealousies on the Systems Board that AIDS was getting too much attention. It was not quite nice in scientific terms. People with no scientific track record were making public pronouncements about the MRC.[13]

The early researchers in the AIDS area in Britain came from a mixed background. Jonathan Weber and Robin Weiss at the Institute of Cancer Research were virologists; Anthony Pinching at St. Mary's and Richard Tedder at the Middlesex were immunologists; Michael Adler at the Middlesex and Charles Farthing at St. Stephen's were specialists in genitourinary medicine. The Social Services Committee report (1987a) noted in 1987 what it called the "haphazard pattern of recruitment of expertise" to AIDS. There were no doubt tensions and differences as in any scientific community; but these new-fledged scientific and medical experts also developed a consistent policy line and means of airing it. Particularly noticeable was the high media profile they adopted to press the case for urgent action on the part of government. Certain of them adopted an overt public lobbying style that was initially characteristic of the AIDS area. In the absence of the type of established policy consultative machinery that would exist in a well-established area of health policy, the experts resorted to the press and to television. In doing this, they were consolidating existing patterns of health reporting, which rely heavily on the small circle of medical "experts." But they were also joined by gay AIDS activists. The Terrence Higgins Trust, in particular, was aware of the value of using the media—it became "pretty clued up about news management" as one activist put it. They and the medical and scientific experts were prepared to be openly critical of lack of action on the part of government or the research councils. Anthony Pinching, for example, in his evidence to the Social Services Committee, attacked the Medical Research

Council's funding of AIDS research—peer review was in fact "peer refusal." Jonathan Weber criticized its role as "leading from behind" (Social Services Committee, 1987b). One commented, "We accepted a public profile to ensure the message was put across."

The type of public reaction that would normally lead to exclusion from the "corridors of power" in this case brought admission to them. For the external policy lobbies were complemented by the "public health" reaction to AIDS within the Department of Health. AIDS was initially dealt with through classic public health routines of monitoring and surveillance. AIDS cases were monitored on a voluntary basis by the Communicable Disease Surveillance Centre at Colindale (part of the Public Health Laboratory Service, whose uncertain future was saved by its role in monitoring AIDS) from 1982 on. CDSC doctors early on developed links with gay activists in the Terrence Higgins Trust. Sir Donald Acheson, the chief medical officer, as a public health epidemiologist himself, was also well aware of the disease's potential for spread. His annual reports made conscious references to the role of the great 19th-century public health pioneers, such as Sir John Simon, medical officer to the Privy Council Office. AIDS was, in his view, a disease that lay in this great tradition of the public health fight against disease. He commented,

While the scourge of smallpox has gone and diphtheria and poliomyelitis are at present under control, other conditions such as legionellosis and AIDS have emerged. The control of the virus infection (HTLV III) which is the causative agent underlying AIDS is undoubtedly the greatest challenge in the field of communicable disease for many decades. (*Annual Report of the Chief Medical Officer,* 1986)

It highlighted, in his view, "the need for the control of the spread of infection to be regarded as an issue of prime importance to the future of the nation."

Acheson, universally hailed for his role in AIDS work by members of the policy lobbies ("if any honours are deserved for AIDS, he deserves one"), had held a meeting in late 1983 with gay activists to register support for the nascent Terrence Higgins Trust and its activities in the gay community. For the rest, his department focused its activities on issuing a number of warning and advisory circulars. The Advisory Committee on Dangerous Pathogens issued one to laboratory workers in 1984; there was the Health Education Council's leaflet, *Facts About AIDS*; and there was advice for doctors in 1985. In 1985 too, the Public Health (Infectious Disease) regulations, made under the Public Health (Control of Diseases) Act of the previous year, were extended to cover AIDS. AIDS was, significantly, not made a notifiable disease. Acheson was strongly opposed to notification; and the strength of the historical record in the area of sexually transmitted diseases was seen to indicate that a voluntary approach would, for the moment, lead to the best results.

The question of potential and actual heterosexual spread of the disease— the threat to the population at large—was the issue that united the AIDS policy community. This was part of the gay lobby's position; it also arose through the blood issue, which first developed in 1983. There had previously been criticism of the government for its failure to develop self-sufficiency in Factor VIII and other blood products after an outbreak of hepatitis B among children at a special school in Hampshire in 1981. The development of self-sufficiency, so critics argued, was being hindered by failure to ade-quately invest in the expansion of the Blood Products laboratory at Elstree and by health service cuts that were preventing the regional health authorities from supplying the laboratory with the extra blood it would need. Heat-treated Factor VIII, introduced originally because of hepatitis, was available by 1984, but there were technical problems involved in getting it into mass production. In the spring of 1983, reports of the possibility of the transmis-sion of the disease through blood first began to appear in the medical press and thereafter in the press in general. In May 1983, a report in the *Mail on Sunday* on hospitals that were using "killer blood" described how two men were in hospital in London and Cardiff, suspected to be suffering from AIDS after routine transfusions for hemophilia (Douglas, 1983). Exact knowledge of the virus and its transmissibility was limited at this stage and the priority was seen, within both the department and the Hemophilia Society—the voluntary organization concerned—as encouraging hemophiliacs to con-tinue with treatment. A DHSS spokesman was quoted in May 1983 as saying that "the advantage of using imported blood products far outweighs the 'slight possibility' that AIDS could be transmitted to patients through Factor VIII" (quoted in Hampshire, 1983). The initial reaction was thus a leaflet, in August 1983, asking high-risk donors not to give blood. Heat-treated Factor VIII was not available from the United States until the end of 1984. Dr. Charles Rizza, an Oxford hematologist, was reported as saying that, until it was available, "I'm afraid our hemophiliacs are in the lap of the gods." The domestic supply came on stream in the following year. By October 1985 too, a British HIV antibody test had been developed and all blood donations began to be screened. The advent of an AIDS dimension to the illegal drugs issue in late 1985 and early 1986 added to the sense of urgency and to the focus on AIDS as a heterosexual disease. In autumn 1986, the McClelland Committee on HIV infection in Scotland declared the dangers of the hetero-sexual spread of the disease to be a greater danger than the spread of illegal drug use itself (Scottish Home and Health Department, 1986).

The new policy lobbies around AIDS were, by late 1984, beginning to coalesce into more established policy advisory mechanisms. The Department of Health began to set up administrative and policy advisory machinery focused on the new disease. The Expert Advisory Group on AIDS (EAGA) first met in January 1985 to advise the Chief Medical Officer (*Annual Report of the Chief Medical Officer for 1985*, 1986, p. 46). Its members came from the clinical and scientific areas of new expertise on AIDS. A "social" group dealing with prevention and health education issues had a mixture of medical and gay activists. There was overlap between the groups. The expert group met seven times in 1985 and set up a number of associated groups—on counseling, screening, resources, a working group on health education in relation to AIDS, a group on AIDS and drug abuse; a surgeon, anesthetist, and dentist subgroup; groups on employment, renal units, artificial insemination; and a group on immunoglobulin. One member early on recalled,

Acheson wanted advice—and pulled names out of a hat of those who'd written about it. . . . It was more effective early on—so many big issues were dealt with on the run. . . . EAGA was a force in developing policies very quickly—screening, blood transfusions, breast-feeding. Everything had to be developed over about two years.[14]

As well as external links, the department also developed its own internal policy machinery on AIDS. In 1985, a direct phone line for professional inquiries was linked to a special AIDS unit in the department. The policy lines that most clearly united the community were a stress on the need for urgent action and the need for public education to stress the heterosexual nature of the disease rather than the "gay plague" angle of the popular press.

The way in which those objectives gained political feasibility in the period of "wartime emergency" from 1986 to 1987 has been discussed elsewhere (Berridge & Strong, 1991a). This section has aimed simply to document part of the early policy history of U.K. AIDS and to show the initial construction of a "policy community" focused on the threat to the general population. It has focused on the policy history, from both within and outside government. The reconstruction of that community as AIDS became normalized and institutionalized is another story. Basically, as one early participant put it, the "old boy network of British science" moved in. But it is also possible to engage with other areas of the social impact of AIDS through historical perceptions. A few possibilities can be suggested.[15] There is, for example, a need to document the lives and perceptions of affected groups who might otherwise be "hidden from history." Relatively few researchers have studied gay culture (as distinct from simply sexual behavior) and the impact of

AIDS; but hemophiliacs have been totally missing from the picture in the cultural sense. In the media's view, they are the "innocent victims" of AIDS; but no one has examined their privatized systems of belief and practice and the impact AIDS has—or has not—made on these.

Paula Treichler has in this volume analyzed the social construction of scientific orthodoxy around HIV; the related question of the "popular culture" surrounding AIDS is also worthy of study. Historians have documented the relationship between popular beliefs about science and medicine and mainstream science; dialectical interrelationships have operated in different forms at different times (Bynum & Porter, 1987). These types of perceptions can also be applied to AIDS—to the interest in "alternative therapies," for example, and the focus on self-help medicine as a form of political activism much as it was in the 19th century. The wider context of popular views is also important. The easy dismissal of widespread public fear in 1985-1986 under the term *moral panic* ignores the construction of alternative theories. Popular views were not simply a reaction to the "gay plague" posture of the tabloid press. Such an interpretation presupposes a form of direct "media effect" on public opinion, which it would be difficult to defend; the relationship between press and public opinion is more of a symbiotic one. It ignores too the long history of popular concepts of disease—in terms of miasma and contagion of moral responsibility for disease. The "enormous condescension of posterity" has been applied to autonomous popular beliefs; these too are worthy of study. Both historical perceptions and historical methodologies can shape the "contemporary history" of AIDS.

Conclusion

Based on the evidence presented here, history has played two quite distinct roles in the AIDS story. Initially, AIDS was a "new" policy area where established interests and policy lines had not yet ossified. In an open situation, history could play a practical rather than a symbolic role. How far that role was justified is a different matter. For what lay behind this form of historical intervention was a Whiggish assumption that there was indeed a "lesson of history" that could be learned, that the past could be used to provide a very specific blueprint for a present-day policy reaction. It implied too that history was incontrovertible "fact" rather than a mass of differing interpretations themselves historically constructed. The belief that historical evidence was some higher form of truth was certainly useful in establishing particular policy positions in relation to AIDS and, in the 1960s (but not in the 1980s), for drugs. But the form of historical relevance adopted was more equivocal in its benefits from the viewpoint of the discipline. It implicitly downplayed some of its subtler strengths in favor of a focus on historical fact and messages that many historians would find problematic. Were historians (along with other social scientists) relapsing into positivism via AIDS?

This does not mean that history has little further role. AIDS in its later stages has, as this chapter has argued, opened up the possibility of other forms of historical input, which also have relevance to the development of the role of history more generally in the study of health policy. History as background is important. Historians can produce the necessary historical perspective. But historical skills can also be applied to provide a critical analysis of almost current developments. Can this type of work bear a relation to policy? History here too can be "policy relevant," although less directly than in the earlier "lesson of history" approach. History can provide some of the key tools for an overall analysis of a particular situation and can demonstrate how interests and strategies, alliances and power struggles, within policymaking can shift over time. The point here is not the "lesson of history" derived from cholera, plague, or the Black Death but a subtler analysis of the nature and determinants of AIDS policymaking. This function for the history of health policy is, it should be noted, more problematic in the United Kingdom than in the United States; policymakers in the former remain to be convinced.

What are the particular tools that history can provide? These are threefold: its use of a chronological approach; a sense of continuity as well as of change; and, within an overall chronology, the ability to interweave different theoretical perspectives and levels of interpretation. AIDS, a "stunning metaphor" in social and welfare terms for other policy areas, according to Denis Altman, has also crystallized some of the debates within the historical profession over the past decade. Historical relevance is one; so too are the debates around chronology. Chronology may not be everything, and historians have now shown that much fundamental work in history cannot be done with a purely chronological approach. Nonetheless, history, more than any other social science, knows how to study the passage of time. Another potential strength (and weakness too) lies in the historian's interest in change and continuity, in an implicit cynicism about proclaimed radical new departures in policy. A historical strength lies in locating policy change in past practice, in seeking out antecedents and preexisting tendencies that feed into policy development. At its worst, this can be an obsessive desire to deny any possibility of real change or the relevance of individual and collective effort; but, at its best, it provides a powerful means of setting policy development in its proper context. In the AIDS area, for example, "new" policies—on research, or illegal drugs, for example—can only be assessed in the light of previous tendencies and policy objectives. One basic historical question is how far AIDS brought about policy change and how far such change was dependent on preexisting interests and tensions.

The final strength of the historical approach lies in an area in which, to observers from other disciplines, it is often considered weak. This is the presumed atheoreticity of the subject. Some historical work is indeed atheoretical and totally empirical in approach; but social historians are mostly theoretically eclectic rather than devoid of broader intellectual context. The borrowing from sociological theory in the 1960s and 1970s is one example, as are also the interest and cross-fertilization with anthropological concerns (MacDonald, 1983). Herein lies a strength (and weakness) of history. The historical approach is unique in its generalizing ability to deal with a range of primary source material bearing on the interplay of policy interests and the development of cultural constructs and to interweave that complex story with levels of theoretical explanation—all within a framework that takes account of the passage of time (Stearns, 1984). The analysis of the social and policy impact of AIDS—and of other issues of health and disease—remains an essentially cross-disciplinary question in which history has a vital role to play; for the value of such collaboration lies not in a blurring of disciplinary distinctions—in John Gagnon's words, a "postdisciplinary stage"—but in a sharpening of perceptions and a greater awareness of the nature of the boundaries (Silverman, 1986).

Notes

1. This section is based on Shirley Lindenbaum's contribution to a session of the conference on which this book is based.

2. The work of the Risse group figured in the conference, AIDS and the Historian, at the NIH in March 1989. For a report, see Berridge (1989).

3. From Martin Levine, in a contribution to the conference discussion.

4. At the conference AIDS and Contemporary History, organized at the London School of Hygiene in April 1990. The earlier sessions specifically addressed questions that AIDS had raised in areas such as research policy, clinical trials, STD policy, and screening. Other sessions dealt with work on the history of AIDS itself. Work from the conference is to be published in Berridge and Strong (in press).

5. Interview (1990), Gay Switchboard worker.

6. Interview (1990), Body Positive member.

7. Interview (1989), Terrence Higgins Trust worker.

8. Interview (1989), former worker, Terrence Higgins Trust.

9. For details of the early trust, see *Capital Gay* (1982-1983).

10. Interview (1990), Body Positive member.

11. Interview (1990), gay activist.

12. Interview (1989), genitourinary medicine consultant.

13. Interview (1990), former member MRC AIDS Working Party.

14. Interview (1990), genitourinary medicine consultant.

15. This section is based on contributions from many of the conference contributors and my summing-up session there.

References

Adams, D. P. (1989). Wartime bureaucracy and penicillin allocation: The committee on chemo-therapeutic and other agents, 1942-44. *Journal of the History of Medicine and Allied Sciences, 44*, 196-217.

Annual Report of the Chief Medical Officer of the Department of Health and Social Security for 1983. (1984). London: Her Majesty's Stationery Office.

Annual Report of the Chief Medical Officer of the Department of Health and Social Security for the Year 1984. (1985). London: Her Majesty's Stationery Office.

Annual Report of the Chief Medical Officer of the Department of Health and Social Security for 1985. (1986). London: Her Majesty's Stationery Office.

Berridge, V. (1984). Drugs and social policy: The establishment of drug control in Britain, 1900-30. *British Journal of Addiction, 79*(1), 17-29.

Berridge, V. (1989). Conference report: AIDS and the historian. *Social History of Medicine, 2*(3), 403-409.

Berridge, V. (1990). *AIDS policies in the Netherlands and Britain.* Report to the European Commission.

Berridge, V. (1991). AIDS and British drug policy: History repeats itself. In D. Whynes & P. Bean (Eds.), *Policing and prescribing: The British system of drug control.* London: Macmillan.

Berridge, V., & Strong, P. (1991a). AIDS policies in the UK: A preliminary analysis. In E. Fee & D. Fox (Eds.), *AIDS: Contemporary history.* Berkeley: University of California Press.

Berridge, V., & Strong, P. (1991b). Essay review: AIDS and the relevance of history. *Social History of Medicine, 4*(1), 129-138..

Berridge, V., & Strong, P. (Eds.). (in press). *AIDS and contemporary history.* Oxford: Oxford University Press.

Brandt, A. M. (1987). *No magic bullet: A social history of venereal disease in the United States since 1880, with a new chapter on AIDS.* New York: Oxford University Press.

Bynum, W., & Porter, R. (1987). *Medical fringe and medical orthodoxy, 1750-1850.* Beckenham: Croom Helm.

Day, P., & Klein, R. (1989). Interpreting the unexpected: The case of AIDS policy making in Britain. *Journal of Public Policy, 9*(3), 337-353.

Douglas, S. (1983, May 1). Virus imported from U.S. hospitals using killer blood. *Mail on Sunday.*

Fee, E., & Fox, D. M. (Eds.). (1989a). *AIDS: The burdens of history.* Berkeley: University of California Press.

Farrell, M. R., Preston, J. A., et al. (1983). Acquired immune deficiency syndrome. *British Medical Journal, 286*, 1143.

Fee, E., & Fox, D. M. (1989b). The contemporary historiography of AIDS. *Journal of Social History, 23*(2), 303-314.

Ferlie, E., & Pettigrew, A. (1989). Coping with change in the NHS: A frontline district's response to AIDS. *Journal of Social Policy, 19*(2), 191-220.

Fox, D. M., Day, P., & Klein, R. (1989). The power of professionalism: AIDS in Britain, Sweden and the United States [Special issue]. *Daedalus, 118*(2), 93-112.

Hall, P., Land, H., Parker, R., & Webb, A. (1975). *Change, choice and conflict in social policy.* London: Heinemann.

Hampshire, J. (1983, May 2). Probe on imports of killer blood. *Daily Mail.*

Living with AIDS [Special issue]. (1989) *Daedalus, 118*(2).

MacDonald, M. (1983). Anthropological perspectives on the history of science and medicine. In P. Corsi & P. Weindling (Eds.), *Information sources in the history of science and medicine.* London: Butterworth Scientific.

McKie, R. (1986). *Panic: The story of AIDS.* Wellingborough: Thorsons.

Muraskin, W. (1988). The silent epidemic: The social, ethical and medical problems surrounding the fight against hepatitis B. *Journal of Social History, 22*(2), 277-298.

Musto, D. (1973). *The American disease: Origins of narcotic control.* New Haven, CT: Yale University Press.

Nyswander, M. (1956). *The drug addict as a patient.* New York: Grune and Stratton.

Porter, R. (1986, December). History says no to the policeman's response to AIDS. *British Medical Journal,* pp. 20-27.

Porter, R., & Porter, D. (1988). AIDS: Law, liberty and public health. In P. Byrne (Ed.), *Health, rights and resources* (pp. 76-99). London: King Edward's Hospital Fund for London.

Scottish Home and Health Department. (1986). *HIV infection in Scotland: Report of the Scottish Committee on HIV Infection and Intravenous Drug Misuse.* Edinburgh: Author.

Scull, A. (1989). Reflections on the historical sociology of psychiatry. In A. Scull (Ed.), *Social order/mental disorder Anglo-American psychiatry in historical perspective.* Berkeley: University of California Press.

Shilts, R. (1988). *And the band played on: Politics, people and the AIDS epidemic.* London: Penguin.

Silverman, S. (1986). Anthropology and history: Understanding the boundaries in history and anthropology—a dialogue. *Historical Methods, 19,* 119-128.

Social Services Committee. (1987a). *Third report: Problems associated with AIDS* (Session 1986-1987). London: Her Majesty's Stationery Office.

Social Services Committee. (1987b). *Problems associated with AIDS: Minutes of evidence* (Vol. 2). London: Her Majesty's Stationery Office.

Stearns, P. N. (1984). History and public policy. In G. J. McCall & G. H. Weber (Eds.), *The roles of academic disciplines in policy analysis* (pp. 91-128). London: Associated Faculty Press.

Steffen, M. (1990). *The policies on AIDS in France.* Paper presented at the Social Policy Association conference, Bath, England.

Street, J. (1988). British government policy on AIDS. *Parliamentary Affairs, 41,* 490-508.

Strong, P., & Berridge, V. (1990). No one knew anything: Some issues in British AIDS policy. In P. Aggleton, P. Davies, & G. Hart (Eds.), *AIDS: Individual, cultural and policy dimensions.* Basingstoke, England: Falmer.

Waterson, A. P. (1983). Acquired immune deficiency syndrome. *British Medical Journal, 286,* 743-746.

Weeks, J. (1988). AIDS: The intellectual agenda. In P. Aggleton, G. Hart, & P. Davies (Eds.), *AIDS: Social representations, social practices* (pp. 1-20). Brighton: Falmer.

4

AIDS, HIV, and the
Cultural Construction of Reality

PAULA A. TREICHLER

Scientific activity is not "about nature,"
it is a fierce fight to construct reality.

—Bruno Latour & Steve Woolgar
(1979/1986, p. 242)

You don't have 500 dollars for the operation?
For 50 bucks I'll touch up the X-ray.

—Groucho Marx

As the AIDS epidemic enters its second decade, its importance as a social
and cultural as well as a biomedical crisis is clear. The Fifth International
AIDS Conference in Montreal in 1989, for example, was titled "AIDS: The
Scientific and Social Challenge" and featured more social and cultural
presentations than in past years. Richard A. Morisset, M.D., chair of the

AUTHOR'S NOTE. Thanks to Anthony Appiah, Ed Bruner, Gertrude Fraser, Colin Garrett, Alan
Harwood, Patty Marshall, Emily Martin, Cary Nelson, Bill Schroeder, Joseph Sonnabend, and
Simon Watney. My thanks also to colleagues in the faculty seminar of the University of Illinois
Unit for Criticism and Interpretive Theory, the Society for the Humanities at Cornell University
(spring 1989), and the Wenner-Gren symposium on AIDS (June 1990).

program committee, wrote in the official program that the conference was expected to be "an extraordinary one" not only for its scope but also for "the profoundly humanistic philosophy guiding it." He continued:

> Anyone who has kept a close watch on the series of International Conferences on AIDS that began in Atlanta in 1985 will have noticed how these encounters have gradually opened up. Originally, you will recall, the meetings dealt almost exclusively with biomedical topics. Yet scientists soon had to admit that AIDS is not simply a medical problem, but also a human drama. (Morisset, 1989, p. 6)[1]

With nearly one third of its panels and papers devoted to "social aspects of the epidemic," the commitment of the Montreal conference was clear.

What is less clear is precisely what it means to describe AIDS as a social or cultural phenomenon or, in a phrase becoming common, a *cultural construction*. To call AIDS "cultural" may mean simply that AIDS—like any great event or crisis—significantly affects social life and symbolic expression. But to call it "culturally constructed" invokes long-standing debates about human knowledge and the nature of the world. This is far from evident in Morisset's opening statement, which characterizes the *problem* as medical, the *drama* as human, and links the recognition of AIDS's *social challenge* to a humanistic philosophy. The anchoring tradition remains biomedical:

> Naturally, we all know that the ultimate solution will eventually come to light in a laboratory. But meanwhile, what can the virologist or microbiologist offer an AIDS victim and his or her loved ones to ease their burden? To help them combat the ignorance and intolerance they face, which are growing day by day? (Morisset, 1989, p. 6)

Here the human sciences, handmaid to the biomedical sciences, do their best to ease suffering and combat ignorance until the laboratory can find the "ultimate solution." The "social challenge," primarily a matter of helping individuals cope with pain and death, is what happens "meanwhile."

The biomedical vision embodied in this conference statement is widely shared and deeply embedded in Western postindustrial culture. The discourses of virology, molecular biology, and immunology permeate the ways we think and talk about the AIDS epidemic. "We report here," wrote the Pasteur Institute research group in *Science* in 1983, "the isolation of a novel retrovirus from a lymph node of a homosexual patient with multiple lymphadenopathies" (Barré-Sinoussi et al., 1983, in Kulstad, 1986, p. 49). Just seven years later, the sprawling exhibitors' area at the 1990 Sixth

International Conference on AIDS in San Francisco was dominated by an immense three-dimensional glass model of the human immunodeficiency virus (HIV). Not only aesthetically stunning, HIV had become an intensely personal experience as well. Andrea Walton, for example, "one of the one thousand people with HIV who attended this week's conference," was profiled by a San Francisco television station; the camera followed Walton as she wandered through the exhibit hall and paused to scrutinize the model glass virus:

> That's my enemy—that's what I fight every day. I'm feeling overwhelmed because it's killing me—and it's actually pretty. There are a lot of things in nature that are deadly and pretty and I guess that's what I'm dealing with. (Saiz, 1990 [film])

Elsewhere in the world, the virus is also experienced and represented in many ways. In a Central African Republic pamphlet on AIDS written in Sango, the immune system is shown surrounding the human figure like a rope; viruses, pictured as beaked and batlike birds, are eating through the protective boundary. In a Brazilian magazine graphic in 1987, HIV attacks cells that look like Caspar the Friendly Ghost, a popular way of illustrating the immune system in 1950s medical textbooks (see Haraway, 1989a). Paul Farmer (1990) shows that understandings of AIDS (*sida*) among villagers in rural Haiti were diverse until 1987, when accumulated knowledge and firsthand experience of the disease led to a shared model based on tuberculosis and, therefore, believed to be caused by a microbe. Benedicte Ingstad (1990), writing about the cultural construction of AIDS in Botswana, notes that, with incidence still low, people sometimes talk about AIDS ironically as the "radio disease"—widely publicized but not yet experienced. Though associated with violation of sexual proprieties, the disease will need to become more common before traditional healers can decide whether it should be diagnosed as a traditional (*Tswana*) disease or as a "modern" disease.

If we think of cultural construction as a symbolic model of reality, these formulations of HIV raise several questions. What kind of correspondence do we presume to exist between the representation of a virus and its reality? Is this reality universal and unchanging? What features of culture determine the form in which reality is constructed? What is the role of language in articulating and popularizing a particular construction? Is any articulation a construction? Do different representations make a difference? Three general takes on these questions are familiar. First, the virus is a stable, discoverable entity in nature whose reality is certified and accurately represented by scientific research; a high degree of correspondence is assumed between reality and biomedical models. Second, the virus is a stable, discoverable entity in nature but is assigned different names and meanings within the signifying systems of different cultures; all are equally valid though not all are equally correct. Third, our knowledge of the virus and other natural phenomena is inevitably mediated through our symbolic constructions of them; biomedicine is only one among many, but one that currently has privileged status. While none of these views is purely realist ("HIV is an autonomous physical reality that we merely label") or purely idealist ("HIV is an abstraction that exists only in the mind"), the first—despite the provisional nature of much scientific inquiry—is characteristic of science and medicine; the second, of a nonjudgmental cultural relativism that nonetheless often assumes the fundamental correctness of Western biomedicine; and the third, of a radical constructionism that foregrounds such mediating processes as language and makes few claims about universal truth.

Medical anthropologists, professionally allied to both the first and the third positions, have tended, by default perhaps, to take the middle ground on this epistemological and ontological continuum: Most seem more comfortable with the notion of a single, stable, underlying biological reality to which different cultures assign different meanings than with the view that everything we know about reality is ultimately a cultural construction. Ingstad, for example, argues that health officials in Botswana should recognize traditional healers' knowledge and influence over villagers' health-seeking behavior. Yet, ultimately, she privileges a Western biomedical account of HIV infection, noting that some healers are cooperative and receptive to modern health information, while

> others are skeptical, prefer to keep a distance, and may promote behavior that is counterproductive to prevention. Considering the seriousness of the AIDS epidemic and the likelihood that the incidence of the disease will increase in Botswana in the near future, it is important that healers be made to feel that they have a role to play in the prevention of this disease. (Ingstad, 1990, p. 38)

The "be made to feel" of this conclusion suggests, perhaps, the moral and intellectual burden of carrying out ethnographic fieldwork driven in part by the threat of a particularly vicious and terrifying infectious disease for which Western health intervention strategies seemingly remain the best form of prevention. As new cases of AIDS around the world continue to escalate, many researchers engaged in cultural analysis are having to develop theory under crisis conditions and, at the same time, efficiently produce data to guide prevention programs. Our growing knowledge of cultural difference and specificity does not make this easy. Pedagogy across cultures involves more than translating prescriptions for behavior change into different languages: Inevitably, we need to know more about the meaning of given practices and conceptions, their place in a community's social and cultural life, the political economy that frames them, and the contingencies that sustain or discourage them.

There are pressing reasons for attempting to clarify the concept of cultural construction. In the face of the epidemic's growing toll, the moral and technical limitations of a facile constructionism are obvious. To paraphrase Pauline Bart, everything is cultural construction but cultural construction isn't everything.[2] "Culture," moreover, figures so insignificantly in the crude realism of most discussions about AIDS that cultural scholars hardly have time to do more than lobby for its inclusion somewhere in the big picture. Yet the AIDS crisis—with its long-term influence over the direction of policy, research, education, legislation—makes it all the more imperative to take seriously the conceptual clashes between different symbolic models and the ways in which biomedicine is itself culturally constructed. Because the question of culture is central to interdisciplinary work on AIDS and to wider struggles against the epidemic, this chapter explores relations between AIDS and culture and seeks to refine our understanding of how AIDS can plausibly be characterized as a cultural construction. The epidemic demonstrates the unique value of the concept of cultural construction and, at the same time, highlights the dangers of using it.

Cultural Construction and
Mannheim's Paradox

> If we are asked: "How can a logical construct like culture explain anything?" we would reply that other logical constructs and abstractions like "electromagnetic field" or "gene"—which no one has ever seen—have been found serviceable in scientific understanding.
>
> —A. L. Kroeber & Clyde Kluckhohn (1952, p. 190)

"Culture," writes Raymond Williams (1983, p. 87), "is one of the two or three most complicated words in the English language." As Williams shows, *culture*'s historical legacy encompasses both material and nonmaterial meanings—for example, both the concrete objects a cultural community produces (pots, books, television sets, glass models of HIV) and the complex of practices, attitudes, beliefs, and ideas that make up its way of life. This is a duality upon which ethnography rests and the reason for the elaborate fieldwork practices aimed at helping the investigator reconstruct the signifying or symbolic system underlying another culture's everyday life. At once useful and problematic in examining the AIDS epidemic, it is one of several dichotomies the term *culture* invokes: Williams notes that culture has served to distinguish *material* from *spiritual* development yet also to distinguish *human* from *material* development. In American anthropology, A. L. Kroeber and Clyde Kluckhohn's (1952) exemplary and instructive semantic history of the word and concept was instrumental in institutionalizing ethnographic, relativist definitions of *culture* over older elitist and chauvinist uses of the term to mean progress toward the practices and values of European civilization. (Alfred G. Meyers, in his appendixes to Kroeber & Kluckhohn [pp. 207-217], notes that anthropologists tend, in contrast, to hold up other cultures as a "didactic mirror" [p. 208] that reflects unfavorably on modern society.) Their review demonstrates too that the term continues to embrace both specialist and nonspecialist meanings.[3]

The term *cultural construction* derives less from the field of anthropology than from the sociology of knowledge. Our current understandings are informed by a number of sources, including Karl Mannheim's *Ideology and Utopia* (1936/1985), a study in the sociology of knowledge that examines the way knowledge is bound up with being. For Mannheim, though all knowledge of the world is finally indirect and partial, any object of knowledge becomes clearer with the systematic and cumulative analysis of different ways of seeing it (from Dilthey: "situational determination" or "seat in life"). These ways of seeing are existentially determined, not mere perspectives but fully naturalized worldviews; identifying them is the task of the scholar or researcher (the "socially unattached intelligentsia"). Political and historical change comes about, in part, through the clash between two ways of seeing the world that Mannheim terms *ideology* and *utopia*. For Mannheim, *ideology* is not the politically tainted doctrine of conventional usage but a serious worldview; it is a position that constructs the world as situationally congruent—that is, so that the status quo is reinforced. *Utopia* constructs the world as situationally transcendent, so that the status quo is challenged. "The world," the same material object, is rendered by ideology and utopia as two very different realities, each of which the world's material data appear to support. Particularly useful is Mannheim's emphasis on the hermeneutic activities that produce different constructions. Both ideology and utopia produce distorted determinations of reality, but ideology works to maintain what is (as ideology renders it) while utopia works to transform reality into its own image. When ideological and utopian visions become locked in sustained opposition over time, proponents of the two camps inevitably become intimately familiar with each other's positions and, therefore, symbiotically and ironically, perfectly situated to engage in a sophisticated exchange of critiques. I return to this symbiosis below.

That Mannheim treated ideology as a subject for serious investigation was important for Peter Berger and Thomas Luckmann's (1967) influential work *The Social Construction of Reality,* originally formulated as a project for sociology though ultimately taken up more vigorously by other fields. Drawing on Dilthey, Mannheim, Weber, and others, Berger and Luckmann argue that we routinely experience the world in the form of multiple realities. Given the constraints of environment and biology on the human animal (i.e., human beings have no species-specific environment), the worlds we inhabit are largely socially—not physically—constructed. We work to create meaning, to achieve and maintain cognitive coherence, because our ability to be in the world at all is at stake (no habitat will do it for us). When problematic sectors of experience threaten to disrupt the totality, we work to integrate them, often by marking them as "finite provinces of meaning" (Berger & Luckmann, 1967, p. 25) through explicit linguistic transitions. Though anchored in its specific set of social determinations, each of these multiple realities is nevertheless experienced as total, nontrivial, and inescapable. The commonsense reality of everyday life occupies a privileged position for Berger and Luckmann; though it is but one reality among many, it offers a realm where our subjective experience of the world seems trustworthy and meanings seem to be unproblematically shared with others. The object of sociological analysis is the self as it goes about creating meaning in everyday life.[4]

Originating in a phenomenological analysis, *The Social Construction of Reality* had immediate resonance throughout the social sciences: The book's very title, its insistence on the validity of multiple socially determined realities, and its analysis of ideology's function in deploying what we think we know to resolve knowledge that has been rendered problematic—all provided a way of thinking about the production of knowledge that moved away from the pervasive realism and totalizing determinism of postwar social science. But, in the United States, Thomas Kuhn had meanwhile published *The Structure of Scientific Revolutions* (1962), a sociology of knowledge in the natural sciences; though more or less cleansed of its continental and phenomenological influences, Kuhn's analysis treated scientific theories as social constructions rather than assigning them (as even Althusser did) to a realm of truer discourse that transcends social history. True, Kuhn ultimately pulled back from the precipice of radical constructivism (enlarged edition, 1970); yet, as a compelling and socially situated account of scientific change, the book's influence and liberatory potential were enormous, in some respects preempting and even superseding the project of Berger and Luckmann.

On such works is founded a dialectical view of the intersections between the real material world and human consciousness—*dialectical* because the known world is determined neither by "reality" nor by the perceiving mind but is a product of the interaction, continually modified first by one, then the other. They also provide a foundation for self-reflexivity in the social sciences, enabling social and cultural critics to characterize positivist accounts (of social life or scientific progress, for example) as themselves "social constructions." Making this argument in *The Interpretation of Cultures,* Clifford Geertz charges that positivist social science is not qualified to analyze symbolic action adequately; it is the ethnographer who is best equipped to attempt "the perfection of a conceptual apparatus capable of dealing more adroitly with meaning." Geertz insisted that the cultural be inserted into the study of the sociology of knowledge, challenging the widespread view that science is radically different from ideology—that, in the recurrent simile of the literature, thought determined by fact is like a crystal-clear stream while ideological thought is like a dirty river. That the study of ideology itself repeatedly and inevitably becomes ideological is what Geertz labels "Mannheim's paradox" and continues (1973, p. 194): "Where, if anywhere, ideology leaves off and science begins has been the Sphinx's Riddle of much of modern sociological thought and the rustless weapon of its enemies."

The Sphinx's Riddle can be read more broadly as the problem of any constructionist approach, for where, if anywhere, does construction leave off and reality begin? That cultural constructionism is itself culturally constructed, the product of particular intellectual interests at a particular point in history, creates the potential for theoretical paralysis or relativism, which may in turn inspire impatience, the embrace of a reliable realism, and charges of idealism, mentalism, armchair speculation, or semantics. But there are differences between the kind of dialectic embodied in cultural constructionism and the conventional realist-idealist dualism. This is made clear by more radical versions of constructionism in which ideas have a life and logic of their own yet are in intimate dialogue with the material data—including the discursive data—of a real world (*a* real world). The point is that these data always engage with an already constructed perceptual and interpretive apparatus, albeit one designed to mitigate or erase its own effects (e.g., scientific method). A constructionist view must, therefore, encompass the apparatus as well as the data. The Sphinx's Riddle is answered then, or at least finessed, by such studies as Karin D. Knorr-Cetina's (1981) application of a rigorous ethnography to the sociology of knowledge; setting out to examine the production of scientific knowledge in a laboratory setting as an anthropologist would study a strange culture, Knorr-Cetina moves away from social explanations for scientific research, in Kuhn's sense, to an emphasis on meaning, discourse, and the discursive construction of knowledge within a given disciplinary culture. Insisting on the manufactured, *made* nature of science, Knorr-Cetina concludes that science must be seen as radically constructive rather than descriptive and that scientific discourse is not qualitatively different from other discourse. Noting the laboratory's concern with "making things work," she emphasizes the etymological connection between *fact* and *fabrication.* One can compare Ludvik Fleck's (1936/1979, p. 98) earlier definition of a scientific fact not as an entity with established ontological autonomy but as that which constrains subsequent scientific discourse: "a stylized signal of resistance in thinking."

Crucial insights here are the recognition of the role of discourse and the insistence that discourse entails concrete practices. Like Foucault's system in which entities are products of the discourse that embodies them, Knorr-Cetina's detailed analysis dissolves any strict dichotomy between material and nonmaterial elements of scientific research (e.g., laboratory apparatus versus "ideas"), between objects and discourse, between science and ideology. Scientific laboratory operations, she argues, are constituted by the exegeses and symbolic manipulations in the laboratory itself; these construct an argument primarily designed to make sense within the field. Written communication—mainly in the form of scientific journal publications—crystallizes the laboratory's entire argument and stakes its claim. Science, as a discursive field of interaction, is directed at and sustained by the arguments of others; writing is, therefore, at the heart of its social and symbolic foundation. But writing is in no simple correspondence with natural reality, and Knorr-Cetina reminds us of Pierce's assertion that manifestation in writing reveals the presence not of an object but of a sign (i.e., not of a referent but of a symbol).

Knorr-Cetina also asserts, quoting Dorothy L. Sayers, that "facts are like cows—look them in the face long enough and they generally run away." But the observer must get close enough to phenomena to glimpse their true character: getting a good hard look requires uncovering the rules of everyday practice and attempting to capture the meanings in the culture being observed. In short, one must go beyond simply the desire to understand or even to describe the other culture; one must let it speak and then give voice to the story it tells. This approach does not guarantee an unconstructed account, indeed cannot, for this is impossible; but it does enable us to achieve a "decentered constructivity." Finally, scientific inquiry and the study of science always take place within a given context, a context that includes the community of one's peers. Knorr-Cetina, departing from conventional notions of peer review as a rational and authoritative evaluation by a scientific elite, argues that a scientific laboratory does not simply enter its product—its publications—into open competition in the scientific marketplace; rather, the publication is shaped from the beginning by the gatekeeping operations of scientific peer review. Gatekeeping thus influences the entire research process, including what research project is selected and how it is pursued.

For Knorr-Cetina, the constructed nature of science is defined through concrete practices situated within the culture of a discipline. Bruno Latour and Steve Woolgar, whose study *Laboratory Life* (1979/1986) builds on Knorr-Cetina's work, further sketch this cultural domain. Observing that *fact* means simultaneously what *is* fabricated and what is *not* fabricated, they maintain that scientific accounts are necessarily provisional and uncertain; this is their essential character, whether explicitly articulated or not. They define (1979/1986, p. 236) the construction of scientific facts as "the slow, practical craftwork by which inscriptions are superimposed and accounts are backed up or dismissed." "It is through practical operations," they continue, "that a statement can be transformed into an object or a fact into an artifact." There is no inherent or persistent difference between material and intellectual dimensions of construction: What is the subject of today's intellectual dispute is incorporated into tomorrow's laboratory furniture. (Compare Antonio Gramsci's rejection, so influential in the development of cultural studies, of the classical Marxist dichotomy between materialism and idealism, Stuart Hall's [1980a, 1980b] discussion of the mediations between discourse and material practice that mass communication routinely produces, or Donna Haraway's [1989b] characterization of Harlow's primate research as the transformation of metaphor into hardware.) Those accounts of phenomena that have come to be taken for granted as reified autonomous objects—"black-boxed," as Bruno Latour (1987) puts it—constitute what is referred to as reality. Characterizing the social study of science as "the construction of fictions about fiction construction," they also define reality discursively as the set of statements considered too costly to modify.[5]

What does this mean in terms of human disease or a "natural" entity like a virus? Where the object of knowledge is a living human being—or even a living host environment for a virus—symbiosis is even more intense. A virus—any virus—is a constructed entity, a representation, whose legitimacy is established and legitimized through a whole series of operations and representations, all highly stylized. Each of these must be critically analyzed on its own terms rather than accepted as though a scientific assertion about a virus stood for a referent rather than a sign. Yet we encounter peculiar difficulties in the cultural analysis of medicine. On the one hand, the biomedical model shares qualities with physics or molecular biology, appearing to describe entities and phenomena that are transcultural and natural. On the other hand, it is the human body—and the perceiving self—that gives the virus its host environment, experiences and reports its effects, and undergoes treatments (and cognitive and affective events) that may change both the environment and the virus.[6]

It is said of Western medicine that the patient comes to the physician's office with an illness but leaves with a disease. Disease is thus taken to represent the medical model, illness the patient's subjective experience or, in anthropological terms, the native's point of view. Current conventional wisdom is that the patient's view must be honored; the physician is, therefore, urged to understand the patient's cultural construction of reality, to read the native's text. This fits nicely into current ethnographic theory. George Marcus and Michael Fischer (1986), for example, argue that *dialogue* is the underlying metaphor for ethnography today. This has a pleasing and contemporary ring to it and seems in one sense perfect: the social in dialogue with the physical, the cultural with the natural. Yet, as Atwood Gaines and Robert Hahn (1985, p. 4) observe, "for many anthropologists, Biomedicine is *the* reality through the lens of which the rest of the world's cultural versions are seen, compared, and judged." And, as Arthur Kleinman notes (in the introduction to Gaines & Hahn, 1985), the entry of the social sciences into medicine has for the most part prompted not dialogue but "an enriched biomedical monologue" characterized by the subversion of social science to medicine's aims. As a model for research or clinical practice, the notion of dialogue breaks down, for in whose words does the body speak?

This question lies at the heart of Michael T. Taussig's (1980) germinal essay "Reification and the Consciousness of the Patient," which addresses at once the moral foundations of the physician-patient encounter and the particular social and historical conditions that cause moral questions to emerge *now* as problematic. Taussig forcefully challenges the recommendation that physicians learn to understand what constitutes illness for people of diverse cultural backgrounds—to understand, that is, the "cultural construction of clinical reality":

like so much of the humanistic reform-mongering propounded in recent times, in which a concern with the natives' point of view comes to the fore, there lurks the danger that the experts will avail themselves of that knowledge only to make the science of human management all the more powerful and coercive. For indeed there will be irreconcilable conflicts of interest and these will be "negotiated" by those who hold the upper hand, albeit in terms of a language and a practice which denies such manipulation and the existence of unequal control. (Taussig, 1980, p. 12)

"It is a strange 'alliance,' " writes Taussig, "in which one party avails itself of the other's private understandings in order to manipulate them all the more successfully." The issue, he argues, is not "the cultural construction of clinical reality" but the "clinical construction of culture." In this view, Western medicine must be seen as an ideological system (in the sense of Mannheim, Berger and Luckmann, and Geertz): It is experienced by its practitioners as inescapably natural, as what *is*, and whatever data they collect will sustain a vision of biomedical knowledge as true. Taken for granted as reality, the underlying system of biomedicine is precisely what need not be examined.

The unfolding journal literature on HIV reads like a case study on this point, documenting, on the one hand, the instability of linguistic signs and their presumed referents and, on the other, the efficient ways in which instability is repaired. The compilation of papers published in *Science* from 1982 to 1985 (Kulstad, 1986), for example, illustrates several ways in which the research laboratory of virologist Robert C. Gallo at the National Cancer Institute (NCI)—"codiscoverer" of HIV with Luc Montagnier of the Pasteur Institute in Paris—was able to stake out fairly ambitious territory: By repeatedly citing each other's work, a small group of scientists quickly established a dense citation network, thus gaining early (if ultimately only partial) control over nomenclature, publication, invitation to conferences, and history. The "Introduction and Overview" chapter of the *Science* collection—written, quite appropriately, by a leading AIDS researcher who is, however, within the NCI network (Max Essex)—serves to stabilize the scientific narrative up to that point: reinforcing some lines of thinking, omitting untidy anomalies, cleaning up terminology. Subsequent articles in journals like *Scientific American* by Gallo and others accomplished the same kind of textual cleansing and fortification. As we would expect, the journal literature on AIDS journal literature (e.g., Small & Greenlee, 1989) documents the increasing reality of "the AIDS virus" as a legitimate object of scientific study and shows that citation evolves an intertextual life of its own. As the *Science* collection suggests, one group of influential papers can significantly shape subsequent citation patterns, fix nomenclature, and stimulate or close off particular avenues of research. But it also suggests that density of signification may tell us as much about a given laboratory's authority in the field to produce statements as about the concrete operations by which it claims to transform statements into scientific objects. This may include the power to influence acceptance or rejection of papers for publication, to shape the language of someone else's publication, to determine the speakers and formats of conference sessions, and to interpret the significance of research for other scientists and the media; the effect is not only to help or hurt individual scientists but to set a gold standard for future discourse. John Crewdson (1989), using the Freedom of Information Act to trace the history of the identifying names given by various laboratories to the AIDS-related viruses and viral strains that ultimately emerged as *HIV*, found that records of Gallo's lab created a chaotic trail of signifiers that often simply disappeared. While much of this may not be rare in scientific investigation and publication, questions and controversies in this case continue to call attention to the apparatus of production, to the practices through which facts are fabricated, and to the tenuous correspondence between objects and signs.

No wonder, then, that "the cultural" becomes precisely what must be repeatedly transcended (or jettisoned) in order to identify and maintain a sense of what is real and universal. In addition, as Philip Setel (1990, p. 18) writes, "Medical literature virtually creates 'culture' as a reservoir of unhealthy practices to be stamped out." Such observations inevitably challenge medicine's narration of the real.[7]

AIDS and HIV in Montreal

> The evidence for HIV is overwhelming. There is
> a primary etiologic agent, the *sine qua non*.
> Take it away and you don't have an epidemic.
>
> —Robert C. Gallo (June 1989)

> We are 10 years into this epidemic and the HIV
> picture remains foggy and blurry.
>
> —Nicholas Regush (June 1989)

AIDS and HIV are now taken for granted as stable observable entities, fully institutionalized through scientific journals, funding incentives, clinical regimens, health policies, educational brochures, books and poems, personal testimonies, and corporate investments. One sees this clearly at the annual international AIDS conferences that have been held since 1985. At rare moments, however, medicine's narration of the real is interrupted long enough to glimpse other narratives. Such a moment occurred at the Fifth International AIDS Conference in Montreal in June 1989. This was by far the largest conference yet: over 10,000 delegates, 1,000 media representatives, 1,000 corporate and organizational delegates, and—uninvited—a few hundred AIDS activists. Quite unexpectedly, several factors converged to challenge biomedical control over the epidemic: specifically, the accepted view that AIDS is caused by the human immunodeficiency virus (HIV) and that HIV acts alone—in Robert Gallo's words, as the "Mack truck" of AIDS. Though the participants in the debate never articulated it in quite these terms, their questions about HIV—how it works, how it does damage, how it can be the sole cause of AIDS—inevitably opened the black box of what had been considered settled and wholly routinized within the apparatus of scientific investigation and reporting. Even as the conference overwhelmingly confirmed (in hundreds of scholarly presentations as well as in the conspicuous presence throughout a huge exhibition hall of the 1,000 corporate and organizational delegates) that this particular virus had probably become a reality too costly to give up, questions about HIV called attention to the cultural construction of AIDS and specifically its construction within the culture of biomedical science.

It is germane to my account to say that most people who do cultural research on the AIDS epidemic have at least a rudimentary theoretical grasp of virology and immunology. The same cannot be said of most scientists' grasp of social and cultural theory. At a press briefing on June 8, for example, Robert Gallo was asked whether he thought the Montreal conference's unusual emphasis on social challenges was overshadowing the science and whether he would come to these annual conferences in the future. He replied that, while his decision to come next year would depend on the final conference program, "I must have heard fifty or one hundred scientists yesterday say there wasn't enough time for science."[8] He continued:

> I appreciate women's rights but I would like a chance to make a choice. We didn't expect this amount of diversity. People from Third World nations need a chance to get together but is here the best place? You can't even find the people you want to talk to here.

For Gallo, the term *social* seems to invoke a range of issues: the amount of conference time allotted to social issues and social sciences as opposed to "science," the visible presence of AIDS activists (whose agenda is apparently what Gallo means by "women's rights"), the "diversity" represented by "people from Third World nations," and the social congestion caused by conference crowds. These characterizations, including the conflation of conventional academic social science with political activism, cropped up repeatedly. Indeed, one could say that, in general, "the cultural" in AIDS discourse is collapsed with "the social" into an amorphous undifferentiated domain containing sociology, anthropology, other cultures, other countries, humanism, the humanities, art, linguistics, economics, the media, morality, ethics, religion, popular culture, politics, political activism, the quilt, and anything else that is not paradigmatic biomedical science or clinical medicine.[9]

Yet, by June 1989, social and cultural questions were periodically disrupting the tidy biomedical narrative. A number of questions about HIV had accumulated and not been fully answered by leading AIDS scientists, at least to the satisfaction of the challengers. Most prominent was the bitter struggle between NCI and the Pasteur over the name, genesis, paternity, and mechanism of the virus, and credit for discovering it. As early as 1983, according to Crewdson (1989), when the Pasteur group submitted a paper to *Nature* that was at odds with Gallo's more well-known representations of the virus, one American reviewer wrote that, if what the French were saying were true, it would be an important paper—but it wasn't true. The paper was rejected; indeed, it ultimately required a patent battle and threat of an international lawsuit by the French to get the true significance and legitimacy of their findings recognized. Many American scientists supported the French, believing that Gallo's laboratory had done sloppy work and perhaps even stolen the Pasteur virus; though their support was often expressed in code or in private, it ultimately spurred international compromises that took into account the interests of the French.

A different challenge came in 1988 when Peter Duesberg (Ph.D.), a retrovirologist at the University of California at Berkeley, contended that no retrovirus could cause the kind of damage being ascribed to HIV. While other scientists' grumblings about "the AIDS mafia" are to some degree discounted as professional sour grapes, Duesberg's relentlessness has led him to be treated as an monomaniacal eccentric whose charges drain time from valuable research. Another long-standing critic has been Joseph Sonnabend (M.D.), a New York City physician who has repeatedly argued that AIDS research has too narrow a focus: Although a number of factors may be involved in the epidemic, he has charged, the government has based all its financing on the assumption that HIV is the sole cause of AIDS. "The HIV hypothesis has consumed all our resources," Sonnabend argues, "and yet hasn't saved a single life." Whether or not HIV is a causal factor, the epidemic in his view is most likely the product of immune suppression caused by dramatic social and environmental changes during the 1970s and the action of other widespread viruses. He has wanted to see these factors investigated as well as the potential role of syphilis, malnutrition, malaria, repeated sexually transmitted diseases (STD), and drug use; he founded the *Journal of AIDS Research* to provide a forum for nonviral research. When it became clear that the viral etiology of AIDS was emerging as triumphant, the journal's editorship was transferred to a virologist and, ironically in view of Sonnabend's original intent, renamed the *Journal of AIDS Research and Human Retroviruses*. At Montreal, Sonnabend participated in a press briefing to announce that a range of community research initiatives were being established to explore many causal factors in AIDS and test a wide range of treatments including nonviral drugs. Meanwhile, the gay journal *The New York Native* published weekly assemblages of counter-evidence, charging that a virtual conspiracy was functioning to champion HIV as the sole cause of AIDS and suppress alternative evidence that would implicate syphilis and/or suggest the role of other viruses.

A common effect of criticism has been to isolate the critics from the scientific establishment, from other journals and science writers, and from many people with AIDS—most of whom have been increasingly inclined to take HIV as an established fact and shift attention to issues of treatment and cure (see Treichler, 1991a). But at the Montreal conference, media criticism of HIV orthodoxy went more mainstream.[10] Nicholas Regush, an experienced Canadian science writer, has contended for some time that AIDS research is dominated by a small coterie of U.S. government scientists who endorse HIV as the cause of AIDS. Regush argued on a Canadian Broadcasting Corporation radio series in 1987-1988 that few journalists (American or Canadian) had critically examined the processes by which the virus theory was constructed and maintained and that even fewer understood or reported the "escalating debate about the actual role of the so-called AIDS virus" (CBC, 1988, p. 2). As early as 1984, Regush himself had come to challenge the orthodox scientific argument on principle:

> I felt that a reasonable argument that HIV could be the cause—*could* be the cause of AIDS—was being translated all too quickly by science and the media as *the* cause of AIDS, and no one seemed to give a damn about really questioning whether in fact that was true or not. (CBC, 1988, p. 2)

Most U.S. science journalists, Regush argued on the CBC program, "are basically fan clubs of certain scientists who believe that HIV is the cause of

AIDS. [The coverage of AIDS] is one of the most disgraceful performances by science writers that I've ever come across" (CBC, 1988, p. 3).

Covering a major basic science session at the Montreal conference, Regush in his column of June 6 (1989a) used the foggy slides produced by a defective projector as a metaphor for the current state of AIDS theory: "We are 10 years into this epidemic and the HIV picture remains foggy and blurry." Pursuing the same theme, his column of June 8 took the form of an open letter to Robert Gallo. Titled "OK, Bob! Are You Going to Talk Turkey About HIV or Not?" the column opened by noting that, although Gallo had not arrived in Montreal in time to deliver his listed conference paper, he had nevertheless reassured Regush by phone that the mechanism of HIV's action was well understood:

> I admit [writes Regush, 1989b] I smiled when you said your lab was researching a dozen ways that HIV could somehow indirectly cause AIDS—considering that you once argued forcefully that direct action of the virus on key immune-system cells was all that was required. You summed up your position by saying that given the right strain of the virus, the right dose and enough time, a person will develop AIDS.
>
> But then you added that it was quite possible that a person could live to a ripe old age with HIV infection and not get AIDS.
>
> Look, Bob, we both know this may sound authoritative to a lot of people, but it really isn't convincing. And frankly, it is getting quite confusing. We really need the scientific details of how this all works. (Regush, 1989b)

In refusing to grant unchallenged authority to scientific assertions and suggesting central contradictions in Gallo's account, Regush is not denying the value of orthodox science. Like the other challengers cited above, however, he emphasizes that scientific accounts are constructed versions of reality rather than simply transparent discoveries. Science writers, accordingly, must not merely act as scribes, reproducing or translating scientific representations into discourse for the general public, but must also oversee the signification process, examining and cross-checking the discourse at multiple points on the assumption that, if the statements in the literature don't hold up, the objects they purport to establish won't either. Examining the structure of language—exposing the seams in the apparent seamlessness of scientific accounts—is the writer's check on reality, carried out on behalf of the public. Thus Regush urges Gallo to present his findings at Montreal: "Bob, we really need you. The HIV-theory side of the conference is in worse shape than I expected." In conclusion, Regush mentions that Peter Duesberg has called him to say he is convinced Gallo doesn't have the data he claims to have: "Prove him wrong, Bob."

Gallo tried to prove him wrong that afternoon, at the press briefing from which I quoted above. In response to a packed house and some rather sharp questions, he reasserted his position that HIV was not simply one factor in a "multi-factorial" explanation of AIDS. "Look," he finally said to his questioners, "I'm in one laboratory. The world is free to find what it wants. Peer reviews do the decision-making, not us." He continued:

> Pasteur, NIH, WHO, NCI—these are not stupid people. The evidence for HIV is overwhelming. There is a primary etiologic agent, the *sine qua non.* Take it away and you don't have an epidemic. This particular epidemic has as its cause HIV. . . . We cannot demonstrate or explain every aspect of the way the virus causes disease. We don't *have* to explain everything to agree upon an agent. We have more evidence about *this* disease, and this agent, than any other in history.

Gallo was asked whether he was sufficiently convinced of HIV as the sole cause of AIDS that other sources of pathogenicity should no longer be explored. "Absolutely," responded Gallo, "they should no longer be explored." When Regush arrived, Gallo broke off his comments to address him: "Mr. Regush," he said, "I'm sorry you were late—I opened my remarks in response to your open letter." From the back of the room, Regush responded, "You were the one who phoned me in the first place." The next day Regush's column did not even bother to discuss Gallo's assertions about HIV, focusing instead on the alternative theories of Joseph Sonnabend and others.[11]

I cite these exchanges in some detail to show how dialogue at this conference between scientists and their critics called attention to and at times even disrupted the machinery by which scientific discourse is produced and accepted. The disruption of media machinery was evident as well. The physical setup of television monitors in the Media Centre enabled reporters, individually or in groups, to follow any major conference paper via closed circuit TV without being physically present at the session; at the same time, the Media Centre was closed to all conference participants except credentialed media representatives, with their official green badges, and their individual "interview subjects." In theory, at least, a reporter could cover the entire conference without ever leaving the Media Centre or encountering a single nonmedia person (see Treichler, 1991b). The chants and actions of AIDS activists were prominent at the conference, however, delaying the opening plenary session by more than an hour and in the process garnering much of the coverage by giving the media what they wanted: the visual, the quotable, and the unexpected. By the third day of the conference, activists had color-xeroxed multiple copies of the official green badges and were regularly attending the closed press briefings inside the Media Centre, including those organized by their friends and colleagues. This "artificial" crowd in turn drew a "real" crowd of "real" media representatives, whose coverage generated more crowds and more coverage, with the consequence of more fully communicating and legitimating nonestablishment perspectives and projects.

This orchestration of simulated identity and its transformation into the real parallels the construction of HIV's own reality. Recall Knorr-Cetina's claim that peer review is not a detached postresearch evaluation process but a continual gatekeeping operation. When Gallo, at his famous 1983 press conference, announced the discovery of "the AIDS virus," he provided it with a proper name—*human T-cell leukemia virus, type III* (*HTLV-III*). This name for the virus was subsequently challenged, even down to what the *L* would stand for; the Pasteur Institute—whose published findings appeared in the same issue of *Science* that Gallo's did—called their virus *LAV,* for *lymphadenopathy virus*, marking its association with lymph gland phenomena rather than leukemia. John Crewdson's book-length analysis in the *Chicago Tribune* in November 1989 reported that Gallo not only peer reviewed grant proposals and manuscripts of close competitors but, in at least one case, changed the wording of a manuscript to bring it into conformity with his own hypothesis that the virus acted like a leukemia virus. While Gallo's network of colleagues at the National Institutes of Health and elsewhere consistently used the name *HTLV-III* in their publications and the French used *LAV* in theirs, a number of other scientists and journals during this period used the name *HTLV-III/LAV* (or *LAV/HTLV-III*) to give recognition to both the NIH and the Pasteur or even to express skepticism about Gallo's claims. The slash helped mark the virus' identity as culturally constructed and disputed. The compromise name *HIV,* recommended in 1986 by the Human Retrovirus Subcommittee of the International Committee on the Taxonomy of Viruses and adopted in the 1987 settlement of the NIH-Pasteur dispute, was a consequence of this turmoil. As Latour and Woolgar (1979/1986, p. 236) conclude from their study of scientific contestation, reality is often "the *consequence* of a dispute rather than its *cause*."

Names play a crucial role in the construction of scientific entities; they function as coherent and unified signifiers for what is often complex, inchoate, or incompletely understood. In turn, names establish entities for the public as both socially significant and conceptually real.[12] The existence of multiple signifiers for the virus, even within the pages of the same journal, reproduced the competition among several laboratories and kept alive a tension over just what the signified consisted of and how it was being constructed. It is in this context that the names *HIV* and *AIDS* are still interesting as one legacy of battles in AIDS research for authority, power, and control over resources, including control over the discourses of the field. Many questions remain about the various signifieds represented by the original array of names; but the existence of *HIV* and *AIDS* as unifying signifiers now makes it possible to proceed *in discourse* as though the questions had been resolved. It takes capital to make capital: As the adoption and acceptance of these terms become increasingly widespread, their linguistic capital continues to accrue.

Montreal did not change AIDS science or science writing but it did call attention to disjunctures in signification, to "the AIDS virus" as a constructed entity across multiple discourses, to the function of metaphors in shoring up favored versions of reality, and to the substantial investment in the notion that reality exists out there to be discovered. In terms of HIV's market currency, the debates over HIV at Montreal did not bring about market failure or anything close to it. But they did bring about scrutiny of the market and, at least in some cases, a more critical examination of individual investment portfolios.

The Reality of HIV and the Apparatus of Production

> In metaphor one has, of course, a stratification of meaning, in which an incongruity of sense on one level produces an influx of significance on another.
>
> —Clifford Geertz (1973, p. 210)

> First umpire: I calls em as I sees em
> Second umpire: I calls em as they are
> Third umpire: They ain't nothin till I calls em
>
> —Baseball saying

We can construct a set of statements about HIV, varying the points and degree of transparency to vary the visibility of fabrication and cultural constructedness:

(1) HIV causes AIDS.

(2) *HIV* is the name scientific culture gives the virus widely believed to cause AIDS.

(3) *HIV* is the compromise name proposed by an international commission to resolve the bitter international dispute over the "discovery" of a virus judged by many to be a causative factor in the infection and immune deficiency that can lead to the specific clinical conditions diagnosed as AIDS.

(4) *HIV* is the acronym adopted in 1986 by the international scientific community to name the virus hypothesized to cause immune deficiency in humans and eventually *AIDS,* another acronym, adopted in 1982, to designate a collection of more than 30 widely diverse clinical conditions believed to be given the opportunity to develop as the result of a severely deficient immune system.

(5) HIV is a hypothesized microscopic entity called a "virus" (from Latin *virus* or "poison") invented by scientists in the 19th century as a way to conceptualize the technical cause and consequences of specific types of infectious disease. A virus cannot reproduce outside living cells: It enters into another organism's host cell and uses that cell's biochemical machinery to replicate itself (in the case of HIV, often years after initial entry), at which point the cell's DNA, with which the virus is integrated, is transcribed to RNA, which in turn becomes protein. Our knowledge of this "life history" has been produced by an intense national research effort focused both on HIV and on drugs designed to disrupt its life history at various points; as the major subject of scientific investigation and pharmaceutical research efforts and major recipient of AIDS research funding, HIV is, therefore, also, as Joseph Sonnabend puts it, "metaphorically representative of other interests."

This comparative exercise illustrates some of the tools of "fiction construction": It suggests that reality is always contextual, always to be read and understood in relation to specific discourse practices, specific metaphors, and the representations and claims (e.g., based on its mechanical operations) in which a specific discipline or subdiscipline specializes. HIV cannot, therefore, be read and understood as "the same" entity in each of the foregoing statements.

In these five statements, we see a move away from the apodictic free-floating assertion of statement (1) toward the explicit linguistic markers that assign statements about reality to specific provinces of meaning—for example, to those of virology and immunology. Different realities are signaled by these differently constructed accounts of viruses. At the same time, the set of statements shows how realities come to be merged and muddled through discursive collapses. Thus statement (1) involves the collapse of *HIV* with two other signifiers: "the AIDS virus" and "the cause of AIDS." The interchangeability of these three terms—precisely what Regush was questioning in his open letter to Gallo—here goes far beyond the discourses of virology and molecular biology. That the universe of scientific investigation and clinical practice with respect to AIDS is now primarily determined by the simple acronym *HIV,* and that HIV has come to seem natural, inevitable, and taken for granted as the cause of AIDS, mark this construction of reality as the hegemonic position from which AIDS research and treatment are typically understood.

The set of statements suggests that "facts are like cows" that in some sense dissolve in the face of close scrutiny only to reemerge as soon as one shifts one's focus. As Foucault (1972, p. 97) writes, "a statement always has borders peopled by other statements," and as Fleck observes, when scientific terms are broken down to show their underlying assumptions, those assumptions must then be broken down to show *their* assumptions, and so on in an infinite regress, with each definition growing larger and more unwieldy. In place of these semantic pyramids, scientific discourse is a form of shorthand in which facts, once admitted, need no longer retain the history of their fabrication.

The statements also reveal that metaphors do important work. Communication and coding metaphors like "transcription" as a vehicle to describe viral replication, for example, import significant elements into the reality claimed about what viruses do. Where tenor meets vehicle, as I. A. Richards (1936) put it, the transaction between the two produces a meaning not attainable without the metaphor because the vehicle brings with it a range of associations that cannot be suppressed or excluded in its new context (a proposition further developed by Max Black, 1962). This gives metaphors a special kind of cognitive power—including the power to shape cognitive processes.[13] In science, Knorr-Cetina (1981, p. 84) observes that some conceptions, including metaphors, may be seen as interesting or useful because they generate puzzles in new ways, represent resources perceived as unrealized, or mobilize various cognitive interests. In contrast to Gallo's Mack truck metaphor, we see in statement (5) a different set of metaphors drawn from the terminology of communication, computers, and high-tech postmodern warfare. Donna Haraway (1989a) argues that it was the move away from the military/industrial complex of metaphors to those of postindustrial information age metaphors of coding and communication that has enabled immunology to claim its current high theoretical status.

Evident in this discussion is the metaphorical and connotative richness of both *HIV* and *AIDS*; indeed, AIDS metaphors are now routinely compared and critiqued to refine their effectiveness and usefulness. For example, Allan M. Brandt (1988, p. 415) describes AIDS (like other epidemic diseases) as a "natural experiment" in how societies respond to disability, dependence, fear, death; society's response reveals its most fundamental cultural, social, and moral values. Mary Catherine Bateson and Richard Goldsby (1988), using an earthquake as an even more specific vehicle for the idea that a sudden serious calamity like a natural disaster at once reveals the stresses and vulnerabilities of a society, write that AIDS reveals the "fault lines" in our society. But June Osborn, speaking on the *MacNeil-Lehrer Newshour* (December 7, 1989), argued that the AIDS epidemic is *not* like an earthquake, which happens all at once and brings normal life to a standstill, but is drawn out over a period of time, never creating for a broad mass of people enough sense of urgency to address it effectively. Note that there are political implications here as well: If an earthquake—or an epidemic like AIDS—is conceptualized as a natural disaster, an act of God, people in some cultures are less likely to expect or demand immediate government assistance than if it is seen as a massive social or public health crisis (in other cultures, the opposite might be true). At the same time, this metaphorical richness is reciprocal, with HIV and AIDS exported to explain other concepts just as other concepts are imported to explain them; indeed, there is no *lingua rasa* to be found. As Nancy Scheper-Hughes and Margaret Lock (1986) so eloquently argue, an illness always constructs its metaphorical double, which speaks truth as faithfully as any biomedical diagnosis. If a term is being used in the culture with increasing breadth and frequency, what I have elsewhere called an "epidemic of signification" is inevitable: No matter how literal and denotative a linguistic form may at first appear, it will develop new meanings almost as fast as we can identify old ones. This makes it difficult to predict what a particular metaphor will actually do. The plague metaphor for AIDS, for example, is now so routine that we cannot really say how meaningful it is unless we can examine exactly how and where it is deployed, how it is understood, and how it is acted upon. The apocalypse metaphor functions very differently in the history of formulations about AIDS in Africa, in contrast to formulations about AIDS in the West or to formulations about AIDS by Africans. To attribute a particular effect to a metaphor too readily closes off inquiry into contradictory senses of metaphors operating in the culture and inquiry into the legacy of diverse historical tropes.

The Montreal conference also introduced and strengthened a way of thinking about AIDS itself as no longer inevitably fatal but as a chronic manageable condition. Though arising from several different discourses (scholarly papers, activist press releases, social issues debates), this view achieved currency only when these discourses coalesced at the conference. The term *AIDS discourse* is not simply descriptive but entails an examination of the context—the entire apparatus—through which utterances about AIDS are produced and interpreted and speaking positions are made possible. The issue is not whether or not HIV "exists" or whether a "cultural construction" is pure discourse. The issue is what the grounds and consequences are in a given context for positing HIV and AIDS as realities and embedding them within various networks of signification, and what body of "craftwork" this represents. Discourses are also in some sense always oppositional. Any given discourse or context, that is, can always by characterized in relation to some other discourse or context as representing a dominant, negotiated, or oppositional position (see Hall, 1980b).

Yet the Montreal conference also makes clear the impossibility of strictly separating a "dominant discourse" from an "oppositional discourse." No discourse is autonomous; it is rather shaped in the light of ongoing day-to-day struggles for survival and legitimacy, in the light of processes of signification, and in the light of what happens when edges touch. Here Mannheim is especially useful: When ideological and utopian visions become locked in sustained opposition over time, proponents of the two camps become intimately familiar with each other's positions—symbiotically dependent upon each other for continuing self-definition but also for continuing critique. Through this symbolism, knowledge, differently produced, has come to be shared to such a degree that a range of collaborative research initiatives has been created. One of the reasons for examining AIDS discourse, and the construction of HIV within it, is to see language in the process of formation—terms and concepts entering and reshaping the discursive field. The scientific culture that constructed the virus is now what most effectively disguises its existence as a cultural construction. Thus reified, HIV exhibits a number of predictable characteristics: It is referred to by a universally agreed upon signifier; conventional representations for it have been developed in journals, the media, three-dimensional glass models, and elsewhere; and its reality continues to be verified through ongoing laboratory and clinical operations (e.g., its structure and life cycle can be described). In addition, HIV is now a taken-for-granted reality in the discussions and plans across many social and cultural institutions and in the lives of many individuals (scientists, persons with AIDS, health care professionals, others). Pervasive in discourse, HIV is used as a weapon both to defend and to attack the current state of science, as a metaphor to explain other phenomena, and as an entity through which further research will be generated. Widely identifiable on computer data bases and indexes, HIV now exists across the discourses of the culture. Both fabricated and fact, HIV has become, in short, a reality that is too costly to give up.

This is all the more reason to keep track of these costs by asking such questions as the following: What are the range of existing discourses in which HIV is mentioned? How is it articulated to the pre-existing issues and codes in those discourses? How do discourses empower people and people empower discourses? To what extent does a "dominant" discourse on HIV continue to be identifiable, under what circumstances and under whose auspices did it emerge, and what kind of resources have been required to sustain its authority? How are authoritative definitions constructed and deployed? Conversely, how are they challenged, evaded, disrupted, or redefined? How does discourse, in other words, work to articulate, codify, maintain, or challenge various forms of authority, power, and control over material resources? And what difference does it make?

Conclusion

The concept of cultural construction can be understood as follows. It is a way of talking about how knowledge is produced and sustained within specific contexts, discourses, and cultural communities; it takes for granted metaphor and other forms of linguistic representation; it presupposes that ideas are produced out of concrete contexts and have concrete effects; it takes for granted hermeneutic activity; it is a complex of ideas and operations sustained over time within a given community; hence it is institutionalized. Though often confused with idealism or more recently with a view that "everything is discourse," the notion of cultural construction is not a matter of arbitrarily envisioning an unknowable material reality but of engaging in highly *non*arbitrary ways with the material world. Although meaning is indeed arbitrary and fluid, this does not mean that it is arbitrary and fluid within a given signifying system. The predictability and stability provided by a given history, society, culture, and set of disciplinary conventions are anything but arbitrary. This point is often misunderstood when a given meaning or idea is termed a *cultural construction.* Within the signifying system, that *is* the meaning. No wonder then that we expend great effort to preserve belief in a given system where meaning appears stable, indeed, even universal. Recognition that reality is culturally constructed makes such belief impossible.

Why does the concept of cultural construction emerge so strongly now? Philosopher Hilary Putnam (1975), asking what precisely it is that language tells us about material reality, posits a "division of linguistic labor," whereby we cede particular realms of reality to acknowledged experts, and suggests that problems and contradictions presented by human disease phenomena may be disguised by the denotative power of medical experts. During a period like the current one in which medical authority is widely challenged, the existing division of linguistic and conceptual labor is inevitably challenged as well. In Montreal and elsewhere, we are seeing a challenge to the "clinical construction of culture" in which "the natives" talk back, articulating their own interests and writing their own texts.

As a crisis named and interpreted through culture, the AIDS epidemic demonstrates the argument that the concepts of *culture* and *cultural construction* encompass both material and nonmaterial phenomena and that analysis must emphasize the ongoing interaction and mutual influence between the two. This task presents two difficulties: The first is that the claims of any analysis always press at the boundaries of their established context, dissolving the evidence of origins and disclaimers as they are taken up, with the force of powerful metaphors, in new discourses. The second is that the material and the nonmaterial cohabit much more intimately and inseparably than we usually suppose. If we take Saussure's famous image of linguistic duality as a sheet of paper with the material on one side and the conceptual on the other, we can also always flip the sheet of paper over, so that what we thought was the material entity is seen also to have a conceptual life and the conception a material life: metaphor into hardware, but hardware into metaphor too. Though ideas and conceptions emerge from material reality, that reality has itself been named and interpreted according to the rules and understandings of scientific culture. That scientific findings are over-determined by culture, however, does not mean they are not deeply engaged with the story material reality has to tell. Cultural constructions are not lies, as the touched-up X ray of the Groucho Marx epigraph that opened this essay is a lie. A lie, to be sustained, requires the invention of an alternate universe: Hence, to be sustained, the touched-up X ray requires the falsification of medical records, the murder of the radiologist, or perhaps the development of new interpretive conventions that redefine what a "bad" X ray looks like.

With numbers of new cases continuing to escalate, the moral limitations of a facile constructionism are evident. Even if we will never know reality, specific tasks, goals, and crises may require us to go with our best shot as though it were real. Yet the enormity of the AIDS crisis should not force us back toward the complacent imperialism of a transparent realism, for this equally abuses the multiple ways in which the AIDS epidemic is experienced, interpreted, confronted. Resisting realism does not mean abandoning the real world but abandoning faith in transparency. This raises a third difficulty, however—another version of Mannheim's paradox: An analysis aimed at revealing the cultural constructedness of a body of theory can hardly avoid acknowledging its own cultural constructedness as well. This certainly complicates the voice with which social scientists are to enter these discussions about AIDS and culture. Features so crucial to scholarly projects in the last two decades—features like irony, satire, self-reflexiveness, and the desire to understand how different groups construct and represent reality—do not compete well in an international crisis against the certainties that anchor other discourses, some of which have been noted here.

Although it is useful to characterize AIDS and HIV as cultural constructions, this by no means liberates us from taking responsibility for the existence of a real, material world and analyzing its intersection with our conceptions and interventions; indeed, so long as the analysis is local, provisional, and contextualized in terms of specific purposes, a serious commitment to a constructionist model undermines rather than reinforces relativism or pluralism. Likewise, the use of the concept of cultural construction intensifies the responsibility to make choices. But if we take seriously the contradictions built into the term *culture* from its earliest days, we can work more seriously with the dialectic these contradictions offer. It is the contradictions that mark the pleasure and danger of cultural theory.

Notes

1. In addition to the conference program, sources for examples of discourse at the conference include texts of lectures, press kits, press releases, published newspaper and journal articles, and the author's notes from press conferences and press briefings.

2. Sociologist Pauline Bart designed a T-shirt in the 1970s with the statement "Everything is data" on the front, "But data isn't everything" on the back. In other words, everything is potentially material for an analysis based on cultural construction, but this enterprise by no means exhausts the world or one's ways of being in it.

3. Kroeber and Kluckhohn trace the two ideologically contradictory meanings that the term *Kultur* acquired in Germany as both in league with and resistant to *zivilisation*: The first meaning was international and progressive and involved the desire to go forward toward democracy; the second was introverted and romantic and represented a fight for Germany's unique cultural heritage (and wish to go backward toward "nature"). We do not know which meaning would

have won out because the word was deleted from German dictionaries until after 1848, by which point its radical connotations had been forgotten.

4. The social and cultural construction of reality, as I am interested in it here, is, of course, addressed in the work of Dilthey, Weber, Merton, Benedict, Sapir, Firth, Halliday, Whorf, Putnam as well as Weber, Schutz, Ricoeur, Mead, Freud, and Giddens; and see Hill (1988), Ortony (1979), Sperber (1985), and Wuthnow, Hunter, Bergensen, and Kurzweil (1984). Kroeber and Kluckhohn's review is a definitive starting point for any discussion of culture. They invoke the old realist/idealist divide—what Ortony (1979), updating the terminology, calls the realist/constructionist divide—only to reject it: "We are not too sure we can properly classify ourselves as cultural realists, idealists, or nominalists" (Kroeber & Kluckhohn, 1952, p. 190). Bourdieu also insists on a radical attention to practice, leading him to the notion of the *habitus*—a term designed to move beyond "the common conception of habit as a mechanical assembly or performed programme" (Bourdieu, 1972/1977, p. 218, n. 47) and instead emphasize a specific intersection in time and space. By emphasizing the situatedness of practice, its unique possibilities within a network of constraints, Bourdieu can envision a system that transcends conventional dichotomies.

5. Given their radical and uncompromising version of construction, Latour and Woolgar no doubt took some pleasure in reporting, in a note to the 1986 (second) edition, that, when the book was originally published, they were forced to remove such disclaimers to certainty as "*all texts are stories*" and "the reader can never 'know for sure' "; the publishers (Sage) said they were not in the habit of publishing anything that "proclaimed its own worthlessness" (Latour & Woolgar, 1986, p. 284). Latour and Woolgar also note their decision to drop the term *social* from the book's original subtitle (*The Social Construction of Scientific Facts*): "By demonstrating its pervasive applicability, the social study of science has rendered 'social' devoid of any meaning. Although this was our original intention, it was not clear until now that we could simply ditch the term" (p. 281).

6. Perhaps because physicians worked so systematically to establish medicine as a science equipped to define reality—anywhere, anytime—their resistance to constructionism is considerable. Indeed, *resistance* is perhaps the wrong word, for it implies a perceived and articulated challenge. It is more accurate to see medicine as an ideological system that works tirelessly and smoothly, in Berger and Luckmann's sense, to keep its reality coherent, a reality that is by definition unchallengeable. Hence, when anthropology and ethnography encounter medicine as a signifying system, they come into contact with a deeply entrenched realism. Nevertheless, a view of medical reality as constructed does now figure in the work of some medical sociologists, historians, linguists, literary critics, and anthropologists. Writings in medical anthropology particularly germane to this essay include Caplan (1987), Gaines (1987), Gaines and Hahn (1985), Marcus and Fischer (1986), Marshall and Bennett (1990), Payer (1988), Holland and Quinn (1987), Rapp (1988), Scheper-Hughes and Lock (1986), Schneider (1980), Sperber (1985), and Wright and Treacher (1982). On anthropology and AIDS, see Farmer and Kleinman (1989), Marshall and Bennett (1990), Parker (1987, 1990), the Symposium on Anthropology and AIDS (in *Medical Anthropology Quarterly* [1986], and Bolton's comprehensive bibliography [1991]).

While some anthropologists would place themselves on one side or the other, others suggest that the division grows out of the way the world is. Dorothy Holland and Naomi Quinn (1987, p. 3) write, for example, "Undeniably, a great deal of order exists in the natural world we experience. However, much of the order we perceive in the world is there only because we put it there. That we impose such order is even more apparent when we consider the social world, in which institutions such as marriage, deeds such as lying, and customs such as dating happen at all because the members of a society presume them to be. D'Andrade contrasts such culturally constructed things with cultural categories for objects such as stone, tree, and hand, which exist whether or not we invent labels for them. An entity such as marriage, on the other hand, is created by 'the social agreement that something counts as that condition' and exists only by virtue of adherence to the rules that constitute it."

Atwood Gaines (1987) summarizes with great confidence the assumptions of a constructionist position in medical anthropology: Medical knowledge is seen as problematic, not given; medical knowledge is not distinct from social knowledge; diseases are not naturally existing entities; the study of medicine and its development must include the study of external social forces. But, in the absence of the detailed cultural context and meticulously circumscribed ground rules established by studies like Knorr-Cetina's, an uneasiness with a constructionist model of biomedical phenomena sometimes emerges. The introduction to Gaines and Hahn (1985, p. 5), for example, includes the statement: "The editors note here a difference between them which also divides anthropologists more widely; in the determination of human affairs, Hahn gives more weight to an external 'real' 'physical' world while Gaines emphasizes particular cultural constructions of reality as sources and guides of human action."

7. Recent ethnographic research on sexuality and sexual identity could be said similarly to challenge epidemiology's narration of the real. See Caplan (1987), Herdt (1981), Kane and Mason (1990), Leonard (1990), Lindenbaum (1984), and Parker (1987, 1990). Gill Shepherd (1987, in Caplan, 1987) describes sexual relationships in Mombasa, Kenya, where "same-sex" behavior indubitably occurs but differs in cultural meaning according to sex, social rank, and age; because same-sex relationships are constituted within this dense network of social and symbolic relationships, they are said not to exist in virtually all nonscholarly literature on "homosexuality" in Africa. See also Bolton (1991).

8. Press briefing reports are based on my field notes.

9. The Montreal conference provides other examples as well. A second understanding of culture at Montreal was reflected in public health and social science papers. In the tradition of Virchow, Sigerist, and Dubos, these accounts emphasize the broad social conditions that encourage and sustain epidemics of infectious disease in various cultures—conditions ranging from poverty, malnutrition, endemic disease, population shifts, and inadequate health care to discrimination, capitalism, colonialism, environmental toxins, cultural and linguistic barriers to communication, government inaction, drug use, and problems of postcolonial development. Here information about social conditions and cultural practice is crucial to defining the epidemic and developing strategies for addressing it; the 1989 conference was enhanced in this respect by the participation of people of color from developing countries (scientists, policymakers, media representatives, and people with AIDS). As the correspondent for the magazine *West Africa* commented, the Montreal conference was a landmark for Third World people ("Symptoms of Global Malady," 1989).

Another understanding emerged in the events explicitly labeled "cultural": educational dramas and dances designed for rural villages in the Caribbean and Central Africa, exhibits of historical and contemporary art on infectious and venereal disease, and panels of writers, television producers, artists, activists, and academics featured in SIDART (a series of panels, exhibits, films, and other cultural events organized in conjunction with the conference). Here, culture—designating, on the one hand, the actual objects and artifacts resulting from cultural production and, on the other, the intellectual apparatus of symbolic production and meaning (signification, cultural difference, cultural production, interpretation, and representation)—addressed what Brazilian writer Herbert Daniel called "the staging of the epidemic"; notions of cultural construction were explicit elements of debate.

10. No doubt in part this is because the Canadian press has a tradition of deflating U.S. puffery. Press coverage relevant to the Montreal conference includes Charles (1989), Crewdson (1989), Dunn (1989), Kuitenbrouwer (1989), Picard (1989), Regush (1989), and Treichler (1991b). See Konetey-Ahulu (1988) for a similar African critique.

11. Questions at these briefings were sometimes passed forward in writing. In this case, the questioner was writer and activist Michael Callen, one of Joseph Sonnabend's AIDS patients and a participant at Sonnabend's press briefing the day before. In asking his question orally, Callen noted that the written version had been torn up rather than read out. (Thus gatekeeping can take place even when no gates are visible.) When a couple of quasi-technical follow-up questions failed to elicit any concession from Gallo that other factors might be involved, Callen started to turn away; but Gallo stopped him, saying with some sarcasm, "Wait a minute, wait a minute—I probably know as much about this as you." He then proceeded to talk at length, concluding: "I don't control who gets funded. If it meets peer review, it gets funded. If you or Duesberg or Sonnabend wants to work on something other than HIV, be my guest."

12. The often amorphous conditions and diverse injuries caused by the stress of repetitive motion are considered a legitimate occupational disease category in Australia but not in the United States. It has been persuasively argued by Andrew Hopkins (1990) that in part this is because the Australians early settled on a single term—*repetitive strain injury* (or *RSI*)—which was conceptually meaningful in terms of its causes; in contrast, the United States has confused the picture with a plethora of terms including the narrow medicalized *carpal tunnel syndrome* and the broader but vaguer *cumulative trauma syndrome,* a term few would readily associate with work-related problems.

13. This is in transition; in abstracts of papers given at Montreal and San Francisco, one finds both military and coding metaphors. See Woese (1967) on the development of coding and language as the metaphors underlying molecular biology; see Haraway (1989a) on the evolution of representations in 20th-century medical textbooks. On metaphor, see Brandt (1988), Geertz (1973), Lakoff and Johnson (1980), Martin (1988), Miller (1989), Ortony (1979), Sontag (1988), Watney (1989), and Williamson (1989).

Consider the ways, as described by Crewdson (1989), that the Pasteur group and the Gallo group approached the problem of identifying "the AIDS virus." From the beginning, Gallo believed AIDS was caused by a leukemia retrovirus like the two HTLV viruses his laboratory had already isolated. The discovery process was, therefore, shaped by this conception: When he introduced infected cells from AIDS patients into cell cultures, he expected them to replicate as a cancer virus like HTLV would; instead, the cultures died. As a metaphor, the tenor of Gallo's conception was that AIDS was caused by a human retrovirus; the vehicle for him was the HTLV leukemia model. The French, meanwhile, began with no such preconception: The tenor was identical but the vehicle was not nearly so narrow. Accordingly, they explored different ways to keep the cell culture alive, discovering before too long that the virus killed cells rather than causing them to replicate; because the French scientists kept adding fresh cells, the cultures did not die.

For a detailed analysis of the Gallo-Montagnier dispute and its status as a continuing narrative, see Feldman (1991).

References

AIDS victims live longer, U.S. doctor says. (1989, June 8). *The [Montreal] Gazette,* p. 1.

Bateson, M. C., & Goldsby, R. (1988). *Thinking AIDS: The social response to the biological threat.* Reading, MA: Addison-Wesley.

Berger, P. L., & Luckmann, T. (1967). *The social construction of reality: A treatise in the sociology of knowledge.* New York: Anchor/Doubleday.

Black, M. M. (1962). Metaphor. In M. M. Black (Ed.) *Models and Metaphors.* Ithaca, NY: Cornell University Press.

Bolton, R. (with M. Lewis & G. Orozco). (1991). AIDS literature for anthropologists: A working bibliography. *Journal of Sex Research, 28*(2), 307-346.

Bourdieu, P. (1977). *Outline of a theory of practice* (R. Nice, Trans.). Cambridge: Cambridge University Press. (Original work published 1972)

Brandt, A. M. (1988). AIDS and metaphor: Toward the social meaning of epidemic disease. *Social Research, 55*(3), 413-432.

Canadian Broadcasting Corporation (CBC). (1988). *Ideas* [January 12, 13] (4ID8-232). (Available from CBC Transcripts, P.O. Box 6440, Station A, Montreal, Quebec, H3C 3L4)

Caplan, P. (1987). Introduction. In P. Caplan (Ed.), *The cultural construction of sexuality* (pp. 1-30). New York: Tavistock.

Charles, R. (1989, June 8). HIV link over-emphasized, say dissidents. *Montreal Daily News,* p. 5.

Crewdson, J. (1989, November 19). The great AIDS quest. *Chicago Tribune,* sec. 5, pp. 1-16.

Dunn, K. (1989, June 8). Look beyond HIV as the cause of AIDS, New York doctor says. *The [Montreal] Gazette,* p. 10.

Farmer, P. (1990). Sending sickness: Sorcery, politics, and changing concepts of AIDS in rural Haiti. *Medical Anthropology Quarterly, 4*(1), 6-27.

Farmer, P., & Kleinman, A. (1989). AIDS as human suffering. *Daedalus, 118*(2), 135-160.

Feldman, J. (1991). *HIV and the Gallo-Montagnier dispute: A narrative analysis.* Paper presented at the Medical Humanities and Social Sciences Seminar, University of Illinois College of Medicin, Urbana.

Fleck, L. (1979). *Genesis and development of a scientific fact* (T. J. Trenn & R. K. Merton, Eds.). Chicago: University of Chicago Press. (Original work published 1936)

Foucault, M. (1972). *The archeology of knowledge* (trans. Rupert Swyer). London: Tavistock.

Gaines, A. D. (1987). *Cultural constructivism and biomedicine: Understanding ethnomedical knowledge and practice.* Unpublished manuscript.

Gaines, A. D., & Hahn, R. (Eds.). (1985). *Physicians of Western medicine: Anthropological approaches to theory and practice.* Dordrecht, the Netherlands: D. Reidel.

Geertz, C. (1973). *The interpretation of cultures.* New York: Basic Books.

Hall, S. (1980a). Cultural studies: Two paradigms. *Media, Culture and Society, 2,* 57-72.

Hall, S. (1980b). Encoding and decoding. In S. Hall et al. (Eds.), *Culture, media, language* (pp. 128-138). London: Hutchinson/CCCS.

Haraway, D. (1989a). The biopolitics of postmodern bodies: Determinations of self in immune system discourse. *Differences: A Journal of Feminist Cultural Studies, 1*(1), 3-43.

Haraway, D. (1989b). *Primate visions: Gender, race, and nature in the world of modern science.* New York: Routledge.

Haraway, D. (1991). *Simians, cyborgs, and women: The reinvention of nature.* London: Free Association Books.

Herdt, G. H. (1981). *Guardians of the flutes: Idioms of masculinity.* New York: McGraw-Hill.

Hill, J. H. (1988). Language, culture, and world views. In F. J. Newmeyer (Ed.), *Linguistics: The Cambridge Survey* (Vol. 4, pp. 14-36). Cambridge: Cambridge University Press.

Holland, D., & Quinn, N. (Eds.). (1987). *Cultural models in language and thought.* Cambridge: Cambridge University Press.

Hopkins, A. (1990). The social recognition of repetition strain injuries: An Australian/American comparison. *Social Science and Medicine, 30*(3), 365-372.

Ingstad, B. (1990). The cultural construction of AIDS and its consequences for prevention in Botswana. *Medical Anthropology Quarterly, 4*(1), 28-40.

Kane, S., & Mason, T. (1990, June). *AIDS research, anti-drug policies, and ethnography.* Paper prepared for the Wenner-Gren Conference, "AIDS Research: Issues for Anthropology Theory, Method, and Practice," Estes Park, CO.

Konetey-Ahulu, F. I. D. (1988). AIDS in Africa: Misinformation and disinformation. In D. Koch-Wesser & H. Vanderschmidt (Eds.), *The heterosexual transmission of AIDS in Africa* (pp. 24-25). Cambridge, MA: Abt Books.

Knorr-Cetina, K. D. (1981). *The manufacture of knowledge: An essay on the constructivist and contextual nature of science.* Oxford: Pergamon.

Kroeber, A. L., & Kluckhohn, C. (with the assistance of W. Untereiner and appendixes by A. G. Meyer). (1952). *Culture: A critical review of concepts and definitions* (Papers of the Peabody Museum, Harvard University, Vol. 47, no. 1). Cambridge: Peabody Museum of American Archaeology and Ethnology.

Kuhn, T. S. (1962). *The structure of scientific revolutions.* Chicago: University of Chicago Press. (Enlarged ed. published 1970)

Kuitenbrouwer, P. (1989, June 3). African girls need AIDS facts from elders: MD. *The [Montreal] Gazette,* p. A8.

Kulstad, R. (Ed.). (1986). *Papers from science, 1982-1985.* Washington, DC: American Association for the Advancement of Science.

Lakoff, G., & Johnson, M. (1980). *Metaphors we live by.* Chicago: University of Chicago Press.

Latour, B. (1987). *Science in action: How to follow scientists and engineers through society.* Cambridge, MA: Harvard University Press.

Latour, B., & Woolgar, S. (1986). *Laboratory life: The construction of scientific facts.* Princeton, NJ: Princeton University Press. (Original work published 1979)

Leonard, T. L. (1990). Male clients of female street prostitutes: Unseen partners in sexual disease transmission. *Medical Anthropology Quarterly, 4*(1), 41-55.

Lindenbaum, S. (1984). Variations on a sociosexual theme in Melanesia. In G. H. Herdt (Ed.), *Ritualized homosexuality in Melanesia* (pp. 337-361). Berkeley: University of California Press.

Mannheim, K. (1985) *Ideology and utopia.* New York: Harcourt Brace Jovanovich. (Original work published 1936)

Marcus, G. E., & Fischer, M. M. J. (1986). *Anthropology as cultural critique: An experimental moment in the human sciences.* Chicago: University of Chicago Press.

Marshall, P. A., & Bennett, L. A. (1990). Anthropological contributions to AIDS research. *Medical Anthropological Quarterly, 4*(1), 3-5.

Martin, E. (1988, April 25). *The cultural construction of gendered bodies: Biology and metaphors of production and destruction.* Paper presented at the Vega Day Symposium in Honor of Fredrik Barth, Swedish Society for Anthropology and Geography, Stockholm.

Miller, D. A. (1989). Sontag's urbanity: Review of *AIDS and Its Metaphors,* by Susan Sontag. *October, 49,* 91-101.

Morisset, R. A. (1989, June 4-9). *Abstracts and program* (Fifth International Conference on AIDS, "The Scientific and Social Challenge," Montreal). Ottawa, Canada: International Development Research Centre.

Ortony, A. (Ed.). (1979). *Metaphor and thought.* Cambridge: Cambridge University Press.

Parker, R. (1987). Acquired immunodeficiency syndrome in urban Brazil. *Medical Anthropology Quarterly, 1*(2), 155-175.

Parker, R. (1990). *Bodies, pleasures, and passions: Sexual culture in contemporary Brazil.* Boston: Beacon.

Payer, L. (1988). *Medicine and culture: Varieties of treatment in the United States, England, West Germany, and France.* New York: Holt.

Picard, A. (1989, June 8). Sole cause of AIDS queried by doctor. *[Toronto] Globe and Mail,* p. A12.

Putnam, H. (1975). *Philosophical papers* (Vol. 2). Cambridge: Cambridge University Press.

Rapp, R. (1988). Chromosomes and communication: The discourse of genetic counseling. *Medical Anthropology Quarterly, 2,* 143-157.

Regush, N. (1989a, June 6). Focusing on cause of AIDS is a game of cat and mouse. *The [Montreal] Gazette,* p. A12.

Regush, N. (1989b, June 8). OK, Bob! Are you going to talk turkey about HIV or not? *The [Montreal] Gazette,* p. A11.

Richards, I. A. (1936). *The philosophy of rhetoric.* London: Oxford University Press.

Saiz, R. (Producer). (1990, June). *AIDS in the 90s* [Film]. San Francisco: Group W Television, Inc., KPIX-TV.

Scheper-Hughes, N., & Lock, M. M. (1986). Speaking "truth" to illness: Metaphors, reification, and a pedagogy for patients. *Medical Anthropology Quarterly, 17*(5), 137-140.

Schneider, D. M. (1980). *American kinship: A cultural account* (2nd ed.). Chicago: University of Chicago Press.

Setel, P. (1990). *AIDS and the body as social space: Epistemologies of distinction and difference.* Unpublished manuscript.

Shepherd, G. (1987). Rank, gender, and sexuality: Mombasa as a key to understanding sexual options. In P. Caplan (Ed.), *The cultural construction of sexuality* (pp. 240-270). New York: Tavistock.

Small, H., & Greenlee, E. (1989). A co-citation study of AIDS research. *Communication Research, 16*(5), 642-666.

Sontag, S. (1988). *AIDS and its metaphors.* New York: Farrar, Straus, and Giroux.

Sperber, D. (1985). Anthropology and psychology: Towards an epidemiology of representations. *Man, 20,* 73-89.

Susser, M. (1973). *Causal thinking in the health sciences: Concepts and strategies of epidemiology.* New York: Oxford University Press.

Symposium on anthropology and AIDS. (1986). *Medical Anthropology Quarterly, 17*(2), 31-40.

Symptoms of global malady. (1989, June 19-25). *West Africa.*

Taussig, M. T. (1980). Reification and the consciousness of the patient. *Social Science and Medicine, 14B,* 3-13.

Treichler, P. A. (1988). AIDS, homophobia, and biomedical discourse: An epidemic of signification. In D. Crimp (Ed.), *AIDS: Cultural analysis/cultural activism* (pp. 31-70). Cambridge: MIT Press.

Treichler, P. A. (1989). AIDS and HIV infection in the Third World: First World chronicles. In P. Mariani & B. Kruger (Eds.), *Remaking history* (pp. 31-86). New York: Dia Art Foundation.

Treichler, P. A. (1991a). How to have theory in an epidemic: The evolution of AIDS treatment activism. In C. Penley & A. Ross (Eds.), *Technoculture* (pp. 57-106). Minneapolis: University of Minnesota Press.

Treichler, P. A. (1991b). Seduced and terrorized: AIDS and network television. In A. Klusacek & K. Morrison (Eds.), *A leap in the dark: AIDS, art, and contemporary culture*. Montreal: Artexte.

Watney, S. (1989). Missionary positions: AIDS, "Africa," and race. *Differences: A Journal of Feminist Cultural Studies, 1*(1), 83-100.

Williams, R. (1983). *Keywords: A vocabulary of culture and society*. New York: Oxford University Press.

Williamson, J. (1989). Every virus tells a story: The meanings of HIV and AIDS. In E. Carter & S. Watney (Eds.), *Taking liberties: AIDS and cultural politics* (pp. 69-80). London: Serpent's Tail.

Woese, C. R. (1967). *The genetic code: The molecular basis for genetic expression*. New York: Harper & Row.

Wright, P., & Treacher, A. (Eds.). (1982). *The problem of medical knowledge: Examining the social construction of medicine*. Edinburgh: University of Edinburgh.

Wuthnow, R., Hunter, J. D., Bergensen, A., & Kurzweil, E. (1984). *Cultural analysis: The work of Peter L. Berger, Mary Douglas, Michel Foucault, and Jürgen Habermas*. London: Routledge & Kegan Paul.

PART II

Method and Theory in Western Society

5

Sex, Lies, and Ethnography

PAUL R. ABRAMSON

This book, and the conference that preceded it, presumes that cultural anthropology and ethnography can make a significant contribution to understanding, and reducing, the AIDS pandemic. This presumption is reasonable because HIV is transmitted behaviorally, prevention of HIV infection can be achieved through education, and there is considerable cultural variability in the transmission dynamics of HIV infection. While many of the chapters contained in this book examine the broader context of these issues, this chapter, in contrast, is narrowly focused. Quite simply, it addresses a very specific problem: conducting research on the sexual transmission dynamics of HIV infection. That is, because research on the sexual transmission of HIV infection will represent a sizable foundation of cultural anthropology's/ ethnography's contribution to this field, I believe that attention should be directed toward examining the methods of this research. Obviously, these methods are the vehicle through which knowledge is accrued and, as such, warrant serious consideration. Therefore, the purpose of this chapter is to provide a critique of the prevailing methods. I hope that this discourse, which is at a very basic level, will strengthen the data obtained and, ultimately,

AUTHOR'S NOTE. Research on, and discussion of, this chapter was supported by Wenner-Gren Foundation symposium 111, AIDS Research: Issues for Anthropological Theory, Method, and Practice, June 25-July 1, 1990, Estes Park, Colorado. This chapter is dedicated to the memory of Philip A. Goldberg (Psychology Professor, Connecticut College), who professed little but taught a lot. Also, I wish to thank Joe Carrier, Gil Herdt, and Don Symons for their helpful comments on this manuscript. Requests for reprints should be sent to Dr. Paul R. Abramson, Department of Psychology, UCLA, Los Angeles, CA 90024-1563.

cultural anthropology's contribution to the broader problems inherent in the AIDS pandemic.

This chapter begins with three beliefs. First, I believe that satisfactory explanations of human sexual behavior require a rigorous sexual science (Abramson, 1990). I also believe that a rigorous sexual science will facilitate explanations of the sexual transmission dynamics of HIV infection (Abramson & Herdt, 1990). Finally, I believe that cultural anthropology, and particularly ethnography, can enhance our understanding of the sexual transmission dynamics of HIV infection and broaden the foundation of a sexual science (Parker & Carballo, 1990; Parker, Herdt, & Carballo, in press).

However, before preceding, I have a confession to make. I know very little about cultural anthropology and even less about ethnography. This limitation is obviously problematic. Yet, I hope to use this deficit to some advantage. Although I lack the knowledge and depth of an anthropologist, I also lack the standard anthropological prejudices. Second, as an outsider I can offer an outsider's perspective, which has the potential to be illuminating and instructive (or the reverse, hopelessly naive). Finally, being an outsider, I have no desire to offend, because I am obviously unaware of traditional polemics. Thus, in summation, though unschooled, I hope to offer an alternative perspective and, if I offend, gain some latitude for my naïveté.

Perhaps, as a start, it might be helpful if I gave my general impression of cultural anthropology and ethnography. I have chosen this strategy because this impression is fundamental to the rest of my discussion. Thus I will start with some basic ideas about cultural anthropology and observational methods and eventually integrate this perspective with both sexual science and research on the transmission of HIV infection.

It is my opinion that cultural anthropology, and ethnography, are both legitimate sciences. In contrast, I believe that observation (including participant observation), as an instrument and process, is largely overrated. These two opinions, I have reason to believe (primarily as a result of my discussions at the Wenner-Gren Foundation symposium), run counter to prevailing anthropological norms (Evans-Pritchard, 1952; Kroeber, 1952; Lévi-Strauss, 1963). As I understand it, ethnographers (and cultural anthropologists) conceptualize, or apologize, that their discipline is neither truly an art nor a science but falls somewhere in between. On the other hand, I sense the discipline presumes to redeem itself through its skillful use of observation and interpretation.

It is not clear to me whether this is an accurate or fair assessment of cultural anthropology. However, it is certainly simplistic—because these issues are often more complex than a novice can comprehend. Yet, these limitations notwithstanding, this portrayal will at least allow me to examine some basic notions about science and ethnography. What follows is admittedly superficial. It merely provides a simple (and by no means novel) framework, drawn primarily from Karl Popper (1957, 1972, 1983), for contending that ethnography (hence cultural anthropology) is a legitimate science and that observational methods (including participant observation) require more critical scrutiny. This discussion is being advanced herein because I believe that it is essential for integrating anthropological research with sexual science, in general, and HIV/AIDS, in particular.

Popper (1983) contends that a theory has the status of belonging to the empirical sciences if and only if it is falsifiable. Second, Popper (1972) defines the aim of science to be the search for better and better explanations. Note, in neither case would these definitions necessarily exclude research and theory in ethnography and cultural anthropology. Thus, within the general arena of science, at least as defined by Popper, ethnography (and cultural anthropology) would presumably have a home.

However, the criticism of cultural anthropology, both within and outside the field, is that the discipline lacks scientific methods. The reliance on observation, some would argue, is prima facie evidence that cultural anthropology, and most certainly ethnography, is not scientific. Again, the work of Popper is instructive in this regard. Popper (1983, p. 7) argues that the method of science consists primarily of rational *criticism*. That is, "scientific theories are distinguished from myths merely in being criticizable, and in being open to modification in the light of criticism." To Popper, there is no such thing as scientific method, let alone a preferred scientific method, such as mathematics or the methods of the physical sciences. Popper (1983, p. 7) offers the following maxim for all of the sciences: "Never aim at more precision than is required by the problem in hand."

To elaborate further, a scientific explanation, according to Popper (1972), is an explanation of the known by the unknown. Lewis Carroll's (1981) infamous conclusion "For the Snark *was* a Boojum" obviously fails in this regard. On the other hand, much of cultural anthropology satisfies this criterion. For example, to use a classic citation, Evans-Pritchard (1937) provides considerable insight, and a broader context (i.e., "the unknown"), for witchcraft (i.e., "the known").

Second, Popper also contends that the explanation must be independently testable (which is another problem with Carroll's inference)—and the greater the severity of the independent tests it has survived, the more satisfactory the explanation (Popper, 1957, 1972). Obviously, longitudinal and time-lag fieldwork (plus independent observers) would provide a reasonable vehicle for achieving these objectives. Thus neither of these requirements would necessarily exclude cultural anthropology and ethnography from the realm of science. Furthermore, because the ethnographic and cultural anthropological literature has had a long tradition of critical debate (e.g., Freeman, 1983), this research, at least according to Popper, is clearly scientific.

Good science means good explanation or theory. And what makes a theory good? As implied above, it is good if it can survive frequent and stringent examinations designed to falsify or refute it. Note, once again, no mention is made of specific methods and models. Further, no mention is made of a quantitative or mathematical foundation. Instead, as mentioned previously, Popper indicates that a theory is powerful if it can provide an "unknown" explanation of a known phenomenon and if it can withstand repeated attempts to disprove it.

Obviously, this is not the only definition of science, and, in fact, it differs in a number of critical ways from the Baconian or Euclidean traditions of science. Also, Popper certainly has his detractors (e.g., Kuhn, 1962). However, in this chapter, it is not my intention to critique the philosophy of science or the underlying dimensions of Popper's writings. Instead, I have a very simple purpose. I am attempting to find a workable definition to support my conclusion that cultural anthropology and ethnography are scientific. (This conclusion is important because it represents a springboard for critically scrutinizing anthropological/ethnographic methods.) And in this regard, the selection of Popper (and his definitions) is a reasonable choice, given his prominence in this area. Furthermore, although my selection is biased (i.e., being chosen to support my own position), it is not obscure.

Now that I have provided a rationale for including cultural anthropology/ethnography within the realm of science, I will turn my attention to the problems of observation. Note that I am not suggesting an alternative to observation per se but instead am attempting to articulate some obvious limitations within observational methods. These limitations are not new; neither is this the first time that they have been raised (e.g., Bacon, 1620/1955; Descartes, 1628/1969). Rather, these limitations are again being discussed because they are particularly critical to the study of human sexual behavior—a behavior that is private, clandestine, and enmeshed in a variety of taboos and restrictions.

Observation is the essential method, and vehicle, for obtaining ethnographic data. To enhance the validity and reliability of observational methods, a variety of fieldwork principles have been established—many of which have a considerable tradition. These include the following: (a) The anthropologist must spend sufficient time in the field; (b) he or she must be in close contact with the people among whom he or she is working; (c) he or she must communicate with them through their own language; (d) he or she should study the entire culture and social life; (e) he or she must put him- or herself in a position that enables him or her to establish ties of intimacy, to observe daily activities from within community life; (f) he or she must live in the village/camp where he or she is physically and morally part of the community; (g) he or she maintains a neutral position—he or she is not there to change a way of life but to learn from it (Evans-Pritchard, 1952); and so forth (see Spradley, 1980, for a more current and thorough description). These principles are obviously designed to maximize familiarity with the individuals under study and minimize interpreter bias. And while these principles are certainly reasonable, and have intuitive integrity, they are nonetheless void of empirical verification. That is, although these principles and procedures may be *preferred* to less rigorous—or more biased—fieldwork, it does not mean that observations (or interpretations) obtained from these methods are inherently valid and reliable. For example, to what extent would equally qualified male and female anthropologists (or Western and non-Western anthropologists), following exactly the same procedures, reach exactly the same interpretations? Rarely, I would presume. And if this is true, then the reliability of such methods—even if scrupulously rigorous (e.g., cross-referencing all informants)—is clearly in question. This problem, by the way, is not unique to fieldwork but is characteristic of all methods that rely upon interpretation. For example, projective tests are notoriously refractory to interrater reliability—even with equally qualified psychologists (Goldberg, 1965). In fact, when high interrater reliability is achieved, it is usually the result of simplifying the scoring categories and requiring raters to carefully study a very simple scoring manual.

Interrater reliability is not the only problem with observational methods. And rather than rehash the standard critique of such methods, or point out the obvious, I will instead examine the extent to which such fieldwork methods are appropriate for the study of human sexual behavior. In this case, I will presume that, although the fieldwork principles mentioned above are certainly flawed, and in need of modification, anything less (e.g., using interpreters) would further weaken the validity and reliability of ethnographic data. That is, I will treat the traditional fieldwork methods as a methodological ideal, which, though less than perfect, can serve as a benchmark for reasonable field research. In this regard, we can examine the extent to which human sexual behavior is amenable to fieldwork methods—or, conversely, what obstacles make the study of human sexual behavior particularly problematic from an ethnographic perspective. Once these issues have been discussed, we can also look at some potential alternatives or solutions.

However, before examining fieldwork methods per se, I will present a perspective that argues that human sexual behavior is refractory to direct assessment. This perspective is drawn from the psychoanalytic and projective testing literature. In contrast to traditional fieldwork methods, psychoanalysis and projective testing have sought *indirect* measures of sexual functioning—in large part as a means of circumventing various problems in the direct assessment of human sexual behavior. While I am not endorsing psychoanalytic or projective methods of assessment, I do believe that these literatures are instructive for establishing a conceptual framework for measuring human sexual behavior. After covering this material, I will then attempt to integrate both the psychoanalytic and the projective literatures with the anthropological literature on fieldwork/observational methods. I hope that combining these three literatures will provide a better understanding of the obstacles to sexual measurement.

Additionally, a fourth area of research will also be introduced—test construction strategies—which should facilitate the development of relevant measures for the study of the sexual transmission of HIV infection. Finally, the test construction strategy will use a fifth area of research—studies of memory within natural contexts—to suggest a simple model, and related investigations, which should enhance the measurement of sexual behavior related to the transmission of HIV infection.

Psychoanalysis and Projective Tests

This section will explore some of the basic tenets of psychoanalysis and projective testing. This material is being introduced as a vehicle for examining sexual histories within the context of the obstacles inherent in the assessment of such information.

The growth of psychoanalysis, and projective tests, was in large part an explicit recognition of human sexuality. According to both perspectives, sexual thoughts, feelings, and experiences were acknowledged as being critical to psychological development and, conversely, to psychological trauma. Furthermore, both believed that, due to cultural restrictions and unconscious dynamics, sexual experiences and thoughts were guarded and covert. Thus, because sexuality was buried or shielded, and, more important, because sexuality was critical to psychological functioning, both psychoanalysis and projective tests created subtle methods of unearthing sexual histories (e.g., free association, the TAT). Finally, both deemed subtle methods to be necessary because both believed that repression and resistance characterize the remembrance or discussion of sexual thoughts, feelings, and experiences.

These conclusions are based in large part upon Freud's emphasis on unconscious thoughts, feelings, and remembrances (produced by the dynamic conditions of infantile sexuality, repression, resistance, the constancy principle, and so on)—which are inaccessible and refractory to standard methods of inquiry, thereby requiring unique methods of access (Breuer & Freud, 1957; Freud, 1935, 1949, 1950; Kris, 1954). The "instruments" that Freud developed to reach unconscious processes included hypnotic suggestion, free association, dream interpretation, and the analysis of transference.

Additionally, the broad appeal of Freud's ideas led to the exploration of more expedient methods of obtaining unconscious material. Without devaluing psychoanalysis, psychologists argued that the sheer number of people in need of psychological diagnosis and treatment demanded quicker and more convenient instruments to gain access to the unconscious. And, in response to this concern, projective tests proliferated (Murstein, 1965).

The projective test hypothesis contends that, by presenting a person with an unstructured stimulus (e.g., inkblots), you induce this person to reveal his or her own way of organizing experience. That is, it is presumed that the individual will project upon this "plastic field" his or her way of seeing life, meanings, significances, patterns, and feelings (Frank, 1939). Additionally, projective tests are also presumed to have the capacity to reveal experiences that the individual is unwilling to express, or unable to express (e.g., "taboo" sexual thoughts), because he or she is unconscious of them (Murray, 1951).

To summarize then, psychoanalysis and projective tests converge on three complementary insights: the significance of unconscious processes, the hidden nature of certain sexual experiences, and the value of unstructured (or nondirective) assessment.

What is the current status of such tests and psychoanalytic therapy? Unfortunately, neither has withstood the passage of time. Projective tests have failed in almost every regard (Murstein, 1965), and traditional psychoanalysis attracts few new adherents. On the other hand, psychoanalytic insights and the projective hypothesis may be more salient than the vehicles, or operational methods, that they employ. That is, the failure of projective tests, or traditional psychoanalysis, does not necessarily undermine the original insights such as unconscious processes. For example, there is certainly a broad and varied literature that verifies nonconscious mental functioning (e.g., the experimental literature on memory—Neisser, 1982; Tulving & Schacter, 1990) and, as such, "unconscious processes" remain a viable psychological concept.

Thus this chapter wants to reintroduce the original insights of psychoanalysis and projective tests for the very specific purpose of facilitating the assessment of sexual behaviors relevant to the global transmission of HIV infection. Furthermore, such insights are also being reintroduced because they are particularly relevant to ethnographic methods, given that the study of human sexual behavior usually negates traditional observational strategies. That is, to gain information about human sexual behavior, if ethnographic research must deviate from the methodological ideal of observation (or participant observation for that matter) and rely upon informants and self-reports, then these insights are now crucial to ethnographic research in this area. However, before discussing this issue more fully, it is important to examine the current alternatives to sexual assessment.

If psychoanalysis and projective tests fail as *methods* of assessing sexual histories, what reasonable alternatives exist? To date, although exceptions remain (see Carrier, 1972, 1976, 1980, 1985; Herdt, 1981; Parker, 1990), the primary method of collecting information about human sexual behavior is the questionnaire or interview (Abramson, 1988; Bentler & Abramson, 1981; Johnson & DeLamater, 1976). While these methods prevail, are they viable and, second, have they been successful?

It is my opinion that such methods, except for the study of sexual attitudes or traits, are superficial at best—because they ignore much of what psychoanalysis has discovered about resistance and unconscious processes. At worst, they are sheer folly. Certainly, the more extensive the interview, the more skilled the interviewer, the more rapport between interviewer and subject, and the more conducive to disclosure the interview situation, the more meaningful the results. However, questionnaire surveys or, worse yet, telephone surveys invite a plethora of methodological problems (thereby being little improvement over projective tests) and serve as testimony to scientific naïveté.

Consequently, given the limitations of the prevailing methods (e.g., surveys) of sexual assessment, alternative methods need to be developed and perfected. And in this regard, ethnographic methods certainly warrant careful reconsideration.

Cultural Anthropological/Ethnographic Perspectives

The opinion stated above about self-report measures is not unique to me or to the psychoanalytic and projective literatures. In fact, the anthropological literature also makes it very clear how difficult it is to obtain accurate records of human sexual behavior due to cultural and psychological conditions that elicit the disapprobation of sexual disclosure (Abramson & Herdt, 1990; Herdt, 1981; Herdt & Stoller, 1989; Mead, 1961). Mead (1961), in her classic description of anthropological methods for sex research, introduces an extraordinary number of obstacles in the study of human sexuality. To start, Mead notes that human sexual behavior is intimately linked with privacy. Thus the process of collecting data, which requires either a public communication or record, runs counter to a basic component of sex (Abramson, 1990; Mead, 1961). Similarly, Mead notes that, in almost every society, sexuality is characterized by gaps in awareness (e.g., accurate descriptions of genitals) and specific taboos (e.g., homosexuality), which further emphasize the intricacy of the systems of inhibition and expression of human sexual behavior. Finally, Mead asserts that (a) there is no cultural rationale for honestly describing one's sexual behavior; (b) there is often a considerable discrepancy between highly institutionalized statements of what should be done sexually and what is really done sexually; (c) there is little opportunity to observe human sexual behavior; and (d) there are few skilled investigators in the field of human sexuality.

To date, although obvious exceptions certainly exist (e.g., Carrier, 1972, 1976; Herdt, 1981; Parker, 1990), little has changed to alter Mead's concerns. In fact, if anything, more methodological issues have arisen, which, in conjunction with cultural prohibitions and unconscious processes, make the assessment of sexual histories an extraordinarily difficult objective.

For example, Abramson and Herdt (1990) note two additional levels of bias in the cross-cultural assessment of sexual practices. The first level concerns the sociolinguistic identification and selection of culturally sensitive categories for constructing question items, with suitable linguistic frames, for their administration to subjects. For example, is there a generic category term for "prostitute"? Is it gendered (compare "hustler" for male and "hooker" for female). How may it be used, in what contexts, and by whom? This example also raises situation-specific meanings and behaviors, which may presumptively bias *responses* to questions about sexual behavior.

A second level of bias concerns the pragmatic administration of sexually related protocols and questions in sociolinguistic context and in culturally sensitive interpersonal ways. Should subjects be interviewed in public or private, for example? Should interviewers be of the same culture, sex, class, and so on as that of subjects? Here this issue confronts the problem of achieving rapport, eliciting accurate and complete responses, and retrospective bias—all of which affect *response rate* in sex research (Abramson & Herdt, 1990).

In summary, the insights (or concerns) of the literatures (psychoanalytic, projective, and anthropological) presented thus far yield a fairly consistent pattern for the assessment of sexual histories: (a) "Surface"-level material is often unreliable; (b) subtle and indirect methods are necessary; and (c) rapport and intimate understanding are critical (Parker & Carballo, 1990). Obviously, these three conclusions—or concerns—are neither satisfied nor minimized in questionnaire or telephone survey research. Instead, such methods operate with either ignorance or defiance of such conclusions (for an exception, however, see Wellings et al., 1990). Finally, although questionnaires certainly have many advantages in administration, scoring, and sampling, they are subject to a large array of methodological problems, including questionable validity and reliability, social desirability effects, participation bias, and memory bias (Abramson, 1988; Catania, Gibson, Chitwood, & Coates, in press)—and so are hardly a recommended alternative for the limitations in psychoanalytic/projective/ethnographic assessment devices.

Thus a paradox exists. Psychoanalysis and the anthropological literature have yielded some robust insights about studying human sexual behavior. Yet their methods are cumbersome and often unreliable. In contrast, questionnaire research has yielded an expedient method for collecting data on human sexual behavior, but this method is often naive as well as unreliable. Therefore, a stalemate has occurred. Neither method is ideal, and both have a variety of problems.

Perhaps it is now reasonable to consider modifications within ethnographic research as a viable research strategy. Certainly, there are many compelling arguments for the inclusion of qualitative data as a supplement to survey research in the area of HIV/AIDS (see Parker & Carballo, 1990). A variety of researchers, in fact, have delineated a number of alternatives, including secondary sources, participant observation, mapping the sexual geography of an area, focus groups, sexual diaries, and so on (Carrier, 1980; Parker & Carballo, 1990; Parker et al., 1991). However, the question still remains: To what extent are traditional fieldwork methods relevant to the study of the sexual transmission dynamics of HIV infection? As mentioned earlier, I believe that observation is largely overrated as an ethnographic method. This statement, however, is not meant to disparage observational research per se, because much of what we know about human sexual behavior results from classic work in this area (e.g., Carrier, 1972; Herdt, 1981; Parker, 1990). Instead, what I want to challenge is the presumption that observation invariably yields valid and reliable data. It seems to me that the opposite is more certainly true, given the overwhelming literature on observer bias (see Heisenberg's uncertainty principle for an analogy in atomic systems). Furthermore, the obstacles to observing human sexual behavior also raise serious concerns about this strategy. Thus two alternatives exist. On the one hand, ethnographers can extend the logic of participant observers to the study of human sexual behavior. The rationale, and ethical issues, involved in this strategy are already addressed in this book (see the Bolton chapter). However, unless multiple male and female participant observers are used, and unless this participant observation is conducted longitudinally and with various age cohorts, this strategy is still subject to the same limitations as observation in other contexts. That is, such observations are limited by biases inherent in the observer as well as biases inherent in the situations selected for participant observation.

On the other hand, if participant observation is not viable for the study of human sexual behavior in a particular culture, then the alternatives (e.g., in-depth interviews and informants) still must be critically scrutinized. That is, just because an anthropologist is now doing in-depth interviews, or is now using selected informants, such data are not ipso facto valid. They may be fascinating, culturally rich, and literate—like much of anthropology—but still not valid. Validity requires rigorous scientific scrutiny. And because I believe that cultural anthropology and ethnography are both sciences, it would violate a basic premise of the scientific enterprise to avoid critical scrutiny of observational methods and their alternatives.

The most obvious alternative to enhancing the rigor of ethnographic in-depth interviews for the study of the sexual transmission of HIV infection is, as implied above, the use of multiple ethnographers (e.g., triangulation, continuous cross-referencing). This means both male and female ethnographers who represent different age cohorts. Again, these ethnographers would have to assess (interview, observe, and so on) the same individuals, or culture, and their consensus, or lack of consensus, would be subjected to both qualitative and quantitative scrutiny. Furthermore, the degree of (or lack of) consensus would exist as a significant source of information about the individuals under study or perhaps the entire culture.

Next, if interrater reliability were high, such teams of ethnographers would have to take measurements (e.g., observations, in-depth interviews) in a threefold fashion: longitudinally, cross-sectionally, and using a time-lag design. The combination of these three approaches would yield prospective data that were not confronted by time of assessment or the cohort under study. Also, such data (especially longitudinal data) would yield information on the developmental processes underlying the full spectrum of human sexuality. Finally, the selection of the behaviors or issues for study, and the integration of sexual data within the broader system (or pattern) of the culture, would produce a unique anthropological perspective on the sexual transmission dynamics of HIV infection—within a more valid and defendable methodology.

These suggestions are, of course, being offered with full recognition of how difficult they are to implement. They are obviously more expensive, more cumbersome—and, quite literally, more of a hassle. However, these complaints are not a sufficient rationale for discarding improved methods. If we are ultimately seeking the "truth" about the sexual transmission dynamics of HIV, we cannot endorse methods that clearly compromise the truth— merely because they are more convenient. Choosing convenience, when the limitations are readily apparent, is analogous to accepting fiction because fact is so much harder to achieve. And, while we usually fail to obtain the truth, the closer we get, the better the explanation, and the easier it is for subsequent investigations to take it one step further. (I am reminded, in this regard, of Goethe's words in *Faust*: "The lofty prize, of science lies, concealed today as ever. Who has no thought, to him it's brought, to own without endeavor" [Kaufman, 1961]).

In addition to using multiple ethnographers, and multiple data collection strategies, attention also needs to be directed toward the specific measurement strategy (e.g., interview questions) and the processes underlying the validity of such data (e.g., can people accurately remember their sexual behavior? Will people honestly report their sexual behavior?). Thus this chapter will now introduce some ideas about designing a specific measure. Second, this chapter will also introduce some relevant findings from memory research conducted in natural settings. Finally, this chapter will conclude with an attempt to integrate the measurement strategy with the memory literature (i.e., a simple "working" model) to suggest several additional avenues of research on the recall of sexual practices relevant to the transmission of HIV.

Developing a Measure

The following measurement strategy derives from the work of Julian Rotter (1960, 1990). It is introduced herein in the hopes that it will prove useful for developing measures of sexual practices relevant to HIV. This perspective is now important—especially to the ethnographer—because traditional fieldwork methods are often impractical (or impossible) in the study of human sexuality. However, as the reader will note, the guidelines are not specific to human sexual behavior. Instead, they relate to instrument construction and are derived from the notion that the development of an instrument (e.g., interview, survey, questionnaire) should use an analysis of the determinants of behavior (i.e., theory) as it relates specifically to instrument (e.g., interview, survey, questionnaire) response behavior. For example, where human sexuality is concerned, theories should incorporate hypotheses about how people respond in interviews (diaries, questionnaires, focus groups, and so on) about their sexual behavior—because the manner in which sexual "facts" are obtained obviously influences the resultant data. Perhaps one could argue that answers to a survey on human sexual behavior do not reflect the actual behavior of the interviewee but, instead, prevailing cultural norms (or myths) or, alternatively, what the interviewee believes the interviewer wishes to hear (Abramson & Herdt, 1990). This later circumstance is also more likely when interviewers are from a different culture, or class, than the interviewee. Thus, as Rotter notes, knowledge of such "instrument-taking behavior" should be explicitly combined with theory as a guideline for constructing a measure and designing a measurement situation.

Rotter (1960) argues that three conditions underlie the methodological failure of social science measures. First, he observes that most instruments fail to provide a good match between the instrument and theory. That is, we rarely devise instruments that measure a carefully defined theoretical construct, of which the instrument behavior can be understood as a logical referent. Second, Rotter argues that social science measures usually fail to recognize the significance of the instrument-taking situation. For example, if theory would predict significant differences in behavior in the presence of authority figures, most social science measures ignore their importance in the instrument-taking situation. Rotter notes that it seems obvious to presume that the examiner/interviewer (e.g., psychologist, sociologist, anthropologist) may have a different social stimulus value in one situation than in another or under one set of conditions rather than another. Thus "instrument behavior" must be fully conceptualized within the specific instrument-testing situation itself. Finally, Rotter discusses a variety of problems with the inferences we make about "instrument behavior." That is, there is often an absence of logic, or an obvious contradiction, in the assumed relationship between what a person does or says (i.e., "instrument behavior") and what is inferred from such behavior. Simply stated, it is often unclear what can be predicted, or should be predicted, from "instrument behavior."

These issues, and limitations, are readily apparent in most measurement strategies for collecting data on human sexual behavior. Although I have beaten this "dead horse" before (Abramson, 1988; Abramson & Herdt, 1990), I'll raise the whip one more time to state that it is clearly evident that almost *all* measures (e.g., interviews, questionnaires) of human sexual behavior lack (a) theoretical grounding, (b) a carefully operationalized theoretical construct, (c) conceptualization to include variability in the "instrument-taking situation," and (d) an explicitly conceptualized relationship between "instrument behavior" and real behavior. Worse yet, human sexuality measures, instead, use the "potpourri" philosophy of test construction, that is, a little of this and a little of that. The presumption being that, if the "mix" is appropriate and it "smells good," it should do the trick. The limitations of this perspective are obvious and need not be elaborated herein.

Of course, a major stumbling block to the construction of human sexuality measures (e.g., interviews, questionnaires) is the absence of a unified theory of human sexual behavior (Abramson, 1990). If the fundamental objective of science is to establish principles that can explain and predict empirical phenomena, a theory is the necessary connection between observation and prediction. Thus, in the absence of a theory, what do we expect our human sexuality measures to predict? Perhaps one might argue that our measures are attempting to accumulate the facts that can be inductively combined into a theory. This is certainly a reasonable proposal, if we could demonstrate that our measures are truly void of theory. But this is not the case. Instead, our measures are driven by vague theoretical notions about childhood sexuality, premarital sexuality, risky sexuality, and so forth. And, given the vagueness of our ideas, it is not surprising that our measures so often fail (Catania et al., in press).

On the other hand, to use Rotter's (1960) advice, it would be better to develop our measures with a specific theory and theoretical construct in mind—making every effort to include questions, or items, that relate broadly to the nomological network inherent in the construct (Cronbach & Meehl, 1955). This measurement strategy would also facilitate explicit predictions about the testing situation and the meaning of test behavior. For example, let us propose a simple and purely hypothetical theory about a specific behavior, that is, that risky sexual behavior is a function of the interaction of sex guilt and exogenous agents (e.g., drugs, alcohol). That is, those who engage in risky sex are people who are sexually restrictive and uninformed but, in the presence of an exogenous agent, act impulsively and without precaution. This simple hypothetical theory now provides fairly explicit guidelines for the types of questions or items we must ask when we study risky sex. Obviously, we want to assess (a) the use of exogenous agents, (b) the use of exogenous agents in conjunction with sex, (c) guilt about sexuality, (d) risky sex, (e) impulsive sex, and so forth. Also, we want to consider how our testing situation would affect the study of this issue. If we believe that sex guilt is a critical variable in predicting risky sex, we must also consider how sex guilt will influence how people will *answer our questions*. Do we need indirect assessment or symbolic assessment (and so forth)? All of which must be tested prior to our final measure. Similarly, we need to hypothesize how other aspects of the testing situation (e.g., interviewer, gender, context) will influence responding—and design our measure accordingly. Finally, we must consider the relationship between the way someone answers our questions and what someone does in the real world. Perhaps sexually guilty people use such questions "confessionally"—which enhances their guilt and provokes a change in their behavior. In this case, this measure of "risky sex" will predict poorly in the future. Other scenarios are also easily visualized and need not be limited to traditional questionnaires but can embrace *every* method that asks questions about sexual practice—thereby further emphasizing the point that we need to consider the relationship between the instrument situation/behavior and real behavior.

These guidelines are being stressed herein because I believe that they will facilitate the construction of better and more meaningful measures (e.g., interviews)—which is now necessary in ethnographic research on human sexuality—and they will provide better and more meaningful data on human sexual behavior, in general, and, in particular, on sexual practices relevant to the transmission of HIV. However, these guidelines are again being offered with full recognition of the obstacles inherent in achieving these objectives. This is not a quick fix. If anything, it is a long and laborious process without any guarantee of success. Which, it is not surprising, is typical of most areas of science. And, in fact, what I see as particularly problematic in the study of human sexual behavior is the desire to jump in and get started (i.e., quickly grind out a interview or set of questions)—without careful scrutiny of issues—and then piloting accordingly. And though I am sympathetic to the pressures of addressing real problems quickly, we can't lose sight of the necessity of an ongoing sexual science that tackles basic issues without regard for their current application (Abramson, 1990). This later approach, I am convinced, will provide us with the tools and theories to tackle "real problems quickly"—as they continually arise (also see Lakatos [1978] for the importance of an ongoing research program).

Memory in Natural Contexts

Which brings me to the last area of research I want to cover: studies of memory in natural contexts. It is surprising that this topic is frequently overlooked in the study of human sexual behavior—within ethnography as well as all other areas of sexual science. Yet, it is basic to every method we use to get information on sexual practices. That is, when asking someone to describe their sexual behavior, we are explicitly asking that person to recall past experience. And this process of recall obviously relies upon memory (or, more precisely, autobiographical or episodic memory; Tulving & Schacter, 1990).

Although researchers interested in human sexuality are not naive to this implication, they often proceed naively when constructing methods for measuring sexual practices. Presumably, such researchers view memory as tangential to the broader issue of collecting data on human sexual behavior. Perhaps memory is considered "reliable," though not perfect, and, as such, is dismissed as part of the method variance in standard assessment procedures.

However, examining the literature on memory, especially in natural contexts, will quickly emphasize the fallacy of that reasoning. For example, Neisser (1982) argues that memory is an extraordinarily complex phenomenon, perhaps even an incoherent notion. The inability to remember can be influenced by a variety of factors, such as retrieval failures, memory decay, or distortion. Even these three factors can be broken down again. For example, problems with retrieval can be distinguished into failure to recall or failure to distinguish. Complicating this issue even further is the possibility of functionally different types of memory in everyday life—all of which has lead Neisser (1982) to propose that we bypass the concept of memory and focus upon the question: How do people use their past experiences in meeting the present and the future?

Neisser's perspective has stimulated a renewed interest in the study of memory outside of laboratory context and stimuli, that is, in a natural setting. This work has yielded some very interesting findings, which are particularly relevant to the measurement of past behavior. For example, Marigold Linton (1975, 1978, 1982) recorded at least two events from her own life, every day, for six years. Each month, she tested herself on her ability to remember, order, and date some of those events.

The results of this very careful but simple study are quite illuminating—especially in demonstrating the very active and kinetic properties of forgetting and remembering. As a first step, Linton notes that newly encoded information is not merely remembered or forgotten but goes through modifications and changes as a result of interacting with previous information in memory. Similarly, new information can also provoke reinterpretation of previously held information. Thus Linton concludes that progressive changes typically occur in both interpretation and evaluation of new information as it interacts with old information or subsequently acquired information. In this regard, Linton draws an analogy between personal remembered histories and cultural/political histories; that is, the importance of a single event can be continuously reinterpreted as different events or contexts occur.

Where sexual behavior is concerned, an obvious parallel exists. It is easy to imagine that memories of sexual experiences vary (i.e., are reinterpreted, distorted, and so on) depending upon age recalled, current relationship status, situational context, and so on. Therefore, it seems reasonable to propose that discontinuity exists for memories of sexual behavior—as it does for other experiences in one's personal history. It also seems reasonable to propose that other factors operate upon remembered sexual experiences (Bozulich, 1990). For example, research indicates that rehearsal (rethinking about an experience)/retrieval strength (Bjork, 1989) and order (being the first or early events in a sequence of experiences) facilitate remembering (Neisser, 1982). Thus experiences that we continually think about, that happened at a salient point (e.g., our "first" such experience), or that are infrequent are better recalled—while the "average" or frequent experiences are more likely to blend or distort. It is interesting that this particular finding emerged in a recent study of sexual practices relevant to the transmission of HIV infection. The reliability of recalled sexual behavior was much higher for *infrequent* sexual practices than for frequent sexual behavior (McLaws, Oldenburg, Ross, & Cooper, 1990). Finally, research also indicates that autobiographical memory is dependent upon the "state" (e.g., on drugs, drinking alcohol) or mood (e.g., happy, anxious) in which the experience occurred (Blaney, 1986; Eich, 1989). That is, an experience that occurs in one "state" (or mood) is better remembered in that state. This finding is obviously important to the assessment of past sexual experience, because drugs, alcohol, and intense pleasure often accompany sexual behavior.

Complicating these issues even further is the finding that emotionality exerts a complex influence on remembering. While it is generally believed that we are better able to remember emotionally important events, Linton (1982) notes that such events can decrease in significance over time, fostering forgetting, while inconspicuous events (e.g., first time you met your spouse) can increase in importance over time, facilitating remembering. Similarly, habituation can reduce the emotional impact of a memory, or life experiences can change, which in turn, will provoke a reinterpretation of the emotional impact of memory. Finally, Linton (1982) also suggests that there are three features that will contribute to the endurance of an emotional event in memory: (a) It must be perceived as strongly emotional when it first occurs; (b) it must remain a focal point in recall; and (c) it must be relatively unique.

Do these three features characterize sexual experience? In some regards, yes. In many circumstances, no. For instance, take the very sexually active adult. How much of his or her sexual practices are unique—strongly emotional—and remain a focal point in recall? Perhaps a very unusual sexual experience would retain these characteristics. However, the recall of a large number of sexual encounters would obviously undergo considerable change, distortion, and reinterpretation—merely as a function of the number of related experiences. Similarly, a variety of other processes would be operating (failure to recall, failure to distinguish, and so on)—raising serious concerns about the accuracy of reports on past sexual behavior.

On the other hand, perhaps a sexually inexperienced person would be better able to recall his or her sexual practices—especially if the behaviors were infrequent—and the three features cited above were applicable. However, it should be noted that most research on the sexual transmission of HIV infection has isolated sexually prolific individuals or groups—because of the obvious implication that they are at higher risk for HIV (Abramson, 1988). Thus those individuals most likely to be targeted for study are the least likely to accurately recall their past sexual experiences.

It would also be erroneous to conclude that these findings are specific to industrialized countries. Surely some of the specific results would be culture dependent but not culturally extinct—in the sense that the basic finding on the discontinuity of memory should extend to all peoples of all places. In fact, Bateson (1958) argued that each culture has a specific cognitive style (i.e., *eidos*), which uses a variety of mnemonic devices in the retention and recitation of oral histories and myths (e.g., visualizing, debating). In this regard, it would be interesting to isolate cross culturally those characteristics that affect memory of specific personal experiences. Where sexual behavior is concerned, it would also be interesting to examine whether people in cultures that put a premium on sexual practices (i.e., these experiences are more salient) are better able to recall such experiences. Of course, complicating this simple question is the fact that behaviors that are more valued are expressed more, thereby adding more memories, which could cause more blending, distortion, and so forth. Thus, although the study of memory has enormous cross-cultural importance—especially in research that relies upon recalled past behavior—it is also extraordinarily complex and requires a careful program of investigation.

Conclusion

In conclusion, I'd like to tie together all of these areas of research into a simple, coherent pattern. This should yield some suggestions for future research on the assessment of sexual practices relevant to the transmission of HIV infection. However, before concluding with this exercise, I want to voice some cautionary remarks about the material presented thus far. First, it should be readily evident that I have merely skimmed the surface of a number of important areas of research. Significant issues have been omitted, and complex issues have been simplified. Moreover, I have often digressed into basic issues that are only tangentially related to the HIV and AIDS. However, this strategy has a very specific purpose. It presumes that this brief summary will act as a divining rod—drawing researchers (and particularly ethnographers) to literatures that I believe can enhance the depth and sophistication of how we approach the study of sexual practices relevant to the transmission of HIV infection.

And speaking of the sexual transmission of HIV, I think the material presented herein yields several directions for subsequent research. As a first step, I believe we need a theory or model of sexual expression that incorporates the dynamics of recall. In the service of that objective, I offer the following. It is a very simple "working" model of the sequence of sexual expression and its implications for sexual measurement. Note that the determinants of sexual behavior are conspicuously missing from this model—and certainly deserve attention. However, a theory of the determinants of sexual behavior is well beyond the scope of this chapter and, perhaps for now, my expertise.

Therefore, the starting point of this model is the exhibition of sexual behavior in thought or action (which I label point A). After sexual behavior is exhibited, I believe that a bifurcation occurs. The source of this bifurcation is the process of recognizing/acknowledging and labeling the behavior as "sexual." It is clear that some sexual behavior is not labeled accordingly (e.g., a person who commits sexual abuse claims it is not sex but affection; a married person kissing his or her secretary claims it is not sex but affection) and, as such, never gets encoded as a sexual experience. Thus it cannot be recalled as sexual. In this case, the exhibition of A yields two *Bs—B1* (in which, because of personal dynamics or cultural beliefs, the sexual behavior is recognized, acknowledged, and labeled as sexual behavior) and *B2* (in which, because of personal dynamics or cultural beliefs, the sexual behavior is *not* recognized, acknowledged, or labeled as sexual behavior). Note that step B also assumes an elaboration process whereby sexual behavior is infused with cultural and personal meaning. Similarly, this step also assumes an omnipotent arbitrator, who, despite cultural variability, can determine (or change his or her mind about) what is ultimately sexual behavior and can further distinguish experiences that people correctly—or incorrectly—label as sexual. This assumption obviously needs more work—especially in carefully defining sexual behavior.

Step *C* involves the storage of sexual experiences in memory—and follows directly from Step B1. It does not follow from Step B2 because this behavior has not been labeled as sexual. However, Step B2 experiences are still obviously stored in memory—but cued differently. Also, if a reinterpretation occurs, Step B2 experiences will become Step B1 experiences, and the sequence to Step C will also occur.

Following Step C, I envision a continuum of substeps within C that reflect recall accessibility (e.g., *C1* is a recent, easily remembered experience; *C20* is an older, harder to remember experience). Furthermore, I presume that memories of sexual experiences can shift upward and downward on this continuum as a function of recency, rehearsal, blending, resistance, repression, and so forth—making the whole process discontinuous. However, I also presume that, at any given point in time, there is a threshold substep C, above which the behavior is potentially recalled accurately and below which the behavior is either forgotten or distorted. I use the phrase "potentially recalled accurately" to signify the psychological process of disclosure, which subsumes the willingness (conscious and unconscious) to recall a sexual experience.

This simple working model suggests the following measurement implications for the assessment of sexual practices: First, we are only able to measure that fraction of A that has been labeled B1—because these are the only experiences that the person has labeled as being sexual. B2 experiences cannot be recalled because they are not personally or culturally deemed sexual. Of B1 that has led to C, we can only accurately measure those experiences that are above the substep C threshold in accessible memory. Thus this model suggests that, from the start, only a fraction of sexual experiences can be accurately recalled because some experiences are not labeled as being sexual and many sexual experiences are below the threshold at which they can be remembered accurately. Finally, drawing upon the psychoanalytic/projective/anthropological/memory literatures, it is also very clear that a variety of processes inhibit the recall and disclosure of sexual experiences—thereby further reducing the fraction of information that can be accurately recalled.

This obviously is not an encouraging model for researchers who hope to fashion quick measurement devices (e.g., questionnaires, interviews for ethnographic study) for the assessment of sexual practices. Instead, it argues for careful study of (a) the process of labeling sexual behavior, (b) the process of encoding and cuing of sexual experiences in memory, (c) the process of remembering sexual experiences over time—having full recognition of the different values of a large range of sexual experiences—and (d) the process of disclosing sexual practices (i.e., type, situation, age, gender, and like determinants). In turn, using Rotter's guidelines, the findings from these studies must then be carefully employed in a theoretically driven measure of sexual practices (which uses both direct and subtle methods) to enhance prediction and understanding of the recalled sexual behavior.

This is certainly no easy task. It is, instead, "Like an eye in the black cloud in a dream" (Ginsberg, 1984). A extraordinarily difficult agenda for a complex and illusive subject.

References

Abramson, P. R. (1988). Sexual assessment and the epidemiology of AIDS. *Journal of Sex Research, 25,* 323-346.

Abramson, P. R. (1990). Sexual science: Emerging discipline or oxymoron? *Journal of Sex Research, 27,* 147-166.

Abramson, P. R., & Herdt, G. (1990). The assessment of sexual practices relevant to the transmission of AIDS: A global perspective. *Journal of Sex Research, 27,* 215-232.

Bacon, F. (1620/1955). *Selected writings* (edited by H. G. Dick). New York: The Modern Library.

Bateson, G. (1958). *Naven.* Stanford, CA: Stanford University Press.

Bentler, P. M., & Abramson, P. R. (1981). The science of sex research: Some methodological considerations. *Archives of Sexual Behavior, 10,* 225-251.

Bjork, R. A. (1989). Retrieval inhibition as an adaptive mechanism in human memory. In H. L. Roediger III & F. I. M. Craik (Eds.), *Varieties of memory and consciousness: Essays in honour of Endel Tulving.* Hillsdale, NJ: Lawrence Erlbaum.

Blaney, P. H. (1986). Affect and memory: A review. *Psychological Bulletin, 99,* 229-246.

Bozulich, D. (1990). *Reliability of self-reported sexual behavior for a sample of gay men.* Unpublished master's thesis, University of California, Los Angeles.

Breuer, J., & Freud, S. (1957). Editor's introduction. In *Studies on hysteria.* New York: Basic Books.

Carrier, J. M. (1972). *Urban Mexican male homosexual encounters: An analysis of participants and coping strategies.* Unpublished doctoral dissertation, University of California, Irvine.

Carrier, J. M. (1976). Cultural factors affecting urban Mexican male homosexual behavior. *Archives of Sexual Behavior, 5,* 103-124.

Carrier, J. M. (1980). Homosexual behavior in cross-cultural perspective. In J. Marmor (Ed.), *Homosexual behavior: A modern reappraisal.* New York: Basic Books.

Carrier, J. M. (1985). Foreword [Special issue, Anthropology and Homosexual Behavior; E. Blackwell, Ed.]. *Journal of Homosexuality, 2*(3/4), xi-xii.

Carroll, L. (1981). *The hunting of the snark.* Los Altos, CA: William Kaufman.

Catania, J. A., Gibson, D. R., Chitwood, D. D., & Coates, T. J. (in press). Methodological problems in AIDS behavioral research: Influences on measurement error and participation bias in studies of sexual behavior. *Psychological Bulletin.*

Cronbach, L. J., & Meehl, P. E. (1955). Construct validity in psychological tests. *Psychological Bulletin, 52,* 281-302.

Descartes, R. (1628/1969). *The essential Descartes* (edited by M. D. Wilson). New York: New American Library.

Eich, E. (1989). Theoretical issues in state dependent memory. In H. L. Roediger III & F. I. M. Craik (Eds.), *Varieties of memory and consciousness: Essays in honour of Endel Tulving.* Hillsdale, NJ: Lawrence Erlbaum.

Evans-Pritchard, E. (1937). *Witchcraft, oracles, and magic among the Azande.* Oxford: Clarendon.

Evans-Pritchard, E. E. (1952). *Social anthropology.* Glencoe, IL: Free Press.

Frank, L. K. (1939). Projective methods for the study of personality. *Journal of Psychology, 8,* 389-413.

Freeman, D. (1983). *Margaret Mead and Samoa.* Cambridge, MA: Harvard University Press.

Freud, S. (1935). *A general introduction to psychoanalysis.* New York: Liveright.

Freud, S. (1949). *Three essays on the theory of sexuality.* London: Standard Edition.

Freud, S. (1950). *Beyond the pleasure principle.* London: Standard Edition.

Ginsberg, A. (1984). *Collected poems.* New York: Harper & Row.

Goldberg, P. A. (1965). A review of sentence completion methods in personality assessment. *Journal of Projective Techniques and Personality Assessment, 29,* 12-45.

Herdt, G. (1981). *Guardians of the flute: Idioms of masculinity.* New York: McGraw-Hill.

Herdt, G., & Stoller, R. J. (1989). *Intimate communications: Erotics and the study of culture.* New York: Columbia University Press.

Johnson, W., & DeLamater, J. (1976). Response effects in sex surveys. *Public Opinion Quarterly, 40,* 165-181.

Kaufman, W. (1961). *Goethe's Faust.* New York: Doubleday.

Kris, E. (1954). Introduction. In *Sigmund Freud's letters.* New York: Basic Books.

Kroeber, A. L. (1952). *The nature of culture.* Chicago: University of Chicago Press.

Kuhn, T. S. (1962). *The structure of scientific revolutions.* Chicago: University of Chicago Press.

Lakatos, I. (1978). *Mathematics, science, and epistemology* (volume 2). Cambridge: Cambridge University Press.

Lévi-Strauss, C. (1963). *Structural anthropology.* New York: Basic Books.

Linton, M. (1975). Memory for real-world events. In D. A. Norman & D. E. Rumelhart (Eds.), *Explorations in cognition.* San Francisco: Freeman.

Linton, M. (1978). Real-world memory after six years: An in vivo study of very long term memory. In M. M. Gruneberg, P. E. Morris, & R. N. Sykes (Eds.), *Practical aspects of memory.* London: Academic Press.

Linton, M. (1982). Transformations of memory in everyday life. In U. Neisser (Ed.), *Memory observed.* San Francisco: Freeman.

McLaws, M. L., Oldenburg, B., Ross, M. W., & Cooper, D. A. (1990). Sexual behaviour in AIDS-related research: Reliability and validity of recall and diary measures. *Journal of Sex Research, 27,* 265-281.

Mead, M. (1961). Cultural determinants of sexual behavior. In W. C. Young (Ed.), *Sex and internal secretions.* Baltimore: Williams and Wilkins.

Murray, H. A. (1951). Uses of the Thematic Apperception Test. *American Journal of Psychiatry, 107,* 577-581.

Murstein, B. I. (1965). *Handbook of projective tests.* New York: Basic Books.

Neisser, U. (1982). *Memory observed: Remembering in natural contexts.* San Francisco: Freeman.

Parker, R. G. (1990). *Bodies, pleasures, and passions: Sexual culture in contemporary Brazil.* Boston: Beacon.

Parker, R. G., & Carballo, M. (1990). Qualitative research on homosexual and bisexual behavior relevant to HIV/AIDS. *Journal of Sex Research, 27,* 497-526.

Parker, R. G., Herdt, G., & Carballo, M. (1991). Sexual culture, HIV transmission and AIDS. *Journal of Sex Research, 28,* 77-98.

Popper, K. (1957). *The poverty of historicism.* London: Ark.

Popper, K. (1972). *Objective knowledge.* Oxford: Oxford University Press.

Popper, K. (1983). *Realism and the aim of science.* Totowa, NJ: Rowman & Littlefield.

Rotter, J. B. (1960). Some implications of a social learning theory for the prediction of goal directed behavior from testing procedures. *Psychological Review, 67,* 301-316.

Rotter, J. B. (1990). Internal versus external control of reinforcement: A case history of a variable. *American Psychologist, 45,* 489-493.

Spradley, J. P. (1980). *Participant observation.* New York: Holt, Rinehart & Winston.

Tulving, E., & Schachter, D. L. (1990). Priming and human memory systems. *Science, 247,* 301-306.

Wellings, K., Field, J., Wadsworth, J., Johnson, A. M., Anderson, R. M., & Bradshaw, S. A. (1990). Sexual lifestyles under scrutiny. *Nature, 348,* 276-278.

6

Mapping Terra Incognita:
Sex Research for AIDS Prevention—
An Urgent Agenda for the 1990s

RALPH BOLTON

Name any behavior, and you could probably get agreement from most anthro-pologists that we ought to know more about it. This attitude drives much research and grant-giving activity, and rarely would any of us be caught saying that too much is known about some topic or other. Sex is curious, however—though perhaps not uniquely so—in that Anthropology seems unable to decide whether it knows too little or too much about it. This uncertainty is a product, I suggest, of a 60-year-old tradition in which behavior, as such, has played a relatively minor role in the analysis and interpretation of cultural systems. By adopting, instead, a discourse based on normative and propositional statements, symbolic structures, and other such abstractions, Anthropology not only lost analytic sight of what individuals do and think, it did not deal conceptually with the serious, interactive play of phenomenal events and cultural formations.

—Donald Tuzin (1988)

A Personal Prolegomenon

On July 14, 1984, I walked into the offices of the newly created Los Angeles Men's Study.[1] This was to be my first exposure to sex research in

AUTHOR'S NOTE. This chapter is dedicated to my friends, Björn, Brendan, Charlie, and Sky, with thanks for all the good times, and to Keith, who lives on in my memory.

the AIDS era. A call had gone out earlier that year for volunteers to participate in a prospective AIDS investigation, and I had responded, motivated in part by a sense of responsibility to my community, which had been hit early and hard by the epidemic, in part by personal fears about becoming a casualty in this disaster, and in part by intellectual curiosity about the research then beginning to try to understand this grim phenomenon. Six years later, I am still a participant in what became the largest prospective AIDS study anywhere, with more than 5,000 volunteer subjects in four centers in the United States (Baltimore, Pittsburgh, Chicago, and Los Angeles), and over 1,500 in Los Angeles alone.

Every six months, we donate blood samples, are physically examined (lymph nodes, skin, weight, reflexes, and so forth), and submit to tests of neurological functioning (e.g., fitting pegs in holes, reciting strings of numbers forward and backward, and recognizing computer-administered word patterns). Prior to each visit, we fill out questionnaires that cover social and psychological coping mechanisms. During the first years, semen samples were also collected, through a process known in the scientific literature as "autostimulation," a polite term for what most of the participants in the study would refer to in their own vernacular as "jerking off," performed in a tiny room papered from floor to ceiling on all walls with pages taken from porn magazines. And, finally, we are interviewed on such topics as our medical history of the preceding six months, current drug and alcohol use, and, of course, sexual conduct.

From the outset, I was intrigued by the questioning about sexual behavior, perhaps pretty standard stuff for sex researchers, but for me at the time something novel:

> Have you engaged in any sort of sexual activities, involving another person, since your last visit?
>
> Since your last visit, have you had some kind of sexual activity with another man?
>
> How many different men, if any, have you had sexual intercourse with since your last visit?
>
> With how many of these men, if any, did you have sexual intercourse for the first time?
>
> Of these men you had sexual intercourse with, how many of them were more or less anonymous (i.e., you did not know how to find them again)?

General questions come first, followed by probes for more specific details:

> With how many men since your last visit did you engage in the following activity, and with how many of them did you do it for the first time:
>
> You put your penis in his mouth?
>
> You ejaculated/came in his rectum?
>
> You used your tongue to touch or lick his anus or rectum ("rimming")?
>
> He put his penis in your rectum?
>
> He put his finger or fingers into your rectum?
>
> You engaged in scat?

And so forth. Over the years, the questions have changed somewhat, of course. In the beginning, no mention was made of the use of condoms when asking about specific sexual practices. Safe sex was in its infancy when the study was designed.

A number of features of this protocol have always struck me as problematic, especially in investigating sexual behavior among gay men who may have had more than a handful of partners during any six-month period. Unless they kept records of what they did with whom, their responses were likely to be at best rough "guesstimates" based on some sort of central tendencies in the enactment of their sexual repertoires. Indeed, even what was meant by "sexual intercourse" was confusing; questions about "sexual intercourse" were preceded by a definition of that concept as used in this study—that is, oral or anal penetrative sex. Thus, in recalling the "numbers," it was necessary to separate those with whom one had penetrative sex ("real" sex?) from those with whom one had other kinds of sex ("vanilla" sex or nonpenetrative S&M, for example). For me at least, this was not a natural division to make; I didn't think of my sexual encounters as dichotomous, divided between those involving penetration versus those without penetration. For individuals in monogamous relationships, for those with few partners, and for those with a highly restricted sexual repertoire, the task may be easy ("Let's see, did I last get fucked in May or June, and was that before or after my last LAMS appointment, hmmm?"), but for others, it could be a computational nightmare. What constitutes sex is highly variable across individuals. For Johnny Rio, the protagonist in Rechy's (1967) novel, *Numbers,* a score was counted if the "trick" touched his penis; for others, counting occurs if at least one partner ejaculated.

Also striking were the questions not asked. How many times one had sex, for instance, of any kind or of specific kinds, was not investigated. It seemed to me that the frequencies of different sexual activities was pertinent, not merely the number of partners with whom one engaged in these behaviors. But then, this neglect of frequencies was a reflection of the misplaced emphasis that existed then, and which still persists among some AIDS specialists, on the dangers of "promiscuity" (Bolton, in press), despite the obvious fact that a high frequency of risky sex with one partner may be more dangerous than high frequencies of safer sex with a large number of partners (Reiss & Leik, 1989). And what about all the other forms of behavior, from massages to nipple torture, which gay men may engage in during sexual encounters? Questions about the broad range of behaviors that constitute a sexual encounter were not asked. Neither was any effort invested in trying to ascertain the meaning of sex in general or of specific sexual practices.

The lacunae in the MACS protocol are legion, but the same is true of the protocols of most AIDS research projects that I have had an opportunity to examine, such as the UCSF Men's Survey, the NIDA "CAPOD" Project Questionnaire, and the Collaborative Howard Brown Memorial Clinic/University of Michigan "Coping and Change" Survey of Chicago Men. The published studies that present the results of investigations into sexual behavior provide little evidence that their authors have gone any deeper into the subject than the ones mentioned above. Their findings on sexual "behavior" generally do not extend beyond the following items:

(1) number of sexual partners during a given period
(2) extent of use or nonuse of condoms
(3) participation in anal sex
(4) participation in oral sex
(5) existence of a primary relationship
(6) attitudes toward safer sex practices
(7) changes in the above
(8) types of sexual partners

In short, AIDS sex research has been extremely narrow, and I conclude that, 10 years into the AIDS epidemic, we have learned little about sexual behavior, even in the population most heavily affected by the AIDS epidemic in the United States, the gay community. My intention in pointing out the deficiencies in what has been done is not to disparage the research that has been conducted or is being conducted. It is, instead, to note the limitations so that we can proceed with research that will expand our knowledge in significant ways. There is a serious danger of remaining in a holding pattern, continuing to replicate the studies done to date without striking out into *terra incognita.*

Sex Research and AIDS:
Epidemiology Versus Prevention

Obviously, there were reasons that past research did not delve deeper into the subject of sexual behavior. One reason, we would like to think, was that few anthropologists were involved, although if Tuzin (above) is correct about anthropologists' aversion to studying behavior rather than normative and propositional statements, it is possible that, even had they taken up this topic, they may not have done research on actual behavior. Indeed, those few anthropologists who have done sex research in relation to AIDS have for the most part not used traditional anthropological methods in their research; after all, most of them were also trained as epidemiologists, and they relied on their epidemiological role rather than their anthropological role.[2] Time pressure was another reason. Baseline data were needed quickly, and that fact implied a methodological approach that could generate data rapidly, usually a survey approach. As a result, superficiality was privileged over complexity. Research focused on high-risk and potentially risky activities. The objectives of this work provided additional justification for quick-and-dirty approaches. One aim of much of this research was to determine how dangerous or safe the more salient behaviors were for the transmission of the etiological agent of AIDS, and for that purpose this line of questioning seemed appropriate. (I shall argue below that, even for this purpose, however, the methods were insufficient.) This work did result in clarifying the relative riskiness of the more prominent forms of sexual behavior among gay men (receptive anal intercourse > insertive anal intercourse > receptive oral intercourse > insertive oral intercourse > mutual masturbation). A second aim was to ascertain the extent of the problem by determining the prevalence of high-risk behavior in various populations and, to a limited degree, to explain participation in high-risk activity, for example, the role of cofactors such as alcohol and drug use (e.g., Ostrow et al., 1989; Stall, 1988), social support (e.g., Vincke, Bolton, Mak, & Blank, 1990), perceived susceptibility (e.g., McCusker, Zapka, Stoddard, & Mayer, 1989), and knowledge of HIV antibody status (e.g., van Griensven et al., 1989; Wiktor et al., 1990).

For epidemiological purposes, the research was productive; for prevention purposes, however, the data generated in this way—except for some of the cofactor research—have been practically useless. Indeed, it is difficult to demonstrate that the knowledge acquired about sexual behavior during the 1980s has been of significant help in promoting prevention, in limiting the spread of HIV. The evidence is quite strong that behavior changes have occurred in large metropolitan gay communities in the United States and in some European countries, and that HIV transmission may even have been halted in those communities. But it is doubtful that the changes occurred because of prevention efforts based on AIDS sex research. Safer-sex guidelines were distributed prior to the confirmation by researchers of the relative risks of different sexual practices, and intensive workshops to promote safer sex were conducted without significant input from studies of sexual behavior. Knowledge of sexual behavior may have contributed to the success of these endeavors, but, if so, it was the personal knowledge of the participants derived from their own experiences that counted, not knowledge acquired by reading the sex research literature.

I would like to suggest that a crucial distinction must be made between *epidemiological sex research* and *disease-prevention sex research*. To date, only the former has been done. Confounding the problems of epidemiology and prevention has had disastrous consequences already during this epidemic in the case of the issue of "promiscuity," where what was important epidemiologically was assumed to be important in prevention. The result was to promote so-called monogamy rather than to concentrate on safer-sex practices (Bolton, in press; Levine & Troiden, 1988; Murray & Payne, 1988). The agenda for the 1990s must be to carry out prevention sex research that goes beyond the limited requirements for epidemiological sex research. This is important because prevention efforts need to go forward under circumstances that were not present in communities where reductions in risk behavior have been accomplished, that is, in communities that have not yet felt the impact of the epidemic as severely as have major metropolitan gay communities, namely, gay communities in other regions and heterosexual communities everywhere. And we need to have more knowledge to reach those hard-core individuals in heavily affected areas whose behavior has not yet changed or who may have a tendency to "relapse" to unsafe practices.

During the past two or three years, several publications have summarized the sex research that has been undertaken in response to the HIV pandemic and/or have presented programmatic statements concerning the kinds of sex research that the authors deem important (Abramson, 1988; Abramson & Herdt, 1990; Gagnon, 1988; Turner, 1989; Turner, Miller, & Moses, 1989).[3] Valuable as these statements are, they do not, in my view, call for the kinds of research methodologies that I believe need to be prominently featured in prevention sex research. In the remainder of this chapter, I shall discuss three methodological approaches to the study of sexual behavior not covered (or only in passing) in the above publications, using my own work in progress to illustrate both the potential and the problems associated with their implementation. In this discussion, I shall focus particularly on sex research among gay men; the reader who is interested in sex research in other populations (lesbians, straight men, straight women, IV drug users in Western societies, or people in non-Western settings) will no doubt find the problems and potentials of the approaches discussed here differentially suitable for use in other settings (for example, more applicable in sex-positive cultures than in sex-negative ones and more applicable among those most at risk—the sexually active—than among those at low risk).

Participant Observation in Sex Research: Going to Where the Action Is

> When persons go to where the action is, they often go to a place where there is an increase, not in the chances taken, but in the chances that they will be obliged to take chances. Should action actually occur it is likely to involve someone *like* themselves but someone *else*. Where they have to go, then, is a place where another's involvement can be closely watched and vicariously enjoyed.
>
> —Erving Goffman (1967, p. 269)

On the Nature of Participant Observation

The hallmark of anthropological research methods is participant observation. I suggest that we desperately need to give priority to this research strategy in the domain of sexuality if we are to produce the knowledge required for successful AIDS prevention efforts. Bernard (1988, p. 148) refers to participant observation as "the foundation" of the anthropological enterprise, but he goes on to note that it is also "the least well-defined methodological component of our discipline." Obviously, there are varying degrees of participation involved in participant observation. At the "narrow" end of the scale is the investigator who is merely present and, therefore, able to observe some phenomenon; studies at this end of the scale barely qualify for inclusion in the category of participant observation. The observer may even be invisible or unknown to the actors in the situation, using unobtrusive measures in the collection of data (Webb, Campbell, Schwartz, Sechrist, & Grove, 1981). At the other end of the scale, one finds situations in which the field-worker "goes native" and eventually drops the observer role entirely. Most anthropological research falls between these two extremes, but, in general, it would appear that the emphasis is placed on observation rather than participation.

Indeed, participation rarely involves actually partaking of the activities being observed. How many anthropologists studying peasant working conditions have actually spent time plowing, sowing, or reaping? More than likely, they sat at the edge of the field and observed. Is that really participant observation? How many of those studying rituals have participated in those events? Goffman has argued (see quotation above) that, to fully appreciate the activities one is observing, it is necessary to engage in them, and I would concur with his assessment, all the more so when the behaviors being studied are not generally ones about which people will speak openly, which is often the case with respect to sex or in situations where the opportunities for observing the behaviors are limited, which is usually true in the arena of sexuality.

Many reasons have been advanced in support of participant-observation research, but quite possibly the most important is that it offers the researcher "an intuitive understanding of what's going on in a culture" (Bernard, 1988, p. 151). Because of the restrictions surrounding sex, this "feel" for the phenomenon may be of exceptional importance when studying sexual behavior. Unless the observer has had wide-ranging sexual experience, it is unlikely that he or she can even know what questions to ask or imagine all of the permutations and complexities of sexual events—all the more so when studying sexual behavior in a culture other than his or her own or one in which sexual behavior is highly elaborated, which is true in some gay subcultures.

Participant Observation in Sexography

The most direct resource available to the sex researcher is his own sexual experience. But a participant-observation study of sex entails several risks. For one thing, the investigator may mistake his personal peculiarities for universal features of social life, painting a portrait of intercourse that his readers will find unrecognizable. For another, he may inadvertently reveal his own sexual preferences and discover, to his embarrassment, that he has exposed himself in public as completely as any confessional writer (for the way a person wants to copulate is thought to manifest his true nature). Finally, he may feel obliged to neutralize sex's sinister properties by using various appurtenances of "scholarly detachment" such as statistics, jargon, and blandness. Otherwise some of his colleagues may feel that his topic has contaminated him personally by seeping across the boundary between research and researcher.

—Murray Davis (1983, p. xxi)

I believe that it is safe to assume that participant observation, even at the most intense level, has been practiced by a few anthropologists who have done sexography—indeed, that some of the very best cross-cultural work on homosexuality has benefited from insights gained through participation—but, because of the risks described by Davis above, not one that I know of has acknowledged the use of this research strategy. But, for the most part, anthropologists have eschewed doing sexography, perhaps because they agreed with Foucault (1983, p. 62) when he said: "I must confess that I am much more interested in problems about techniques of the self and things like that rather than sex . . . sex is boring." Averting their gaze from sex itself, with its messiness, complications, and research difficulties, most anthropologists interested in sexuality have opted to concentrate on issues of gender, identity, roles, rituals, and symbolism almost to the exclusion of sexual behavior.

A few studies in which participant observation was involved can be cited (limiting the list to those involving homosexuality). The most famous of these, by a sociologist, was Laud Humphreys's (1970) study of tearoom sex; his monograph unleashed a whirlwind of criticisms from other scholars, but not because of any alleged full participation in the events he described, which in print Humphreys never acknowledged doing (as far as I am aware). One level or another of participant observation is evident too in the work of Gilbert Herdt (1987), Joseph Carrier (1971), Esther Newton (1972), Kenneth Read (1980), Serena Nanda (1990), and Walter Williams (1986). Sexual behavior per se, I believe it fair to say, is not the focus, however, of any of the publications of these scholars, with the possible exception of Carrier's work.[4]

I would like to propose that we must go beyond the narrow concept of participant observation if we are to study sexual behavior. In part this is essential because sex is generally private and not available for observation except through participation. There are exceptions, of course, especially perhaps in gay subcultures of the West in which narrow participant observation is possible in a variety of public or semipublic settings, for instance, parks, bathhouses, and J/O clubs. It is time that anthropologists live up to their methodological pretenses.

An Illustration: Research in Brussels

In the fall of 1988, I began a period of fieldwork in Belgium that extended over eight months (September through January, 1988 to 1989, and May through August 1989). This research was sponsored by the Fulbright Commission of Belgium and Luxembourg. The proposal submitted to the commission called for doing a profile of the impact of AIDS on Belgian society and the influence of Belgian culture on the national response to the epidemic. Assigned to the Institute of Epidemiology of the Ministry of Public Health, I worked closely with the head epidemiologist responsible for monitoring the Belgian AIDS situation. As part of my goal of understanding the gay community's response to AIDS, I planned also to carry out a study of sexual cognition (discussed below) in the Belgian gay community, a project for which I had been unable to obtain funding from any source despite extensive searching for support.

To carry out this research agenda, it was necessary to do participant observation, and I spent most of my time, at all hours of day and night (Brussels never closes down), in settings where gay men in Brussels hang out: bars, saunas, restaurants, parks, tearooms, streets, and private homes. I talked to people (in French or English, depending on the relative fluency of the person with whom I was speaking). There were no structured interviews, and I tended not to steer conversations toward the subjects of greatest interest for my research. Indeed, I soon learned that it was taboo to mention AIDS in settings such as bars—bars were for fun and relaxation, not for taking up depressing topics. Sex, on the other hand, was an acceptable subject for conversation. Generally, I spoke with anyone who was willing, but I talked at greater length with individuals in key positions in the commercial gay scene—bartenders, for example, who have vast knowledge about the members of the community who frequent the settings in which they work.

In time I became integrated fully as a member of the gay community of Brussels. This transition was a function not merely of my omnipresence in gay settings but also of the nature of the Brussels situation. In the "capital of Europe" (headquarters of the EEC and NATO), non-Belgians are hardly a novelty. And the Belgian gay community itself is multiethnic, in any case, integrating better than the rest of Belgian society the two major ethnic groups the country comprises, the Walloons and the Flemish. Indeed, I more readily integrated into this community in a few months than I ever was able to when doing fieldwork over two years in an Andean village. But, in a sense, this was "my" community, not a strange or foreign one. There exists an international gay community that is analogous to the Jewish one, made up of different nationalities, living in a diaspora of sorts, but united by a feature of their lives, their homoeroticism, that they consider to be of great importance, one that gives them a set of similar experiences in life and one that separates them from their conationals. While the social science literature is replete with debates over which takes precedence, ethnic identity or class affiliation, there can be little doubt that, for many gay men, sexual orientation overrides nationality, race, ethnicity, and class. But perhaps the critical feature of being accepted in this community was the fact that I did not merely observe but participated fully in all aspects of gay life. And the key domain of gay culture, some would say the central ritual, is sex.

My presentation of self was simple and straightforward: I was a gay man doing research as a medical anthropologist on AIDS and sex. In the minds of most of the people I met, I suspect that my former role was more salient than the latter one. I never took notes in public, relying instead on my memory to write up in the privacy of my own apartment what I had learned. The physical product of this work is a set of qualitative field notes (approximately 500 pages, 8 by 11, single-spaced) in which I recorded observations, conversations, and experiences.

Although I believe that, as a result of this fieldwork, I gained a basic, but by no means complete, understanding of the sexual lives of the people I met, it is difficult to condense and present that information, and I won't attempt to do so here. However, I would like to discuss one of the findings of this participant-observation research that I regard as important and that alone justified the work and validated the approach I used (and invalidated other research methodologies).

At the ministry, I was given free rein, and, indeed, I spent little time at the office. The epidemiologist in charge approved of my efforts to learn as much as possible about gay life in Brussels ("If you sat around the office, we'd feel you weren't working, but if you are in the field, we are confident that you are," he noted one day when I explained my absences). The ministry had no one doing research on the community, and no funds were available for such investigations (and perhaps even less of an inclination to do them on the part of the political authorities who ultimately control the activities of scientists in public health). Early on during my stay, I became curious about one of the conclusions that I read in a position paper published by the institute. On the basis of surveys that had been done, it was concluded that gay men in Belgium knew how HIV is transmitted and that they had changed their risk behavior sufficiently to make it unnecessary to expend further efforts on AIDS education and prevention in that segment of Belgian society.

I was skeptical of that conclusion on a number of grounds. First, very little AIDS education had been carried out in Belgium. The gay community had discussed the problem in its publications, a few posters and pamphlets had been distributed, but not much else had been done. There had been no "stop AIDS" projects, for example. The number of cases was relatively low. It hardly seemed reasonable that gay men had altered their behavior on the basis of so little effort and in the absence of overpowering evidence of the dangers in the form of friends sick or dead from AIDS. Saunas were open and active; AIDS was not being discussed in the bars. I suspected a massive case of denial, on the part of both the authorities and the gay community.

The evidence to call into question the ministry's conclusion could be found after a few months in the records of my personal sexual encounters with Belgian men as well as in my conversations with gay men ("Oh yes, everyone says they do safe sex, but my friends are all engaging in risky behavior, every one of them," one informant told me). It became clear that unprotected anal intercourse was still widely practiced, as were unprotected oral sex and rimming. Poppers were still popular, in bed as well as on the dance floors.[5] In my casual sexual encounters with men I picked up in gay cruising situations, my approach during sex was to allow my partner to take the lead in determining which sexual behaviors to engage in. Low-risk activities posed no problem, of course, but to discover which moderate and high-risk behaviors they practiced, I assented to the former (oral sex, for example) while declining the latter (unprotected anal intercourse). Inasmuch as I personally do not engage in high-risk sex, I would proceed during a sexual encounter to the point at which the next logical step was a high-risk behavior; it was the rare partner who would mention refraining or who would ask for a condom to be used when he was to be the recipient partner in anal sex or when his indicated (verbal or nonverbal) desire was to be the insertive partner in anal sex.

Given the nature of some of my evidence, I presented only an oral report to the institute's chief epidemiologist, with a recommendation that, instead of decreasing prevention efforts in the gay community, it was imperative that those efforts be drastically enhanced. Whether or not that recommendation will be implemented remains to be seen, but at least the ministry now has a different understanding of the risks being taken by Belgian gay men than the one held previously based on other types of research.

It was not difficult to discover how the ministry had been misled into thinking that the problem was solved. There had been a couple of surveys, albeit with admitted problems in sampling and other features. One survey, conducted by a private AIDS organization, showed that one third of the respondents were still practicing risky sex; however, the organization decided, for strategic reasons, to stress the finding that one third were never engaging in risky sex, and another third were only doing so occasionally. Was the glass half full or half empty? They chose to say that it was half full; to head off a backlash against the gay community, they decided to emphasize the responsible response being made by gay men, even if that meant reduced government support for what they recognized as an urgent need for more prevention activities. Their own data suggested that two thirds of their respondents were at some risk of infection, and that may have been an underestimate given the tendency for respondents in such studies to give an answer that they feel is acceptable. As the epidemic proceeds, it is likely that there will be an increasing tendency for respondents to surveys to give socially acceptable rather than honest answers to questions about their sexual behavior.

Problems in Doing Sexographic Participant Observation

The problems associated with doing in-depth participant observation in sexographic research are legion, but they do not preclude such work. The inherent risks of this approach must be weighed seriously against the benefits to be derived therefrom and the cost in human lives of not meeting the challenge of finding out what is happening sexually in a community.

Ethical issues. All participant observation has the potential for posing ethical dilemmas that an ethnographer must take into consideration. In sex research, the problems are intensified by Western cultural attitudes toward sexual behavior, the extremely personal nature of the phenomenon, the privacy that ordinarily surrounds it, and the fact that it is encompassed by a vast array of religious proscriptions. I believe that none of these poses an insurmountable barrier to doing participant-observation sexography. The research described above, for example, did not, as far as I am concerned, violate provisions of the statement on the "Principles of Professional Responsibility of the American Anthropological Association" ("Proposed Draft Revision" in the *Anthropology Newsletter,* 1989, pp. 22-23). No deception was involved in any phase of the research, and the behaviors engaged in were consonant with those that are normative within the community being studied; moreover, my research objectives were subordinate to my participation as a member, albeit temporary, of the community I was studying. In practice, that means that I never engaged in any behavior that I would not have engaged in had my research objectives been different. To state that my personal life as a member of the community being studied took precedence over my professional life may seem odd, but in general my view has been that the personal/professional boundary is an imaginary one, especially when one is working in one's own culture or subculture. If I had a sexual encounter with someone, it was because the encounter was desired for its own sake by both my partner and me. That I derived "data" from the event (in which I was a full participant, not merely a detached observer) was in some senses incidental. That I then wrote field notes may make it seem unusual, but writing—and even publishing—about one's sexual encounters is not that uncommon among gay men, many of whom keep some sort of record of their experiences, though perhaps not in the detail found in my notes.

The most basic responsibility of the field-worker is to protect informants from negative consequences. In this research, the anonymity of informants was guaranteed. In a community in which closeted individuals have the right to remain closeted, anonymity and confidentiality are, indeed, of the utmost importance and cannot be compromised.

Some anthropologists may interpret the use of this research methodology as a violation of the responsibility specified in the Principles of Professional Responsibility for the "good reputation of the discipline." In my view, that interpretation is misguided, conflicting as it does with other principles such as the "responsibility to contribute to the formation of informational grounds upon which public policy may be founded." In the midst of a major health crisis, the responsibility of anthropologists should be to provide the kinds of data and analysis necessary to deal intelligently with the problem, even if that means doing some research that will meet with disapproval from intolerant segments of the public. The reputation of the discipline can only be enhanced by significant contributions to the solution of societal problems.

Funding. I need not dwell long on the issue of financing this kind of research. Based on my experience in seeking funding for a less sensitive methodology (discussed next) dealing with gay male sexuality, I hold little hope that applications that mention this type of work will be funded. Observational studies that involve settings where sex takes place (saunas, for example), even absent participation, are also likely to fail to be approved. The best one can do is to piggyback participant observation onto research projects based on other, more acceptable methodologies.

Ethnographer identity. Clearly, this type of research is not suitable for many anthropologists. It would most likely be precluded for anyone in a monogamous, sexually exclusive relationship. Indeed, equivalent sexual orientation is probably necessary for even less comprehensive participant observation. Gagnon (1988, p. 598) has pointed out: "In an earlier era, it was thought that a homosexual could not study homosexuality because of his or her bias." This viewpoint needs to be turned on its head. I do not believe participant-observation research could be done in gay settings on sexual behavior by a heterosexual male, and such research could not be done at all by a female—lesbian or straight. This is not to deny that nongays could obtain some data and produce some insights on the subject through research involving interviews, but it is certain that many gay men will not discuss their sexuality honestly and openly with anyone but other gay men. (Personal communication from a MACS investigator who must remain anonymous indicates that some participants admitted lying to the interviewer when the interviewer was a woman.)

It is self-evident that religious or moral values would make this methodology unavailable to some scholars, and it is conceivable that certain forms of participant-observation research should not be engaged in by investigators who are themselves HIV positive.

Presentation of results. How to present the results of research based on participant observation involving sexual encounters is a difficult question for several reasons. First and foremost is the imperative to protect the anonymity of informants. As noted above, their privacy and their right not to be harmed must not be compromised in any way. While underscoring the importance of this requirement, I do not believe that it is difficult to do this. On the other hand, the ethnographer faces the daunting problem of deciding how much to reveal about himself, because, of necessity, this type of research is likely to require self-revelation on matters that are normally private. The risks of the ethnographer may be greater than those of informants, especially in an age of postmodern ethnography, with its insistence on full disclosure of the role of the field scientist in the construction of ethnographic texts (Roth, 1989). It may be that the career risks are significant, and, therefore, this methodology may be inadvisable to individuals without tenure (though I might add that any form of sex research can be dangerous to the career of a young scientist; AIDS probably has not changed that). At the current time, physicians are coming under attack for refusing to take risks in treating HIV-infected patients; I believe that it would be hypocritical for anthropologists to refuse to take risks with less ominous potential consequences.

Some Additional Points on
Participant Observation in Sexographic Research

"Going where the action is" may generate valuable insights that cannot be obtained any other way. Contrary to the assumption that much of gay male sexuality is deficient in intimacy, the time spent together during and after sex frequently results in a degree of intimacy that exceeds what is attained by many monogamous couples (gay or straight) after years of living together. It is in the après-sex milieu of a casual sexual encounter when people often open up and speak honestly and profoundly about their lives, sharing thoughts with a partner that may never be voiced in any other context.

But, in addition, "going where the action is" offers the opportunity to engage in immediately significant applied anthropology, *action anthropology* in all senses of the term. It is in the setting of a sexual encounter that the most effective safer-sex education may take place. This alone can justify the research strategy I am advocating, a combined research/applied approach that saves lives directly. This is especially significant in encounters with individuals who are not part of the gay community, who have not had access to the safer-sex materials produced and distributed among those who are out of the closet, and who have not been socialized into the safer-sex norms that have become part of the gay subculture in many major metropolitan areas.

Mapping Eros: Thinking About Sex

A Cognitive Approach to Sex

While participant observation allows us to obtain needed data on actual behavior, we need also to more systematically get inside the heads of the people whose behavior we are studying. Actual sexual behavior may occupy only a small portion of an individual's time, but thinking about sex is much more common, unconstrained by the practicalities of actually doing it. As has often been noted, the most significant sex organ of all is the one that lies between the ears. We need to understand how people think about sex, how they classify sexual practices, what connotations they place on specific sex acts. In short, we need to investigate and decipher the cognitive structures of the domain of sexuality. Both participant observation and the study of sexual encounters (discussed below) provide important evidence for the behaviors of sex, but, if we are to be effective in promoting risk reduction, we will need to know how people think about sexual practices, those they engage in themselves and those they do not.

Humans respond differentially to the idea of specific sexual practices: sexual acts may be considered good/bad, safe/unsafe, boring/exciting, masculine/feminine, and so forth. In naturally occurring conversations, one can obtain some insights into how people classify sexual behaviors and the meanings they attach to them. However, more rigorous techniques are called for if we are to obtain comprehensive maps of the sexual domain. Models of this type of research can be found for other domains in the work of psychologists such as Charles Osgood and Harry Triandis and their associates (Osgood, Suci, & Tannenbaum, 1971; Triandis et al., 1972) and of anthropologists such as Roy D'Andrade and A. K. Romney and their associates (D'Andrade, Quinn, Nerlove, & Romney, 1972; Wexler & Romney, 1972) and of John M. Roberts and his associates (Roberts & Chick, 1979, 1984; Roberts, Golder, & Chick, 1980). D'Andrade et al. (1972), for example, mapped the domain of disease categories, while Roberts and Chick (1979) performed a behavioral space analysis of eight ball.

A recent study from Australia is the closest example in the literature of the approach I am proposing. Connell and Kippax (1990) developed an inventory of sexual practices that covered the entire repertoire of their informants, 535 men who have sex with men. Then they asked informants to indicate whether or not they had tried each of the practices and how they had enjoyed them. This allowed them to rank practices on enjoyment and to explore the interrelationships of the practices. The article is a major contribution, but its reach is still not wide enough inasmuch as the connotations of sexual practices are explored only with respect to the "pleasure" associated with each. The approach that my colleagues and I have followed is somewhat different.

An Illustration: Research in San Francisco and Flanders

In 1986, David Jaramillo and I conducted a pilot study on the sexual concepts of a small sample of gay men in San Francisco and a still smaller sample of gay male college students in Southern California (Bolton & Jaramillo, 1988). Lists of sexual concepts were first elicited from informants, and, from these lists, a composite list was constructed. From the composite list, we drew a set of 30 items to be used in obtaining the cognitive data. Table 6.1 contains the items that were used. We employed the semantic differential technique with the set of adjective scales shown in Table 6.2. Informants were asked to rate each of the sexual concepts on each of the adjective scales, and that constituted our data set, to which we applied various multidimensional scaling techniques to explore the similarities and dissimilarities between specific concepts and to discover the basic dimensions that structure the domain of sexuality in the minds of these informants. Figure 6.1 shows how the concepts appear on a dendogram. In Table 6.3, one sees the results of a factor analysis, showing five factors to be significant in the organization of this domain for the San Francisco informants, which we labeled as follows:

Factor 1: Appropriate/inappropriate
Factor 2: Anonymity
Factor 3: Orifice/genitalia
Factor 4: Condom
Factor 5: Sadism

Table 6.1. Sexual Concepts

1.	Touching/caressing
2.	Anal intercourse/fucking someone without condom
3.	Sex in bathrooms/t-rooms
4.	Anal intercourse/getting fucked without condom
5.	Voyeurism
6.	Sex in bathhouses/clubs
7.	Anal intercourse/fucking someone with condom
8.	Anal intercourse/getting fucked with condom
9.	Sex with strangers
10.	S&M passive/bottom
11.	Oral-anal sex/rimming (giving)
12.	Masturbation/jacking-off (yourself)
13.	Oral-anal sex/rimming (receiving)
14.	Sex in parks/alleys
15.	Watersports/golden shower/piss (receiving)
16.	Being touched/caressed
17.	Kissing/social
18.	Exhibitionism
19.	Sex with relatives
20.	Fisting (anal penetration-giving)
21.	Group sex/orgy
22.	Masturbation/jacking-off (mutual)
23.	Fisting (anal penetration-receiving)
24.	S&M active/top
25.	Watersports/golden shower/piss (giving)
26.	Kissing/French/deep kissing
27.	Sex with lovers
28.	Oral sex/getting sucked
29.	Phone sex
30.	Oral sex/sucking someone

Table 6.2. Adjective Scales

Evaluation	Potency	Activity	Stability	Unassigned	Novelty
Interesting-boring	Hard-soft	Fast-slow	Lasting-transient	Private-public	New-old
Natural-artificial	Strong-weak	Easy-difficult	Careful-careless	Butch-fem	Young-old
Healthy-sick	Rugged-delicate	Active-passive		Dominant-submissive	Usual-unusual
Pleasant-unpleasant	Heavy-light	Emotional-unemotional			
Sensitive-insensitive	Free-constrained	Hot-cold			
Safe-dangerous					
Clean-dirty					

Table 6.3. Factor Loadings of Sexual Behaviors

Factor 1	.907 Masturbation/yourself
	.895 Kissing/social
	.892 Masturbation/mutual
	.870 Touching
	.863 French kiss
	−.837 Fisting/receiving
	−.818 Sex/relatives
	.805 Sex/lovers
	−.754 Watersports/receiving
	−.742 Fisting/giving
	−.738 S&M passive
	.733 Oral/receiving
	.697 Being touched
	−.596 Watersports/giving
	.592 Voyeurism
Factor 2	.887 Sex/parks
	.886 Sex/baths/clubs
	.845 Sex/t-rooms
	.817 Group sex
	.810 Exhibitionism
	.657 Sex/strangers
Factor 3	.892 Anal passive w/o condom
	.861 Rimming/giving
	.860 Rimming/receiving
	.832 Anal active w/o condom
	.601 Oral/giving
	−.511 Phone sex
Factor 4	.928 Anal passive w/condom
	.833 Anal active w/condom
Factor 5	.773 S&M active

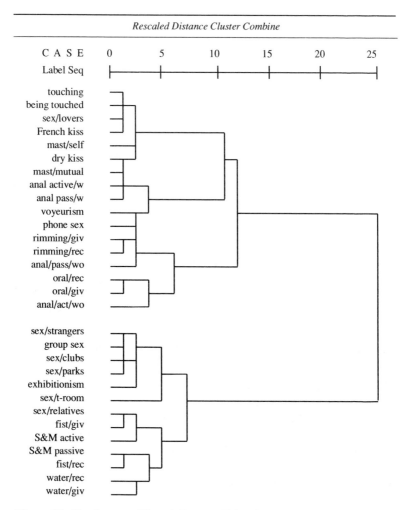

Figure 6.1. Dendogram of Sexual Concepts Using Complete Linkage

Figures 6.2 and 6.3 show the structure of the domain when Factor 1 is plotted against, respectively, Factor 2 and Factor 3. The factor loadings of the adjective scales on the five dimensions are shown in Table 6.4. When we compared the results of the student sample with the San Francisco sample, we discovered that there were significant differences in how respondents structured the sexual domain (Table 6.5). It was quite clear that the student structure corresponded more closely than did the structure of the San Fran-

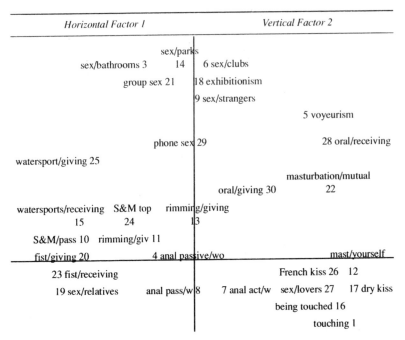

Figure 6.2. Two-Dimensional Plot of Sexual Concepts on Factors 1 and 2

cisco sample with safe-sex guidelines, which had been in existence throughout the sexually active portion of the lives of the former.

On the basis of the pilot study, which had numerous problems, we designed a more sophisticated study that has since been carried out in Flanders, Belgium. In that study, we again elicited from informants a list of sex behaviors that may occur during a sexual encounter (see Table 6.6). The list contained almost 100 items, what we might call, following Lévi-Strauss (1963), "sexemes" or, following Colby (1973), "sexons," that is, the elementary units of behavior that constitute meaningful elements in sexual encounters.[6] From this list, we developed two overlapping subsets of items for use in a semantic differential test, which was administered by computer to 379 gay Flemish men. The data from this investigation are still being analyzed. In addition to the semantic differential data, we elicited from these men in-depth information on relationships (sexual, peer, familial), sexual practices, social support, coping, knowledge of AIDS, health, and other topics, and we obtained serological data by collecting blood specimens. Our goal is to explore their conceptualization of sexual behaviors, to examine relation-

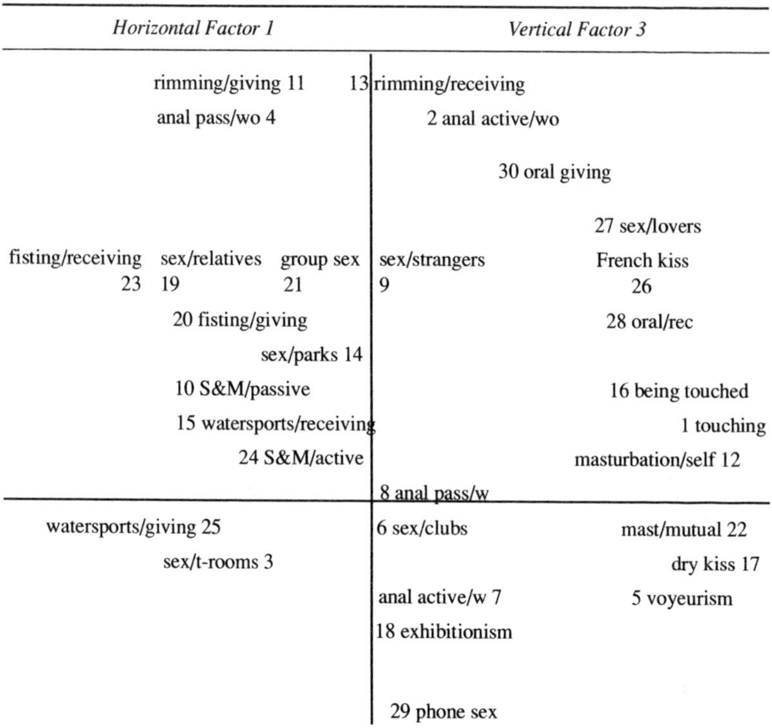

Horizontal Factor 1		Vertical Factor 3

rimming/giving 11   13 rimming/receiving
anal pass/wo 4   2 anal active/wo

                                           30 oral giving

                                                      27 sex/lovers

fisting/receiving sex/relatives group sex   sex/strangers   French kiss
          23   19   21   9   26
                    20 fisting/giving   28 oral/rec
                              sex/parks 14
                    10 S&M/passive   16 being touched
                    15 watersports/receiving   1 touching
                              24 S&M/active   masturbation/self 12
                                            8 anal pass/w

          watersports/giving 25   6 sex/clubs   mast/mutual 22
                    sex/t-rooms 3   dry kiss 17
                                      anal active/w 7   5 voyeurism
                                      18 exhibitionism

                                      29 phone sex

Figure 6.3. Two-Dimensional Plot of Sexual Concepts on Factors 1 and 3

ships between their cognitive structures and self-reported behaviors, to test hypotheses concerning relationships between cognitive structures and social and psychological variables, and to discover whether different types of cognitive structures exist within the population of gay men in Flanders.

At this point, it is difficult to say exactly what will come out of this analysis. We believe that this data set constitutes the most detailed information on how gay men think about sex that has ever been collected, but clearly the work is exploratory and heavily descriptive. One of the products that we hope will emerge is an instrument that will be more useful than behavioral questionnaires themselves in determining the effectiveness of AIDS prevention programs (persistent distortion on a semantic differential test is less likely to occur, we believe, than it is in response to questionnaires asking about the individual's behavior, although this is a hypothesis that we still need to test). We also hope that, if a limited set of types of semantic structures

Table 6.4. Factor Loadings of Adjective Scales

Factor 1	.937 Safe-dangerous
	.932 Clean-dirty
	.879 Healthy-sick
	.862 Careful-careless
	−.764 Unusual-usual
Factor 2	.846 Private-public
	.843 Emotional-unemotional
	.807 Lasting-transient
	−.807 Fast-slow
	.748 Sensitive-insensitive
	.666 Light-heavy
	.547 Strong-weak
Factor 3	.873 Interesting-boring
	.756 Hot-cold
	.726 Natural-artificial
	.704 Pleasant-unpleasant
Factor 4	.778 Dominant-submissive
	−.649 New-old
	.622 Active-passive
	.596 Free-constrained
	.500 Butch-fem
Factor 5	.839 Rugged-delicate
	.710 Hard-soft

emerge from the data, that information will be helpful in designing educational materials targeted toward individuals with different sexual cognitive maps.

Studying Sexual Encounters: The Basic Unit of Analysis

HIV transmission occurs as a result of specific sexual acts, but those acts do not take place in a vacuum. Rather, they occur in the context of a sexual encounter, and the dynamics of the sexual encounter may itself determine

Table 6.5. Factor Loadings of Sexual Behaviors: Student Data

Factor 1	.928 Sex/lovers
	.929 French kiss
	.900 Being touched
	.844 Touching
	.838 Masturbation/mutual
	.822 Masturbation/yourself
	.801 Kissing/social
	.739 Oral/receiving
	.702 Oral/giving
	.500 Anal passive w/condom
	−.522 Watersports/receiving
	−.370 Watersports/giving
	.361 Exhibitionism
	.336 Anal active w/condom
	.249 Voyeurism
Factor 2	.875 Fisting/giving
	.840 Anal active w/o condom
	.768 S&M passive
	.765 Fisting/receiving
	.741 Rimming/giving
	.673 S&M active
	.642 Sex/relatives
	.634 Anal passive w/o condom
	−.390 Phone sex
	.261 Rimming/receiving
Factor 3	.938 Sex/clubs
	.895 Sex/parks
	.857 Group sex
	.824 Sex/strangers
	.722 Sex/t-rooms

Table 6.6. A Partial List of Erotic Behaviors That May Occur During Gay Male Sexual Encounters

1.	Anal intercourse, insertive, without a condom
2.	Anal intercourse, insertive, with a condom
3.	Anal intercourse, receptive, without a condom
4.	Anal intercourse, receptive, with a condom
5.	Oral sex, insertive, without a condom
6.	Oral sex, insertive, with a condom
7.	Oral sex, receptive, without a condom
8.	Oral sex, receptive, with a condom
9.	Stimulating the nipples/breasts, hard
10.	Stimulating the nipples/breasts, soft
11.	Having your nipples/breasts stimulated, hard
12.	Having your nipples/breasts stimulated, soft
13.	Using a cock ring
14.	Masturbating yourself
15.	Masturbating your partner
16.	Being masturbated by your partner
17.	Simultaneous mutual masturbation
18.	Kissing on lips
19.	French kissing
20.	Biting/nibbling your partner in the neck area
21.	Having your partner bite/nibble you in the neck area
22.	Licking the testicles of your partner
23.	Having your testicles licked by your partner
24.	Having your testicles taken into partner's mouth
25.	Taking your partner's testicles in your mouth
26.	Sucking on your partner's toes
27.	Having your toes sucked
28.	Being tickled in sensitive areas
29.	Tickling your partner in sensitive areas
30.	Having your testicles squeezed or tugged
31.	Squeezing or tugging on your partner's testicles
32.	Using tit clamps
33.	Having your partner employ dildo/vibrator on you
34.	Using a dildo/vibrator on your partner
35.	Caressing your partner's back
36.	Having your back caressed
37.	Giving your partner a full body massage
38.	Receiving a full body massage
39.	Hearing your partner talk dirty
40.	Talking dirty to your partner
41.	Watching porno videos
42.	Watching your partner masturbate
43.	Having your partner watch you masturbate
44.	Sucking on your partner's fingers
45.	Having your fingers sucked

(*continued*)

Table 6.6. (*continued*)

46.	Fingering your partner's anus
47.	Being fingered anally by your partner
48.	Using cream or lotion for masturbation
49.	Being the S in S/M activities
50.	Being the M in S/M activities
51.	Slapping your partner's butt/thighs
52.	Having your own butt/thighs slapped
53.	Hugging each other
54.	Expressing appreciation verbally to your partner
55.	Having your partner verbally express appreciation for your actions
56.	Golden showers, active
57.	Golden showers, passive
58.	Dressing in leather
59.	Having your partner dress in leather
60.	Dressing in women's clothing
61.	Having your partner dressed in women's clothing
62.	Standing up during sexual activity
63.	Sitting down during sexual activity
64.	Kneeling during sexual activity
65.	Lying down during sexual activity
66.	Being lightly caressed on the entire body
67.	Lightly caressing your partner's entire body
68.	Heavy kneading of your partner's body/muscles
69.	Putting a condom on your partner
70.	Having your partner put a condom on you
71.	Ejaculating
72.	Having your partner ejaculate
73.	Engaging in sex with multiple partners (four or more)
74.	Having sex with more than one person (threeways)
75.	Swallowing your partner's semen
76.	Having your partner swallow your semen
77.	Ejaculating inside your partner during anal sex
78.	Having your partner ejaculate inside you during anal sex
79.	Rimming your partner
80.	Having your partner rim you
81.	Fisting, top
82.	Fisting, bottom
83.	Frottage, body rubbing
84.	Fucking your partner between the thighs
85.	Getting fucked between the thighs
86.	Having sex
87.	Abstaining from sex
88.	Engaging in scat (active)
89.	Engaging in scat (passive)
90.	Showering before sex
91.	Showering after sex

whether or not a risky behavior transpires. Sexual encounters are exceedingly diverse, ranging from brief and simple sexual episodes to extremely complex events with a duration of hours. Contrary to the impression one gets from reading the sexual research literature, that sex consists of little more than "fucking and sucking," the number of "sexemes" called into play in the course of a single encounter may be enormous. What is needed is a science of sexual encounters. I am not aware of any significant corpus of scientific literature that takes as its focal concern the sexual encounter.

We need to know what actually happens when two (or more) people have sex, from beginning to end, from first contact until separation. Fortunately, for those who wish to understand gay male sexual encounters, there is a body of literary work that does describe encounters, and, from this literature, one can learn a great deal about gay male sexual behavior. I would certainly send a safe-sex educator to the writings of Camus (1981), Leyland (1986), Leyland and Judell (1984), Mains (1984), Stambolian (1984), Townsend (1972), McDonald (1981, 1982a, 1982b), and Preston and Swann (1986) before I would recommend any of the writings based on sex research. The descriptive accounts by these gay authors may be partly based on fantasy rather than actual occurrences, but I suspect that they come closer to reality than do retrospective reports on sexual episodes given by informants to researchers. Indeed, even pornographic films could be used in the study of sexual encounters despite the obvious fantasy elements that these depictions contain.

How to obtain accurate accounts of sexual encounters is a difficult question. Some accounts can be obtained through participant observation, of course, but they will be influenced to some degree by the participant observer himself. The content of a sexual encounter always involves some sort of negotiation (usually implicit rather than stated) between or among the participants in the encounter, each of whom brings to the encounter his own past experiences, his cognitive structure, his emotional needs. This is what makes each encounter slightly different than all others. Indeed, it is often stated that, when you have sex with someone, you are having sex with all of the other people with whom that partner has had sex; usually this is stated to emphasize the danger of contracting a venereal disease, but it also means that his prior sexual experiences will color his behavior in his sexual encounter with you. It can be pointed out that this fact adds a degree of richness as well as danger to the encounter; it may account for the fact that sexuality is a highly elaborated domain in the gay subculture. Sexual repertoires are more likely to be constricted among those whose range of sexual experience is narrow.

There is one concept within the sexology literature that is related to the sexual encounter approach that I am urging. I refer to the notion of "sexual scripts" (Gagnon, 1973; Gagnon & Simon, 1973; Hoffman, n.d.; Simon,

1973; Simon & Gagnon, 1984, 1987). To determine the nature of sexual scripts, it is essential to have a large number of accounts of sexual encounters. Given the large number of sexemes that exist in the repertoire of gay men, it is likely that a broad array of sexual scripts exists among gay men. It is entirely plausible, however, that the patterning seen in sexual encounters is not random, but that, similar to the situation in the domain of color terms, it may be that we will discover basic sexemes and nonbasic sexemes that reoccur in a limited set of configurations (Berlin & Kay, 1969). In the words of one of our San Francisco informants (Bolton & Jaramillo, 1988):

> At some point in the act of sex there *will* be cocksucking! That is probably the only sex act that will happen positively. Of course, touching the partner as well as yourself is understood (and I don't mean on the hand), tits, cock, balls, and ass, to be explicit. Hugging and kissing should be included unless you are in a public area or bathhouse. Then it can be a rather cold encounter. A good body massage can be a real turn-on. Fucking, unfortunately, is not all that common. I personally feel if there is no fucking, there really was *no* sex. But that is my personal opinion. Here is my list of what I conceptualize gay male sex to be, in order—1) touching [cock, tits, ass, chest], 2) cocksucking, 3) maybe a little kissing and then fuck, 4) if the person has an exceptionally nice ass, and is clean, then we have a new situation! There is nothing more sensual than eating a beautiful *clean* ass. Then fuck the shit out of it or get the shit fucked out of it!

The concept of sexual scripts may prove to be extremely valuable; however, its value will only be realized if the basic data used to "construct" these scripts are accounts of real occurrences. I am skeptical of those constructed on the basis of photo stimuli or other test materials because they represent generalized conceptualizations that do not respond to the complex situational determinants that come into play (as noted in the informant's account above). They are likely to represent idealized scenarios that have relatively little relevance to real-life situations.

It should be pointed out that what I am calling for here is also extremely different than sexual histories. Recalling sexual data has been shown to be problematic for some sexual practices, even when the recall period covers only one month (McLaws, Oldenburg, Ross, & Cooper, 1990); obtaining data on sexual encounters that occurred even longer in the past is likely to be fraught with even greater unreliability. Conceivably, the kind of data I am suggesting is important could be collected from informants who were trained to record their sexual encounters in depth. An overly simplified description of what this type of recording might look like is contained in Coxon's (1988) discussion of the use of sexual diaries for mapping sexual behavior.

I would like to give an example of how such data might be useful, even for epidemiological purposes. On the basis of data gathered via the instruments used in the prospective studies, it was determined that HIV can be transmitted by receptive oral sex. But the number of documented cases of transmission by this route is extremely small. And the determination that transmission must have occurred due to oral sex was done by a process of elimination, that is, informants steadfastly denied that they had engaged in anal sex, receptive or insertive. An analysis of a hypothetical sexual encounter might suggest that other routes were possible. For example, let's say two men have sex; they begin by having oral sex; then they turn to masturbating together, each masturbating himself; one climaxes before the other; the one who has climaxed then assists his partner by inserting his fingers in his partner's rectum. By definition, there was no anal intercourse. Was HIV transmitted by oral sex? I leave it to the reader to imagine the possibilities. If we study the sequencing of sexual behaviors during an encounter, we will be able to contribute information that is useful both epidemiologically and for prevention efforts.

Conclusions

In the above discussion, I have urged that consideration be given to the privileging of three related methodological approaches to the study of sexual behavior: participant observation, cognitive mapping, and the recording and analysis of sexual encounters. Despite important differences, these three approaches have one aspect in common—they attempt to provide a context for the sexual behaviors we seek to understand, and they attempt to see these behaviors from the point of view of the actor. They attempt to get at what sex means to its participants. In this, they contrast sharply with almost all the sex research done since the beginning of the AIDS pandemic. They are, I would assert, more appropriate to the tasks of designing and implementing prevention programs.

Previous research may be faulted on many grounds, but the most serious of these is that it has emphasized danger over pleasure. Sex consists of both pleasure and danger, but, by focusing on risks, too many of the positive dimensions of sexuality have been ignored along with the richness and complexity of behavior in this domain. Sex research has been the servant of repressive, antisexual forces because of this narrow vision. AIDS has reduced the scope of sexual freedom that was once enjoyed, but the goal of sex research should be not to assist in imposing a sexophobic ideology on people who are at risk but to help to restructure and re-create a sexuality that is life-sustaining and beneficial. It is precisely because the prevention programs developed within the gay community, without the benefit of research, emphasized the wealth of possibilities for leading a highly enjoyable sex life in spite of AIDS that those efforts have paid off in halting the spread of HIV. Those programs have helped to liberate the imagination and experiences of gay men rather than to restrict them.

The approaches I have outlined are intended to generate information about the creativity and diversity of sexuality, not to reinforce the stereotypical ideology so prevalent in Western cultures that defines "sex" as involving exclusively "sucking and fucking." Weeks (1985), in his critique of the work of the early sexologists, noted that sexual science in the 19th century formed part of a "grappling for control" over sexuality rather than a truly oppositional force, and he argues that its claims to enlightenment and scientific neutrality are suspect. Current debates and research on sexuality suggest that his argument applies as well to the current situation, with sexologists generally serving as the shock troops in the service of a Jehovanist sexual ideology with its emphasis on the only acceptable sex being vaginal sex in a faithful, monogamous, heterosexual union (Davis, 1983). This repressive, antipleasure stance will not contribute to ending the epidemic; indeed, it may worsen the situation because of its unacceptability. If our research is to be effective, it must help to create a new sexuality, one that is thoroughly grounded in and that expands upon the richness of sexual behavior actually being practiced.

We have already lost a decade, which can never be recaptured. I am not optimistic that we will get done the work that needs doing to make as powerful a contribution as we as anthropologists could make to AIDS prevention. Few among us are doing sex research, let alone the kinds of work that I view as critical. Under these circumstances, it may be that the best work done in prevention by anthropologists is being done by applied anthropologists working in AIDS education, drawing upon their anthropology and, in the case of gay men, in their lifetime experience within the gay community; they may be saving more lives than all the rest of us combined.

Notes

1. I wish to express my gratitude to Gail Orozco for her assistance with the preparation of this manuscript.

2. I refer to M. Gorman, R. Stall, and K. O'Reilly, for example. It is a curious phenomenon that ethnographic components have been much more conspicuous in the work of AIDS researchers studying intravenous drug users than in that of those interested in the sexual transmission of

HIV among non-IVDUs. Parker's work in Brazil, Lang's in Houston, and Carrier's in Mexico and Orange County, California, are exceptions. Even more notable is the shying away, even by gay anthropologists, from investigating the epidemic in gay communities. For references to the publications of these authors, see Bolton, Lewis, and Orozco (1991).

3. I have managed to obtain a copy of a working draft of a WHO document titled "Guidelines for Qualitative Research on Sexual Behaviour and Lifestyle Changes of Gay and Bisexual Men." That document does not explicitly mention "participant observation," but it does call for observational studies on sexually significant social settings. A revised version of this document has been published since this chapter was written (Parker & Carballo, 1990).

4. The role of the ethnographer's sexuality in fieldwork was the subject of a symposium at the 1990 annual meeting of the American Anthropological Association in New Orleans. For an insightful discussion of the problems associated with the compartmentalization of the ethnographer's professional and private lives and of the complications involved in writing up materials when the border between private and professional is blurred, consult the paper by Wafer (1990).

5. The riskiness of oral sex as well as rimming for the transmission of HIV is probably extremely low in both cases, although, in most safe-sex guidelines, both tend to be listed as high-risk behaviors. They do present serious risks of contracting other diseases such as gonorrhea as well as parasitic diseases.

6. Lévi-Strauss referred to the basic units of myths as "mythemes," and Benjamin Colby called the elementary units of folktales "eidons."

References

Abramson, P. R. (1988). Sexual assessment and the epidemiology of AIDS. *Journal of Sex Research, 25,* 323-346.

Abramson, P. R. (1990). Sexual science: Emerging discipline or oxymoron? *Journal of Sex Research, 27,* 147-165.

Abramson, P. R., & Herdt, G. (1990). The assessment of sexual practices relevant to the transmission of AIDS: A global perspective. *Journal of Sex Research, 27,* 215-232.

Berlin, B., & Kay, P. (1969). *Basic color terms: Their universality and evolution.* Berkeley: University of California Press.

Bernard, H. R. (1988). *Research methods in cultural anthropology.* Newbury Park, CA: Sage.

Bolton, R. (in press). AIDS and promiscuity: Muddles in the models of *HIV* preventions. *Medical Anthropology.*

Bolton, R. (with M. Lewis & G. Orozco). (1991). AIDS literature for anthropologists: A working bibliography. *Journal of Sex Research, 28,* (2), 307-346.

Bolton, R., & Jaramillo, D. (1988). *Gay men, gay sex: A behavioral space analysis.* Paper presented at the 87th annual meeting of the American Anthropological Association, Phoenix, AZ.

Camus, R. (1981). *Tricks: 25 encounters.* New York: St. Martin's.

Carrier, J. (1971). *Urban Mexican male homosexual encounters: An analysis of participants and coping strategies.* Unpublished doctoral dissertation, University of California, Irvine.

Colby, B. N. (1973). Analytical procedures in eidochronic analysis. *Journal of American Folklore, 86,* 14-24.

Connell, R. W., & Kippax, S. (1990). Sexuality in the AIDS crisis: Patterns of pleasure and practice in an Australian sample of gay and bisexual men. *Journal of Sex Research, 27,* 167-198.

Coxon, T. (1988). Something sensational . . . the sexual diary as a tool for mapping detailed sexual behavior. *Sociological Review, 36,* 353-367.

D'Andrade, R., Quinn, N. R., Nerlove, S. B., & Romney, A. K. (1972). Categories of disease in American-English and Mexican-Spanish. In A. K. Romney, R. N. Shepard, & S. B. Nerlove (Eds.), *Multidimensional scaling: Theory and applications in the behavioral sciences* (pp. 9-71). New York: Seminar.

Davis, M. S. (1983). *Smut: Erotic reality and obscene ideology.* Chicago: University of Chicago Press.

Foucault, M. (1983). How we behave. *Vanity Fair, 46,* 61-70.

Gagnon, J. H. (1973). Scripts and the coordination of sexual conduct. In J. K. Cole (Ed.), *The Nebraska Symposium on Motivation.* Lincoln: University of Nebraska Press.

Gagnon, J. H. (1988). Sex research and sexual conduct in the area of AIDS. *Journal of Acquired Immune Deficiency Syndromes, 1,* 593-601.

Gagnon, J. H., & Simon, W. (1973). *Sexual conduct: The social sources of human sexuality.* Chicago: Aldine.

Goffman, E. (1967). *Interaction ritual: Essays on face-to-face behavior.* New York: Pantheon.

Goffman, E. (1989). On fieldwork. *Journal of Contemporary Ethnography, 18,* 123-132.

Herdt, G. (1987). *The Sambia: Ritual and gender in New Guinea.* New York: Holt, Rinehart & Winston.

Hoffman, V. (n.d.). *An analysis of safer-sexual practices using sexual scripts.* Unpublished manuscript, Claremont Graduate School, Claremont, CA.

Holleran, A. (1988). *Ground zero.* New York: New American Library.

Humphreys, L. (1970). *Tearoom trade: Impersonal sex in public places.* Chicago: Aldine.

Levine, M. P., & Troiden, R. (1988). The myth of sexual compulsivity. *Journal of Sex Research, 25,* 347-363.

Lévi-Strauss, C. (1963). *Structural anthropology.* New York: Basic Books.

Leyland, W. (1986). *Hard: True gay encounters* (Vol. 2). San Francisco: Gay Sunshine.

Leyland, W., & Judell, B. (1984). Hot acts: Homosexual encounters from "first hand." San Francisco: Gay Sunshine.

Mains, G. (1984). *Urban aboriginals: A celebration of leathersexuality.* San Francisco: Gay Sunshine.

McCusker, J., Zapka, J. G., Stoddard, A. M., & Mayer, K. H. (1989). Responses to the AIDS epidemic among homosexually active men: Factors associated with preventive behavior. *Patient Education and Counseling, 13,* 15-30.

McDonald, B. (Ed.). (1981). *Meat: True homosexual experiences from S.T.H. writers* (Vol. 1). San Francisco: Gay Sunshine.

McDonald, B. (Ed.). (1982a). *Flesh: True homosexual experiences from S.T.H. writers* (Vol. 2). San Francisco: Gay Sunshine.

McDonald, B. (Ed.). (1982b). *Sex: True homosexual experiences from S.T.H. writers* (Vol. 3). San Francisco: Gay Sunshine.

McLaws, M. L., Oldenburg, B., Ross, M. W., & Cooper, D. A. (1990). Sexual behaviour in AIDS-related research: Reliability and validity of recall and diary measures. *Journal of Sex Research, 27,* 265-281.

Murray, S. O., & Payne, K. W. (1988). Medical policy without scientific evidence: The promiscuity paradigm and AIDS. *California Sociologist, 11,* 13-54.

Nanda, S. (1990). *Neither man nor woman: The Hijras of India.* Belmont, CA: Wadsworth.

Newton, E. (1972). *Mother camp: Female impersonators in America.* Chicago: University of Chicago Press.

Osgood, C. E., Suci, G. J., & Tannenbaum, P. H. (1957). *The measurement of meaning.* Urbana, IL: University of Chicago Press.

Ostrow, D. G., VanRaden, M., Fox, R., Kingsley, L., Dudley, J., & Kaslow, R. (1989). *Drug use and sexual behavior change in a cohort of homosexual men.* Unpublished manuscript.

Parker, R., & Carballo, M. (1990). Qualitative research on homosexual and bisexual behavior relevant to HIV/AIDS. *Journal of Sex Research, 27,* 497-525.

Preston, J., & Swann, G. (1986). *Safe sex: The ultimate erotic guide.* New York: New American Library.

Proposed draft revision of the Principles of Professional Responsibility. (1989). *Anthropology Newsletter, 30,* 22-23.

Rabinow, P. (1977). *Reflections on fieldwork in Morocco.* Berkeley: University of California Press.

Read, K. E. (1980). *Other voices: The style of a male homosexual tavern.* Novato, CA: Chandler and Sharp.

Rechy, J. (1967). *Numbers.* New York: Grove.

Reiss, I., & Leik, R. K. (1989). Evaluating strategies to avoid AIDS: Number of partners vs. use of condoms. *Journal of Sex Research, 26,* 411-433.

Roberts, J. M., & Chick, G. E. (1979). Butler County eight ball: A behavioral space analysis. In J. H. Goldstein (Ed.), *Sports, games and play: Social and psychological viewpoints* (pp. 65-99). Hillsdale, NJ: Lawrence Erlbaum.

Roberts, J. M., & Chick, G. E. (1984). Quitting the game: Covert disengagement from Butler County eight ball. *American Anthropologist, 86,* 549-567.

Roberts, J. M., Golder, T. V., & Chick, G. E. (1980). Judgment, oversight, and skill: A cultural analysis of P-3 pilot error. *Human Organization, 39,* 5-21.

Roth, P. A. (1989). Ethnography without tears. *Current Anthropology, 30,* 555-569.

Simon, W. (1973). The social, the erotic, and the sensual: The complexities of sexual scripts. In J. K. Cole (Ed.), *The Nebraska Symposium on Motivation.* Lincoln: University of Nebraska Press.

Simon, W., & Gagnon, J. H. (1984). Sexual scripts: Permanence and change. *Society, 22,* 52-60.

Simon, W., & Gagnon, J. H. (1987). A sexual scripts approach. In J. H. Geer & W. T. O'Donohue (Eds.), *Theories of human sexuality* (pp. 363-383). New York: Plenum.

Stall, R. (1988). The prevention of HIV infection associated with drug and alcohol use during sexual activity. In L. Siegel (Ed.), *AIDS and substance abuse* (pp. 78-88). New York: Harrington Park.

Stambolian, G. (1984). *Male fantasies/gay realities: Interviews with ten men.* New York: Sea Horse.

Townsend, L. (1972). *The leatherman's handbook II.* New York: Modernismo.

Triandis, H. (with V. Vassiliou, G. Vassiliou, Y. Tanaka, & A. V. Shanmugam). (1972). *The analysis of subjective culture.* New York: Wiley-Interscience.

Turner, C. F. (1989). Research on sexual behaviors that transmit HIV: Progress and problems. *AIDS, 3*(Suppl. 1), S63-S69.

Turner, C. F., Miller, H. G., & Moses, L. E. (Eds.). (1989). *AIDS: Sexual behavior and intravenous drug use.* Washington, DC: National Academy Press.

Tuzin, D. (1988). *Intercourse, discourse and the excluded middle: Sex and the anthropologist.* Paper presented in the symposium "Anthropology Rediscovers Sex" at the 87th annual meeting of the American Anthropological Association, Phoenix, AZ.

Van Griensven, G. J. P., de Vroome, E. M. M., Tielman, R. A. P., Goudsmit, J., de Wolf, F., van der Noordaa, J., & Coutinho, R. A. (1989). Effect of human immunodeficiency virus (HIV) antibody knowledge on high-risk sexual behavior with steady and nonsteady sexual partners among homosexual men. *American Journal of Epidemiology, 129,* 596-603.

Vincke, J., Bolton, R., Mak, R., & Blank, S. (1990). *The effects of social support, locus of control, and stress on high-risk behavior patterns.* Paper presented at the annual meeting of the Society for Cross-Cultural Research, Claremont, CA.

Wafer, J. (1990). *Identity management in the textual field.* Paper presented at the annual meeting of the American Anthropological Association, New Orleans, LA.

Webb, E. E., Campbell, D. T., Schwartz, R. D., Sechrist, L., & Grove, J. B. (1981). *Nonreactive measures in the social sciences.* Boston: Houghton Mifflin.

Weeks, J. (1985). *Sexuality and its discontents: Meanings, myths & modern sexualities.* Boston: Routledge & Kegan Paul.

Wexler, K. N., & Romney, A. K. (1972). Individual variations in cognitive structures. In A. K. Romney, R. N. Shepard, & S. B. Nerlove (Eds.), *Multidimensional scaling: Theory and applications in the behavioral sciences* (pp. 73-92). New York: Seminar.

Wiktor, S., Biggar, R. J., Melbye, M., Ebbeson, P., Coclough, G., DiGiosia, R., Sanchez, W. C., Grossman, R. J., & Goedert, J. (1990). Effect of knowledge of human immunodeficiency virus infection status on sexual activity among homosexual men. *Journal of Acquired Immune Deficiency Syndromes, 3,* 62-68.

Williams, W. L. (1986). *The spirit and the flesh: Sexual diversity in American Indian culture.* Boston: Beacon.

7

Anthropological Witnessing for African Americans: Power, Responsibility, and Choice in the Age of AIDS

ERNEST QUIMBY

Acquired immunodeficiency syndrome (AIDS) is a metaphor for life, death, sex, and drugs. It has disproportionately affected African Americans. This is especially so for crack-cocaine and intravenous drug users (IVDUs), women, children, and gay men. However, African American organizations have been relatively slow in responding to the human immunodeficiency virus (HIV) epidemic because they encounter several precarious dilemmas in their philosophies, constituencies, outreach practices, and limited resources. Unique difficulties and dynamics are experienced. Since 1987, I (a sociologist) have ethnographically pursued two key research questions: How are African American organizations responding to the epidemic? What are the implications for intervention and prevention efforts?

This chapter is not a presentation of my research, which has been reported elsewhere (Friedman, Quimby, Sufian, Abdul-Quader, & Des Jarlais, 1988; Quimby, 1987, 1989a, 1989b; Quimby & Friedman, 1988, 1989). The aim here is to conceptually discuss factors that anthropologists and sociologists consider as they study and intervene on behalf of peoples threatened by HIV.

AUTHOR'S NOTE. I am indebted to the Wenner-Gren Foundation for Anthropological Research and to the participants who shared critical insights at the foundation's 1990 international symposium on AIDS research.

Undocumented references are personal communications to me or information otherwise obtained by me. To ensure anonymity, names and identifying descriptions have not been used.

Contextual Perceptions and Definitions

Two competing, sometimes conflicting, models analyze public health problems: clinical and social context perspectives. Each has strengths, weaknesses, defenders, detractors as well as different levels and sources of funding. Both approaches, plus quantitative and qualitative information, are necessary for reducing HIV infection. As people argue for academic turf, folks in the trenches are being psychically battered.

To people of color, HIV infection, and mobilizing organized responses to reduce its spread, may be culturally circumscribed existentialist absurdities. Prevention, treatment, and other forms of intervention center on bread and butter, ideological dilemmas, and crucial, conceptual metaphors organizing experience and defining socially constructed reality. They involve notions of liberation versus containment, actualization versus eclipse, empowerment versus powerlessness, responsibility versus denial, affirmation versus stigma, authenticity versus fraudulence. These are all points of a continuum in the struggle for a meaningful, stable presence in the midst of a precarious existence—what Black folks call "trying to make it real; but compared to what?" They are shaped by a series of dualities, myriad consciousness-influencing choices between race and class, Africa and America, Black and White, male and female, gay and heterosexual. A health worker summed it up this way: "AIDS is just another drop of suffering in our population." Despite her condemnation of drug dealing and illegal drug use, an African American female businessperson and broadcaster once jokingly asked, "Sex, drugs, and money, what more could a colored woman want?" Another African American female talk show host referred to drugs as "a bag of goodies." Yet patterns of drug use have greatly increased HIV progression among African Americans and Latinos (Brown, Evans, Murphy, & Primm, 1986; Brown, Murphy, & Primm, 1987).

Seemingly forced into a hyphenated existence, people of African descent living in predominantly White nations are maneuvered into opting between denial or assertion, avoidance or engagement, passivity or action, being conscious historical participants or being mechanically moved by historical currents. Thus it is with AIDS in America. Given media portrayal of a disease mainly of peril to gays and addicts, many African Americans are fearful of being associated with its culturally stigmatizing consequences.

Meanwhile, the epidemic continues to spread. For those with access to care, HIV infection is frequently treatable, albeit incurable. Despair is being replaced with endurance and hope. But, for the poor and those deemed socially useless, it is deadening. There is a sense of utter futility. As of January 1990, the U.S. Centers for Disease Control (CDC) reported 121,645 AIDS cases in the continental United States, Guam, U.S. Pacific Islands, U.S. Virgin Islands, and Puerto Rico; 33,419 were Black (U.S. CDC, 1990a). The total included 2,055 pediatric cases (children under 13 years old); 1,076 were Black (compared with 454 White, 507 Hispanic, 9 Asian/Pacific Islander, and 4 American Indian/Alaskan Native children). Of the Black children, 92% had been exposed to a mother who was infected primarily because of her own contaminated intravenous (IV) drug use or having had unprotected sex with an IV drug user. The contact/exposure categories for Black adolescents and adults included 37% for male homosexual/bisexual, 39% for intravenous drug use (female and heterosexual male), and 7% for male homosexual/bisexual and IV drug use.

By August 31, 1990, the CDC reported 142,426 national cases; 41,166 were Black (U.S. CDC, 1990b). Generally, Whites accounted for more cases, but with decreasing incidence, although more Black women and children had AIDS than comparable Whites. (See the Appendix tables: "AIDS Transmission Categories in the U.S. by Racial/Ethnic Group.")

Some of these figures could be plotted on socioeconomic and geopolitical maps showing general social problems: unequal, inadequate, or inaccessible services; poor formal education and high unemployment, which lead to further underdevelopment and dependency; entrenched racism, sexism, and homophobia. Poor health is a structural feature of African American existence (U.S. Department of Health and Human Services [DHHS], 1985). It is made worse by culturally appealing advertisements inducing drug use (notably tobacco and alcohol) and malnutrition (through nutritionally deadly "fast-food" diets).

HIV is a spectrum of illnesses, reflecting particular social-psychological and structural issues for Blacks and Latinos (U.S. CDC, 1986). AIDS will not be contained without focusing on sociological, service, and psychosocial issues (Mays & Cochran, 1987). Increasingly, there is recognition of the relationship of AIDS to conditions of existence. If lives are to be saved by helping to change values, attitudes, and behavior, then the material circumstances within which people live need to be altered. This reality has been clearly noted in HIV policy suggestions that "focus on the critical need for drug-treatment, health care, delivery of culturally appropriate AIDS-related social services and education, the development of Black professionals in AIDS research and service provision, foster care, case management and housing" (New York State Governor's Advisory Committee for Black Affairs, 1987).

Historical Context

AIDS raises the specter of a people believing themselves to be free but actually haunted by yet another burden not of their choosing and possibly beyond their capacity to fully cast off. To make sense of this, it is necessary to take a historical look. HIV infection struck the United States in the 1980s, a period of extreme conservatism coupled with a cultural and ideological stress on individualism, laissez-faire approaches toward public policy, deregulation, and privatization. "Yuppies" and "bubbies" were symbols for progress and security. Revolution got redefined not as a shift in the class that exercises state power but as a qualitative change in the nature of the tactics to be used by those who have historically held power and exercised authority. Thus Reaganomics was hailed by some as revolutionary, as a dramatically new emphasis on and legitimation of the triumph of self-sufficiency, indulgence, and nonreliance on federal intervention. Social security was regarded as what could be done for oneself.

All this seemingly required the demise of social welfare. It meant the abandonment of liberalism, a philosophy now on the defense, and renewed quests for order, stability, and "traditional" cultural values. Battles against disruptive and threatening elements were started. Accordingly, drugs became a metaphor guiding and shaping attitudes, values, and behavior.

The launching of a new "war on drugs" pitted White soldiers and propagandists against poor communities and people of color. Illegal users of illicit chemicals had to be blocked from contaminating the society. Deviance had to be checked. African American communities got attacked. They were characterized by economic underdevelopment, unemployment, deteriorating health, and erosion of gains predicated on equal opportunity. Besieged by violence, crime, crack-cocaine, racist media, and declining social services, working-class neighborhoods bought into a cultural orientation that stigmatized and criminalized chemical dependency. Victories in the new offensive required training and deployment of professional elites and political troops drawn from the ranks of the offending racial, cultural, ethnic, or other groups. Hence, as some cities were experiencing demographic changes and greater numbers of African American elected officials, selected urban areas became sites of gentrification for upwardly mobile Whites and a limited number of qualified African Americans. However, while formal, but not necessarily the most important, symbols of local governance were passed to African American mayors, city administrators, and state council members, the leadership found itself presiding over urban shells. Industries relocated overseas. Public education stagnated. Municipal hospitals closed. Public transportation sputtered. Subsidized housing declined. Recreational facilities vacated. The national political administration relegated responsibility to local governments even though their economies were in fiscal decline. Still, funds were found for more prisons, police, and mechanisms of surveillance and control.

Inner city became a euphemism for crime, violence, disorder, disruptive Blacks, and life-styles deemed illegitimate and immoral by those in power or arrivistes courting the anointment of gatekeepers within public and private corridors of power. Drug wars were perceived as selective battles against African American males specifically and working-class people generally. Partly in reaction, intense and prolonged discussions and updated versions of older ideological currents resurfaced among African Americans. Nationalism, socialism, Black capitalism, entrepreneurship, Islam, Christianity, and other perspectives were debated. Competing groups lobbied for strategies and tactics that reflected their interests and constituencies. Heterosexual African American organizations were fearful of being identified with White gays. Cultural nationalists and integrationists were wary of one another. African Americans, Latinos, Asian Americans, and Native Americans have historically been suspicious of White liberals. Central to these dynamics was (and still is) a debate over the nature and meaning of culture and power.

Then came AIDS. It appeared in a context of political struggles for and cultural adaptations to survival, acceptance, mobility, development, and liberation. Unresolved questions were argued: Where to go? Why? How to get there? What alliances should be formed? What route to take, separatist or assimilationist? New debates arose around unsettled concerns: the roles of women and their relationship to each other and to men, reproductive rights, sexual orientation, and how to handle those "deviants" who were further blemishing an already stigmatized people. One African American organizer said sadly, "It looks like every bad disease affects us."

In some areas, HIV infection became increasingly one of color and class. Yet Black professionals, working-class communities, and leaders tended to avoid ownership of responsibility to grapple with the illness. An activist rationalized the difficulty by saying, "AIDS is a political hot potato." Those who did opt for affirmation risked stigmatization. Moreover, they were shut out if they struggled for broader issues of empowerment. No matter what choice was made, African Americans remained marginal—were kept marginal—in the arenas of AIDS and drugs research, planning, and evaluation. By the late 1980s, in New York City, AIDS was declared to be a leading killer of African American women in their prime reproductive years. Also in New York, it was a cause of mortality among narcotic users (Stoneburner et al., 1988). Deaths and illnesses were linked to HIV-induced immunosuppression (Des Jarlais, Friedman, & Hopkins, 1985; Des Jarlais, Friedman, & Stoneburner, 1988; Selwyn et al., 1988). There were official pronouncements about the potentially devastating toll on Latinos and Blacks. Yet, the New York City Health Department's monthly AIDS surveillance meetings focused on the interests of White gays, White lesbians, and White heterosexuals.

What then to do? African American liberation was not conceptually or ideologically on national and neighborhood agendas. Power brokers, administrative gatekeepers, and persons driven by myths and realities of upward mobility blocked attempts to link AIDS with survival, genocide, and power. AIDS was perceived as being stigmatizing to neighborhoods groping for legitimation, higher status, recognition, and governmental recourse. Media helped with the blemish, portraying African American males as the nation's worst urban nightmares.

Added to all this was an interpretation of Christianity that depicted sexuality as exclusively a moral concern. Black churches officially condemned homosexual and nonmarital sexual relations. Yet, congregations and pulpits had some known gay men and promiscuous heterosexuals. Paradoxically, along with national surveillance data, organized gay men and lesbians of color were among the first who drew national attention to the increasing incidence of AIDS among Blacks and Latinos. Conferences were held in 1986 by the Third World Advisory Task Force and the National Coalition of Black Lesbians and Gays. The major nationally established religious, civil rights, and Black advocacy groups did not attend, although some individual African American religious leaders and bodies have since endorsed HIV reduction efforts. Thus, in 1987, the Southern Christian Leadership Conference (SCLC) held national and regional conferences on "AIDS and the Black community."

Signification

Queries have been sparked among African Americans. Do people have multiple identities within multiple cultural contexts? For instance, how, in what ways, and to what extent do gay men of color identify themselves—on the basis of sexual orientation, class, ethnic culture, or experience of political marginality (and among yet other possibilities)? Can united fronts be created between groups with varying and perhaps even subjectively competing subcultures? How can a community or cultural group become actively empowered if the institutional resources and symbolic imagery are controlled by others?

Answers are elusive. It seemed to be easier, politically safer, and more acceptable to highlight IV drug-related HIV issues rather than also address those of homosexuals with HIV infection. A gay African American AIDS educator indicated, "There's an illusion that the only AIDS cases in the minority communities are of intravenous drug users." One social service worker noted, "Most gay people in the Caribbean community don't want to admit they are gay and come forward for services." According to one sarcastic AIDS educator, "There are no gays in Puerto Rico, only men who have sex with men."

African Americans talk of "signifying." How can the signifiers and signification (both official and culturally based) be channeled to help stop the epidemic? As the disease has spread, so have its metaphoric portrayals. It was originally equated with gay White males, then gays generally, followed by intravenous drug users, heterosexuals, Africans and Haitians, and now African Americans. No longer conceptualized as a fatal, terminal, hopeless illness, HIV is now considered a chronic, manageable disease. For those with adequate support systems, concepts about dying have been supplemented by visions of living with AIDS. But who or what determines the concepts?

These are anthropologically important considerations. Contaminated intravenous drug use is not the only threat to immunosuppression posed by substance abuse. There have been dramatic increases in sexually transmitted diseases and probable HIV infection because of crack cocaine's highly addictive properties. Chemical dependency, including alcohol abuse, can impair judgment, resulting in a dangerous exchange of blood, saliva, semen, and vaginal secretions for money or more chemicals. From the vantage point of an anthropology of AIDS or public health, how do socialization and psychopharmacology affect people at various stages of chemical use? What norms and identities are generated by specific users of specific drugs? Do intravenous and other drug users have subculture(s)? Are there patterns of urban U.S. drug use and sexual expression that have implications for risk reduction?

What we currently know about expressions of sexuality is inadequate. New conceptualizations and methodologies are needed. An urgent social scientific task is how to identify, demonstrate, and otherwise situate sexuality and sex research within the multidimensional contexts of people's lives.

This leads to the problem of shedding the myth of value-free science, yet maintaining balance between objectivity and subjectivity. Some researchers argue that it is imperative to ground studies from the participants' perspectives. Social scientists grope with how to do research that is both theoretical and applicable to solving social problems. Knowledge and information per se do not change behaviors. AIDS is completely preventable. However, the outsider's attitude of empowering others can be paternalistic. This is not the same as assisting people in their own empowering process. Empowerment may mean confronting the unwillingness of those with power to give it up or to share it. This is risky politically, professionally, and perhaps even financially.

One effect of AIDS and AIDS research on culture and power is that social scientists are reformulating their definitions and methods of studying these two concepts. They are not separable. Culture implies a rationalization of and claims to ways of being and interacting, that is, feeling, thinking, communicating, acting. Power is implicit in social life and notions of cultural legitimacy and illegitimacy, in meanings of and reactions to normality and deviance. The notion of subterranean subculture as immoral, illicit, or illegal has been negatively applied to politically marginal or powerless groups such as gays and drug addicts. As such, it reflects an aspect of labeling by dominant groups and classes in society.

What then is the social scientist's role? A function of ethnography is to show how power is embodied in social structures, relationships, and symbolism. Rooting human relations in systems of control requires a practical integration of culture and power. Anthropology can understand cultural systems and meanings and locate them in the contexts of perceived and/or objective powerlessness and subjugation. In so doing, power needs to be conceptualized as more than a predicate or footnote. Consequently, anthropology is compelled to develop a method for studying power.

Problems of African American Mobilization

Anthropology is descriptively important for applied purposes. It also has crucial value for contributing to social movement theory as it specifically relates to AIDS mobilization efforts and African Americans. In this regard, among some of the principal issues to be clarified are the following: community outreach work, government reactions to mobilization, and factors affecting efforts to organize groups. Anthropology could raise significant questions and help flush out answers. For example, what appears to be the more successful model of effecting behavioral change for which specific target group(s): a centralized or grass-roots approach? Applied lessons from neighborhood development efforts may increase mass participation. Recruitment and service delivery from the bottom up may be more effective than traditional top-down methods. Sometimes well-intentioned outreach work is inappropriate and lacks credibility and authenticity.

Research among African Americans supports the use of community members to effect change. HIV infection is both problem and symptom. It requires community and organizational infrastructures along with individual, neighborhood, and group empowerment. Specific tactics vary depending on who is being targeted and for what purposes. A general strategy is cultural empowerment, that is, the capacity of groups to progressively develop and contribute to healthy environments and well-rounded personalities. It highlights cultural continuity between the various participants (e.g., lay clients and professionals).

Some organizers have been involved in previous movements. They developed networks and formulated ideological perspectives that inform their activities. How do such experiences affect meaningful action? How are meanings derived from and revealed in social movements around AIDS? For that matter, what is a social movement? Social activism in itself does not constitute a movement. Alcoholics and Narcotics Anonymous focus on change within individuals, not social change of conditions. Although effective and popular, they are not social movements. Is AIDS activism only a movement among (White) gays? What equivalents of ACT UP are there among African Americans or IV drug users?

Definitions aside, organizing has been rather weak for addicts and African Americans for various reasons. Efforts to mobilize both have been especially difficult partly because of perceived government reactions to the HIV epidemic. According to some activists and health care workers, government regards people of color and addicts as acceptable casualties. The moral, political, and ideological climate (of conservatives and liberals) has blocked distribution of condoms and experiments to distribute "clean needles." Needle exchange programs and condom usage have been regarded as genocidal or unwarranted governmental interference. One counselor severely criticized needle exchanges, saying, "I don't understand why you would want to exchange one form of slavery for another." Campaigns by organizations, such as the Association for Drug Abuse Prevention and Treatment, Inc. (ADAPT)—a Brooklyn-based voluntary group of former addicts and professional substance abuse workers—to get addicts to use "clean works" have been opposed because it is supposed that they promote illicit and unhealthy behavior.

Engaging IV drug users has also been problematic because they are not a group, are politically unorganized, and lack a constituency. For instance, one of the Brooklyn AIDS Task Force's main difficulties has been in sensitizing local politicians to put AIDS on their agendas. When it held a community conference in October 1987 to sensitize local leaders and neighborhood residents to AIDS issues, no elected officials attended. Moreover, a controversy arose because the meeting had no workshops on gays. This omission was severely criticized by an emotional White gay audience member who interrupted a speaker. During the heated exchange, the keynote speaker and panel chair accepted angry criticism but argued that, because IV drug use is a main transmission route for minorities, it was time for addicts to be recognized and organized the way gays have been.

There are still other restrictions on mobilizing. Suspicion is strong. Many African Americans and IV drug users argue that AIDS may be a conspiracy directed against them. Governmental authorities and most researchers publicly dismiss such views. Nevertheless, distrust remains. Activists also criticize the insufficiency and type of substance abuse rehabilitation facilities. One respondent wanted to know, "What good is drug treatment if we don't teach people to do something once they've finished treatment?" Numerous patients and service providers complain that a demotivating precondition for entering treatment is the loss of jurisdiction over one's life. In addition, bureaucratic delays, perceived social indifference, neighborhood resistance to being sites for drug recovery programs, and restrictive case management approaches tend to block motivation to collective organizing by and among addicts. An additional demobilizing issue is the greater stress by middle-class African American organizations on education and social mobility compared with the priority given to HIV infection by emerging grass-roots organizations.

African American institutions and subcultures have not responded to AIDS as readily as have White gays. White and Black gay mobilization against HIV infection has been successful in accomplishing educational, cultural, and political objectives (Altman, 1986; Patton, 1985; Stall, Coates, & Hoff, 1988). Black people face vital constraints: limited availability of and supervision over economic and political resources, relative decline of the Black liberation movement, ideological confusion, extensive cleavages by class, religion, and cultural origin, lack of trained and organized personnel who are knowledgeable about AIDS, and epidemiologically different risks of exposure to HIV.

Health is a socioeconomic and political issue. Public health policy is shaped by and influences definitions, goals, institutions, cultures, and activities that are primarily outside the African American community. A group has to be predisposed or readied for mobilization. Otherwise, it may reflect the view of a prominent African American politician who asked, "Why don't we round up all the known drug addicts and put them away some place?" Effective outreach encompasses information and attitudinal change as well as community development.

My research suggests several main themes. First, African American organizational avoidance and resistance to AIDS work are partly reflections of White denial, dominant political hesitancy, and inappropriate public health education. An educator explained, "You can't confine AIDS to a ghetto and expect them to respond to your brochures and commercials the way you want them to." Second, Black people's responses differ according to class, gender, education, culture, and politics. An African American AIDS program director stated, "People who run AIDS programs don't know very much about us." Third, external pressures, internal dynamics, and structural characteristics of working-class areas retard organizing and outreach efforts (e.g., institutional insufficiency in resolving related problems of racism, unemployment, crippling miseducation, and poverty; an already overburdened and inadequate health care system; fears held by formal and informal leadership of controversies about sexuality and drug issues; and conflicting attitudes of religious officials). According to one male, "We're more likely to be shot by that cop standing over there than dying from AIDS."

The chief theoretical and empirical research questions are these: Why have Blacks not mobilized earlier and more effectively? What has been done? And why does there seem to be disorganization, lack of significant mobilization, and confusion concerning Black responses to the HIV epidemic? Answering these questions adequately requires the development of a social science of AIDS. AIDS has a racial dimension that has been sketched elsewhere yet remains to be more fully described and analyzed.

Data on the epidemic's history reveal a critical situation. Nationally, infected African Americans are overrepresented in five major categories: drug users, homosexuals, bisexuals, women, and children. Yet sheer numbers do not galvanize sustained organizational response. Denial, avoidance, and immobilization are related to structural and cultural variables that are not being addressed and evaluated.

Drugs and AIDS mobilization research illustrate at least four interrelated issues. First of all, efforts are restricted by competing priorities, alternating demands, mistrust, blurry political agendas, and deep divisions within and between organizations. Cleavages and rifts are obstacles to community development, communication, and the formation of policy positions. These problems are reflected in the difficulties African American groups have in recognizing the importance of HIV issues for gays, the absence of powerful self-organization by African American gays, and the relative lack of involvement of White gay groups in antiracist politics or in AIDS service delivery in African American neighborhoods. Second, the emergent Black community is limited by racially restricted access to power coupled with internal differences and unresolved debates on drugs and sexuality. Third, prior to AIDS, compared with Blacks, White gays were more mobilized and had community structures plus supportive institutions more readily adaptable to coping with HIV-related issues. (This does not mean that White gays are a homogeneous group.) Finally, low levels of organization and mobilization in the early 1980s also stem from several other factors, notably destruction and co-optation of radical segments of prior movements and the depressive and immobilizing effects of the national political climate since the mid-1970s.

HIV reduction activities by African American and Caribbean Blacks are based on three main stances: (a) AIDS is regarded as a public health concern mainly for White gays originally and currently for intravenous drug addicts; therefore, let health officials deal with the problem. (b) HIV causes and solutions are fundamentally moral issues; consequently, religious convictions and/or righteous living will settle the problem. (c) AIDS is ultimately a political matter; hence solutions involve struggling for access to and better usage of power and resources.

However hesitant or problematic, responses to AIDS have been attempts to integrate and resolve these potentially conflicting tendencies. Although organizational reactions recently reflect greater awareness, they are still fairly diffuse and somewhat unstructured. No national or regional group has generated mass support. Efforts and ideological positions are not yet unified.

It appears that persistent ambiguity and failure of effective responses also stem from the marginality of and prejudice toward the most directly affected segments. As one former addict put it, "They don't care whether junkies die." He and many others argue that the general public believes AIDS helps solve the predicament of what to do with addicts, homosexuals, and babies born by too many poor women of color. The epidemic seems to be attacking those who are the least empowered. In this sense, perhaps AIDS is selective.

Despite posturing, there seems to be a serious reluctance by some African American professionals to work cooperatively. Several of the very charges labeled against some Whites have been made of some Blacks: egoism, individualism, "wanting to have it all for themselves," unwillingness to share information, failure to assist less established organizations and individuals, monopolizing access to funds, operating an old boys' network, freezing less traditional grass-roots leadership and groups out of the process, channeling grants to the same recipients, networking for personal gain rather than collective solutions, and making a profitable career on the basis of others' suffering.

Particular factors influence African American responses to AIDS. Stemming the epidemic requires that they be documented and strategically addressed. In so doing, invaluable lessons may be learned about resolving new problems. Among the more important dynamics are the following: contradictory socialization about sexuality, living, dying, and drug use; racism; sexism; homophobia; addictophobia; unwillingness and inability of White and Black leadership to confront and address the specific impact of AIDS on Blacks; ideological conflict; inflexible, hesitant, or undefined roles of traditional community and national organizations; confusion about goals and objectives; conflicting interests; competing constituencies; personal or organizational hegemony; class tension; ethnic or cultural disputes; ethnocentrism; professional alienation from working-class communities and street people; and differences in levels and types of support by and for intravenous drug users, gays, and heterosexual males and females.

Anthropology's Potential Role

Anthropological study could yield descriptions of the roles of power, authority, marginality, and struggles for variously defined liberation surrounding HIV and addiction. A preexistent gay liberation movement provides an insightful context for AIDS activists and research (Shilts, 1987). As with gays and lesbians, a central problem for organizers of addicts is how to get validation both as outsiders and as insiders. Addicts themselves are organizationally fragmented, stigmatized, and stereotyped. Therefore, their ability to be politically recognized and considered is undercut. Independent action runs the risk of governmental resistance (generally by co-optation or confrontation). These points were vigorously raised at the three CDC-sponsored national conferences on HIV infection and AIDS among U.S. racial and ethnic minorities held between 1987 and 1989. None was held in 1990. Yet IV drug users have a potential for informing and creating effective public policies, carrying out risk reduction efforts, providing services, and engaging in subcultural change.

Anthropology has the ability to demonstrate common denominators and differences among specific categories of people being mobilized to adopt risk reduction behaviors. Insights gained from research on strategies used to engage addicts may have value for other segments of the population. Social science has identified variables affecting organizing among IV drug users, which have been determined through ethnography, a method developed by anthropologists. Several of these factors may not be unique to IV drug users. Among the more salient factors are the following: ideological disputes over goals, specific objectives, and methods of organizing; community and family opposition to drug use and users; tension between service providers and organizers; establishment of trust between researchers and subjects; perception by outsiders of drug users not solely as objective categories or individual cases but as social actors; homelessness; access to resources (e.g., meeting sites, supplies, finances); splits over race and class; repression; reliance on and restrictions imposed by funding agencies; and burn-out in limited and overworked leadership. Several factors may be particular to chemical dependency, including pharmacological effects of drugs on users; effects of drug addiction on use of time and labor (e.g., energy spent on obtaining drugs, criminal activity, exchanging sex for drugs); subculture of addiction; and inducements (e.g., meals or showers) to draw users into programmatic activities.

Serious concerns arise as anthropologists study cultural life—how to objectify subjects and maintain detachment in the midst of a human drama requiring compassion and scientific assistance? Does value neutrality engender applied research? How can action-oriented social science research be legitimated and valued? How can social science be appreciated when biomedicine is regarded as the valued method of research on HIV? These tend to be matters of reconciling philosophical positions with data gathering techniques and uses. They also have significance for who gets grants. However, at the empirical level of linking culture and power, three specific questions may be asked about organizing selected groups as opposed to doing outreach and service for them: Does organizing lead to greater risk reduction than outreach? Does organizing become self-sustaining? Does it spread to other members of the same population segment (e.g., other IV drug users) in a neighborhood or a city?

Health professionals agree that a person is not at risk because of who he or she is but because of what he or she does. However, the evidence for that supposition has yet to be convincingly demonstrated. Using ethnography and surveys, concrete achievements that engage targeted persons may be documented by mobilizers and outreach workers. These could center on the purpose, number, and types of meetings; topics; demographics of participants; activities; emerging leadership; perceived levels and types of empowerment; impact on behavior; and statistical reduction of incidence and prevalence rates in specific locales and groups.

Returning to issues for social movement theory, what are the factors that hinder organizing heterosexual African Americans and gays around AIDS issues? Answers may be linked to the cultural use of power as well as the political use of culture by both groups. AIDS has had a differential impact on the social categorization, political behavior, and cultural life of gays and African Americans (which are not mutually exclusive). It altered and was changed by gay institutions, subcultures, and support networks, some of which were previously unnoticed (Adam, 1987). In some cases, new lifestyles and organizations were formed. This has not been true for African American organizations, which are still grappling over whether and how to mobilize around HIV. For both groups, prior cultural and ultimate political liberation movements developed around issues of identity, autonomy, and self-determination. Social conceptions of gender roles and racial stereotyping affected self-images. They also shaped the formation and use of networks as well as relationships between the state and community-based organizations.

In the United States, between 1983 and 1985, there were media and public sensationalism and hysteria over AIDS. Gays, along with lesbians (first White ones and then those of color), mobilized to obtain treatment and to counter stereotypes. Unlike African Americans, for White homosexual activists, mobilizing against HIV infection was perceptibly linked to broader issues of survival and development. Since then, White gay groups have been able to negotiate the public health bureaucracy better than African American organizations. However, both experience state attempts to impose notions of sexuality and morality. Messages related to oral sex, adolescent sexuality, bisexuality, conspiracy, and genocide have tended to be censored. Gays can be sexual but not intimate; heterosexuals may be intimate though not sexual. Male bonding and unapproved heterosexual intimacy are portrayed as socially and individually dangerous—suspiciously deviant acts ultimately corrected or terminated by the final solution of death. Overly simplistic dualities are substituted: safe versus unsafe sex, promiscuity versus fidelity, and risk groups (Blacks, gays, Haitians, and Central Africans) versus implicitly not-at-risk groups (middle-class heterosexuals). Persons with AIDS (PWAs) are designated victims and victimizers.

Where government and community-based organizational relationships become more cooperative, co-optation is observed. Institutionalization of an AIDS establishment and the politics of funding pressure local organizations into becoming models of state bureaucracy. Efforts to develop support care systems lead to organizing around larger public health issues such as medical insurance. Public health and community social support systems have also become intertwined. A passive, compliant model of clients appears to be desired for organizational funding. In Weberian terms, there has been a shift from charismatic authority to rational, bureaucratic forms of local organization.

Partly out of response to state models of health care and because of desperation, gay and heterosexual activists, particularly White PWAs and HIV-infected persons, have initiated alternative care and treatment systems and protocols. Some are underground networks of PWAs and their supporters. Others are primarily of PWAs. When there has been no establishment of trust between outside organizers and service populations, mobilization has been extremely difficult, often nonexistent, or minimally sustained. This apparently is the case with relationships between White gay groups and traditional heterosexual African American organizations.

What is the additional significance of these issues for anthropology in addition to those already illustrated? Anthropology has the potential for helping to deemphasize the tendency to overly medicalize health and illness. New perspectives other than deified biomedical constructions are wanted to help explain people's behavior. Unlike psychology and sociology, anthropology has been relatively slow in researching HIV issues. It abdicated responsibility to shape a humanistic and holistic formulation of HIV treatment and prevention. Yet, because of its emphasis on culture and the fact that

HIV infection may be conceptualized as a medical and cultural problem, anthropology could advance our understanding of the social context of mobilization efforts to contain the pandemic.

Considerations toward a model of anthropological inquiry into AIDS might include, but not be restricted to, the following: relating epidemiology to social ecology; comparing AIDS projects (e.g., social work versus civil rights models); describing preexistent resources and those generated by AIDS/HIV activism; assessing federal versus local roles in legitimating or invalidating organizations; analyzing the impact of governmental and private funding (e.g., in providing or disrupting stability); illustrating conflicts between programs that stress status quo maintenance and those that challenge dominant structural interests; providing empirical data on the differential organizational capacity of groups to mobilize community resources to identify and secure their own objectives; describing the impact of networks on self-image, political advocacy, and service provision; identifying and explaining dynamics of task forces, consortia, united fronts, and coalitions; clarifying the impact of culture and political socialization on organizational theory and practice (e.g., identifying those norms and symbols that help to coalesce and legitimize organizations); and empirically describing variables responsible for organizational cohesion among culturally different groups.

HIV infection has forced anthropologists to reexamine the relationship of culture and research to power. They have contemplated their contributions to debates about deconstructionism and activism by social scientists. The epidemic has become a potential metaphor for advancing or containing the liberation of groups. It also represents an opportunity for scientists to galvanize around other problems. Within the profession and among outsiders, there is a need to increase the hearing of alternative voices and to empower research. In the competition between social and biomedical science, anthropology craves to be empowered. It—not too unlike African Americans as a racial group—is in a struggle for representation and discourse as a way of negotiating power.

For stigmatized groups (such as White gays or heterosexual Haitians), as well as undervalued anthropologists (and sociologists), empowerment is partly achieved through cultural and professional discourse. Whether by community activists or professionals, the mastery of imagery, political agitation, and ideological or theoretical expression ultimately lead to appeals to and for authority. As it relates to AIDS, one role of explanation in applied anthropology is to help subjugated people gain dominion over their devalued culture. A fundamental task of theory is to help vitalize conscious activity, to help direct action. In the process, explainers and theorizers attempt to gain command of the message and the medium. Alternative explanations are sometimes dismissed and negatively labeled.

Theoretical constructions and presentations are means of representation. In rejecting explanations that deviate from official or dominant orthodoxy, there can be a tendency toward arrogance. Representations may be metaphors for powerlessness and marginality. So-called conspiracy theories reveal thought and behavior. They express a history of objective oppression and exploitation. Rather than being discounted as paranoid ideation or naive simplification, it may be fruitful for social scientists and health activists to regard them as powerfully coherent organizers of data and experiences.

Thus a central issue, again, is who determines and portrays the construction of reality and representation within affected communities? For social scientists, a related matter is ascertaining how groups gain access to and manage imagery. AIDS research has the potential for scientifically helping to incorporate personal and group experience into theory. The anthropologist as social partisan may also communicate theory into personal experience. As a scientist, she or he has to wrestle with how to integrate objectivity with subjective intention. In the age of AIDS, how can a discipline or researcher be objective within a subjective context? Theory is not neutral.

Theoretical development can be subversive, that is, challenging to and undermining cherished hypotheses. Another view is that alternative voices are not threatening per se. They may supplement rather than replace older ones. In either case, a lifesaving task is to operationalize conceptual knowledge. The point is to act rather than becoming neutralized by or infatuated with analysis.

Accordingly, interdisciplinary and interorganizational work could be undertaken. It would be grounded in the cultural (theoretical and symbolic) representations of the groups being studied and assisted. The most advanced analytical tools and rigorous procedures are required. This could be accomplished by interdisciplinary research, although there is a danger of getting trapped in and perpetuating other agendas. Thus interdisciplinary and interorganizational activities require each party be able to identify and set its own agenda. Cultures have to be able to represent themselves.

In the cultural realm, groups have unequal and differential access to vehicles of formal representation such as the media. Putting facts in ever-broader contexts and constructions is dependent on a sense of history, order, structure, and power. Sometimes groups lack authoritative endorsements of their claims to factual validity. Amidst conflict and contention, rumor and gossip may function to forge alternative perspectives and provide social stability. Anthropologists could enunciate the meanings of cultural communication among politically isolated urban and rural folk.

Urgent Tasks

In documenting how community forces enhance or retard mobilization around HIV issues, social science learns a lot about culture and power. It also helps save lives. Anthropology and sociology could provide evidence and description of efforts that impede or facilitate the following processes that collectively might reduce the rate of new infections:

(1) peer-based education around cultural messages and goals developed within the community;

(2) community dialogue, conflict, and resolution about how best to respond to the disease;

(3) group support for risk reduction measures that conform to emergent norms and values;

(4) recruitment and organization of volunteer labor to assist the ill and their relatives; and

(5) community protection from HIV-related public policies that might hurt it.

Metaphors and Ideologies

There are no clear answers for these issues. Indeed, anthropologists are groping for clear questions. In the meantime, people are living and dying. Tension exists between different explanatory models of culture and its relationship to health. Additional tension exists among explainers and between them and their subjects. There is continuous incongruity between theory and practice—reflecting an insurmountable gap between existence and description—symbolically imagined by metaphor and presumptively depicted through research.

Recognizing their limitations, social scientists can be less presumptuous observers and clearer social participants. Bearing witness involves power, responsibility, and choice. It is a way of remembering, honoring, enabling others and ourselves to become more effective describers and makers of history. In so doing, anthropologists assume roles as players and observers. This duality reflects an ambiguous and sometimes contradictory nature of social participation by professionals. Deconstructing restrictive conceptual frameworks and empowering new visions include the demonstration of cultural relativism and documentation of cultural history.

For African Americans, reconciling the double consciousness of heritage can lead to a sense of cultural schizophrenia, a split between various chosen and assigned identities. HIV has rendered African Americans both visible and invisible. AIDS, sexuality, and drugs have become ways of organizing experiences often through denial or ownership. For some persons, there has been an urgency to struggle for ideological and cultural clarity. There have been attempts to help nourish communities and subcultures that exist and that are coming into being. Thus there is acknowledgment of and appreciation for White and Black gays and lesbians who helped publicize the issue of HIV infection among heterosexual Blacks. For others, including too many African American sociologists, there is still avoidance of AIDS issues at conferences and universities.

Complicating matters is the representation of AIDS as a disease of White and Black gays and street addicts of color. Imagining HIV infection as afflicting poor Latinos and Blacks seems to permit the middle class a false sense of estrangement: Do we wait out the epidemic until it reduces the undesirable and disinherited among us or do we confront the issues that AIDS and HIV signify? AIDS is conceptually linked to metaphors and ideologies that themselves contain cultural assumptions.

Does AIDS serve the painful function of reminding the Black middle class of its own cultural disenfranchisement and political feebleness? Historically, the African American professional sector has not been an entrepreneurial or ownership class. It has moved into positions of prominence as hired functionaries following civil rights and Black Liberation struggles. Its cultural cues come not only from its African American heritage but also from its Euro-American yearnings. This sector profits from and is hurt by the medicalization and criminalization of individual deviance. By sensationalist and racist labeling of behavior and distorted equivalences, alleged deviance is shifted to whole groups. Symbolic transformation is exemplified in the mass media imagery of cities being terrorized by marauding gangs of young Black males. There are simultaneous calls for Afrocentricity, for mentors "who have made it," and for the death penalty. Symbolic codes are established: *inner city, drug dealing, crime, violence,* and now *AIDS* become terms and ways of organizing perceptions of and feelings toward racial and ethnic groups. African American elites perceive themselves to be forced into association and disassociation with the so-called underclass (itself a conceptual code that obscures structural causes of behavior). The salaried Black and

White middle class lives a tenuous existence. Both professional segments may have a reliance on sustaining problems and channeling people into social containment institutions.

Concluding Considerations

AIDS is geographically and socially being increasingly shown as an epidemic of people of color. Yet committed African American professionals report they are shut out or minimally included in research protocols, significant funded research, prominent publications, and other spheres of influence. If segments of African America's molders of cultural life disown the epidemic, while others are excluded from participating in its representation and resolution, who can be catalysts for progressive empowerment and change?

While White gays increasingly linked safety and freedom around their mobilizing to confront HIV issues, African Americans tended to view avoidance as a way of protecting their social status. Personal distancing from the crisis may be a mechanism for defining one's life and managing dynamics of racism, sexism, paternalism, and neocolonialism. How does a group "own" a problem if it is unable to exercise power and choice? How do organizations negotiate stable and sensible meanings in a context of varied ideologies, conflicting images, and often incoherent narratives about AIDS? When institutional resources are controlled by Whites, it may be difficult for people of color to assume cultural responsibility for helping to plan, implement, and evaluate policies and programs.

For many African Americans, drugs and AIDS are perceived as problems not because of their devastation but because they cause potential embarrassment. They are reminders that social mobility is fragile and linked to the representation of African to White America. Drug and AIDS wars may be perceived not as battles against plagues but as offensives against selected groups of people. Mobilizing around political metaphors about crucial crusades enlisting disposable colored elites is fraught with contradictions. African Americans, not unlike applied anthropologists, ask sober questions about the relationship of AIDS to culture and power: Who defines AIDS? Did cultural and/or political values, norms, and behavior create AIDS? Can culture eliminate AIDS (e.g., through biomedicine or new conceptions of morality)? Whose interests do science and research serve? What clues and lessons do we have from history?

HIV infection and AIDS dramatize linkages between individual action and social context. As an investigator of society, anthropology is becoming a clearer science of cultural and political construction. If it wishes to bear witness in the age of AIDS, it will have to consciously choose between either serving traditional powers or illuminating cultures of the dispossessed.

Despite their clear differences, there are some similarities between the social movements of African Americans, gays, and women. If studied and applied, they might provide instructive lessons for consistently mobilizing efforts to reduce the spread of HIV infection. Each has stressed self-empowerment, political socialization, the development of empirically based theory grounded in activism, situating programmatic and spontaneous activity in a useful theory of struggle, ideological clarity, supremacy over the symbols of group identity and representation, respect for cultural constructions of reality, and recognition that struggles for competing notions of survival, development, and liberation lead to changes in meanings, strategies, and tactics. Regardless of race, gender, or sexual orientation, studying AIDS involves the dynamics of class, power, and culture.

As anthropologists and sociologists appreciate and document these variables, they will have a far greater potential to address social dynamics of mobilization. They may even overcome their own closeted feelings of marginality and develop a sense of greater worth.

Appendix

The Appendix tables are based on a total of 146,746 U.S. cases of AIDS reported to the CDC through August 31, 1990, which includes Guam, U.S. Pacific Islands, Puerto Rico, and the U.S. Virgin Islands. Excluding U.S. dependencies, possessions, and freely associated independent nations, the U.S. total was 142,426.

Table 7.1. AIDS Transmission Categories in the United States by Racial/Ethnic Group: White and Black

	White (not Hispanic)		Black (not Hispanic)	
	Cumulative Number	(%)	Cumulative Number	(%)
Adults/Adolescents:				
homosexual/bisexual male	61,586	(76)	14,486	(36)
intravenous (IV) drug abuser	6,309	(8)	15,617	(39)
homosexual male & IV drug abuser	5,703	(7)	2,624	(7)
hemophilia/coagulation disorder	1,078	(1)	84	(0)
heterosexual cases	1,564	(2)	4,523	(11)
transfusion, blood components	2,426	(3)	576	(1)
other/undetermined	1,908	(2)	1,958	(5)
subtotal	80,574	[100]	39,861	[100]
Children:				
hemophilia/coagulation disorder	87	(16)	17	(1)
mother with/at risk of AIDS	322	(59)	1,200	(92)
transfusion, blood components	130	(24)	52	(4)
undetermined	7	(1)	36	(3)
subtotal	546	[100]	1,305	[100]
Total	81,120		41,166	

Table 7.2. AIDS Transmission Categories in the United States by Racial/Ethnic Group: Hispanic and Asian/Pacific Islander

	Hispanic		Asian/Pacific Islander	
	Cumulative Number	*(%)*	*Cumulative Number*	*(%)*
Adults/Adolescents:				
homosexual/bisexual male	9,078	(41)	662	(75)
intravenous (IV) drug abuser	9,039	(45)	37	(4)
homosexual male & IV drug abuser	1,393	(6)	16	(2)
hemophilia/coagulation disorder	99	(0)	15	(2)
heterosexual cases	1,271	(6)	31	(3)
transfusion, blood components	336	(2)	68	(8)
other/undetermined	1,116	(5)	57	(6)
subtotal	22,332	[100]	886	[100]
Children:				
hemophilia/coagulation disorder	22	(3)	3	(25)
mother with/at risk of AIDS	554	(85)	4	(33)
transfusion, blood components	55	(8)	5	(42)
undetermined	20	(3)		
subtotal	651	[100]	12	[100]
Total	22,983		898	

Table 7.3. AIDS Transmission Categories in the United States by Racial/Ethnic Group: American Indian and Alaskan Native

	American Indian/ Alaskan Native		Total	
	Cumulative Number	(%)	Cumulative Number	(%)
Adults/Adolescents:				
homosexual/bisexual male	112	(55)	86,113	(60)
intravenous (IV) drug abuser	34	(17)	31,114	(22)
homosexual male & IV drug abuser	26	(13)	9,776	(7)
hemophilia/coagulation disorder	8	(4)	1,288	(1)
heterosexual cases	10	(5)	7,418	(5)
transfusion, blood components	3	(1)	3,417	(2)
other/undetermined	12	(6)	5,095	(4)
subtotal	205	[100]	144,221	[100]
Children:				
hemophilia/coagulation disorder			129	(5)
mother with/at risk of AIDS	5	(100)	2,091	(83)
transfusion, blood components			242	(10)
undetermined			63	(2)
subtotal	5	[100]	2,525	[100]
Total	210		146,746	

References

Adam, B. D. (1987). *The rise of a gay and lesbian movement*. Boston: Twayne.

Altman, D. (1986). *AIDS in the mind of America*. Garden City, NY: Doubleday.

Brown, L. S., Evans, R., Murphy, D., & Primm, B. J. (1986). Drug use patterns: Implications for the acquired immunodeficiency syndrome. *Journal of the National Medical Association, 78*, 1145-1151.

Brown, L. S., Murphy, D. L., & Primm, B. J. (1987). Needle-sharing and AIDS in minorities. *JAMA, 258,* 1474-1475.

Des Jarlais, D. C., Friedman, S. R., & Hopkins, W. (1985). Risk reduction for the acquired immunodeficiency syndrome among intravenous drug users. *Annals of Internal Medicine, 103,* 755-759.

Des Jarlais, D. C., Friedman, S. R., & Stoneburner, R. L. (1988). HIV infection and intravenous drug use. *Reviews of Infectious Diseases, 10*(1), 151-158.

Friedman, S. R., Quimby, E., Sufian, M., Abdul-Quader, A., & Des Jarlais, D. C. (1988). Racial aspects of the AIDS epidemic. *California Sociologist, 11*(1-2), 55-68.

Mays, V. M., & Cochran, S. D. (1987). Acquired immunodeficiency syndrome and Black Americans: Special psychosocial issues. *Public Health Reports, 102,* 224-231.

New York State Governor's Advisory Committee for Black Affairs. (1987). *AIDS in the Black community: Programmatic directions for New York State* (Preliminary Report of the Human Services Subcommittee). New York: Author.

Patton, C. (1985). *Sex and germs: The politics of AIDS.* Boston: South End.

Quimby, E. (1987, October 1). [Testimony at Public Hearings held by the Human Services Subcommittee]. New York State Governor's Advisory Committee for Black Affairs, New York City.

Quimby, E. (1988, November 9-12). *Brooklyn's newest entrepreneurs: Drug dealing by Caribbean youth.* Paper presented at the annual meeting of the American Society of Criminology, Chicago.

Quimby, E. (1989a). Precarious dilemmas: Mobilizing Blacks against AIDS. In L. S. Harris (Ed.), *Problems of drug dependence* (National Institute on Drug Abuse Research Monograph 95, DHHS Pub. No. [ADM]90-1663). Washington, DC: Government Printing Office.

Quimby, E. (1989b, August 6-8). *Policy research implications of Caribbean drug dealing.* Paper presented at the annual meeting of the Society for the Study of Social Problems, Berkeley.

Quimby, E., & Friedman, S. R. (1988, August 21-23). *Emerging Black responses to AIDS in New York City.* Paper presented to the annual meeting of the Society for the Study of Social Problems, Atlanta.

Quimby, E., & Friedman, S. R. (1989). Dynamics of Black mobilization against AIDS in New York City. *Social Problems, 36*(4), 403-415.

Selwyn, P. A., Feingold, A. R., Hartel, D., Schoenbaum, E. E., Alderman, M. H., Klein, R. S., & Friedland, G. H. (1988). Increased risk of bacterial pneumonia in HIV-infected intravenous drug users without AIDS. *AIDS, 2*(4), 267-272.

Shilts, R. (1987). *And the band played on: Politics, people, and the AIDS epidemic.* New York: St. Martin's.

Stall, R. D., Coates, J., & Hoff, C. (1988). Behavioral risk reduction for HIV infection among gay and bisexual men. *American Psychologist, 43,* 878-885.

Stoneburner, R. L., Des Jarlais, D. C., Benezra, D., Gorelkin, L., Sotheran, J. L., Friedman, S. R., Schultz, S., Marmor, M., Mildvan, D., & Maslansky, R. (1988). Increasing mortality among narcotic users in New York City and its relationship to the AIDS epidemic. *Science, 242,* 916-919.

U.S. Centers for Disease Control (CDC). (1986). Acquired immunodeficiency syndrome (AIDS) among Blacks and Hispanics: United States. *MMWR, 35,* 655-666.

U.S. Centers for Disease Control (CDC). (1990a, February). *HIV/AIDS surveillance report.* Atlanta: Author.

U.S. Centers for Disease Control (CDC). (1990b, September). *HIV/AIDS surveillance report.* Atlanta: Author.

U.S. Department of Health and Human Services (DHHS). (1985). *Report of the Secretary's Task Force on Black and Minority Health: Vol. 1. Executive summary.* Washington, DC: Government Printing Office.

8

The Implications of Constructionist Theory for Social Research on the AIDS Epidemic Among Gay Men

MARTIN P. LEVINE

> The aims, then, of a sociological approach to homosexuality are to begin to define the factors—both individual and situational—that predispose a homosexual to follow one path as against others; to spell out the contingencies that will shape the career that has been embarked upon; and to trace out the patterns of living in both their pedestrian and their seemingly exotic aspects. Only then will we begin to understand the homosexual. This pursuit must inevitably bring us—though from a particular angle—to those complex matrices wherein most human behavior is fashioned.
>
> —Simon & Gagnon (1967, p. 185)

In this chapter, I examine the implications of constructionist theory for social research on the HIV (human immunodeficiency virus) epidemic within the gay community. My aim is to review the status of the existing social inquiry on the HIV epidemic among gay men; identify the cultural definitions of sexuality, homosexuality, and HIV disease embedded in this research; and conclude by proposing a constructionist approach to AIDS research.

Constructionism (symbolic interactionism) constitues a major theoretical paradigm within the social sciences (Coser, 1977). Drawing upon basic axioms within 20th-century European philosophy and the history of science

(Kuhn, 1962; Law & Lodge, 1984), constructionism includes three basic assumptions (Denzin, 1989). First, social reality is socially constructed: The objects that constitute social life lack intrinsic meaning. Instead, these objects take on meaning through human actions. The cultural definitions, symbols, and identities attached to these objects are thus acquired through the process of social interaction. Second, human interaction entails mental processes in which individuals fashion a point of view that accords with the behavior of other actors. These mental processes involve the manipulation of symbols, words, meanings, and languages. Consequently, social interaction is symbolic, emergent, negotiated—and frequently unpredictable. Third, self-reflexive conduct distinguishes human beings from other forms of life. Individuals are capable of shaping and directing both their own actions and those of other people.

The constructionist perspective transformed social science thinking about human sexuality (Gagnon & Simon, 1973). It challenged us to see the conceptual categories through which individuals interpret eroticism are not, as previously thought, as biologically or psychologically determined but are socially constituted (Simon & Gagnon, 1987). Culture, that is, provided the conceptual meanings through which people distinguished sexual feelings, identities, and practices. It thus effectively claimed that these definitions were culturally relative (Plummer, 1975).

Constructionism directly challenged the essentialist approach to homosexuality, which prevailed within the social sciences (Troiden, 1988). Essentialism regarded homosexuality as a form of gender inversion that arose from such presocial forces as genes, hormones, instincts, or specific kinds of developmental psychodynamics (Richardson, 1981). In other words, it viewed same-sex desire and its perceived behavioral pattern of gender nonconformity as "a manifestation of some" biological or psychological "inner essence" (Greenberg, 1988, p. 485). It regarded homosexuality as a distinct and separate form of being, with modes of expression that transcended time and place (Troiden, 1988).

Conversely, constructionism interpreted homosexuality as a conceptual category that varied between cultural and historical settings (Troiden, 1988). Definitions of same-sex eroticism were viewed as cultural inventions that were specific to particular societies at particular times. It also held that conceptualizations of homosexuality determined the forms same-sex eroticism took within a given a society (Greenberg, 1988). In other words, the social meaning of homosexuality shaped the domain of emotion, identity, and conduct associated with sex between men.

The anthropological and historical record supports constructionist propositions concerning the behavioral patterns associated with human sexuality (Ford & Beach, 1951; Gregerson, 1983). The enormous variation in the social meaning and organization of heterosexual and homosexual eroticism shown in this record discounts the possibility of a presocial origin for these behavioral patterns (Gagnon & Simon, 1973; Troiden, 1988). Instead, the historical and cross-cultural variability demonstrates how cultural definitions organize the forms of sexual expression both between and within the sexes (Adam, 1985).

Social Research on the
HIV Epidemic Among Gay Men

Epidemiological and public health concerns have largely framed the theoretical perspectives, research questions, and methodologies used in social inquiry on the HIV epidemic within the gay community. Epidemiological interest lay primarily in uncovering both the determinants and the distribution of HIV disease among gay men. Hence epidemiologists initiated studies of the social attributes and risk behaviors associated with the disease (Institute of Medicine, 1986). At first, mainly heterosexual researchers, typically physicians with public health or epidemiological backgrounds, conducted descriptive studies that used case reports and survey questionnaires to provide data regarding the geographic, sociodemographic, and life-style attributes of the original HIV cases (Oppenheimer, 1988). The survey instruments reflected to a great extent assumptions about a causal relationship between the illness and behavioral features of the urban gay life-style (Murray & Payne, 1988). The raging epidemic of sexually transmitted diseases during the 1970s within urban gay communities made many investigators suspect that the new disease was attributable to the prevailing life-style of drugs, discos, and anonymous sex (Oppenheimer, 1988). Hence the survey schedules usually asked numerous questions about erotic conduct and substance abuse.

Subsequent epidemiological inquiry became more analytic in orientation and designed case control and prospective studies to identify the specific risk factors associated with HIV infection and the rate of progression through the sequential stages of the disease (Institute of Medicine, 1986). Although more social scientists participated in the research, the investigators remained chiefly heterosexual physicians. Only a handful of gay men worked on these studies, but many were deeply or partially closeted. The case control studies attempted to identify the nutritional, residential, and life-style attributes that distinguished the gay AIDS (acquired immune deficiency syndrome) cases from the healthy gay or heterosexual controls (Oppenheimer, 1988). Generally, the gay cases were recruited from the practices of gay physicians. The prospective studies attempted to examine processes of disease progression over time among large cohorts of individuals thought to be at high risk for infection; survey questionnaires, physical examinations, and specimen collections (for laboratory and serological purposes) were used. Typically, the prospective studies enrolled large community-based convenience samples of gay and bisexual men who were recruited primarily from gay organizations, health facilities, or gathering places that were located in areas with elevated rates of HIV disease (Institute of Medicine, 1986). Only one study used a population-based (probability) sample that also included a heterosexual cohort (Winkelstein et al., 1987).

Public health interest lay primarily in prevention, that is, halting the spread of the disease among gay and bisexual men. Consequently, prevention-oriented investigators implemented prospective (longitudinal) or cross-sectional (at one point in time) studies of the magnitude and correlates of changes in those sexual practices or life-style features known or suspected to be associated with the transmission of HIV (Turner, Miller, & Moses, 1989). Again, most of the researchers were heterosexual physicians and social scientists. However, some were closeted or openly gay men, including a few of the principal investigators. Furthermore, most of the prospective studies were piggybacked onto broader investigations of the natural history of the disease. These studies commonly used self-administered questionnaires and community-based convenience samples of gay and bisexual men living mainly in epicenter areas (Turner et al., 1989). Only two prospective studies in San Francisco used probability-based samples (Communication Technologies, 1987; Winkelstein et al., 1987), and one prospective study in New York used face-to-face interviews (Bauman & Siegel, 1986; Siegel, Bauman, Christ, & Krown, 1988; Siegel, Mesagno, Jin-Yi Chen, & Christ, 1989).

Public health or psychological models of behavioral change shaped most of the attempts within these studies to identify the correlates of changes in risk practices. These models were drawn from either preexisting theories of health conduct or the attitudinal basis of social behavior. The models derived from theories of health conduct assumed that already identified predictors of health conduct were also correlates of changes in risk behavior for

HIV (Siegel et al., 1988). The recognized predictors of health behavior included (a) knowledge about the disease, (b) perception of vulnerability to the disease, (c) beliefs about the efficacy of health care, (d) accessibility to health or preventive care, (e) dispositional barriers to health or preventive care, (f) degree of affiliation within a social network, (g) normative structure of the social network, and (h) demographic characteristics such as age, class, race, residence, and relationship status (Cummings, Becker, & Maile, 1980). The assumed correlates of risk behavior for HIV were (a) knowledge of HIV etiology, transmission, and prevention; (b) perceived risk of HIV disease; (c) perceived efficacy of HIV risk reduction behavior; (d) perceived difficulty in sexual impulse control; (e) belief in biomedical technological cures or prevention for HIV disease; (f) degree of integration into gay social networks; (g) perceived peer support for HIV risk reduction; and (h) perceived level of emotional support from peer group (Emmons et al., 1986; Siegel et al., 1988).

The studies found that the predictors derived from models of health behavior poorly explained alterations in risk behavior for HIV (Becker & Joseph, 1988; Siegel et al., 1989; Stall, Coates, & Hoff, 1988). For example, Joseph et al. (1987) reported that the predictors taken from this model accounted for only 30% to 50% of the variability in longitudinal risk reduction behavior observed in their cohort of gay and bisexual men. The predictors used in their study included (a) knowledge of AIDS, (b) perceived risk of AIDS, (c) perceived efficacy of behavioral change, (d) perceived difficulty with sexual impulse control, (f) belief in biomedical cure or prevention for AIDS, (g) perceived social norms supportive of behavioral change, and (h) gay social network affiliation. Moreover, they believed that the inclusion of initial risk reduction behavior in their linear regression model explained most of the observed effect:

> Closer inspection of these results suggests, however, that this is primarily due to the inclusion of S1 behavior in the model; as has frequently been reported in analyses of longitudinal or panel data, many behaviors are relatively stable across time, and initial behavior is one of the strongest predictors of subsequent behavior. (Joseph et al., 1987, pp. 86-87)

Joseph and her associates (1987) also found that the effects of these predictors diminished over time. The cross-sectional analysis indicated a relationship between knowledge of AIDS, perceived risk of AIDS, perceived efficacy of behavioral change, perceived difficulty with sexual impulse control, belief in biomedical cure or prevention for AIDS, and perceived social norms supportive of behavioral change—with reductions in HIV-related risk practices. Nevertheless, the number and magnitude of these relationships either diminished or disappeared in the longitudinal analysis. To clarify, all of these factors except that of perceived efficacy had no effect on risk reduction from the first to the last assessment interval. In addition, the effect of perceived efficacy was greatly reduced.

Notwithstanding, several studies reported a strong association between two predictors derived from health behavior models and longitudinal risk reduction. These predictors included perceived peer support for HIV risk reduction and perceived level of emotional support from peer group. For example, Joseph and her co-researchers (1987) found that perceived social norms supportive of behavioral change was highly related to risk reduction over time. In addition, Siegel et al. (1989) reported an equally strong relationship between perceived adequacy of peer emotional support and longitudinal risk reduction.

Attitudinal models of behavioral change also shaped efforts within one of these studies to determine the correlates of risk behavior. Communication Technologies (1987) researchers assumed that the factors specified in Fishbein's (Ajzen & Fishbein, 1980) theory of the attitudinal basis of social behavior affected risk practices. Fishbein maintained that an individual's intention to behave in a certain manner reflected that person's beliefs about the attitudinal and normative status of this behavior. Indeed, an individual's beliefs informed that person's attitude toward the behavior, which may be either positive or negative. An individual's beliefs about the normative standing of a behavior in the eyes of other people and groups similarly influences that person's perception of the normative prescriptions and proscriptions affecting the behavior.

Following Fishbein, Communication Technologies (1987) investigators examined the extent to which beliefs about the risk, enjoyability, and normative status of HIV risk behavior influenced anal and oral risk practices with secondary partners during the 30-day period before the interview among a probability-based sample of gay and bisexual men in San Francisco. They found that enjoyability and perceived social norms significantly influenced participation in unprotected intercourse. For example, the correlation coefficient between enjoyment of anal intercourse with the exchange of semen and engagement in this practice was +.26. Similarly, the enjoyment of other unsafe practices was linked to participation in this act. The correlations between oral-anal relations, anal fisting, and oral intercourse with ejaculation—and anal sex with ejaculation—were, respectively, +.18, +.15, and +.13.

It is surprising that the researchers reported that the effect of enjoyability weakened for unprotected oral sex. The correlation between enjoyment of oral intercourse with the exchange of semen and the practice of this behavior was +.16. This effect reversed for enjoyment of safer erotic practices. The correlations between enjoyability of mutual masturbation, anal intercourse without ejaculation, oral sex without ejaculation, protected anal intercourse, and deep kissing—and oral sex with ejaculation—were, respectively, −.23, −.19, −.15, −.13, and −.13.

Furthermore, these investigators found significant associations between perceived social norms and engagement in unprotected sex. They reported, for example, that the correlation coefficient between the belief that friends disapproved of anal sex without a condom and anal intercourse with the exchange of semen was −.21; again, the relationship declined for unprotected oral sex. The correlation between the belief that friends disapproved of oral sex without a condom and oral intercourse with ejaculation was −.13.

Moreover, the researchers found little relationship between perceived risk of intercourse with semen exchange and participation in this behavior. The correlation between perceived risk of oral sex with ejaculation and the practice of this act was −.08. However, this association weakened for unprotected anal sex. The correlation between perceived risk of anal sex with ejaculation and engagement in this practice dropped to −.03.

Public health concerns about prevention also elicited efforts to evaluate the effect of HIV antibody testing and prevention campaigns upon risk behavior within the gay community (Office of Technology Assessment, 1988). Typically, these studies examined the impact of antibody testing or particular educational interventions on risk reduction among a community-based convenience sample of gay and bisexual men through self-administered questionnaires (Valdiserri, 1989).

Finally, public health interest in care for individuals with HIV disease fostered attempts to investigate HIV-related volunteering, coping behavior, emotional reactions, and social support (Morin, 1988). Again, through self-administered questionnaires or in-depth interviews, the studies explored these issues among either clinical or community-based samples of HIV-infected gay or bisexual men who frequently resided in areas that were the foci of the epidemic (Institute of Medicine, 1986).

Cultural Definitions Embedded in
Social Research on the
HIV Epidemic Among Gay Men

Epidemiological and public health-oriented social inquiry on the HIV epidemic within the gay community reflected prevailing cultural conceptualizations of homosexuality, sexuality, and HIV disease. An essentialist construction of same-sex eroticism informed much of the early epidemiological research on this epidemic. According to this definition, presocial forces engendered both homosexual desire and behavioral patterns: "Homosexuality" was a monolithic entity characterized by a common origin and life-style.

The background and training of the original band of epidemiological investigators predisposed them to hold an essentialist point of view. The initial researchers were chiefly heterosexual physicians (Astor, 1983) and, therefore, "outsiders" (Merton, 1972) to the gay world, who were recruited largely from the Centers for Disease Control's Division of Venereal Disease Control (Oppenheimer, 1988). Their medical schooling led them to hold essentialist constructions of homosexuality. Typically, they discounted social science findings concerning cross-cultural and historical variability in the social meaning and organization of homosexuality and the diversity of the sexual habits of U.S. gay men (Greenberg, 1988). Same-sex eroticism was regarded instead as either a psychologically or a physiologically induced pathology characterized by hyperpromiscuity.

The investigators' professional experiences corroborated essentialist assumptions about the erotic patterns of gay men. Prior to the epidemic, most of these researchers studied sexually transmitted diseases among gay men (Oppenheimer, 1988). It is not surprising that this research brought them into contact with gay men who were quite sexually adventurous and active. Hence they viewed multiple partners and esoteric acts such as anal fisting as characteristic of gay men's sexuality (Batchelor, 1984).

Most of the original epidemiological theories about the etiology of AIDS reflected essentialist constructions of homosexuality. Many investigators reasoned that the agent causing the disease was related to either a presocial determinant of same-sex desire or the urban gay life-style (Oppenheimer, 1988). For example, some felt that the genetic or hormonal determinants of homosexuality caused AIDS. Typically, they linked the disease to hypothesized genetic abnormalities in the immune system of gay men. Others thought that the urban gay life-style of promiscuity and recreational drug use was responsible for AIDS (Murray & Payne, 1988). The disease in this view was associated with either an unknown sexually transmitted agent or the ingestion of drugs or semen thought to cause immunosuppression.

Essentialist constructions also appeared in the initial epidemiological definitions of risk groups. At the onset of the epidemic, epidemiologists defined gay men as a group that was at high risk for AIDS. They based this classification on the early epidemiological findings that showed that the initial AIDS cases were overwhelmingly sexually active gay men who consumed recreational drugs. However, this categorization reflected essentialist perceptions about the behavioral patterns of gay men. It assumed that most gay men were at risk for the disease because they were commonly hyperpromiscuous drug users.

Essentialism blinded these researchers to the diversity of behavioral patterns within the gay community. Gay men vary widely in their sexual and drug habits (Bell & Weinberg, 1978; Jay & Young, 1977; Saghir & Robins, 1973). Only a small minority of gay men were promiscuous and took drugs. Furthermore, only those men within this minority who lived in areas with elevated rates of AIDS were at risk for the disease. In sum, the assumption that all gay men were at risk reflected a distorted view of the erotic and drug use patterns of gay men and the spatial distribution of the virus.

Moralistic and medical constructions of HIV disease to a large extent also informed much of the public health-oriented research on the epidemic among gay men. The available literature reveals four major definitions of HIV disease both among and within the societies affected by the epidemic: the moralistic, contagion, conspiratorial, and medical constructions. All four definitions differ in regard to the etiology, transmission, and prevention of the illness.

The moralistic definition maintains that HIV disease is a moral problem. In this view, the illness emerges not from a virus but from immoral actions. Disease results not from HIV as such but from promiscuity, homosexuality, and drug use. Obviously, this construction confuses etiology with transmission. It associates the cause of the disease with some of its behavioral routes of transmission. Predictably, of course, this definition sees traditional morality as the chief means of prevention. It considers abstinence from drugs, sodomy, adultery, and premarital sex as the only way to avoid infection.

The contagion definition views HIV disease as a public health problem. According to this construction, HIV is a highly contagious virus that can be casually transmitted in a manner similar to the common cold. Consequently, effective prevention requires the segregation or quarantine of individuals infected with HIV.

The conspiratorial construction regards HIV disease as a political problem. In this view, the epidemic constitutes politically planned genocide for socially stigmatized peoples. In other words, homophobic, racist, and classist elites either launched or inadequately responded to the epidemic to kill morally, racially, or economically devalued populations. The genocidal crusades supposedly took two forms: In the first, the U.S. elite instructed the Central Intelligence Agency to invent and disseminate HIV as part of a germ warfare campaign against gay men, drug addicts, promiscuous heterosexuals, racial minorities, welfare recipients, and the populations of Africa and Latin America. In the second, national elites prevented North American and European governments from providing adequate funding for HIV-related care, research, and prevention in order to decimate gay and Third World communities. It is not surprising that this definition sees political protest and pressure as the mechanism for forcing North American and European governments to provide the needed resources for care, research, and prevention.

The medical construction views HIV disease as a medical problem. According to this definition, medical science has established both the etiology and the transmission of the illness. A multitude of medical studies indicate that the disease results from a newly discovered virus, called HIV, which is transmitted by the exchange of infected body fluids such as blood, semen, and vaginal secretions during such behavioral practices as needle sharing and unprotected (without a condom) intercourse. In addition, this construction views behavioral change as the most effective means of prevention. In the absence of an immediate cure or treatment, halting the behavior implicated in the transmission of the virus through explicit and culturally specific educational interventions constitutes the most effective procedure for preventing infection.

The moralistic and medical constructions of HIV disease influenced the risk classifications for sexual behavior used in public health-oriented research on the epidemic. The moralistic definition considered promiscuity to be a high-risk behavior. The medical model defined this practice as primarily unprotected intercourse. These classifications were uncritically incorporated into most studies of the changes in erotic conduct among gay men. These studies usually measured the frequency and correlates of promiscuity (partner numbers) and unprotected intercourse.

The classification of promiscuity as a risk behavior was scientifically indefensible (Murray & Payne, 1988). As the medical evidence makes abundantly clear, promiscuity was not implicated in the transmission of HIV. The virus was not spread through numbers of sexual partners but through the erotic acts performed with these partners. Risk was not associated with how many partners an individual had but with the erotic acts that person engaged in with these partners.

The medical construction also affected the way in which intercourse was conceptualized. The medical definition regarded intercourse as a health behavior because it could potentially transmit HIV. Moreover, it categorized intercourse as either healthy or unhealthy on the basis of this potential. Protected intercourse was healthy because there was a low risk of transmission. Conversely, unprotected intercourse was unhealthy because it carried a high risk of transmission.

Most of the studies of the correlates of changes in erotic behavior used the medical construction of intercourse. They construed intercourse as a "health behavior" similar to smoking, drinking, eating, and wearing a seat belt. This medicalization of intercourse accounts for the use of models of health behavior within these studies. These studies assumed that the already identified predictors of health conduct were also correlates of changes in risk behavior among gay men because they conceptualized intercourse as a health behavior.

The use of theories of health behavior can be faulted on three grounds: First, these theories denuded intercourse of its social, cultural, and psychological meanings and motivations. Typically, people participated in intercourse for reasons that have more to do with these meanings than with health concerns. Second, these theories stripped intercourse of its interpersonal context. Models of health behavior were predicated upon individual actors making solitary decisions about health-related practices. However, decisions around intercourse were fundamentally dyadic. Choices around intercourse always involved negotiations with another person. Third, these theories denuded intercourse of its noncognitive motivations. Models of health behavior assumed that individuals take health-related actions on the basis of cognitive assessment of such factors as the possible costs and benefits of this practice. Nevertheless, decisions around intercourse are often influenced by deep-seated psychological needs that may lie outside the individual's immediate awareness.

Conclusion

The constructions embedded in social inquiry on the HIV epidemic among gay men led to the crucial questions about the disease being inadequately formulated. Essentialist constructions of homosexuality led epidemiologists to distort the social reality of HIV infection within the gay community. The belief that AIDS was linked to a presocial determinant of same-sex desire wastefully misdirected initial research efforts into the etiology of the illness. In addition, the classification of homosexuals as a risk group for AIDS foolishly ignored the diversity of erotic, residential, and drug use patterns among gay men.

These essentialist definitions also impeded attempts at HIV prevention. As several studies indicated, the perception that AIDS was a gay White disease seriously hindered prevention efforts within the Black and Hispanic communities and among sexually active heterosexuals, especially adolescents and college students (Valdiserri, 1989). Moreover, the perception that AIDS was an illness associated with the urban gay life-style impeded prevention crusades within the gay community. Many gay men justified engaging in unprotected intercourse on the grounds that neither they nor their partner was promiscuous, took drugs, or lived in cities that were the foci of the epidemic (Stall et al., 1988).

The medical construction of HIV disease also distorted efforts at prevention. The medicalization of sexual intercourse as health conduct prompted the use in prevention of models of health behavior change and decision making. However, these models were inapplicable because they stripped intercourse of its social, cultural, and psychological meanings and motivations. It is not surprising, then, that these models could not adequately explain risk behavior among gay men. Indeed, the most commonly identified correlates of behavioral change within this population were social in nature. As many studies demonstrated, age, ethnicity, peer norms, relationship status, and geographic location were associated with risk reduction (Stall et al., 1988).

The constructionist approach to this research must recontextualize the behavior involved with HIV disease in several ways: First, this approach directs our attention to the psychic and sociocultural meanings and motivations attached to intercourse among gay men. Second, this approach presupposes the use of methodologies better suited for capturing the domain of meaning and motivations associated with HIV illness. To date, most research has used survey instruments constructed from a priori assumptions about the nature of the problem typically held by outsiders to the gay community. Constructionism demands the use of qualitative techniques that can tap into the definitions of the situation prevailing among gay men. Third, this approach broadens the research questions asked about the effect of HIV within the gay community. Until now, these questions have reflected epidemiological and public health interests, either the distribution and determinants of the disease or the magnitude and correlates of behavioral change among gay men. A focus on the subjective experience raises entirely new questions such as those concerning the loss of a way of life or cultural community. Ultimately, our understanding of these meanings and motivations will take us to the matrix from which all sexual behaviors are derived—the sociocultural order.

References

Adam, B. D. (1985). Age, structure, and sexuality: Reflections on the anthropological evidence on homosexual relations. *Journal of Homosexuality, 11,* 19-33.

Ajzen, I., & Fishbein, M. (1980). *Understanding attitudes and predicting social behavior.* Englewood Cliffs, NJ: Prentice-Hall.

Astor, G. (1983). *The disease detectives.* New York: New American Library.

Batchelor, W. F. (1984). AIDS: A public health and psychological emergency. *American Psychologist, 39,* 1279-1284.

Bauman, L. J., & Siegel, K. (1986). Misperception among gay men of the risk for AIDS associated with their sexual behavior. *Journal of Applied Social Psychology, 78,* 329-350.

Becker, M. H., & Joseph, J. G. (1988). AIDS and behavioral change to reduce risk: A review. *American Journal of Public Health, 78,* 394-410.

Bell, A. P., & Weinberg, M. S. (1978). *Homosexualties: A study of diversity among men and women.* New York: Simon & Schuster.

Communication Technologies. (1987). *A report on designing an effective AIDS prevention campaign strategy for San Francisco: Results from the fourth probability sample of an urban gay community.* San Francisco: San Francisco AIDS Foundation.

Coser, L. A. (1977). *Masters of sociological thought: Ideas in historical and social context* (2nd ed.). New York: Harcourt Brace Jovanovich.

Cummings, K. M., Becker, M. H., & Maile, M. C. (1980). Bringing the models together: An empirical approach to combining variables used to explain health action. *Journal of Behavioral Medicine, 3,* 123-145.

Denzin, N. K. (1989). *The research act: A theoretical introduction to sociological methods.* Englewood Cliffs, NJ: Prentice-Hall.

Emmons, C., Joseph, J. G., Kessler, R. C., Wortman, C. B., Montgomery, S. B., & Ostrow, D. G. (1986). Psychosocial predictors of reported behavior change in homosexual men at risk for AIDS. *Health Education Quarterly, 13,* 331-345.

Ford, C. S., & Beach, F. A. (1951). *Patterns of sexual behavior.* New York: Harper & Row.

Gagnon, J., & Simon, W. (1973). *Sexual conduct: The social sources of human sexuality.* Chicago: Aldine.

Greenberg, D. F. (1988). *The construction of homosexuality.* Chicago: University of Chicago Press.

Gregerson, E. (1983). *Sexual practices: The story of human sexuality.* New York: Franklin Watts.

Jay, K., & Young, A. (1977). *The gay report: Lesbians and gay men speak out about sexual experiences and lifestyles.* New York: Summit.

Joseph, J. G., Montgomery, S. B., Emmons, C., Kessler, R. C., Ostrow, D. G., Wortman, C. B., O'Brien, K., Eller, M., & Eshleman, S. (1987). Magnitude and determinants of behavioral risk reduction: Longitudinal analysis of a cohort at risk for AIDS. *Psychology and Health, 1,* 73-96.

Kuhn, T. S. (1962). *The structure of scientific revolutions.* Chicago: University of Chicago Press.

Law, J., & Lodge, P. (1984). *Science for social scientists.* London: Macmillan.

Merton, R. K. (1972). Insiders and outsiders: A chapter in the sociology of knowledge. *American Journal of Sociology, 78,* 9-47.

Morin, S. F. (1988). AIDS: The challenge to psychology. *American Psychologist 43,* 838-842.

Murray, S. O., & Payne, K. W. (1988). Medical policy without scientific evidence: The promiscuity paradigm and AIDS. *California Sociologist, 11,* 13-54.

Office of Technology Assessment. (1988). *OTA Staff Paper: How effective is AIDS education?* Washington, DC: U.S. Congress.

Oppenheimer, G. M. (1988). In the eye of the storm: The epidemiological construction of AIDS. In E. Fee & D. M. Fox (Eds.), *AIDS: The burdens of history* (pp. 267-301). Berkeley: University of California Press.

Plummer, K. (1975). *Sexual stigma: An interactionist account.* Boston: Routledge & Kegan Paul.

Richardson, D. (1981). Theoretical perspectives on homosexuality. In J. Hart & D. Richardson (Eds.), *The theory and practice of homosexuality* (pp. 5-37). Boston: Routledge & Kegan Paul.

Saghir, M. T., & Robins, E. (1973). *Male and female homosexuality: A comprehensive investigation.* Baltimore: Williams & Wilkins.

Siegel, K., Bauman, L. J., Christ, G. H., & Krown, S. (1988). Patterns of change in sexual behavior among gay men in New York City. *Archives of Sexual Behavior, 17,* 481-497.

Siegel, K., Mesagno, F. P., Jin-Yi Chen, & Christ, G. (1989). Factors distinguishing homosexual males practicing risky and safer sex. *Social Science and Medicine,* pp. 561-569.

Simon, W., & Gagnon, J. H. (1967). Homosexuality: The formulation of a sociological perspective. *Journal of Health and Social Behavior, 8,* 177-185.

Simon, W., & Gagnon, J. H. (1987). A sexual scripts approach. In J. H. Geer & W. T. O'Donohue (Eds.), *Theories of human sexuality* (pp. 363-384). New York: Plenum.

Stall, R. D., Coates, T. J., & Hoff, C. (1988). Behavioral risk reduction for HIV infection among gay and bisexual men: A review of the results from the United States. *American Psychologist, 43,* 878-885.

Troiden, R. R. (1988). *Gay and lesbian identity: A sociological analysis.* Dix Hills, NY: General Hall.

Turner, C. F., Miller, H. G., & Moses, L. E. (Eds.). (1989). *AIDS: Sexual behavior and drug use.* Washington, DC: National Academy Press.

Valdiserri, R. O. (1989). *Preventing AIDS: The design of effective programs.* New Brunswick, NJ: Rutgers University Press.

Winkelstein, W., Jr., Samuel, M., Padian, N. S., Wiley, J. A., Long, W., Anderson, R. E., & Levy, J. A. (1987). The San Francisco Men's Health Study: III. Reduction in human immunodeficiency virus transmission among homosexual/bisexual men, 1982-86. *American Journal of Public Health, 76,* 685-689.

9

"IV Drug Users" and "Sex Partners": The Limits of Epidemiological Categories and the Ethnography of Risk

STEPHANIE KANE
THERESA MASON

In the popular and scientific discourse on HIV and AIDS in the United States, the epidemiological concept of "risk group" has sustained an inordinate influence throughout the first decade of the epidemic. Questions about who gets a disease and to what group they belong are initial investigative ques-

AUTHORS' NOTE. Research was funded by the National Institute on Drug Abuse (NIDA) through National AIDS Demonstration Research (NADR) grant 5R-18-DAO-5285 and contract 271-87-8208. Portions of this chapter were presented at the annual meetings of the American Anthropological Association in Washington, D.C., in a session organized by Mason and Kane titled "Ethnographic Inquiry and Social Action: The AIDS Crisis." An earlier version of this chapter was presented at the Wenner-Gren symposium, AIDS Research: Issues for Anthropological Theory, Method, and Practice, in Estes Park, Colorado, June 25-July 11, 1990. Mason thanks the leadership and staff of the Health Education Resource Organization (HERO) in Baltimore, who helped direct and conduct the project under a subcontract with the University of Illinois. She also thanks the following individuals on the Baltimore project for research assistance and discussion, particularly Dottie Estes, Benita Paschall, Vernessa Murphy, Myron Johnson, James Maxwell, Carolyn Smith-Bey, Mickey Applegarth, and Patricia Brager. Kane thanks the people on the Chicago project, especially Claude Rhodes for his wisdom and experience, and Wendell Johnson, Dana Nicholas, Oscar Tanner, Sinia Harper, and Lessie Jean Williams for research assistance and discussion. We both gratefully acknowledge the support of Wayne Wiebel, the principal investigator. We would also like to thank the Wenner-Gren Foundation for Anthropological Research for making the symposium and this publication possible.

tions and should give way soon to questions about risk factors and behavior (Frankenberg, 1990). This shift has been slow and difficult in the case of the HIV/AIDS epidemic. Much critical commentary has been devoted to the reasons for and effects of this phenomenon, including the distancing, stigmatizing, and blaming of already stigmatized individuals and groups (e.g., see Crimp, 1987; Fee & Fox, 1988; Watney, 1987).

This chapter examines some problems that the emphasis on social groups as risk groups poses, for ethnographic research that is undertaken as part of larger epidemiological and prevention projects. The problems might be more positively framed as challenges and issues that confronted us as we pursued research and writing on "IV drug users" (Mason) and their "sex partners" (Kane), respectively. Ethnographic representations of some contexts of risky behaviors are provided by each author as illustrations of the complex social, economic, and political realities constituting risk of HIV infection and AIDS.

Background of the Research

Starting in 1987 and during the course of the next several years, the National Institute on Drug Abuse (NIDA) funded research demonstration projects around the United States and Puerto Rico to target IV drug users, their sexual partners, and prostitutes for the purpose of preventing HIV transmission through education and behavior change. One of the more successful and widely emulated models was developed by Dr. Wayne Wiebel (1988) at the University of Illinois at the Chicago School of Public Health. The model, known as "Indigenous Leader Outreach to IV Drug Users," is based on work conducted at the University of Chicago in the 1970s, which combined epidemiological and ethnographic research methods to study and intervene in outbreaks of heroin use known as "epidemics" (Hughes, 1977; Hughes & Jaffe, 1971). The model assumes that street-based drug distribution sites where users go to purchase (*cop*) illegal drugs are key nodes in the social networks of drug injectors. Former drug users known and respected by active users in these areas are employed as HIV educators to return to their former *hangouts* near *copping* areas and act as catalysts for the cultural changes necessary to reduce the prevalence of high-risk behaviors. Ethnographers play a crucial role, as our research helps determine the factors influencing high-risk practices such as "needle sharing" or unprotected sexual intercourse. In addition, ethnographic researchers assess the nature and extent of the cultural change occurring as a result of prevention education.

In 1987, Wiebel established three storefront field stations in ethnically diverse high drug sales and use areas in Chicago as part of the first set of

NIDA research demonstration grants. Ethnographers were placed at each field station as managers and researchers. A year after the project was established, Wiebel received a contract from NIDA to replicate the project in Baltimore, Maryland; Denver, Colorado; and El Paso, Texas. One of the authors, Mason, was hired in 1988 as the ethnographer to help the staff of a well-respected AIDS service organization known as HERO to establish and evaluate the project in Baltimore. Kane was hired later that year to conduct ethnographic research on sex partners of IV drug users at the Chicago project.

The Challenge: Turning Epidemiological Categories into Ethnography

The range of issues that confront ethnographers undertaking such an epistemologically complex and politically charged task is broad. In this chapter, we will address two kinds of problems we faced when provided with risk group categories as the social unit of our research.

In the case of the category of "IV drug users," one prominent concern of Mason's was the potential for the imagery and language of cultural analysis to further exoticize, stereotype, and isolate an already despised sector of communities (Mason, 1989). This posed ethical and representational challenges, given the significance of one's own interpretations for assessing the efficacy of public health programs in a political climate increasingly unfavorable to the illegal behaviors that define the "group" of drug injection users. The most salient limitation of the risk group category "sex partner" that Kane faced was the lack of correspondence between this category and any shared social scene and identity as such as well as the limitations imposed on her methodologies, given the separate risk group structure of the project (Kane, 1991).

We devised theoretical and methodological frameworks for the research to counter the abstract and fragmented categories of risk groups. It became clear that the research and analysis must take place in an expanded field, which includes the political economy of the epidemic and the research itself (see Koptiuch, in press). There must be a strategic self-consciousness about the construction of one's own narratives, particularly as they compete with and counter the simplifying narratives of epidemiology and of popular media. Finally, the social practices described must be grounded in the specific details of people's everyday lives, and yet they must include attention to the complex and broader constraints affecting the behavior that places people at risk for HIV infection.

Research on Injection Drug Users:
Baltimore (Mason)

The funding and design of the Baltimore project, as with most of the NIDA demonstration research projects, focused initially on the risk category "IV drug users" and, more specifically, on those who were not currently in drug treatment programs. Mason's role as "Ethnographic Coordinator" was to assure that all facets of the education and the evaluation research were socially and culturally grounded in the understanding of the "norms" and practices of drug injectors in the targeted copping areas.

It quickly became evident to Mason that her research was entering a realm of politically charged public discourse wherein she was as likely to be in dialogue with the press, policymakers, and politicians as with her fellow social scientists. This was so because the risk group category that was to be the basis of her ethnographic research coincided with a criminal category that, in the imagery and structure of current political discourse, was made increasingly to represent a major threat to the well-being of the social, and now—due to the HIV epidemic—physical, body of the "general population." Anticrime and antidrug rhetoric exploded into full military metaphor with the institution of the most recent "war on drugs" by the Bush administration in Washington in 1989, and the consequent drama of television and print media coverage further emphasized the terror and threat that drug users and dealers in the inner cities posed for law-abiding and conventional citizens.

Mason worked with a team of former addicts in targeted *copping* areas in two of the poorest neighborhoods in a city of poor neighborhoods. One was in an African American public housing project and the other was in a predominantly European American neighborhood of mixed residential and commercial buildings. Administrative duties and related demands of the job prevented her from spending the majority of her time in these neighborhoods in the classical tradition of fieldwork. Still, she was able to *hang out* in the areas where drug users congregated—usually accompanied by at least one other worker—to become familiar to and with a number of the regulars. Although she was expected to focus her interviewing on those who injected drugs, observations and conversations with people in public areas and in the homes of some provided a window into the broader contexts of the lives of those who habitually pursued illegal drugs. Observing the complex social and market ties that bound users with varying degrees of involvement in the drug life to one another and to those who did not use illegal drugs, Mason found the concept of a drug subculture to be of limited value in accounting for many of the situations of risk she was encountering.

To be sure, in the areas where she worked, there were the classic hallmarks of a culturally distinct scene present among a segment of those habitual drug users she met: an insider's body of knowledge, rules of appropriate behavior, an argot. However, understanding the effects of the drug market and low enforcement practices on relationships and exchanges among drug users appeared more germane to understanding much HIV-related risk taking. Although the well-known ethnographies of the subculture of heroin users in earlier eras clearly demonstrated the shaping effects of the illegal drug business and the law (e.g., Agar, 1973; Preble & Casey, 1969), their effects have not been foregrounded in much recent AIDS literature (exceptions include Koester, 1989). The current political climate requires a special awareness of the potential distortions inherent in the language of cultural interpretation, for conveying both the nature of the contemporary illegal drug use phenomenon and the political and policy implications of one's interpretations.

About Using Others' Needles:
Stories from Two Drug Injectors

The situations of two drug injectors as they attempt to incorporate the implications of messages about risk reduction for HIV into their lives are described below. Mason encountered both as she accompanied the outreach team into a predominantly African American public housing project in 1988-1989.[1] The educational strategy depended on sustaining regular contact with the large number of residents, visitors, and those just passing through who constituted the targeted street drug distribution network. Both of the individuals described here were part of that network, although they identified and participated in the *drug game* in distinctly different ways. In such neighborhoods, unemployment and poverty have become concentrated as a result of intended and unintended consequences of housing and other public and private sector policies in recent decades. And it is in these areas that the illegal drug distribution system offers a range of advantages and services to purchasers in addition to the drugs themselves. Residents and other regulars can transform special knowledge and social connections into the financial means to support basic needs or, more likely, an addiction or more casual drug use (*pleasuring*) by helping guide people to the best drugs, making the purchases for them, and perhaps offering a place for them to get high. Such services spring up around neighborhoods where drugs are sold because of the pervasive fear and risk of arrest for possession, a fact that makes it highly desirable to minimize time and space covered with drugs or paraphernalia on one's person. Hence a kind of drug-centered social life flourishes around the business—often mixed with social—exchanges between drug users and nondrug users alike in these neighborhoods and from other parts of town. The residents and regulars who provide the services are often acting as buffers between those less knowledgeable about the drug game and the criminal justice system, because their "service" involves taking a constant risk of arrest and incarceration.

Mike's dilemma: "Dope has become part of my life." "Mike" had talked with the street outreach health educators on a number of occasions before Mason first spoke with him in the fall of 1989. The team had helped him get into a four-day "detox" program that summer, but this did not provide a serious alternative to his 25-year addiction to heroin. It merely helped him to cut back his use. In the meantime, he was making an effort to acquire a medical assistance card so that he could afford a more intensive form of treatment. From the first moment we met, Mike was expressing fears about his health. Some health professional had warned him about a form of hepatitis that could be contracted by drinking after someone else from a bottle or glass, a practice that is common among his friends and associates who *hang out* and drink wine in the projects. This advice exasperated him, because he was already a "nervous wreck" about HIV, because he *knows* it only takes one time with a dirty needle to get it. He said he already has to worry about keeping his own *works* (needle and syringe), cotton, and water, and he has become *afraid* when he *hooks up with* (pools his money with) someone to go and buy some *dope* (heroin).

Mike was engaged in an internal struggle between his desire to get off drugs and his dependence on heroin and *the life* to which he was already deeply connected through his constant pursuit of the drug over the years. He was 42 years old at the time and had been shooting drugs since he was 17. "I enjoyed it then and I enjoy it now. And as bad as I want to stop, I mean I really want to stop, but it's so much shit that's happening in my life that—I don't know. Maybe I said that wrong. Dope has become part of my life, it's just become part of my life."

By saying that dope is part of his life, Mike isn't just referring to his physical dependence on the drug, although he says that he can't make it through the day without getting his *blast* (shot) in him. His self-image, his reputation, are tied up with his mastery of the knowledge and skills needed to survive in the rough world centered on illegal drugs. Respect is very important to him, and he feels he has the respect of older and younger people in his community. As he put it:

> I often wonder if I wasn't a *dope fiend*—which I am—I wonder if I would have that same type of respect. I have respect because of the things I have done during my years of *shooting* dope. I know everything about it, the ups, the downs and the turnarounds. I know all about it, and I often wonder if people would respect me if it was just me, Mike!

Mike sees his participation in the drug world as a career; but, in the eyes of the law, and of the "square world," he is a criminal. But, from his perspective, he is simply *maintaining,* keeping up a good appearance, surviving, and making his *hustles work* for him so that he can avoid *being sick* (going through withdrawal)—taking care of himself.

An important part of taking care of himself these days is avoiding arrest. Like many older addicts—and surviving into his forties qualifies him as "older"—Mike has a criminal record, in fact, is on parole. That means he risks spending a longer time in prison if he is arrested, and he doesn't have that much time left. This limits his *hustling* to such activities as *copping* drugs for others, trading on his street skills and reputation. He says, "I can cop for people because people trust me with their money. No one can say that I ever *burnt* them [conned them out of drugs]!" Though he has occasionally worked temporary labor, Mike is uncomfortable in the "legit" world. He has specialized over the years in using his likable personality and "gift of gab" to develop relationships that brought him money. Though he has been a stickup man, he stresses that his skills lay in selling drugs and being a "ladies man" (somewhat like a pimp, only he insists, more "gentlemanly and kind"). He deplores the violence and disrespect that he says the young boys have brought into *the game.* It is anathema to his sense of respect, standards of skill in hustling, and desire to survive. The increasing dominance of violence and youth in the streets only adds to his growing dissatisfaction with that world.

It is ironic that Mike says he has always wanted to avoid looking like a *dope fiend.* That means he tries to be clean and well shaved, he dresses nicely, and he is careful to avoid scarring his body with *tracks.* His maneuvering around the stigmatized image of the addict is an important survival strategy, for, as elsewhere, image counts for a lot in the streets. It has taken on an even greater significance in his efforts to avoid arrest as he gets older.

The police look at me like, "This guy don't look like no *dope fiend!*" I don't even carry myself like one, I don't *hang* . . . even though I be in the projects, I don't be . . . when they come down I be with the guys drinking wine. It's all part of my staying out of jail. I might have a *bag of dope* in my pocket, ten bags, or whatever, but I hang with the people they don't fuss with.

Mike knows it's a risk to buy drugs, to even *hang* in the projects. But he's there a lot, because that's where he can use his knowledge and connections to spot people coming through and *cop* for them, thereby garnering drugs and a little money for himself. It's also where he says he feels most at home, with people he's known all his life. He lives with his *main woman* (in epidemiological parlance, his noninjecting sex partner) in a lower-middle-class neighborhood on the other side of town. He says there's plenty of drug use there, although it's more hidden, and he makes money by *copping* cocaine for some of his neighbors in the projects they so fear and despise. He speaks of his neighbors with a mixture of scorn for their complacency and a yearning for their respect.

In sum, because of the structure of the drug game, officially defined outside the law but in fact intricately shaped by it, Mike is having trouble pulling out of that world, even though the costs of not doing so appear greater and greater to him. His woman is always on him to get out, and he feels the distance it creates between him and his brothers and sisters and his six grown children now more than ever. "I stay away from them because I'm 42 years old and I should have done better by now."

And added to all that are his growing fears about his health, dominated by his fear of HIV. Just as the nature of the *drug game* keeps pulling him, so it creates strains on his ability to control his risk of contracting HIV. He says he prefers getting high at home. "My woman know what I do, my kids are grown, you know, so I can just go ahead in, and do what I got to do." As he described it:

I don't need nobody to get high with me. I can *hit* [inject] myself. I got my own *jank* [heroin]. And I can get high by myself. Now, if I should be say like crosstown somewhere, and I have to get high in a *shooting gallery* or someone else's place, then I will. [Mason: Why should you have to?] Because, it may be a situation where, they may have *sixties* [$60 bags of heroin] over there, so we supposed to be 30/30—$30 apiece. I may not have but $20, he got $40. So I got to go with him, so if he chooses to go to a shooting gallery, I got to go to a shooting gallery. So he *dumps* the whole thing [puts the heroin in a cooker to mix with water and heat it up]. I always keep my bleach with me all the time, since this thing came up about the bleach thing. I always keep my bleach and things, even if I got old *tools* [needle and syringe], because I have used old *tools*. But I always make sure I dump them and dump them in the bleach. I clean them as best I can in the bleach. Because I really believe that this bleach thing is helpful—it's saving lives! I really believe that—mine! So I use it! Over and over. I might shoot dope in an empty house—if I have to—I just may! You may go into a spot and they say "Well, boy, you can cop, but you got to do it here!" So that's why I always keep my bleach with me—all the time! [He is referring to bleach in 1-ounce plastic containers that our project and others distribute for the purposes of sterilizing paraphernalia.]

These examples of everyday situations where an addict may be faced with the necessity of injecting with works used by someone else were commonly described among adult users with whom Mason spoke. They demonstrate how the epidemiological term *sharing* can be misleading in its connotations of a subcultural ritual bonding. Rather, they reveal much about the vicissitudes and serendipities of acquiring and injecting drugs in an illegal world where even the most skilled and aware are in a constant struggle to maximize control over their lives.

For those like Mike, who have come to recognize the reality of the threat that AIDS poses for them personally, this struggle for control has become an even more formidable challenge to their survival skills. For the many kinds of risks he sees living the life he has lived, Mike has techniques for diminishing or avoiding risks. When Mason asked him what the difference was between taking those risks and the risk of getting AIDS, he replied forcefully: "You can't fight AIDS. You're dead. It's simple, direct, and it's to the point. You get AIDS you're dead." Mason objected that you're also dead when you get shot, and he replied: "No, no, no! You might get shot in the arm! I'll go against a person with a gun, than a person where I know that has dirty *tools*! I got a chance with that gun! I ain't got no chance with no AIDS!"

Ella: Risk reduction in everyday life. "Ella," who was 32 when Mason met her, had been shooting cocaine for four years, though she started using drugs now and then when she was 15. Unlike Mike, she does not think of herself as a *dope fiend*, and she is adamant about not hanging out in the public areas of the projects, areas where she says the "sure 'nuff dope fiends" are. "I'm not saying I'm this and that, but I ain't hanging with them." She told a story about how she had been waiting for the *drug man* down in the park once, and among the others waiting one woman was getting real impatient, exclaiming: "Where are they?" Ella soothed her, told her not to worry, they'd be there soon. The woman turned to her and said, "Well, I don't know what you worrying about! *Bippers* [snorters] don't *be* in a hurry!" Ella said, "I was real pleased. She didn't think I *fired* [shot drugs]. And I don't look like I do. That made me feel real good!" Ella, even more than Mike, distances herself from the image of the out-of-control addict who injects. She even puts vitamin E on the spots where she injects to avoid the telltale scars known as *tracks*.

In recent years, cocaine has become more and more popular as a drug to *shoot* in the neighborhoods where Ella has lived. The image of cocaine as a more acceptable, nonaddictive "rich man's high" lent getting high the sheen of respectability that allowed increasing numbers of men—and especially, they say, women—to be drawn into shooting drugs. A factor contributing to its popularity is the drop in price—around the nearby projects and outside Ella's rented row house, it was sold as cheaply as *nickel caps* ($5 capsules). As Ella told Mason during an interview, "We're not really addicted, me and my husband, just psychologically. When we get money we buy, but not every day. Because we don't have money to buy cocaine all the time." Cocaine may be cheap and plentiful in the poor neighborhood where Ella was living with her husband and three of her four children. She said she can just go out the door anytime and there it is. But the low unit cost is deceptive, because the *rush* with the highly *cut* (adulterated) cocaine sold around there lasts so little time, and the desire to keep doing it is so great, it winds up costing more, sometimes up to $200 to $300 on a binge, says Ella. "When I *do dope,* I get the urge to clean up, dress up the kids, we go places. When I *do caine,* all I want to do is sit up in my room and do *caine* all day. It bring you down. It bring you to your lowest point." The market reflects this difference in the effects of the drugs. People who sell *dope* (heroin) keep relatively regular daytime hours. Cocaine is sold at all hours of the day and night, to accommodate people on a *run*.

Ella has been with the father of her children for eight years, and he has seldom been able to hold a job for long. She eventually admits that he hits her, once broke her jaw, but she is afraid to leave him, because she says he is a decent father to her children and because she's afraid to be on her own. She is devoted to her sons, aged 3, 6, 7, and 15, and suffers tremendous guilt and worry that this delicate psychological and material balance she maintains in their lives will be thrown off and she will lose her children. She is estranged from her own mother, who has disapproved of her drug use over the years, and Ella says she will not help her with the children as a result. Even though her mother-in-law is supportive, she can't take the children because she is already caring for the four children of another daughter caught up in drugs. This makes it difficult for Ella to finish training programs, to get a job, or to get into a long-term detox or residential drug treatment program, which is what she periodically feels she needs. She worries about leaving her kids, worries about the 9-year-old getting pulled into *holding* (carrying drugs) for the dealers, who look for boys his age to minimize the threat of arrest. She feels like a failure for her inability to get off drugs completely, to turn her life around, and yet sometimes it seems like drugs are the main thing she and her husband have together, other than the children. To Ella, the contradiction of drug use is that it seemed to hold her family together and yet simultaneously threaten to destroy it.

When Mason first met them, Ella and her husband Ben were renting a row house near the projects, where the drug activity was heavy all the time, but they tried to confine their drug use to their home. A few friends from the nearby projects or from other parts of town might drop by to share their drugs or money in exchange for a place to get high away from the greater risk of arrest in areas nearer the center of activity or from spouses who didn't know about or disapproved of their shooting drugs. Some were *vics* (victims) who didn't know how to *cop* drugs and who trusted that Ella and Ben wouldn't let them *get burned.* They had heard the message about the danger of HIV infection through used syringes and needles, had relatives and friends who had died or were ill with the disease, and Ella said they each kept their own *works.* Still, despite precautions and in the course of everyday social life, the threat of infection suddenly became a more dramatic presence.

As Ella explained to the outreach team whom she had searched out with her frantic questions, one day she brought a woman who she *thought* was a friend home with her to get high. She had let the woman use her *tools* to shoot up and had used her husband's tools herself. Later on he came home and used one set of their tools to get high without cleaning them first, but he couldn't remember which one. They had since learned the woman had AIDS but had been afraid to tell her for fear of rejection. Not long after this incident, Ella and Ben began to use heroin to cut their expenses and their cocaine *habits* ("heroin will last you longer") and then *chilled out* (cut out drugs) completely. They went so far as to give up their row house to get away from the constant temptations of drugs in the area. All of this was motivated to a great extent by their fear of HIV infection, but, ironically, the move only transformed their risk. They moved in with his mother in another part of town. But, after a period of staying off drugs, helped by his mother who got them involved in church as a therapy, they began to *get high* again. Before, when they had their own place, they could simply stay there to *shoot up.* Now, they were forced to go to a friend's house or to a *shooting gallery* run by a friend as his way of getting drug money. They rented *tools* at the *gallery*, but Ella described the *gallery* as a clean one, where their friend had separate cups of water for everyone and directed people to the bleach as soon as they got their *tools.* (These *shooting gallery* practices, along with Ella and Mike's risk reduction, are indicators of the effects of outreach education projects such as ours.)

Overcrowding and tensions at her mother-in-law's house led Ella to move in with an aunt and precipitated a several-month-long period of homelessness for Ella, in which she struggled resourcefully to put together at least five temporary housing arrangements for herself and her children before she finally was able to get an apartment of her own again, where her husband joined them. During that time, she intermittently *shot* drugs, sometimes *hooking up with* people she didn't know to buy drugs and *get high*. She admits that, though she is careful to use either her own *tools* or the bleach, she can't say that there hasn't been a time or two where she's slipped up. As with her drug use, so it is with the risk of HIV infection—she struggles but sometimes feels unable to control it.

Subcultural Rituals Revisited

The common allusions in the popular media, policy reports, and social science research to the "ritual bonding" functions of needle sharing among drug injectors have contributed to the illusion of an autonomous subculture of IV drug users (Mason, 1989). Implicit in that image, we would suggest, is the notion that it is the subcultural "norms" that create the risk behavior in question. This reductionist notion of culture has had problematic repercussions in the popular depictions of public health interventions on behalf of drug users. It often supports the conclusion that nothing external to the subculture can be done (e.g., by health educators or policymakers) to bring about change in the extent of injection-related risk taking.[2]

The stories illustrating Mike's and Ella's situations provide a different angle on the issue. If one moves beyond the narrow framework of risk group—us and them, normal and abnormal—as a means of grasping the task of risk reduction, it becomes possible to view the larger conditions that produce situations of risk. The pervasive implications and repercussions of the laws designed to control the use of heroin and cocaine, for example, cannot be ignored by depicting them as a kind of backdrop to the real drama of risk behavior. Their effects on Mike's life are vast, indeed, have created a world he depends on, even as it threatens him. Ella and her family are forced to live in neighborhoods where most anyone can be at special risk of HIV infection and where efforts at change can bring additional risks that threaten the tenuous arrangements designed to protect. In sum, ethnographic perspectives on HIV risk must push the questions beyond an isolated concern with risky behavior to ask the more complex and difficult questions of how and why risk situations such as drug-dominated neighborhoods and economic exchanges are produced.

Research on Sex Partners:
Chicago (Kane)

As in all the federally funded AIDS demonstration research projects, and like that in Baltimore, research in Chicago was funded and organized according to an epidemiologically constructed typology of risk groups. The target population of the larger Chicago project was IV drug users of both genders who were not in treatment. But, as with projects that targeted IV drug users in treatment (Des Jarlais, Wish, & Friedman, 1987; Mondanaro, 1987), male IV drug users far outnumbered females in the Chicago sample. To make up in part for the disproportionate focus on men in IV drug user studies, and to expand research to include the "next wave" of the epidemic, sex partner studies targeting women were initiated nationally. *Sex partners* are defined as persons who have had sexual relations with intravenous drug users of the opposite sex. It is a residual category in that it does not include sex partners of IV drug users who are either IV drug users themselves or homosexuals. Kane was assigned to do ethnographic research on the sex partner category.

Although the primary goal was to reach women, research has established that heterosexual transmission of HIV is bidirectional with respect to gender, that is, men can transmit HIV to women and women can transmit HIV to men (Padian, 1987). It is important to note, however, that recent trends reveal a higher rate of male to female transmission as compared with female to male. Still, an unknown number of female IV drug users who are not in treatment have non-IV drug using male sex partners who are at risk of infection. As a consequence, male sex partners were not turned away when they were found. Actually, it was a struggle to find and recruit verifiable sex partners of either gender (also see Sterk, Friedman, Sufian, Stepherson, & Des Jarlais, 1989). As it turned out, a small sample of sex partners with a roughly 1:1 sex ratio (17 men and 18 women) was recruited.

Kane's assigned purpose, then, was to study the social context of risky heterosexual behavior in and around the IV drug user scene, primarily on Chicago's ethnically African American Southside. The storefront that served as the research station on Chicago's Black Southside was successful in becoming an extension of the street scene: IV drug users frequented the front rooms, talking, playing bridge and dominos—in general, reproducing forms of social interaction that take place every day on corners, in homes, prisons, abandoned buildings, and *shooting galleries*—except for the drug taking and selling, of course. In the back rooms, project staff carried out the business of interviewing and drawing blood. Although the station was an interesting place to do participant observation in the IV drug using scene, much to Kane's chagrin, participant observation of sex partners proved to be unrealistic. This was not due to the general and unpredictable danger of doing ethnography in ghetto streets, an activity that, as Philippe Bourgois's (1989) article in the *New York Times Magazine* communicates, requires more savvy, persistence, and courage than most ethnographers are prepared to demonstrate. Instead, it was due to the conceptualization of sex partners as a category of persons at risk.

Risk group categories are useful in tracking and predicting the course of the epidemic, although this too has been the subject of some debate (e.g., Murray & Payne, 1989; Treichler, 1988). As a starting point for ethnography, however, the category of sex partners presents a unique challenge: one that marks the limits of risk group typologies as a conceptual and pragmatic AIDS research strategy (Kane, in press), and one that forces ethnography to invent and develop new methods to critically mediate between scientific and local points of view. Unlike gay-identifying men or IV drug-identifying users who do constitute social scenes and networks, no such preexisting social ground can be assumed for sex partners. They are individuals who happen to share a particular kind of experience but not necessarily with each other. Having a relationship with an IV drug user does not imply having any kind of connection with someone else who happens to have a relationship with an IV drug user.

So much for traditional forms of participant observation. There are no "natural laboratories" already set up for ethnographic exploration here. The research context is an artifact of the epidemiologically rationalized bureaucratic penetration of the street world. As such, ethnographic method is narrowed to a predominantly discursive mode with its own rituals and secret codes appropriate to a setting created for AIDS research and intervention. And due to the prevailing tendency to use epidemiological categories as the basis for stereotyping all kinds of Others who could get AIDS (but, of course, not Us as ethnographers), one finds that one must orient one's analysis as much in opposition to the category that inspired funding for one's research as toward explicating the social and cultural dimensions of life for persons who find themselves so categorized.

The shrinking of ethnographic method around the interview form is not unyielding of data. Nor is it unprecedented in the history of anthropology (for instance, in ethnoscience). And limiting data collection to the interview form does counter, logistically and analytically, some of the unwieldy complexity of social interaction in urban environments. Still, without grounding in some kind of firsthand experience, it is more important than ever to be both accurate in conveying the complexity of any given situation and politically conscious in one's interpretations.

Being in the Life:
Stories from Two "Sex Partners"

Being in the life is an expression urban Americans use to refer to their involvement in activities oriented around the trade of drugs and sex. *The life* is a distinct state of being, a thorough reorganization of experience. A binary logic obtains: You are immersed in *the life*, or you are not, you tend toward the square. If you live in a community in which drug and sex trades prevail, either you work actively to distance yourself from the persons, places, and activities associated with *the life* or you tend to get drawn in. As exemplified by the IV drug user Ella from Baltimore, it is difficult to maintain a participant position on the edge or maintain what is called a "double life" for very long. But through time, it is possible to phase in and out of *the life*, as addicts in and out of recovery do, and it is also possible to have a steady partner who is in *the life* though you are not. In sum, there are social, spatial, and temporal distances constructed between *the life* and the square world, but there is back-and-forth movement between them. There have always been risks involved in *the life* (e.g., illness, financial ruin, prison), and the effects of these risks have tended to weigh on the families and friends of those in *the life*. With the advent of HIV and AIDS, the ante has been upped for everyone, even those who are only indirectly involved.

To communicate how being in *the life* may be experienced in Southside Chicago, and how that experience affects the level and kind of risk of HIV infection, Kane presents the discourse of two intelligent, young Black people who are involved in the life to different degrees. Their descriptions and explanations of the unique constellation of events and predispositions that compose their lives were articulated in confidential, tape-recorded ethnographic interviews in the storefront.

The 34-year-old man and 27-year-old woman whose discourse is presented here—we'll call them Thomas and Madison—are not representative of the Black community on the Southside or even of the sample of men and women Kane interviewed. But they are part of a large group of drug users who prefer a synthetic form of heroin called *karachi*. Karachi may be unique to Chicago, but common names are creatively applied to the same compounds in different places, so it's hard to say for sure. Although they say *karachi* is synthetic heroin, other chemicals such as quaalude and phenobarbital may be included in the mix (which may make it harder to kick than heroin alone). Karachi does not dissolve well in water, so it is sought after by people who *toot* (snort) drugs and disdained by people who *shoot* drugs. People who *toot* drugs, like Thomas and Madison, are not at risk of being directly infected with HIV through reused needles, but they may be indirectly affected by having unprotected penetrative sex with those who do place themselves at such risk. Thomas and Madison each had had a steady sexual relationship with an IV drug using partner, which was why they were recruited into the study of sex partners.

Madison's occasional karachi use. It was in the spirit of an entrepreneur that Madison got *hooked* on karachi: "I seen that it was fast money, cause the dope fiends are out there, you know, and all you have to do is find something that you don't do yourself. Then maybe you can make some money. But by me having it, I found myself doing more. I got to doing it everyday." About the time she started *tooting* karachi, Madison's boyfriend of a year and a half, in desperate need of cash, revealed his *habit* of *shooting*. She'd never seen the *track* marks because, as he told her and she told Kane, he had been *shooting* under finger- and toenails:

> He took his shoes off and his socks and he show me where he *shot dope* at. I didn't want to see him hurting like he was so I went on ahead and gave him the money. But I always told him, "I don't care what you do just please don't ask me to do that. I don't care what you do. That's you. But don't come to me and say 'Aw baby, you should *shoot* this, and try this.' Don't do that. Cause when you do that, you really done fucked up. I'm gonna be through with you for real." And he say, "Aw, I wouldn't even want you to get into this." But still, every chance he get, he was *shooting* this *shit*.

By the time of her interview, three years had passed since she had met her boyfriend, during which time she had enrolled in methadone treatment. This helped her to cut back from habitual to occasional use. She describes the change with treatment:

> Everyday I had to get *high*. But now, if I get *high*, it's not because I have to, it's because I want to get *high*. It's a mind thing. But the other times, I had to get *high* or I wouldn't feel well, you know. I couldn't get up. I couldn't do this. I couldn't do the daily things that needed to be done until I got *high*. But now, I don't get *high* every day. It's helping me to deal with life a little better cause I just used to run and run and get *high*.

Constant movement, circulation between drug-related social connections, is a major feature of the urban drug scene, a pressing dynamic motivated by the desire to replace the state of illness, accompanying the lack of a drug, with a state of wellness or being *high*, accompanying the presence of a drug. Desire for the drug may persist even after the pharmacological aspect of addiction is conquered. On any given day, Madison might still run into some of her old druggy friends on the bus, and they might say, "Oh, so and so got a good *blow* [drug that is *tooted*] over there." And that ticks something off in her mind. She goes along thinking that she wasn't going to get *high*, but after she has run into these people, and they told her how it was a good one, it just clicks in her head, "I got to get a *blow*. I'm going over there." That's if the money is already in her pocket, the money is burning her, and she's got to get it out. A bag of *karachi* costs $20 and the *high* lasts three to four hours. She's got no kids and no job, and if the time it takes to *cop* drugs is also considered, *karachi* pretty much takes care of another day of her life. And, if she lets it, it will take care of everything, until she hits rock bottom.

When you're immersed in the *life*, it seems like nothing else of interest is going on in the world. That's why they also call it "the fast lane." But the drug scene itself is heterogeneous. There are many ways to be addicted and many different scenes in which to do it. Patterns of circulation and consumption among drug users (even "polydrug" users) tend to be organized by preferred type of drug and method of ingestion. So, for example, although Madison and her steady boyfriend shared a common interest in heroin-related compounds, and were dependent on what must be a similar high psychopharmacologically, because he *shot* his and she *tooted* hers, the social networks in which their drugs were distributed and used were distinct. *Karachi* is not easy to *shoot*, and they say the heroin sold to *shooters* often has quinine in it to *boost the rush,* but that makes it too *hot* (painful) to *toot.* So if Madison and her boyfriend wanted to get high when they were together, they had to split up: "We had to separate. He went his way with his money and I went my way to *cop* my drugs because there's two different kinds of drugs."

In such ways, Madison and her boyfriend acknowledged and marked in practice the difference in their drug use. She has negotiated a position that put her at some distance from his acts of *shooting*. She doesn't want to see it, but she knows he does it, and he knows that she knows. Reflexively and within limits, they agree to accept each other's realities. That the history of their relationship does include a negotiation of drug-related difference, we suggest here, provides the conditions necessary for the renegotiation of the sexual aspect of their relationship so that they might deal with the problem of HIV transmission, that is, its intersecting pathways of needles and sex. Madison has never used condoms with her IV drug using boyfriend, or another "intimate friend," with whom she also practices mostly vaginal and rarely oral sex. On New Year's Day she resolved to start using condoms, but that didn't help New Year's Eve, which was the last time she had seen her steady IV drug user partner. Because she was trying to pull back from the drug scene altogether, Madison also wants to break up with her boyfriend. She feels that this would help her recovery from addiction. At the same time, it would eliminate him as a source of AIDS-related risk. She's not dependent on him for anything, not drugs, not money, not housing (she rents her own room in the house of some people she knows), so she has the power to decide her own fate. And if they do continue on together, because his *shooting* behavior has already been acknowledged and negotiated in practice, they have a better chance than most of addressing AIDS-related risks more directly.

"You know I stay in the streets a lot, right?" As he tells it, the mother of Thomas's son, and the woman he felt closest to, died of breast cancer last year after spending her last few months stealing cocaine from friends and neighbors. After this, Thomas slipped deeper than ever into *the life* and, at the time of interview, was *tooting karachi* two to three times every day. His addiction has made him more dependent on the women who care about him, which has made him more vulnerable to the conditions they set. This, as it turns out, may also put him and his sex partners at greater risk of HIV infection.

His retired mother takes care of his son. Thomas explains with affection:

You know how grandmothers is: "You should be here to do this here 6081 [his research code number]." She constantly putting the pressure on me, but thanks be to God that the boy have a grandmother. . . . I be's there. I be's there mostly, maybe on Sundays or something, you know. But I'm not there like I should be, you know. I basically be in the streets with this *habit*. I'm trying to get *dope*, have *dope*, and keep *dope*. That's what I'm basically doing. If I really wasn't on this *karachi* like I am, I could stay at home. But I can't be at home *sick*.

Unlike Madison, who wakes up just about every morning in her own home, Thomas has no home of his own. He's not homeless either.[3] Whenever he has enough *dope* to stay off the street, he retires to his mother's home or to the home of a sex partner who is his mother's friend and neighbor. In addition to these links to the square, churchgoing world (Thomas is a self-proclaimed "backsliding minister"), he has a long-standing sexual and economic relationship with a female companion in *the life*. Although his activities are oriented around his *karachi* habit, as far as Kane can tell from what he said, his mother and his mother's friend may not acknowledge his condition. In the interview passage quoted here, Thomas describes how his mother's friend is aware of subtle changes in demeanor and habit when he's high on *karachi* but seems to have little idea of what's really going on. Kane chose this passage because Thomas talks about how his sleeping patterns are altered by *karachi*. It is an example of the way habitual drug use can have widespread, indirect, and unforeseen effects on everyday life.

But one thing she don't know anything about . . . she's a woman of God . . . she don't know anything about the karachi. But she done noticed that my complexion changed and my voice and that I can sit up in a chair without coming to bed you know. Like high off this karachi. You don't want to put the high to bed, you know. You just want to sit up and enjoy it. So while she's in bed, I might be in a chair looking at TV. "Why don't you come on to bed baby? You're asleep anyway." But she don't understand. I don't want to put this *high* to bed, see. And then, you know, like a lotta times you be sleep, you can sleep your *high* off and you wake up *sick*. That's just like I came in the house day before yesterday at 12:00. I didn't get to bed until about 5:00. I say I was sleep about 5:15 and then I was up at 9:00. See I popped up. I didn't get nothing but about three, three and a half hours worth of sleep. But I didn't wake up sick. Now if I would have just laid there with her into a real, real real deep sleep and didn't get up till 1:00, I would have gotten sick. You following what I'm saying? So I still had energy. And one thing about the *karachi*, you know the older you get really the less sleep your body need? You know it ain't that your body really need eight hours worth of sleep. You know I stay in the streets a lot, right? Sometimes I can go to sleep in the car. Not just go to sleep and take my clothes off, but like if I'm out there with my lady while she busy *dating* or something, I can lock the doors and, you know, take the *nod*. Take a cat nap. And some of those naps be just as good as if I was at home on the couch with my clothes on. So, you know, I gets my rest, you know, cat nap.

The passage describes how natural rhythms of activity and rest are readjusted to accommodate the driving, erratic pace of the street, stealing his night's sleep even when he's off the street. "His lady busy *dating*"—that's his other sex partner who is engaging in prostitution. He's known her since high school, she even paid for his tuxedo at the prom 17 years ago. He lays it out:

She's a prostitute. She have a *habit*. She *shoot* her *dope*. She do way more *dope* than me. She do hard *dope*. That's strictly for *shooting*. She makes sure she gets her *dope* first and then she's good to go. And then if I'm around, catch up with her, if she with me, she gone give money for me to get *dope*. It's just that simple.

It sounds like Thomas spends most of his time trying to cross paths with this woman. He has a car and also gets *dope* by giving rides to others who are going around the city to *cop*. Again, the theme of constant movement and interpersonal connection ties together narratives of the drug scene. And, as for sex, Thomas really doesn't engage in sex that often, once a week or less, and prefers oral sex to vaginal sex because, in his words, it is more safe and more convenient (that is atypical). His use of condoms is governed by the tenor of his illicit relationships. With his steady partner who shoots drugs and works sex, he says:

> She do not *turn no date* without any condom. She don't do that. She don't do that period. She don't do that. And it has been times when she came off the stroll from working some *dates* that we had sex. Naturally, I didn't use no rubbers. That would offend her.

That he can't use condoms with his IV drug using partner is governed by conventions between prostitutes and their lovers that AIDS researchers have documented in places as diverse as New York City (Wallace & Beatrice, 1989), Amsterdam (Hoek, Haastrecht, & Coutinho, 1989), and Barcelona (Casabona, Salinas, Sánchez, Lacasa, & Veranni, 1989). In exchange for his intimate friendship, marked by an absence of condoms, and technical support (he says he watches her back when she dates and/or steals), he is provided with the *karachi* he needs. He relies on her sex trade for his *karachi*; for his health, he relies on her consistent use of condoms with clients and her use of sterile needles for shooting. I'm not sure it's as simple as he'd like to think. At this phase of extreme addiction, he has no power to reverse the risky condom convention or free himself from it altogether (see also Kane, 1990).

In turn, his risk extends to the churchgoing lady, with whom, because of conventions in the square world, he also had never raised the issue of condom use. He says: "Well you know, by me being her brother in the Lord, you understand, she know that what we're doing ain't really right. It's a secretive type affair. And by her knowing my mother and respecting my mother, it's like a hush, hush thing." Because of its illicit character, the subjects of sex and condom use are also "hush hush" things. Thomas and the churchgoing lady occasionally engage in sex, but discursively, they share only a fraction of each other's realities. The relation between life in the church and life in the street is veiled. The danger of HIV infection is, with all the other unwanted elements of the street world, left behind the veil. In contrast, Thomas says he has no problem using condoms when having casual sex with younger women. He explains: "See with them condoms, you need to start off using them. That's what you really need to just get into a habit. See people just ain't into a habit to just start off using them."

Thomas's sexual risk, and the risk he extends to others, are determined by the conditions and expectations particular to each relationship. His situation suggests that, as *karachi* addiction intensifies, his power to negotiate AIDS-related risk reduction diminishes. But then again, his sexual desire might diminish as well.

Repercussions

Involvement in the life reorganizes aspects of everyday experience in ways that vary with the kind and extent of drug use. Differences in drug use can be recognized and negotiated, as with Madison who toots and her boyfriend who shoots. And, as we suggest, this sets up the conditions necessary to renegotiate sexual practice in the relationship. Or differences in drug use can be veiled, as with the square churchgoing lady and Thomas who toots, and this makes it more likely that conditions conducive to HIV transmission will persist.

And it's not just activities more obviously related to drug use, such as buying, selling, and taking drugs, that are of concern. Addiction to a drug such as *karachi* has repercussions throughout a person's life. There are all kinds of unintended consequences, even sleep and activity cycles are altered. Many such activities were problematic but manageable before AIDS. Now, the very techniques of social management, such as veiling what one would rather not see, contribute to the situation of crisis within which we find ourselves. By focusing on the interconnectedness of risky behaviors, and the ways that risky behaviors are integrated into social practice, ethnographers may be able to account for the complex conditions and influences that underlie humanity's openness to HIV infection in different times and places.

Conclusion

In this chapter, we present some of the difficulties that the epidemiological concept of "risk group" poses for ethnographic research on the social context of the AIDS epidemic. In the United States, these difficulties are linked to the politics of a stigmatized disease that disproportionately affects already stigmatized and oppressed sectors of society. As Sanders (this volume) argues in his interpretation of German cultural images surrounding the plague, stigmatizing diseases require a discourse that creates images of clear boundaries between the "normal" and the "diseased." As Emily Martin's work (1987) dramatically shows, the discourse of science is not always independent of popular image-making processes. Indeed, in contemporary discourse on AIDS, boundary images inscribed in the epidemiological classification of risk groups have shaped popular conceptualizations of the disease. Perhaps it is the popular acceptance of this logic that has led to the continued use of the risk group classification despite attempts to refocus research and intervention on behavior (see Treichler, 1988, 1989, for related discussions). In the case of the "IV drug user" risk group, this boundary is sharpened by the discourse of the "war on drugs," which implies an opposition between the citizenry and the enemy. In the language of the disease, the "sex partner" symbolically partitions off the threatening image of the addicts from the "general population." This simplifying logic serves the need that many people feel to retain a sense of safety and distance from the epidemic. However comforting these images of distance may be to some, our analysis reveals how they can obscure the actual determinants of viral transmission.

The static and fragmented sense of the social dimension of HIV risk conveyed by risk group categories is inevitably challenged by ethnography. The narratives presented here illustrate the impossibility of understanding risk behaviors in isolation from their larger underlying conditions and dynamics. When viewed in context, risk behaviors can be seen as interrelated survival techniques. This is strikingly apparent when risk behaviors are enacted in the context of a drug subculture dependent upon a vast illegal economy. Analysis of how risk behaviors are partially determined by drug marketing and distribution systems as well as the criminal justice system in the United States is an important step in understanding the determinants of risk behaviors. It is also necessary to recognize that knowledge of the risk of HIV infection must be incorporated into the complex emotional and personal aspects of people's lives. A fuller grasp of the contexts of risk behavior must lead one to the conclusion that information and education—while crucial—are insufficient in and of themselves as policy tools in the struggle against AIDS.

Transcription Note: Italicized words index the lexicon of the drug subculture which has not yet been widely incorporated into popular English, although, like *shooting galley*, may commonly appear in recent social science literature. Underlined words index emphasis.

Notes

1. Both of the individuals whose situations Mason describes are Black, but this fact is not central to this analysis. They were selected because they were particularly articulate on the topic of risk reduction and because Mason was well acquainted with their situations.

2. This conclusion is not inevitable. De Jarlais, Friedman, and Strug (1986) and Friedman, Celan, and Des Jarlais (1987) relied on this cultural model of needle sharing and at the same time remained vocal advocates of education and needle exchange.

3. Discussion with Wendell Johnson (personal communication, 1989) has given me the insight into the importance of defining the "homelessness" of urban Black men pragmatically.

References

Agar, M. (1973). *Ripping and running: A formal ethnography of urban heroin addicts.* New York: Academic Press.

Bourgois, P. (1989, November 12). Just another night on crack street. *New York Times Magazine,* pp. 53-94.

Casabona, J., Salinas, R., Sánchez, E., Lacasa, C., & Veranni, P. (1989, June). *Prevalence and risk factors for HIV-1, HIV-2, HTLV-1 infection in prostitutes in southern Catalonia.* Poster session presented at the Fifth International Conference on AIDS, Montreal.

Crimp, D. (Ed.). (1987). *AIDS: Cultural analysis, cultural activism.* Cambridge: MIT Press.

De Jarlais, D., Friedman, S., & Strug, D. (1986). AIDS and needle sharing within the IV drug use subculture. In D. Feldman & T. Johnson (Eds.), *The social dimensions of AIDS: Method and theory.* New York: Praeger.

Des Jarlais, D., Wish, E., & Friedman, S. (1987). Intravenous drug use and heterosexual transmission of human immunodeficiency virus: Current trends in New York. *New York State Journal of Medicine, 87,* 282.

Fee, E., & Fox, D. M. (Eds.). (1988). *AIDS: The burdens of history.* Berkeley: University of California Press.

Frankenberg, R. (1990). *Radical approaches to risk and culture in British community epidemiology: Targets, relative risk, and "candidates" and the impact of HIV/AIDS.* Paper presented at the Wenner-Gren symposium, Estes Park, Colorado.

Friedman, S., Celan, B., & Des Jarlais, D. (1987, September). The special problems of intravenous drug users as persons at risk for AIDS. *Medical Times, 115*(9), 39-102.

Hoek, A. van den, Haastrecht, H. J. A. van, & Coutinho, R. A. (1989, June). *Heterosexual behavior of intravenous drug users.* Paper presented at the Fifth International Conference on AIDS, Montreal.

Hughes, P. (1977). *Behind the wall of respect: Community experiments in heroin addiction control.* Chicago: University of Chicago Press.

Hughes, P., & Jaffe, J. (1971). The heroin copping area: A location for epidemiological study and intervention. *Archives of General Psychiatry, 24,* 394-400.

Kane, S. (1990). AIDS, addiction and condom use: Sources of sexual risk for heterosexual women. *Journal of Sex Research, 27*(3), 427-444.

Kane, S. (1991). Heterosexuals, AIDS, and the heroin subculture. *Social Science and Medicine, 32,* (9), 1037-1050.

Koester, S. (1989). *When push comes to shove: Poverty, law enforcement and high risk behavior.* Paper presented at the annual meetings of the Society for Applied Anthropology, Santa Fe, NM.

Koptiuch, K. (in press). Third Worlding at home. *Cultural Anthropology.*

Martin, E. (1987). *The woman in the body: A cultural analysis of reproduction.* Boston: Beacon.

Mason, T. (1989). *The politics of culture: Drug users, professionals, and the meaning of needle sharing*. Paper presented at the annual meetings of the Society for Applied Anthropology, Santa Fe, NM.

Mondanaro, J. (1987). Strategies for AIDS prevention: Motivating health behavior in drug dependent women. *Journal of Psychoactive Drugs, 19*(2), 143-149.

Murray, S., & Payne, K. (1989). The social classification of AIDS in American epidemiology. *Medical Anthropology, 10,* 115-128.

Padian, N. (1987). Heterosexual transmission of AIDS: International and national projection. *Review of Infectious Disease, 9,* 947-960.

Preble, E., & Casey, J. (1969). Taking care of business: The heroin user's life on the street. *International Journal of the Addictions, 4,* 1-24.

Sterk, C., Friedman, S. R., Suffian, M., Stepherson, B., & Des Jarlais, D. C. (1989, June). *Barriers to AIDS intervention among female sexual partners of male intravenous drug users.* Paper presented at the Fifth International Conference on AIDS, Montreal.

Treichler, P. (1988). AIDS, gender, and biomedical discourse: Current contests for meaning. In E. Fee & D. Fox (Eds.), *AIDS: The burdens of history* (pp. 190-266). Berkeley: University of California Press.

Treichler, P. (1989). AIDS and HIV infection in the Third World. In B. Kruger & P. Mariani (Eds.), *Remaking history* (Dia Art Foundation Discussions in Contemporary Culture No. 4). Seattle: Bay.

Wallace, J., & Beatrice, S. (1989, June). *Sex and drug practices in the illicit sex industry as related to the spread of AIDS.* Paper presented at the Fifth International Conference on AIDS, Montreal.

Watney, S. (1987). *Policing desire: Pornography, AIDS, and the media*. Minneapolis: University of Minnesota Press.

Wiebel, W. (1988). Combining ethnographic and epidemiologic methods in targeted AIDS interventions: The Chicago model. In *Needle sharing among intravenous drug abusers: National and international perspectives* (National Institute on Drug Abuse Monograph No. 80; DHHS publication (ADM)88-1567; pp. 137-150). Rockville, MD: U.S. Department of Health and Human Services.

PART III

Cross-Cultural Studies

10

Sexual Diversity, Cultural Analysis, and AIDS Education in Brazil

RICHARD G. PARKER

The rapid spread of the international AIDS pandemic has brought us face to face with the limitations in our knowledge concerning a whole range of different subjects. In few areas, however, have the gaps in data and understanding been more pronounced than in the case of human sexuality and sexual diversity. Even in nations such as the United States, where research on sexual behaviors might be thought to be more or less well developed, the discussion of sexuality in relation to AIDS has been carried out largely in terms of data such as the Kinsey reports, now nearly 50 years out of date (see Turner, Miller, & Barker, 1988; Turner, Miller, & Moses, 1989; Wilson, 1988). The situation is even worse in many of the regions where the spread of AIDS has been most pronounced, as in central Africa, where the discussion of sexual behavior has had to rely on largely unsystematic reports scattered through the ethnographic literature (see Brokensha, 1988; Conant,

AUTHOR'S NOTE. Research on the social dimensions of AIDS in Brazil has been made possible by grants from the Wenner-Gren Foundation for Anthropological Research, the Joint Committee on Latin American Studies of the Social Science Research Council, and the American Council of Learned Societies, with funds provided by the National Endowment for the Humanities and the Ford Foundation, and, most recently, the Foundation for the Support of Research in the State of Rio de Janeiro (FAPERJ). Special thanks to Manuel Carballo, Carmen Dora Guimarães, and Gilbert Herdt as well as the other participants in the Wenner-Gren Foundation for Anthropological Research Conference on AIDS research for their helpful discussions concerning many of the issues examined in this chapter.

1988; Hrdy, 1987; Larson, 1989). Precisely because the spread of HIV has most commonly taken place through sexual contacts, the profound limitations in our cross-cultural knowledge concerning sexual behavior have made it virtually impossible to fully understand the dynamics of the epidemic or to design educational and informational intervention programs that will respond effectively to the risks that it poses (Abramson & Herdt, 1990; Herdt, 1988).

By now, then, the urgent need for extensive cross-cultural research on sexual practices is clearly evident (Carballo, 1988; Gagnon, 1988; Turner et al., 1989). To even begin to understand the dynamics of the international AIDS pandemic will require current data on the most basic aspects of sexual conduct in different social contexts (Abramson & Herdt, 1990; Carballo, Cleland, Carael, & Albrecht, 1989; Gagnon, 1988). We need dependable information on the number of sexual partners and the frequency of sexual intercourse, on the ways in which partners are chosen and the types of intercourse that are practiced, on the prevalence of other sexually transmitted diseases and the use of condoms, and on any number of other details of sexual behavior that have thus far remained largely obscure (Carballo et al., 1989). Perhaps most important, if we are to understand the radical differences that seem to characterize the epidemiology of AIDS in different areas, we need data that will allow us to compare and contrast not only distinct societies but also distinct social groups within any given society to begin to understand the kinds of variations that have marked the spread of the pandemic.

As central as the need for concrete, quantifiable, cross-cultural data on the incidence of specific sexual practices clearly is, however, it is just as clearly not enough. Understanding the spread of AIDS in relation to a fuller understanding of sexual behaviors is without question an initial step in developing a more effective response to the epidemic. In and of itself, however, it will tell us only part of what we need to know to begin to develop effective, socially and culturally sensitive, intervention programs. If they are to be useful in developing strategies and materials for AIDS interventions, quantifiable data on the incidence of particular sexual behaviors must ultimately be situated within a more qualitative context—within the social and cultural systems that give these practices meaning for specific social actors. We must begin to understand not only the empirical frequency of certain sexual acts but the emotional power that they hold for the participants and the wider systems of meaning that make them significant. We must also focus, in short, on what might be described as the erotic dimensions of sexual experience—

the erotic significance that is invested in particular sexual practices within different social and cultural contexts (Parker, 1987, 1989, 1991).

This focus on the question of erotic meanings obviously opens up a whole range of theoretical and methodological dilemmas, as it necessarily involves the examination of among the most private and subjective areas of human experience. It would be a mistake, however, to conclude that the erotic dimensions of sexual experience are, therefore, somehow beyond the grasp of interpretation and understanding. On the contrary, in sexual life as much as in any other area, subjective meanings are ultimately built up out of the intersubjective cultural systems that exist in specific social settings (Parker, 1991; see also Geertz, 1973, 1983). Precisely because erotic meanings take form within a wider cultural context, it is possible to gain access to them through the interpretation of the symbolic systems that shape them (Parker, 1987, 1989, 1991). Without in any way minimizing the complex psychological processes that are involved, it is nonetheless possible to approach the erotic much as we would examine a system of religious beliefs or a particular political ideology (Parker, 1991). And, on the basis of such an examination, we can perhaps begin to develop an understanding of sexual life that will be directly relevant not only to understanding the transmission of HIV and the spread of AIDS but to the task of designing effective information and education programs aimed at responding to the epidemic.

In the pages that follow, I will try to develop these points more fully, and to ground the discussion more specifically, by drawing on a number of examples from contemporary Brazil, where I have been able to conduct ethnographic research on sexual life for a number of years now (see also Parker, 1987, 1989, 1991). Drawing on these examples, I will try to briefly sketch out what we might describe as an ideology of the erotic: the system of cultural representations and symbolic constructs that shape a particular reading or understanding of erotic experience in the specific context of Brazilian culture. Having laid out some of the key terms of this erotic ideology, I will then turn to the ways in which it shapes or structures the possibilities of erotic practice, the erotic scripts or scenarios, present in contemporary Brazilian life. Finally, I will try to suggest at least some of the ways in which an understanding of these erotic meanings, a sense of their accessibility to qualitative research and interpretation, and a respect for their cultural specificity and detail can lead, in very basic and pragmatic terms, to more effective intervention and health promotion strategies in response to the risks of HIV transmission.

Erotic Ideology

In Brazil, as in other complex and diverse societies (and as in virtually all of the societies where the spread of the AIDS epidemic has been pronounced), sexual life takes shape less in the singular than in the plural—it is molded by diverse social institutions as well as by multiple, and often contradictory, cultural discourses (see Parker, 1991). It is characterized by a number of analytically distinct systems of meaning or cultural frames of reference that tend to intertwine in the flow of daily life but that nonetheless offer a variety of diverse perspectives or vantage points for shaping sexual practices and interpreting their significance. Taken together, these different systems map out the sexual universe in Brazil, defining the range of imaginable sexual practices and classifying them in terms of their social acceptability or normality. The very classification of certain practices as acceptable or admissible and others as prohibited or forbidden, however, simultaneously opens up the possibility of some form of transgression in which the rules and regulations that structure sexual conduct in normal daily life can be called into question, undercut, and even overturned. Perhaps more than anything else, it is this notion of transgression that defines the ideology of the erotic in contemporary Brazilian culture (Parker, 1987, 1989, 1991).

At the most general level, this notion of transgression, in Brazil at least, plays upon a culturally defined distinction between notions of public and private conduct. Its central role in defining an ideology of the erotic is captured in folk expressions such as *em baixo do pano, tudo pode acontecer* (beneath the sheets, anything can happen) or, perhaps even more common, *entre quatro paredes, tudo pode acontecer* (within four walls, anything can happen). While a whole range of regulations and restrictions may govern sexual interactions in public life, in private, when one is somehow hidden from the prying eyes of the wider society, a very different set of possibilities is opened up. At least within this particular ideological configuration, quite literally anything is possible. The rules and regulations of normal daily life cease to function in the intimacy of sexual interactions, and a freedom of sexual expression that would be strictly forbidden in the outside world takes shape in the privacy of erotic practice (Parker, 1989, 1991).

At the same time that such expressions articulate a clear distinction between public and private norms in contemporary Brazilian culture, however, they simultaneously subvert this very opposition by hinting at the unexpected possibilities of sexual pleasure. Through a series of symbolic inversions, they play upon a basic symbolic opposition between the *casa* or "house" and the *rua* or "street" as central to the organization of daily life.

The house, on the one hand, tends to be linked to a whole set of notions related to femininity and the proper limits of female sexuality. It is normally understood as the domain of the family and of familial values. While it may be a world inhabited first and foremost by women, it is also associated with at least some form of traditional, patriarchal authority and is seen as the site of a kind of domestic (or domesticated), properly reproductive sexuality. The street, on the other hand, stands as a far more impersonal domain of work and struggle. It offers both individual *liberdade* or "freedom" as well as *tentação* or "temptation" and *perigo* or "danger" (Parker, 1989, 1991).

In erotic ideology, however, the normal relationship, the sharp dichotomy, between these two domains is temporarily undercut or inverted, as the sexual freedom (and the sense of risk) of the street momentarily invades the secluded space of the house—or, for that matter, the controlled sexual functions associated with the family life of the house escape controls and play themselves out in the impersonal (and hence, once again, dangerous or risky) world of the street. The normally clear-cut distinctions between inside and outside, between private and public, suddenly give way, and the structures of normal daily life can be overturned, relativized, and rearranged. It is in these moments that the widest range of sexual experiences takes shape, that everything becomes possible (Parker, 1989, 1991).

With its implied mixture of both temptation and danger, this notion of *tudo* or "everything" is a key to what is described as *sacanagem*—a complex cultural category with no adequate English translation (Parker, 1989, 1991). Its meaning is in fact highly varied, contradictory, and constantly shifting. Traditionally, it seems to have carried a set of essentially negative connotations and was used, perhaps most commonly, with reference to homosexual practices. While this earlier association seems to have become considerably less current, especially in more modern, urban settings, *sacanagem,* along with the verb *sacanear,* is still widely used throughout Brazil to refer to "trickery" or "injustice" (much like the English notion of having been "screwed over" by someone or something). At the same time, however, especially during the course of the past decade, the notion of sacanagem seems to have gradually acquired a number of more positive connotations. It now has a playful side, as well, and is often used to refer to the friendly "teasing" of one's colleagues or fellows. And nowhere is this more evident than in contemporary usage, in which sacanagem has become a general term or category referring to a whole range of sexual possibilities—and, perhaps above all else, to those aspects of sex that are considered especially marginal, prohibited, or dangerous (Parker, 1987, 1989, 1991).

Ultimately, then, this concept of sacanagem seems to link notions of aggression and hostility, play and amusement, sexual excitement and erotic practice, into a single symbolic complex. Whether used positively or negatively, whether referring to injustice or violence, to joking, to teasing, to obscenities or sexual innuendos, to pornographic or erotic materials, or, ultimately, to specific sexual practices themselves, sacanagem seems to be focused, above all else, on breaking the rules of proper decorum—the rules that ought, within the established order of things, to control the flow of normal daily life. In virtually all of its meanings, it implies at least some form of symbolic rebellion or transgression—overturning the restrictions governing normal social interaction. It is in the totalizing sense of *tudo*—of *fazendo tudo* or "doing everything" that would normally be prohibited—that this transgression is most clearly manifest. In thinking about sexual behavior, within the terms of this erotic ideology, it is the idea of *fazendo tudo* that most clearly defines the range of sacanagem (Parker, 1989, 1991).

At once transgressive and totalizing, then, this notion of fazendo tudo thus becomes central to even the physical experience of sexual excitement and erotic pleasure. The idea of sacanagem, for example, can be linked to the notion of *tesão*—another key category in Brazilian sexual culture that can be translated only through a series of approximations but that is used almost interchangeably as the most common way of describing both *desejo* (desire) and *excitação sexual* (sexual excitement or sexual arousal). Indeed, it is through the notion of tesão that desire actually seems to invest itself in the excitement of the body, at once diffuse and focused, describing the heightened sensation of all the body's various surfaces while at the same time glossing the more specific hardening or erection of both the penis and the clitoris. Indeed, tesão can even refer to the sensations of sexual contact itself—the perceived *calor* or "heat" produced by the friction of bodies, and even the mild *dor* or "pain" of sensations that have become momentarily too intense. In the symbolic construction of sexual interactions, then, tesão thus merges unavoidably with (and seems to be necessarily linked to) the very experience of sexual *prazer* or "pleasure." It is in the physical sensations of tesão that the possibilities for sexual pleasure are rooted. And it is in the totalizing and transgressive logic of erotic ideology and sexual sacanagem that both excitement and pleasure take shape (Parker, 1991).

What such notions suggest, of course, is that the very experience of sexual excitement and erotic satisfaction is ultimately defined not merely as just a physical sensation but as a cultural construct. While we tend to think of such experience as somehow linked to biological being, the terms of this erotic frame of reference would suggest a rather more complicated understanding in which even the most intimate feelings and sensations of the physical body are unavoidably merged with the symbolic forms or cultural representations that actually shape sensual experience. This system of erotic meanings, in turn, constitutes or conditions the range of possibilities inherent in erotic practice. It structures actual sexual behavior in a number of quite specific ways by creating a context of meaning in which sexual interaction is socially and culturally scripted (Gagnon & Simon, 1973; Simon & Gagnon, 1984). To fully understand the sexual universe in any given social and cultural setting, understanding this context, and the scripting of erotic practice that it makes possible, may ultimately be every bit as important as detailed data on the incidence of particular behaviors.

Erotic Scripts

Precisely because the body and its possibilities are themselves culturally constructed, sexual practices can never be treated as somehow simply given in nature—or, for that matter, limited by nature. What one society may conceive of as sexually possible, another may not, and the experimentations that might open up the widest conceivable range of imaginable practices are rarely initiated entirely by individuals. On the contrary, it is the cultural construction of potential practices that allows individuals to imagine them. In contemporary Brazil, it is perhaps above all else within this erotic frame of reference that the possibilities of sexual practice are imagined and the erotic meaning of particular behaviors takes shape (Parker, 1991).

Focusing on the transgression of those rules and regulations that would otherwise define the range or prohibited sexual practices, then, what I have described as an ideology of the erotic in contemporary Brazilian culture offers its own distinct interpretation of sexual life. When compared with the world of normal daily life, it seems to function, in a sense, as a kind of alternative model of the sexual universe in which anything is possible—in which prohibition is itself prohibited, and even the most taboo desires and practices can thus be seen as especially exciting and satisfying. It is perhaps hardly surprising, then, that this alternative model should place central emphasis on the widest possible range of sexual behaviors as a key to the constitution of meaningful (exciting and satisfying) erotic practice. It is this wider range of sexual possibilities, rather than some more delimited segment of it, that is especially meaningful within this erotic frame of reference. And it is the fullest range of meaningful possibilities suggested by this frame of reference, in turn, that particular individuals can draw upon in shaping their own erotic meanings.

In transgressing and undercutting the restrictions and prohibitions of normal daily life, erotic ideology perhaps most clearly calls into question the notion of some form of genital (hetero)sexuality as the only really legitimate form of sexual expression. In the constitution of erotic meanings, a whole range of otherwise prohibited possibilities are articulated and invested with positive, rather than negative, value. From early childhood on, masturbation, oral eroticism, and anal eroticism, as well as same-sex relations and any number of other variations, all take shape as possible alternatives for the structuring of erotic practice—alternatives that may or may not be realized in the conduct of any given individual but that are nonetheless clearly articulated within the ideology of the erotic as at least conceivable or imaginable. Indeed, in keeping with the transgressive logic of sacanagem itself, these otherwise marginal sexual practices in fact become absolutely central to the erotic scripts produced in Brazilian culture.

Masturbation, for example, is clearly among the earliest of sexual practices to take on an explicitly erotic meaning. As in the case of so many other significant domains of sexual experience, the vocabulary that can be drawn on to speak of masturbation is itself an indication of its significance. While the verb *masturbar-se* (to masturbate oneself) is frequently used, particularly to speak in public or in polite company about issues related to masturbation, it nonetheless remains a fairly technical term with relatively formal or even medical overtones. Far more common, in popular culture, are expressions such as *tocar punheta* for males or *tocar siririca* for females. The verb *tocar* is used in Portuguese to mean both "to touch" and "to play" (an instrument), and this combination of touching while at the same time mastering a pleasurable technique is clearly central to an understanding of masturbation (Parker, 1991).

As in the case of other erotic techniques, however, it is important to stress that the practice of masturbation is not simply given in nature. On the contrary, it must be learned and, among both males and females, seems to be dependent on a whole set of meanings that are most commonly transmitted through information passed on during childhood or early adolescence by one's friends and associates. Given the divisions of gender, in turn, the learning of masturbation is simultaneously tied to a setting that carries a whole range of bisexual or homosexual connotations as well. The transgressive logic of masturbation itself becomes linked to the context of transgression in which it is learned, and while the interactions involved in this process, and the fantasies that are built up in relation to it, may, at one level, serve to confirm or reaffirm the accepted norms of heterosexual desire, they can also function, on another level, to undercut the distinctions between homosexuality and heterosexuality that are articulated in the discourses of normal daily life.

While masturbation may be most commonly understood as a form of *auto-erotismo* (autoeroticism), then, it is important, as well, to understand the extent to which it can also be integrated into a wider structure of interaction. The same-sex settings that serve as the context for learning about the sexual meanings associated with masturbation can be transformed in more intimate explorations of homosexual desire. Given the continued significance of female virginity in the official sexual ideology of normal daily life, as well as the desire to avoid unwanted pregnancy, masturbation can also become a central part of the sexual scripts of young males and females as well—a technique for avoiding a particular set of consequences that is simultaneously invested with erotic significance. Even later in life (and perhaps especially in keeping with the wider logic of sacanagem), both same-sex and opposite-sex mutual masturbation can serve as a form of sexual contact in certain public settings where the danger of being discovered might limit interactions involving more extensive disrobing or intertwining. In virtually all of its manifestations, then, masturbatory practice undercuts what might be described as the utilitarian logic of a reproductive sexuality and reproduces the transgressive vision of erotic ideology.

This same vision can certainly be found, as well, in the elaboration of oral sexuality. From early infancy on, the mouth is clearly associated with a variety of sensual pleasures. During childhood and early adolescence, it is increasingly invested with meaning as central to the scripting of erotic behavior. Even for very young children, the romantic *beijos* (kisses) that pass across the screens in movie theaters or on television are among the earliest models for structuring sexual conduct. The fact that the beijo can be applied to any part of the body is quickly perceived as well: To kiss not only the lips, but the genitals, is a common enough extension of the early sexual play of children. As children grow older, it is a relatively easy step to the notion that kissing everywhere, even remote recesses of the body, is especially exciting and erotic. This eroticization of the mouth, in turn, is incorporated into an elaborate imagery of food and eating that is central to ideology of the erotic. The sensual pleasures of the palate are metaphorically linked to the pleasures of erotic practice, and the very verb for the act of eating (*comer*) becomes the most common expression for speaking about sexual intercourse. As an extension of this imagery, verbs such as *lamber* (to lick), *chupar* (to suck), and *sugar* (to suck up) are all invested with erotic meanings, and the fact that they constitute especially exciting forms of sexual conduct is constantly reaffirmed in the language of popular culture (Parker, 1991).

As in the case of masturbation, notions of *lambendo* (licking) and *chupando* (sucking) are central to the early sexual explorations of adolescence. Like masturbation, the importance of oral sex, especially for males, is often learned in the context of same-sex interactions—with members of one's peer group, from older males, or what have you—and can sometimes be integrated with homosexual play or experimentation. And, like masturbation, as well, oral sex can offer young couples an important alternative to vaginal intercourse that can be used extensively to circumvent the restrictions placed upon sexual conduct. Indeed, its practice is often taught to young females by their male partners, and, like masturbation, it can come to play a central role in the sexual scripts of both males and females as early as the initial sexual explorations of adolescents. The erotic possibilities of the tongue and the mouth can thus become intimately linked to the notion of sacanagem: to the idea of sexual practices that escape the rules and regulations of conventional life and that are all the more exciting precisely because of this.

As primary as this emphasis on oral eroticism may be, however, it can hardly compare with the emphasis placed on anal eroticism and anal intercourse. For a variety of reasons, anal intercourse is constructed, within this ideological frame, as perhaps more powerfully erotic than any other single aspect of sexual conduct. Like both masturbation and oral sex, anal eroticism is given a key role in early sexual play. For boys, for example, it is the key focus for same-sex explorations such as *fazendo meia* (literally, "doing half") or *troca-troca* (again, literally, "exchange-exchange"), games in which partners are said to take turns masturbating, fellating, or, perhaps most commonly, anally penetrating one another. Like both masturbation and oral eroticism, as well, it is often used to avoid the loss of virginity or the dangers of unwanted pregnancy. Indeed, a whole range of techniques (from strategies for assuring the compliance of partners to the use of different substances for lubrication) related to anal intercourse tend to dominate informant reports of early adolescent sexual behavior, and it is clear that anal intercourse functions as a kind of special case within this particular frame of reference (Parker, 1987, 1988, 1991).

While anal intercourse may have special importance for young people, its significance is hardly less evident even later in life, when the problems associated with virginity and (more problematically) pregnancy give way, and vaginal intercourse becomes common and expected. On the contrary, particularly for men—but also, it would seem, for many women as well—

anal eroticism continues to be associated with the transgression of taboo. Indeed, precisely because one's earliest transgressions are invested with a surplus of meaning, and are thus remembered as especially exciting and pleasurable, anal intercourse continues as unquestionably central to the structure and significance of erotic practice. The scripts that are constructed around anal eroticism are reconstituted and reconstructed throughout later life, investing anal intercourse with a surplus of meaning and giving it a special place within the wider system of erotic meanings.

That anal eroticism should be especially important in this system of meanings is perhaps not surprising. More than any other form of sexual contact, it is especially well suited to breaking down the divisions and separations of normal daily life (between males and females, for example, or homosexuality and homosexuality) in creating an alternative erotic universe. Perhaps even more clearly, precisely because the restrictions and taboos associated with the anus and its functions are perhaps more extreme than in the case of any other part of the body, nowhere is the transgressive logic of the erotic more powerful than in the eroticization of anal intercourse. It is fully in keeping with this logic that anal intercourse should be given special importance within this system of meanings and that the *bunda* (literally, the "behind" or "ass") of both men and women should be treated as almost a national fetish reproduced in a whole range of images and media (Parker, 1991).

Ultimately, then, masturbation, oral sex, and anal intercourse all take shape, in the language and practice of popular culture, as key elements within an erotic vocabulary in contemporary Brazilian life. Invested with erotic meaning through the sexual scripts learned during childhood and adolescence, these practices maintain their significance during adulthood. Precisely because of the numerous prohibitions that inscribe them, they fit perfectly into the transgressive structure of the erotic—a world of sacanagem, tesão, and prazer. While it might be tempting, in light of this, to downplay the importance of vaginal intercourse and genital sexuality within the polymorphous world of erotic pleasures, however, nothing would be more inaccurate. On the contrary, genital practices are very much a positive ideal. The point is not that genital sexuality is unimportant in erotic ideology but that it is integrated equally within a wider set of practices rather than set above these practices as somehow more valuable or correct (Parker, 1991).

Some sense of the degree to which genital sexuality is incorporated into a wider structure of erotic practice is perhaps implicit, for example, in the use of the verb *transar* (roughly, "to transact") as perhaps the most totalizing designation for sexual interaction. Much like the notion of sacanagem, *transar* seems to link a set of at first somewhat unlikely meanings. On the one hand, *transar* can refer to economic exchanges, to having financial dealings with someone, to selling or dealing a product, and so on. *Uma transação* is "an economic transaction," and *a transa* refers to "a deal," "an agreement," or "an arrangement." At the same time, however, *transar* is perhaps the most commonly used term for speaking of a sexual interaction or transaction. *Uma transação* also refers to "a sexual affair" or "fling"—or perhaps even the person with whom one had sex. *A transa* refers to the "sexual transaction" itself—to the sexual act. *Transar* can thus be used as a synonym for a whole range of other terms that designate sexual intercourse. But it in fact includes even more than this. *Transando* may refer to *fodendo* (literally, "fucking"), *trepando* (screwing), but, at the same time, it need not even include penetration. A transaction limited to mutual masturbation is still uma transa—and in the right circumstances, transgressive and dangerous, can be even more exciting than uma transa focused on fodendo. A transação focused on *esfregando* or *roçando* ("rubbing"—i.e., the friction of two bodies rubbing together) can be every bit as pleasurable as trepando (Parker, 1991).

Ultimately, then, even the structures of sexual practice, the very acts that individuals perform, or think about performing, whether alone or with partners, thus emerge less as products of nature than as constructs of culture. While the physiology of the body may perhaps place certain limits on the possibilities that can be encoded in cultural symbols and played out in social action, the fact of the matter is that these limitations, whatever they might be, are actually far less important than the systems of meaning that construct the body and its pleasures in any given cultural context. What one social group conceives of as possible, another may not. And what particular individuals can or cannot imagine is shaped, as much in the sexual realm as in any other, by the intersubjective symbols and meanings of the world in which they live. In short, it is the social and cultural construction of potential practices that allows individuals to imagine them and, perhaps, to integrate them into their own experience. In contemporary Brazilian culture, at least, it is here, in this erotic frame of reference, that among the most important meanings of sexual behavior actually take shape (Parker, 1987, 1989, 1991).

Sexual Meanings and AIDS Education

There is a good deal more that might be said about all of this. In Brazil, as elsewhere, how such culturally constituted erotic scripts are internalized and reconstituted at an intrapsychic level, and how they in fact come to structure the interactions of sexual partners, are key questions that must ultimately be examined in far greater detail (see, for example, Simon & Gagnon, 1984). The processes of sexual learning that lead from such intersubjective symbols and meanings to the world of subjective experience have only barely begun to be explored and should perhaps be the focus of central attention in seeking to build a fuller understanding of sexual life more generally (see Gagnon & Simon, 1973; Simon & Gagnon, 1984).

Even without having resolved such issues, however, the key point that I would nonetheless like to emphasize here is the significance that attention to erotic scripts and meanings might potentially have in developing a more effective response to the spread of HIV through AIDS education and health promotion. In Brazil, as in so many other settings, it perhaps comes as no surprise that early AIDS education efforts, developed with almost no reference to the kinds of cultural meanings described here, seem to have had relatively little impact (see Parker, in press). While recent studies of knowledge, attitudes, and beliefs related to HIV and AIDS have demonstrated a fairly high level of both concern and information, they have documented little in the way of concrete behavioral change along the lines that might be thought to most effectively reduce the risk of HIV transmission in the future (Parker, in press; Parker, Guimarães, & Struchiner, in press).

In Brazil, as in most other societies, the central focus of AIDS education and health promotion during the course of the past decade has clearly been the dissemination of objective information about the risks of HIV transmission. Regardless of the specific media employed, or the particular groups being targeted, the underlying assumption has been that individuals, given objective information, will respond by making rational choices that will result in behavioral change and risk reduction. That the very perception of risk, and the ways in which social actors respond to it, is culturally shaped or constructed has been largely ignored, and the kinds of sexual meanings described here have scarcely entered into the design or planning of intervention strategies or health promotion materials. Indeed, to the extent that sexual and erotic meanings have been discussed at all, it has largely been in terms of what policymakers understand as their essentially biological basis and their irrational effects. Erotic experience has been treated as little more than a function of individual nature and an irrational barrier to reasoned decision making and risk reducing behavioral change.

The reading of erotic ideology developed here, however, might well suggest an alternative approach. The interpretation and understanding of such meaningful systems might in fact provide a kind of theoretical foundation for the elaboration of health promotion strategies that would move beyond the simplistic transmission of information and toward the development of responses to HIV and AIDS that would be integrated into the context of local sexual culture. Treating erotic meanings, along these lines, as part of a socially and culturally constituted system that ultimately shapes individual perception and behavior in highly patterned ways, we might then seek to approach the erotic less as a barrier to effective, rational, individualistic decision making than as a guide to the design of more meaningful AIDS intervention strategies.

In the case of Brazil, for example, an understanding of this system of meanings clearly carries a number of implications that could serve as a focus for health promotion in the future. Perhaps most important, given an ideology of the erotic focused so heavily on the importance of transgression, on a certain kind of danger or risk, as central to the constitution of desire, excitement, and, ultimately, sexual pleasure, it seems reasonably clear that interventions focused on risk reduction and safer sex as part of a reasoned response to objective information will necessarily confront a number of difficulties. Rather than treating this cultural system as an impediment to the reduction of risk, however, a more effective strategy might be to seek to draw on it by focusing on the eroticization of practices that actually result in effective risk reduction.

Precisely because of the elaboration of erotic meanings within Brazilian culture, the possibilities for promoting risk reduction as part of erotic experience, rather than as a logical result of rational decision making, are in fact culturally appropriate. In designing strategies and materials for AIDS education and health promotion, then, central attention should be given to the possibility of drawing on meanings and practices already invested with erotic significance to present risk reduction as erotically satisfying. In terms of the erotic scripts already present in Brazilian sexual culture, for example, it would be entirely feasible to focus on the promotion of a range of nonpenetrative sexual practices such as masturbation or oral eroticism, not simply because of their possibilities for risk reduction but because of their already established link to notions of sensual pleasure.

At the same time, given the profound erotic significance of both vaginal and, in particular, anal penetration, and acknowledging that discouraging such practices would be both unlikely and potentially even counterproductive, attention might be given to the possibility of drawing on the wider system of erotic meanings to promote the use of barriers such as condoms—already present in erotic culture as *camisinhas de Vênis* (Venus's little shirts).

Indeed, precisely because erotic ideology builds up a sharp distinction between reproductive and nonreproductive sexual behaviors, AIDS interventions and health promotion might draw upon a preexisting system of meanings by integrating accepted methods of HIV risk reduction, such as condom use in both vaginal and anal intercourse, as part of a mode of sexual expression that is presented as itself fundamentally transgressive and exciting rather than rational and restrictive.

Ultimately, what should be stressed is the extent to which an understanding of erotic ideology and meaning might serve as a kind of map or guide to health educators, AIDS workers, and even policymakers in seeking to develop culturally sensitive and psychologically meaningful intervention programs. In limited, but important, ways, some steps in this direction have already begun to be taken in Brazil, particularly by local-level community groups and AIDS service organizations seeking to develop materials for homosexually active men and both female and male sex workers that have drawn on erotic images and popular language in seeking to promote safer sexual practices (Parker, in press). Indeed, there is already some evidence to suggest that, in such settings, the use of explicit, erotically focused materials has begun to have an impact in stimulating a number of different forms of risk reduction such as condom use and the adoption of nonpenetrative practices (Parker et al., in press). Such successes are still highly limited, and the political problems involved in extending these approaches to other population groups are clearly extensive (Parker, in press). But preliminary data emerging from recent research nonetheless suggest that, in Brazil, as elsewhere, risk reducing behavioral change in the face of HIV and AIDS may have relatively less to do with objective information and rational decision making than with a range of other social and cultural factors, such as the construction of erotic meanings, that must ultimately be more fully understood if we are to hope to build a more effective response to the HIV/AIDS epidemic in the future.

Conclusion

For nearly a decade now, the AIDS epidemic has called attention to our fundamental lack of knowledge concerning a whole range of human behavior, and nowhere has this been more evident than in the case of human sexuality. The result has been an impressive increase in research activities aimed at responding to this lack of knowledge and understanding through the collection of data on a whole range of different aspects of sexual conduct (see Coxon & Carballo, 1989). The vast majority of this research, however, has been focused on the collection of quantitative data concerning the specific sexual behaviors that are thought to be most frequently linked to the transmission of HIV. In spite of the recent publication of a number of important case studies (see, for example, Carrier, 1989; Schoepf, 1990), relatively less attention has been given to the more qualitative investigation of the social and cultural contexts that shape these behaviors or the symbols and meanings that they hold for their participants.

In turning to the task of transforming research findings into effective interventions capable of responding to the spread of HIV and AIDS, however, questions related to context and meaning may ultimately prove to be centrally important—more important, in fact, than knowledge of behavioral frequencies or calculations of empirical risk. Data on the social construction of sexual identities, on the cultural meaning of sexual conduct, or the erotic significance of different sexual practices in distinct social settings may seem to be less easily systematized and analyzed than more quantifiable behavioral data. As I have tried to suggest in looking at the social construction of erotic practice in contemporary Brazil, however, issues as apparently intangible as the fluctuations of desire and the peculiarities of arousal in different social and cultural contexts are nonetheless open to a particular kind of cultural analysis or interpretation that may well offer important insights that would otherwise be missed—and that may prove to be crucial to the design and implementation of meaningful AIDS education and intervention programs.

In spite of a number of encouraging developments in biomedical research, in the development of therapies for the treatment of AIDS, and even in preliminary research on potential vaccines that may someday be used to inhibit HIV infection, it is nonetheless clear that behavioral interventions will continue, during the foreseeable future, to be central to fight against the AIDS pandemic. If they are to succeed, however, interventions must ultimately respond to the nuances of cultural particularity and detail. They must be based on an understanding of sexual experience as rooted in cultural meanings and social systems. The task of building a foundation, through social research and cultural analysis, for a more effective response to HIV and AIDS in the future, has barely begun. It would be almost impossible to overstate its urgency.

References

Abramson, P. R., & Herdt, G. (1990). The assessment of sexual practices relevant to the transmission of AIDS: A global perspective. *Journal of Sex Research, 27*, 215-232.

Brokensha, D. (1988). Overview: Social factors in the transmission and control of African AIDS. In N. Miller & R. C. Rockwell (Eds.), *AIDS in Africa: The social and policy impact* (pp. 167-173). Lewiston/Queenston: Edwin Mellon.

Carballo, M. (1988). International agenda for AIDS behavioral research. In R. Kulstad (Ed.), *AIDS 1988: AAAS Symposia papers* (pp. 271-273). Washington, DC: American Association for the Advancement of Science.

Carballo, M., Cleland, J., Carael, M., & Albrecht, G. (1989). A cross national study of patterns of sexual behavior. *Journal of Sex Research, 26*, 287-299.

Carrier, J. M. (1989). Sexual behavior and spread of AIDS in Mexico. *Medical Anthropology, 10*, 129-142.

Conant, F. P. (1988). Using and rating cultural data on HIV transmission in Africa. In R. Kulstad (Ed.), *AIDS 1988: AAAS Symposia papers* (pp. 199-204). Washington, DC: American Association for the Advancement of Science.

Coxon, A. P. M., & Carballo, M. (1989). Research on AIDS: Behavioural perspectives. *AIDS, 3*, 191-197.

Gagnon, J. H. (1988). Sex research and sexual conduct in the era of AIDS. *Journal of Acquired Immune Deficiency Syndromes, 1*, 593-601.

Gagnon, J. H., & Simon, W. (1973). *Sexual conduct: The social sources of human sexuality*. Chicago: Aldine.

Geertz, C. (1973). *The interpretation of cultures*. New York: Basic Books.

Geertz, C. (1983). *Local knowledge*. New York: Basic Books.

Herdt, G. H. (1988). AIDS and anthropology. *Anthropology Today, 3*, 1-4.

Hrdy, D. B. (1987). Cultural practices contributing to the transmission of human immunodeficiency virus in Africa. *Review of Infectious Diseases, 9*, 1109-1119.

Larson, A. (1989). The social context of HIV transmission in Africa: A review of historical and cultural bases of East and Central African sexual relations. *Review of Infectious Diseases, 11*, 716-731.

Parker, R. G. (1987). Acquired immunodeficiency syndrome in urban Brazil. *Medical Anthropology Quarterly, 1*, 155-175.

Parker, R. G. (1988). Sexual culture and AIDS education in urban Brazil. In R. Kulstad (Ed.), *AIDS 1988: AAAS Symposia papers* (pp. 169-173). Washington, DC: American Association for the Advancement of Science.

Parker, R. G. (1989). Bodies and pleasures: On the construction of erotic meanings in contemporary Brazil. *Anthropology and Humanism Quarterly, 14*, 58-64.

Parker, R. G. (1991). *Bodies, pleasures, and passions: Sexual culture in contemporary Brazil*. Boston: Beacon.

Parker, R. G. (in press). AIDS education and health promotion in Brazil: Lessons from the past and prospects for the future. In J. Mann, H. Fineberg, & J. Sepulveda (Eds.), *AIDS prevention through education: A world view*. Oxford: Oxford University Press.

Parker, R. G., Guimarães, C. D., & Struchiner, C. J. (in press). The impact of AIDS health promotion for gay and bisexual men in Rio de Janeiro, Brazil. In *The impact of AIDS health promotion directed to gay and bisexual men*. Geneva: World Health Organization.

Schoepf, B. G. (1990, November). *Sex, gender, and society in Zaire*. Paper presented at the International Union for the Scientific Study of Population seminar on Anthropological Studies Relevant to the Sexual Transmission of HIV, Sonderborg, Denmark.

Simon, W., & Gagnon, J. H. (1984). Sexual scripts. *Society, 22*, 53-60.

Turner, C. F., Miller, H. G., & Barker, L. F. (1988). AIDS research and the behavioral and social sciences. In R. Kulstad (Ed.), *AIDS 1988: AAAS Symposia papers* (pp. 251-267). Washington, DC: American Association for the Advancement of Science.

Turner, C. F., Miller, H. G., & Moses, L. E. (Eds.). (1989). *AIDS, sexual behavior, and intravenous drug use*. Washington, DC: National Academy Press.

Wilson, R. W. (1988). Measuring risk behaviors in population-based surveys. In R. Kulstad (Ed.), *AIDS 1988: AAAS Symposia papers* (pp. 237-243). Washington, DC: American Association for the Advancement of Science.

11

Use of Ethnosexual Data on Men of Mexican Origin for HIV/AIDS Prevention Programs

JOSEPH M. CARRIER
J. RAÚL MAGAÑA

In response to the AIDS epidemic, applied anthropologists working in county health care agency settings have unique opportunities to use their skills as ethnographers to assist health care professionals create successful educational intervention programs that may help prevent the spread of HIV in different ethnic groups. They can also use their ethnographic skills to help health care colleagues better understand ethnic and sexual orientation differences that may be important to the delivery of their services to clients diagnosed as having AIDS and those infected with HIV but asymptomatic.

The following description of our work with the Orange County Health Care Agency in California during the past several years illustrates the kind of contributions that anthropologists can make to help curtail the AIDS epidemic. We focus in this chapter on our work as ethnographers because we believe that, as a result of the paucity of relevant cross-cultural data on sexual behaviors and the behaviors of intravenous drug users, one of the most

AUTHORS' NOTE. We would like to thank the following persons for helpful comments on earlier drafts of this chapter: Peter Burrell, Michael Lawrence, Paul Abramson, Ralph Bolton, and Gilbert Herdt. The views expressed in this chapter are the authors' and do not necessarily represent those of the Orange County Health Care Agency or other funding agencies. The chapter is published by permission of the *Journal of Sex Research* (*JSR*), a publication of The Society for the Scientific Study of Sex.

important contributions anthropologists can make is to carefully map out the *range* of those behaviors in different ethnic groups and play the role of knowledgeable informant to health care colleagues. We further believe that, whenever feasible and appropriate, anthropologists should assist colleagues in estimating the *distribution* of those behaviors in different ethnic groups. Written research reports are also important in this setting, but they usually must play a secondary role to the agency's major objective of providing health services to its clients.

The Setting

Located in southern California, the Orange County Health Care Agency serves a county with the third largest population in the state—currently with an estimated 2.2 million inhabitants. Signs in the health care agency are written in three different languages: English, Spanish, and Vietnamese. They reflect the ethnic diversity of the population that is currently estimated to be a little less than 75% Anglo, 20% Latino, and 4% Asian; Blacks and Native Americans make up less than 2% of the total. A majority of the Latinos live in barrios located in the north-central part of the county.

The location of the county has special relevance to the AIDS epidemic in that its proximity to northern Mexico (only a little over a one-hour drive from Santa Ana, the county seat, to the border) has resulted in a Latino population that is primarily of Mexican origin and is made up of two different groups, those born in the United States versus those born in Mexico. The actual number of undocumented Mexican male immigrants in the county is unknown. Their number may vary at any point in time because part of this population are sojourners who move back and forth across the border to supplement incomes of their families at home. Because of this fluctuation, Latino males are believed at times to make up as much as one fourth of the county's male population. Over the past several years, Latino males have made up a large majority of the clients using the health care agency's special diseases (STD) clinic.

Health Care Agency and AIDS

The Orange County Health Care Agency has primarily addressed the AIDS epidemic by using the facilities of the STD clinic, where they operate an Alternative Test Site (ATS) for serologic testing for HIV antibodies and monitor and treat people with AIDS and those seropositive (HIV positive) but asymptomatic, and by setting up an AIDS Community Education Project (ACEP) and an outreach program for IV drug users. The county's chief epidemiologist and the head of Special Diseases Treatment Services (SDTS) are in charge of the various programs and convene weekly meetings of personnel dealing with AIDS to inform and coordinate AIDS activities in the agency.

People identified as being HIV positive but asymptomatic at the ATS are immediately given the option of joining an experimental program funded by the State Office of AIDS, which provides, depending on income, a free or low-cost workup by medical doctors and nurses at the clinic, a monitoring of their immune system and general health over time, and limited psychological counseling. People with AIDS (PWAs) who need treatment but cannot afford private care are provided free medical services. When appropriate, AZT and aerosolized pentamidine medications are provided to them at no cost through a federally funded program. At the end of September 1990, one fifth of "HIV-positive-only" patients reported by the county (183 of 914) are Latinos (OC Reports, 1990).

Estimates of the course of the epidemic in the county are made from trends of the number of people diagnosed with AIDS and from seroprevalence statistics generated from people coming to the ATS. These statistics are broken down into the same categories used by the Federal Centers for Disease Control (CDC) and into some additional categories not used by the CDC; for example, the data are shown by homosexual and bisexual orientation as well as by ethnicity and by that the segment of the population being tested for the federal amnesty program, mostly Mexican immigrants.

AIDS and HIV Infection in Orange County

As of the end of September 1990, 1,635 persons have been diagnosed with AIDS (PWAs) in Orange County, and 1,031 have died. As is the case nationally, a large majority of them are adult males reporting homosexual (67.5%) or bisexual (18.0%) behavior; the largest minority are adult males and females reporting IV drug use (5.1%). Adult males and females reporting heterosexual behavior account for only 2.9% of the total; and only 9 pediatric cases have been diagnosed, less than 1% of the total. The percentage distribution of the cumulative total number of cases by ethnicity is as follows: 82.2% Anglo, 12.3% Latino, 2.9% Black, and 2.8% other/unknown (OC Reports, 1990).

Reflecting a statewide trend, the number of Latino AIDS cases reported have trended upward at a faster rate than Anglo cases; from 8.8% of the total reported in January to June 1987 (11 of 125) to 15.1% of the total reported in January to June 1989 (27 of 179; OC Reports, 1989).

A total of 35,157 individuals have had their HIV antibody status checked at Orange County's ATS since the program began in June 1985 to the end of May 1990. The seropositive rates by ethnic group for cumulative total tested during this time period are as follows: Anglo 3.8% (n = 22,348), Latino 3.8% (n = 5,730), Black 5.3% (n = 1,032), Asian 2.0% (n = 664), and other 2.0% (n = 461). Of the cumulative total number of males tested during this time period, 6,023 reported themselves as being homosexual and 1,930 as being bisexual; the HIV positive rates were 19.4% and 9.7%, respectively. Seropositive rates for IV drug users during this time period were 4.5% for males (n = 2,089) and 2.3% for females (n = 1,339; OC Reports, 1990). Although we must be cautious in using the results of HIV testing programs for predicting infection rates in the general population because of the self-selection of individuals being tested, they nevertheless give some idea of the relatively different rates of HIV infection that may exist between different segments of diverse populations.

Undocumented Laborers, Prostitutes, and AIDS

One of the first concerns that the AIDS Community Education Project had to address was the implications for HIV transmission of sexual relationships that had existed for many years between female prostitutes and immigrant male laborers in the predominantly Mexican barrios of north-central Orange County. In the past, these sexual relationships had resulted in two epidemics of syphilis and one of chancroid. Although the epidemics were brought under control, many of the patients in the county's STD clinic continued to be immigrant Mexican males with syphilis and gonorrhea who had been infected mainly in sexual encounters with female prostitutes. And research findings indicated that the AIDS virus could be transmitted through heterosexual intercourse and that genital ulcer diseases, like syphilis and chancroid, could be important cofactors in its transmission.

Given these findings, it seemed reasonable to conclude that the risk of HIV infection might be high and that some kind of educational intervention might help prevent the spread of HIV within these two high-risk groups. But, to successfully plan and carry out an educational intervention, it was also clear that detailed information was needed on the social and sexual behavior of both groups of participants. A review of the small amount of available information, however, in general only revealed that a large majority of the men were immigrants from Mexico and that many of the female prostitutes were IV drug users who solicited clients door to door in Latino barrios.

The first step in designing the educational intervention was to map out the kinds of behaviors in both groups that were most likely associated with HIV transmission. Both field observations and interviews were used in carrying out this mapping. Respondents, obtained through the STD clinic, provided information on the location of meeting places for prostitution. Prostitutes were then systematically observed at some of the major locations, and several of them were informally interviewed. After gathering sufficient basic information from this method, 38 female prostitutes and 50 of their immigrant male clients were formally interviewed. The interviewees were recruited both from patients at the STD clinic and from attendees of various ACEP outreach programs.

The following are some highlights of research findings on behaviors in both groups that may be associated with AIDS. They thus have special relevance for the development of educational intervention strategies that might reduce the risk of HIV infection among individuals in these groups. Some of the intervention strategies based on these findings will also be described below.

The data suggest that the major sexual outlets for Spanish-speaking undocumented male workers are female prostitutes. Most workers come to Orange County alone or with other single men, leaving wives or girlfriends back in Mexico. They work primarily in male-dominated jobs such as farm labor or gardening and, therefore, have little opportunity to meet women at the job place. Typically, they live in low-income neighborhoods in apartment complexes with an overabundance of other unattached males and few available female companions.

Fearful of being detected by U.S. immigration officials, they are reluctant to spend time in public places. Many of them, as a result, prefer to engage in sex with female prostitutes who come to their places of residence. Others, however, describe getting together with other men to drink at bars or parks and making contact with prostitutes at these locations. None describes going out on the street to look for sex partners. Rather, they rely on female prostitutes who come to them.

Most of the prostitutes are IV drug using Anglo women; some are Latino and Black, but they are a small minority. The ethnographic data confirm previous reports that they exist as a substratum of prostitutes that cater only to immigrant Latino males by going to the neighborhood gathering places, crowded apartment house complexes, and labor camps where they live.

The interview data suggest that the sexual behaviors of the prostitutes and their clients are relatively conservative. They engage almost exclusively in vaginal intercourse in the missionary position. Fellatio is occasionally requested, but Latino men consider cunnilingus to be unusual sexual behavior; both practices cost clients more than vaginal intercourse. Neither prostitutes nor clients report practicing anal intercourse. The prostitutes say they particularly like the fact that most Latino men come to climax rapidly (Magaña, in press).

One important part of their sexual behavior related to potential HIV infection is infrequent use of condoms. Both prostitutes and clients reported using condoms sometimes but not regularly. A number of reasons were cited for this lack of use. Latino males reported their fear that, if they tried using condoms, prostitutes might think they had syphilis or gonorrhea and reject them. Prostitutes reported a similar fear that they might be rejected by customers if they insisted on using condoms. And some noted their reluctance to carry them because they could be used as probable cause for arrest or, if the prostitutes were arrested, could be used as evidence to confirm their profession in court.

Another high-risk sexual behavior practiced by many prostitutes with their clients is serial intercourse. The interview data revealed that it was not unusual for some of them to have unprotected vaginal intercourse with five or six males one after the other with no douching between clients. This means that the men may be coming in contact with one another's semen, thus risking being infected with HIV should one or more of them be seropositive.

Still another risk factor for HIV transmission within these two groups is that, judging from their medical histories, there is a high likelihood that many of them will also be infected with other sexually transmitted diseases. Genital ulcer diseases, as previously noted, have been identified as important cofactors in the heterosexual transmission of the AIDS virus when neither condoms nor nonoxynol-9 lubricants is used.

One additional fact needs to be mentioned about the IV drug using female prostitutes: Many of them have been infected with HIV as a result of sharing contaminated needles. As of June 1989, 53 women have been identified as seropositive through the health care agency's jail testing program. A majority of these women are believed to support their drug habit through prostitution and may thus be part of the prostitute group described above.

Based on the data collected, it was obvious that educational programs were needed to help prevent the spread of HIV among the men and women in these two high-risk groups by bringing about some basic changes in their sexual behavior. And, given that most of the seropositive IV drug using female prostitutes got infected through sharing needles, educational intervention was also warranted to get them into drug treatment programs or at least to inject their drugs safely.

In setting up educational intervention programs, the following factors were taken into account. First, because neither group could be reached in ordinary ways, new methods for getting messages to them had to be found; they could not be educated through such routine channels as churches, schools, or community groups. Second, because both the men and the women in these groups generally have limited reading skills, and the men only understand Spanish and have little formal education, whether spoken, written, or on film, intervention messages would have to be accomplished in easily understandable English or Spanish in nontraditional ways. And third, because under the California Penal Code both the sexual behavior and the IV drug use are against the law, special care would have to be taken when carrying out the educational intervention not to compromise the prostitutes, their clients, or the legal obligations of the health care agency.

Two educational intervention programs were launched: one for IV drug using female prostitutes, the other for their Latino male clients. IV drug using female prostitutes were a target not only because they appeared to make up a majority of the prostitute population but also because the drug habit meant they could be at risk from sharing needles as well as from unprotected sex with multiple sex partners. Prostitutes recently out of jail were used as outreach workers to teach their colleagues about AIDS and the high risk of HIV infection through sharing contaminated needles and unsafe sex. They passed out information and condoms to prostitutes both at places where they worked in barrios and at the county's methadone treatment center. They also urged them to come to the ATS for seroprevalence testing. Additionally, county health care educators continued their program of HIV testing and providing information on AIDS at the county jail.

A totally different approach was used for Latino male clients. The fact that most of them have very little formal education had profound implications for the design of the HIV/AIDS education and prevention programs. There is evidence, for example, that people who have not had extensive experience with formal education lack syllogistic reasoning ability when the syllogism is stated out of context (Laboratory of Comparative Human Cognition, 1986). This means that they may be unable to make inferences based on a general premise.[1]

Messages to Latino clients of female prostitutes, therefore, had to be concrete and rooted to a temporal reality, and printed materials on AIDS and HIV infection had to be developed at a low reading level so that they could be easily understood. Also taken into account was the fact that studies in cross-cultural settings had further demonstrated that individuals with low educational attainment absorb new information best when it is presented in ways that relate it to their current environment and life circumstances. Educational materials for this group thus had to rely more on symbols than on the written word (Magaña, in press).

AIDS educational intervention for the Latino males was thus modified to take into account the sociocultural differences they had with the majority Anglo male population in the county. As part of this adaptation, a *fotonovela* was created by ACEP in Spanish and English about the dangers of HIV infection and how to avoid becoming infected with the virus.

Fotonovelas tell a story by using photographs in a comic strip format. They are very popular reading material in Mexico and elsewhere in Latin America in general for those segments of the population with low educational attainment.

The fotonovela proved to be successful as a means of communicating about high-risk behavior and HIV infection not only to Latinos in Orange County but also at the state level. California's State Office of AIDS distributes the Spanish version, with only a few modifications, at all of their Alternative Test Sites for individuals wanting to know their HIV antibody status.

The fotonovela and other culturally relevant materials available in Spanish were used by health care educators and volunteer outreach workers to convey information about HIV infection and AIDS to groups of Latino males who were likely to use the services of female prostitutes. Presentations were made at all of the Latino labor camps in the county and at "health fairs" at locations where many of them work. Prostitute outreach workers also distributed information at some of the places where they solicit customers. Given that the majority of its patients are Latino males, the county's STD clinic is also a logical place to disseminate information on AIDS and safe sex. STD communicable disease investigators, however, have only been recently allowed to inform patients about AIDS in addition to other sexually transmitted diseases.

Because of insufficient seroprevalence data, no formal evaluation can be made of the county's educational intervention programs to help prevent the spread of HIV/AIDS. The available data suggest, however, that, up to now, no large-scale transmission of HIV from female prostitutes to their Latino clients has taken place. Seroprevalence tests of 50 sexually active immigrant Mexican male farm workers carried out by ACEP in the fall of 1987, for example, revealed that none was HIV positive at that time. And since then, two blind seroprevalence studies of 3,000 males coming to Orange County's STD clinic from September to November 1988 and March to July 1989, the majority of whom are Latino, have found low seropositive rates: Less than 2% of the males in each study group were seropositive.

Mexican Male Homosexual
Behavior and AIDS

Another concern that the AIDS Community Education Project had to address was the fact that, because the Anglo "gay community" in Orange County was the first and hardest hit by the AIDS epidemic, ongoing educational intervention programs of the health care agency and Gay and Lesbian Center were slanted toward Anglo gay men and thus could not be assumed to be effectively reaching men of Latino origin involved in homosexual encounters. Although the largest percentage of AIDS cases in the county were Anglo men infected through homosexual behavior (80%), the second largest risk group were Latino men (12%) infected the same way; and a sizable percentage of the 500 Latino men who reported homosexual behaviors at Orange County's ATS, 16%, have tested positive for the AIDS virus (OC Reports, 1989).

It should also be noted that a large majority of Latino males in California are of Mexican origin (85%); and a large majority of those 15 years of age or older are estimated to be either Mexican born (45%) or first-generation U.S. born (40%), the remaining generations making up only 15% of the total. This means that the consistently high HIV infection rates of Mexican males involved in homosexual behavior in Mexico, from 20% to 30% judging from seroprevalence surveys done in 1986 and 1987, are relevant to the spread of AIDS in California (Carrier, 1989).

Because data were not available on the homosexual behavior of men of Latino origin in California, comparisons of Anglo and Latino male homosexuality could not be made and thus no direct assessment done of ongoing AIDS educational programs in Orange County. A comparison, however, of some findings on Mexican male homosexuality (Carrier, 1985) with some on Anglo male homosexuality (Bell & Weinberg, 1978; Hooker, 1965) revealed some important cross-cultural differences in homosexual behavior of relevance to HIV/AIDS prevention programs.

A major difference of particular relevance to the spread of HIV is that the available data suggest that Mexican men generally have strong preferences for playing either the anal receptive or insertive sexual role and for anal intercourse over fellatio, whereas Anglo men, on the other hand, generally do not have strongly developed preferences for playing one sexual role over the other and do not necessarily look upon anal intercourse as the preferred or ultimate sexual technique in homosexual encounters.

The dichotomization of sexual role preferences by Mexican men means that conceptually there are at least two different male groups with homosexual contacts: By societal standards, the one playing the anal receptive role is considered homosexual; the one playing the anal insertive role may not be. One important outcome of this dichotomization with respect to the spread of HIV/AIDS is that a larger percentage of Mexican males may be involved in bisexual behavior than Anglo males. Additionally, because this segment of the Mexican male population may not consider themselves homosexual or bisexual, they may represent a potentially difficult group to reach through educational intervention. One obvious conclusion is that one should not expect them to be reached through programs designed for Anglo gay men.

As a result of these findings, a study of Mexican and Mexican American male homosexuality was initiated. Major research questions are these: How does the homosexual behavior of Mexican males change when they move to California? How does the homosexual behavior of Mexican American males change with acculturation? And how are these behaviors related to the spread of HIV/AIDS in Orange County and elsewhere in California and the United States?

Some findings from a preliminary analysis of interview and observational data gathered in the study, which is still in progress, indicate that, even though immigrant Mexican male patterns of sexual behavior are somewhat modified by new and quite different sociocultural factors, their homosexual behaviors in California continue to be mainly patterned on their prior sexual experiences in Mexico. As a result of selective acculturation by individuals of Mexican origin to mainstream Anglo American patterns of sexual behavior, however, considerable behavioral variations exist among Mexican American males involved in homosexual encounters.

A major determinant as to whether Mexican American homosexual behavior tilts toward Anglo American or Mexican homosexuality appears to be the extent to which their sexual socialization in adolescence was mostly with Mexican or Anglo American sex partners. Socializing mostly with Anglo American males whether at school or in the neighborhood, for example, increases the likelihood that they will select them as sex partners and will be affected by and/or adopt their sexual preferences and techniques. Socializing mostly with Mexican and Mexican American males, on the other hand, increases the likelihood that their first sex partners will be Mexican or Mexican American males and their sexual preferences and techniques will be more similar to the Mexican than the Anglo American. And, even if they select Anglo Americans as sex partners, their sexual preferences and techniques may be more similar to the Mexican than the Anglo American.

These preliminary findings indicate that any effective educational intervention must take into account the reality that there are several different target populations of males of Mexican origin in California that may be involved in high-risk homosexual behavior. And each one may require different outreach strategies.

A large number of homosexually involved immigrant Mexican males, for example, who consider themselves heterosexual, bisexual, or homosexual, may be most effectively informed about AIDS and the high risk of HIV infection associated with anal intercourse when they are treated at a STD clinic or tested at an Alternative Test Site and through special outreach when grouped on certain street corners and parking lots while waiting for work as day laborers.

They may also be informed via radio. A series of radio soap operas focused on AIDS and HIV infection through unsafe sex were broadcast in Spanish last fall. The target audience of the broadcasts were preliterate monolingual Spanish-speaking Mexican migrant farm workers in the southwestern United States. Our ethnographic data on the different types of Mexican male sexual encounters in Mexico and California were used in the development of the homosexual parts of these radio "novelas."

Gay-identified Mexican and Mexican American men who go to search for sexual partners in Latino gay bars or pornographic bookstores, on the other hand, may be most effectively reached at those locations. The "Core Program" is currently conducting this type of outreach in seven Latino gay bars located in Los Angeles County and is distributing several "gay" comic books on AIDS, HIV infection, and safe sex in Spanish titled *Chicos Modernos*.

Still another useful strategy would be to focus on educating homosexual Latino males playing only the receptive role or playing both roles in anal intercourse about HIV infection and AIDS and get them not only to practice safe sex but to also act as volunteer outreach workers and pass the information on to their sexual partners. The available data suggest that populations of Mexican-origin men playing the anal receptive role are in general more sexually active and have higher HIV infection rates than men who only play the anal insertive role, the majority of whom may be bisexual and thus also have female sexual partners (Carrier, 1989).

Anthropologists as Knowledgeable Informants

Another contribution that anthropologists can make in a health care agency is to play the role of knowledgeable informant about behavioral and attitudinal differences between different ethnic groups for colleagues to assist them in carrying out their ongoing health care programs. We have used our knowledge about cultural differences in attitudes about homosexual behaviors between Anglo and Latino men, for example, to assist in crisis counseling of seropositive men of Mexican origin who, although infected through homosexual anal intercourse, did not consider themselves to be and thus did not want to be labeled or treated as being either homosexual or bisexual.

In training sessions, we have also informed STD communicable disease investigators about these differences. Rectal lesions may thus take on a new meaning when a Latino client denies having had any homosexual encounters. And one cannot assume that a penile lesion was gotten only through heterosexual intercourse.

Additionally, as a final example, we have been asked to use our knowledge about Latino and Anglo differences in attitudes toward death and dying to assist in the counseling of Latino people who have AIDS and those who are seropositive but asymptomatic. In these counseling sessions, the anthropologist plays a unique role in that he not only helps the Latino client in distress but also sensitizes culturally uninformed Anglo counselors about important cultural differences.

Some Observations

One of the most important contributions that anthropologists can make to help control the spread of HIV/AIDS through educational intervention is to provide program directors with accurate ethnographic data on the range of sexual behaviors of targeted populations. Because data available on any given population's sexual behavior may be limited, it will be necessary in many instances to do basic fieldwork to map and decode certain domains of behavior for relevant subgroups of the population. Surveys of the distribution of sexual behaviors must also be done, but it is our belief that meaningful questionnaires can be put together only after the range of sexual behaviors has been mapped and decoded.

Another area in which anthropologists can make a significant contribution is by helping design educational interventions for programs targeted toward

people having low scholastic attainment levels or for people who are preliterate. Anthropologists in general have a good feeling for and often a good
knowledge base about nonformal education as well as traditional educational
techniques and approaches. Thus, when the emphasis of educational campaigns or educational intervention is on nonformal education, anthropologists acquainted with traditional learning systems can provide effective input
into the development of these campaigns.

One final observation: Ethnographic and survey data, as well as those
from the clinical interview, suggest that the issue of voluntary partner
notification appears to be an acceptable strategy for Latino populations. Our
ethnographic data from Latino men and women indicate that cluster elicitation with unacculturated Latino populations may be a more effective technique for preventing the spread of AIDS and providing medical treatment for
HIV-related infections than contact tracing, which provides at best only one
possible source of HIV infection.

Role Preference and the AIDS Epidemic

Sexual role preference between males involved in anal intercourse—that
is, a preference for being receptive or insertive—has been shown to be an
important cross-cultural explanatory variable in male homosexual behavior
(Carrier, 1977). The available data suggest that there is a high correlation
between anal intercourse and role playing; and, in societies where a majority
of homosexually involved men appear to develop sexual role preferences,
such as Mexico, Brazil, Turkey, and Greece, anal intercourse is the ultimate
objective of homosexual encounters (e.g., see Carrier, 1971; Parker, 1987).

The available data also suggest that English and Anglo American men do
not have strongly developed preferences for anal intercourse over fellatio
and for the playing of one sexual role to the exclusion of the other (e.g., see
Bell & Weinberg, 1978, pp. 106-111; Westwood, 1960, pp. 130-131). These
findings have led sociologists to wrongly assume that "sexual role preference" is not an important variable in the study of male homosexual behavior.
For example, Gagnon and Simon (1973, p. 245) assert that "the notions of
'active' and 'passive' in homosexual relationships are more obscuring of the
actual conditions of the behavior than they are enlightening"; and Bell and
Weinberg (1978, p. 111) note "that speculation about sexual 'roles' (e.g.
active/passive) may simply be missing the point."

Taking into account "homosexual role separation and spread of AIDS,"
three Greek epidemiologists (Trichopoulos, Sparos, & Petridou, 1988,

p. 965) recently pointed out "the potential importance of role separation (active vs passive) among male homosexuals as a population variable in models of the AIDS epidemic." They conjecture that, because "receptive anal intercourse is by far the most important risk factor for HIV seroconversion" and that "insertive anal intercourse may be no more conducive to HIV seroconversion than insertive vaginal intercourse," then

> if all male homosexuals were either active or passive, but never both, the proportion of male homosexuals would not be critical to understanding the past or predicting the future spread of AIDS. Those practicing insertive anal intercourse would not be at increased risk because of the inherently low risk of their practice; those practicing receptive anal intercourse would not be at very high risk because of the low prevalence of HIV among their sexual partners, and they would not transmit the infection further. (Trichopoulos et al., 1988, pp. 965-966)

They go on to note that, although this polarity may not be completely realistic, "countries in south-eastern Europe, the Middle East, and, possibly, other parts of the world may provide various degrees of approximation to it." They further conclude that "the slower spread of AIDS in the eastern Mediterranean and Middle East may be accounted for not only by differences in classical AIDS variables such as promiscuity and intravenous drug abuse, but also by a more clear homosexual role separation" (Trichopoulos et al., 1988, p. 966).

Wiley and Herschkorn (1989), with elementary models, quantitatively explore some implications of homosexual role separation and AIDS epidemics. They keep their models relatively simple by assuming that

> the population in question is closed to births, deaths, and migrations, that the incubation period for AIDS has effectively an exponential distribution . . ., that the variation in rates of sexual activity across individuals is minimal, and that the probability of infection from the receptive to the insertive partner in unprotected anal intercourse is nil. (Wiley & Herschkorn, 1989, p. 435)

They note that, with perhaps the exception of the last one, "relaxation of these assumptions would not alter the qualitative implications of the models developed" (p. 435).

Wiley and Herschkorn (1989, p. 447) conclude that, given the assumptions noted above,

> as expected, role differentiation in anal intercourse and mixing preferences affect the course of an AIDS epidemic in crucial ways. As Trichopoulos and his col-

leagues (1988) have inferred, if HIV can be transmitted sexually only from an infected insertive partner to a receptive partner in unprotected anal intercourse, an epidemic will be of smaller size in a population with a correspondingly smaller segment which takes both roles. In fact, with a small enough size dual-role subpopulation, an epidemic may not occur at all.

They also conclude that their

simple models imply that role separation with respect to sexual behavior should be considered carefully in the construction of models of HIV epidemics among homosexual men. This point is especially relevant when such models are applied to populations where ethnographic accounts indicate a rigid stratification according to roles in anal intercourse; it is also important where there is evidence of a trend from role separation toward more catholic preferences in sexual activity. (Wiley & Herschkorn, 1989, p. 448)

Note

1. The findings on syllogistic reasoning reported by Cole and his colleagues do not reflect a deficit theory within a hierarchical mode of development. They simply explain that, if syllogistic reasoning is viewed within the context of a cultural ecology where the cognitive process is irrelevant, then the need to develop it is absent. This does not imply that people cannot learn syllogistic reasoning. See Laboratory of Comparative Human Cognition (1986).

References

Bell, A. P., & Weinberg, M. S. (1978). *Homosexualities: A study of diversity among men and women.* New York: Simon & Schuster.

Carrier, J. M. (1971). Participants in urban Mexican male homosexual encounters. *Archives of Sexual Behavior, 1,* 279-291.

Carrier, J. M. (1977). Sex-role preference as an explanatory variable in homosexual behavior. *Archives of Sexual Behavior, 6,* 53-65.

Carrier, J. M. (1985). Mexican male bisexuality. In F. Klein & T. Wolf (Eds.), *Bisexualities: Theory and research* (pp. 75-86). New York: Haworth.

Carrier, J. M. (1989). Sexual behavior and spread of AIDS in Mexico. *Medical Anthropology, 10,* 129-142.

Gagnon, J., & Simon, W. (1973). *Sexual conduct: The social sources of human sexuality.* Chicago: Aldine.

Hooker, E. (1965). An empirical study of some relations between sexual patterns and gender identity in male homosexuals. In J. Money (Ed.), *Sex research: New developments* (pp. 24-52). New York: Holt, Rinehart & Winston.

Laboratory of Comparative Human Cognition. (1986). Contributions of cross-cultural research to educational practice. *American Psychologist,* pp. 1049-1058.

Magaña, J. R. (in press). Sex, drugs and HIV: An ethnographic approach. *Social Science and Medicine.*

OC Reports. (1989). *Special computer tabulations of Latino STD & ATS clients.* Orange, CA: County of Orange, Health Care Agency.

OC Reports. (1990). *AIDS surveillance and monitoring program HIV reports.* Orange, CA: County of Orange, Health Care Agency.

Parker, R. (1987). Acquired immunodeficiency syndrome in urban Brazil. *Medical Anthropology Quarterly, 1,* 155-175.

Trichopoulos, D., Sparos, L., & Petridou, E. (1988, October 22). Homosexual role separation and spread of AIDS. *The Lancet,* pp. 965-966.

Westwood, G. (1960). *A minority: A report on the life of the male homosexual in Great Britain.* London: Longman.

Wiley, J., & Herschkorn, S. (1989). Homosexual role separation and AIDS epidemics: Insights from elementary models. *Journal of Sex Research, 26,* 434-449.

12

Women at Risk:
Case Studies from Zaire

BROOKE GRUNDFEST SCHOEPF

This chapter explores issues of race, gender, and class in the context of the AIDS epidemic in Central Africa, where the principal mode of HIV transmission is by means of heterosexual intercourse, and slightly more women than men are affected. It draws upon research conducted by Project CONNAISSIDA on AIDS in Zaire from 1985 to 1990. In Africa, AIDS risk is not confined to any special group; it is not only a disease of poor women engaged in commercial sex work ("prostitutes") and long-distance truck drivers. Men and women in these occupations are at very high risk in the cities and towns of Central Africa. However, they do not form bounded groups; their social networks extend into virtually every social milieu and along the trade routes to all but the most remote villages. Because AIDS affects the general population of sexually active adults and adolescents, narrowly focused prevention strategies are not likely to stop the spread of infection.[1] Vignettes composed from case histories of women who are at risk of HIV infection indicate a need to decenter prevention strategies from the current public health communications framework promoting individual behavior change by means of messages aimed at designated "target groups."[2]

AUTHOR'S NOTE. This research was supported in part by grants from the Rockefeller Foundation, Health Sciences Division, and the Wenner-Gren Foundation for Anthropological Research. Grateful acknowledgment of support does not imply responsibility for data or conclusions. The chapter includes material abridged from "At Risk for AIDS: Women's Lives in Zaire," a colloquium presented at the Henry A. Murray Research Center, Radcliffe College, Cambridge, December 12, 1989. This version has benefited from critique by Paul Farmer.

The collaborative study rapidly discovered that culturally constructed gender roles and sexual meanings are crucial to understanding the spread of HIV (Schoepf, Payanzo, Rukarangira, Schoepf, & Walu, 1988). Ethnography and group dynamics methods[3] were used to discover how to help people change their behavior to reduce their risks of AIDS. In a setting where infection is spreading rapidly,[4] this was our first goal (Schoepf, 1986b, 1988b; Schoepf, Rukarangira, & Matumona, 1986). Working first with two women's groups in a low-income neighborhood, then with separate groups of men, women, and adolescents, and, finally, with "traditional" healers, culturally appropriate forms of personal risk assessment and community-based risk reduction support were devised (Schoepf, in press-a, in press-b; Schoepf, Walu, Rukarangira, et al., 1991, in press-a, in press-b). The practice methodology conveyed information in accessible form at the same time that it produced data on the cultural construction of this new disease.[5]

I have sought to place the ethnographic findings in the broader context of research on the political ecology of disease—its social production in specific historical times and places (Feierman, 1985; Hartwig & Patterson, 1978; Schoepf, 1986b, 1988a, 1988b, 1988c; Turshen, 1984). AIDS in Central Africa is a *disease of development,* in the sense of the term coined by Hughes and Hunter (1970), and of underdevelopment (Schoepf, Rukarangira, Schoepf, Walu, & Payanzo, 1988). Because the spread of the new virus is determined by the international political economy and social structures, as well as by the actions of individuals and groups variously situated in society, AIDS may usefully be viewed as socially produced.[6] The study of societal response, including AIDS control policies, has led to interest in the cultural politics of AIDS in the context of relations between Africa and the West (Schoepf, 1986a, in press-c). AIDS brings to the fore in public discourse expressions of ideological representations that support and reproduce already constituted gender, color, class, and national hierarchies. A "political economy and culture" approach to critical medical anthropology is useful in exploring intersections of structure and agency at many levels.

Previous studies of epidemics in Africa have used historical methods, including archival sources and oral history, to discover relationships between disease and socioeconomic change. AIDS offers a unique opportunity for anthropologists to observe response to a new, fatal disease as it occurs in different social settings (Schoepf, 1986b). Ethnographic methods can be used to generate textured firsthand accounts, to probe for meanings, and to compare responses within and across cultures. The research is transdisciplinary, incorporating basic premises from several fields, including public health, social psychology, and development studies, informed by anthropological perspectives. The collaborative team afforded opportunities to test ideas in dialogue with colleagues whose understandings enriched my own.[7]

The vignettes presented in this chapter were composed from life histories of women collected between 1985 and 1989. They indicate how and why infection is spreading during this period of deepening economic crisis. Placing life stories in a broader perspective and attending to the different voices of actors variously situated socially is a fundamental strategy of cultural anthropology. The method of seeking views "from within and below" (Huizer & Mannheim, 1979) helps to break through the distorting mirrors of perception that are molded by dominant paradigms in the sciences and by the social situations of investigators (Schoepf, 1979, 1989).

Case histories, life stories, autobiographies, and correspondence written by and about African women have constituted a minor theme in African Studies since Mary Smith's *Baba of Karo* was published in 1954. Such texts have received renewed interest as means to examine the interplay of social structure and conscious social action by individuals and groups (Geiger, 1986). They allow scholars to focus on the attempts of concrete human beings to make history under conditions not of their own making. They also show how large-scale processes of sociocultural change act in local contexts. Attending to people's perceptions of their lived experience, we may hope to surpass "the somewhat rigid structuralism which characterized much of . . . African historiography in the 1970s" (Marks, 1989, p. 39). In other words, historians of Africa have emerged from the one-sided "economistic" caricatures of dependency and mode of production theories.[8]

> Correspondence, autobiographies and life histories serve: to move us beyond the aridity of an unpeopled political economy to the ambiguities of everyday life . . . [so that] we see the overarching constraints of social structure on human agency, and the complex relationship of individual psychology to a culture-bounded social order. (Marks, 1989, p. 39)

Such texts present "not so much an historical world but a certain consciousness of the world" (Stephen Clingman, cited in Marks, 1989, p. 40). If autobiographies and novels are shaped by the consciousness of their authors, biographies, personal narratives, and case histories are shaped by the double selection operated by two tellers of stories: the informant and the ethnographer (Davison, 1989; Mizra & Strobel, 1989; Romero, 1988). Identifying the social contexts of narrative production is important (Kluckhohn, 1945) but not sufficient. Newer work suggests "the need to recognize both the agenda of the narrator and that of the interpreter as distinct and not always compatible" (Personal Narratives Group, 1989, p. 264; Mbilinyi, 1989).

In this case, however, compatibility appears to be high. My political agenda was made explicit to key informants. I sought to contextualize the social epidemiology of AIDS in Zaire as a means of widening discussion of international disease control policy. Because they resonate with people's daily experience, I hypothesized that life histories could raise awareness of the broader issues of gender relations and development strategies that are involved in preventing the spread of HIV, particularly among men. The women who told their stories were aware of these aims. A summary of political economy, gender roles, and the epidemiology of AIDS in Kinshasa, Zaire, helps to situate the vignettes. The objective is to indicate the usefulness of a methodology that, departing from informants' own perceptions, links micro-level ethnography and macro-level political economy analysis (Schoepf & Schoepf, 1981, 1987).[9]

Social Epidemiology of AIDS

Disease epidemics generally erupt in times of crisis, and AIDS is no exception. Zaire, like most other sub-Saharan nations and much of the Third World, is in the throes of economic turmoil. Propelled by declining terms of trade and burdensome debt service, the contradictions of distorted neocolonial economies with rapid class formation have created what appears to be a permanent, deepening crisis. Zaire's crisis began early with the fall of the price of copper, the major export, in 1974.[10] Per capita incomes are ranked among the world's lowest and, in 1987, were estimated to average $150 per year (World Bank, 1989). Average figures mask wide disparities in wealth. Many families in Kinshasa eat only once a day, and malnutrition is widespread (Houyoux, Kinyavwidi, & Okita, 1986; Schoepf, 1988a; Walu, 1987). Throughout the continent, poor women and children have experienced most severely the effects of structural adjustment policies and the deepening crisis (Gladwin, 1991; UNICEF, 1989). In Zaire, as elsewhere in the region, economic crisis and the structure of employment inherited from the colonial period shape the current configuration, contributing to the feminization of poverty and consequently to the spread of AIDS (Schoepf, 1988a; Schoepf & Walu, 1991; Schoepf, Walu, Rukarangira, et al., 1991).

The 19th-century slave trade and the early colonial period witnessed much brutality and intense social disruption. Women slaves were highly prized within Africa. Slavery lasted well into the 20th century, and freed women worked for meager subsistence. Throughout the colonial period, most wage labor was reserved for men, whose wages were too low to support families. Women were relegated to crop production and childbearing, the latter made more frequent as a result of colonial policies (Schoepf, in press-c). Women who escaped to the cities resorted to petty trade and selling services, including sex. While some were able to achieve substantial economic independence and social freedom in informal sector occupations (see Comhaire-Sylvain, 1968; LaFontaine, 1974), the majority were poor (Bernard, 1972). Even following Independence, few wage labor opportunities for women were created. At the same time, widespread insecurity, added to labor-intensive production techniques, low crop prices, and gender inequality within households, made the villages particularly unattractive to women (Schoepf, 1978, 1981).

Currently, Zaire's cities contain as many women as men, but women constitute only 4% of formal sector workers. An estimated 40%-60% of urban men are without waged employment. They, and the majority of women who are without special job qualifications, resort to informal sector occupations. These include petty trade, food preparation, market gardening, sewing, smuggling, and prostitution—occupations that yield very low incomes for most of those who practice them (Schoepf, 1978, 1981; Schoepf & Walu, 1991). Produce trade and smuggling take place over long distances within Zaire and across its borders. Multiple partner sexual relationships regularly accompany such trade (Rukarangira & Schoepf, 1991).

One result of the crisis at the macro level is to render the already crowded informal economic sector increasingly less profitable for many small operators (Schoepf, 1988a; Schoepf, Walu, Rukarangira, et al., 1991; Walu, 1987). Moreover, many women who formerly could rely upon steady contributions from partners or from their extended families report that both sources are dwindling because they too are hard-pressed to make ends meet. Women often seek occasional partners, *pneus de rechange* (or "spare tires"), to meet immediate cash needs. As economic conditions continue to worsen, the social fabric is tearing apart, and sexual strategies that maximize returns become increasingly important.

The presence of AIDS was identified in 1983. Infection is concentrated mainly in the cities but is spreading along the trade routes outward to the rural areas. It is not surprising that young urban women are at highest risk for AIDS in Central Africa. More than 90% of poor prostitutes—women whose major source of subsistence comes from the sale of sex to multiple casual partners—are reported to be infected in several cities of Central and East Africa. In Kinshasa, the rate among sex workers rose from 27% of 287 women sampled in 1984 (Mann et al., 1988) to 40% of the first 500 women attending a new screening clinic for sexually transmitted diseases (STDs) in 1988 (Dr. Rukarangira, interview with Dr. N. Nzila, July 1988).

However, commercial sex workers are not the only women at risk. Samples of women delivering infants in Kinshasa in 1986 found between 5.8% and 8.4% to be infected (N'Galy, Ryder, & Bila, 1988; N'Galy, Ryder, & Quinn, 1989; Ryder et al., 1989). Nearly 40% of infants born to seropositive women were infected, and most died before the age of 2 years. Most of the mothers were married. Younger mothers aged 20 to 30 years were most likely to be seropositive, while rates among unmarried women in this age group were higher still, with 16.7% of hospital workers and 11.1% of textile factory workers infected in 1986. Most are single and are paid below-subsistence wages. In sum, not only sex workers but many women of childbearing age are at high risk, as are young girls just becoming sexually active.

Discourse About Women and AIDS

The first two women on record as having probably died of HIV infection contracted in Zaire were a "free woman," that is, a woman not living under the control of a father, brother, or husband, from Equateur Region, and a surgeon from Denmark who worked in the same region in the 1970s. The contrast in the implicit constructions of these two women's lives in the biomedical literature are striking. The texts and their silences tell us something about cultural constructions of AIDS.

The Zairian woman is reported to have lived for some years in Kinshasa, where she is assumed to have been a prostitute, supporting herself by selling sex to multiple partners. She then returned to the village, where her blood was collected in 1976 as part of a cluster sample drawn by a CDC team studying the new Ebola hemorrhagic fever, which erupted suddenly in the mission village of Yambuku. This woman died several years later of AIDS-like disease, as did a 15-year-old youth. The blood of three other people tested also showed antibodies to HIV (Nzila et al., 1988).

The Danish woman worked for several years at a mission hospital in the great forest. Because surgical gloves were in short supply, she often operated ungloved. Swollen glands without apparent cause were followed by a series of unusual infections, a cough, fever, and constant fatigue. Too weak to work and worried by her inconclusive diagnosis, she returned to Denmark, where repeated workups failed to establish a cause or a name for the mysterious symptoms. Her condition was described by a physician-friend who observed her long illness (Bygbjerg, 1983). The anonymous African woman is mentioned in an epidemiological report.

Juxtaposing the two texts of these presumed cases from the "pre-AIDS era" allows us to compare their underlying premises. The Zairian "free woman" is assumed to have acquired and transmitted HIV infection to others as a result of sexual intercourse. The Danish surgeon (also a "free woman" in the technical meaning of the term) is assumed to have acquired the disease from patients' blood. The report is silent about the possibility that she might have transmitted infection to others. Different constructions of characteristics implicitly attributed to the women on the basis of gender, class, and color emerge.

The resulting dichotomies are Cartesian in their simplicity: White woman/ Black woman; missionary/sinner; heroic work/dirty work; innocent victim/ perpetrator; valued, named/unvalued, unnamed; good woman/bad woman. In short, they form the prototypic we/other couplet, redoubled by the saint/ whore dichotomy of Western sexual morality. The possibility that an African sex worker might have acquired the infection from a blood transfusion is not entertained.[11] The possibility that a White professional woman might have become infected through sexual intercourse is not entertained either. Unprotected by gloves or condoms, the occupations of both women carry considerable risk. Nevertheless, either of them might have become infected in the manner assumed for the other.[12]

Communication systems mirror, reinforce, and reproduce social systems of unequal power. Biomedical discourse is replete with culturally constructed metacommunication. It enters into clinical decision making and shapes the ways patients, physicians, and the public view themselves and others (Schoepf, 1969, 1975, 1979). The new disease syndrome, laden with emotionally charged issues of sex, blood, and death, is not only the newest disease metaphor in Western society. It has unleashed stigmatizing metadiscursive practices and social action in the international arena (Chirimuuta & Chirimuuta, 1987; Konotey-Ahulu, 1989; Prewitt, 1988; Schoepf, 1986a, 1988b, 1990a, 1990b; Waite, 1988; Watney, 1989).

Western popular and biomedical accounts of AIDS contain examples of racist constructions of African culture; these in turn have provoked defensive responses from African leaders and peoples (Schoepf, in press-c). Africa has been designated as the source of AIDS; exotic customs have been held responsible for passage of the virus from monkeys to humans, and the sexuality of Africans has been characterized as "promiscuous" and different than that of peoples elsewhere. Western racism has contributed to denial of AIDS by African leaders and slowed efforts to halt the spread of infection, as both leaders and publics have defended African personhood against the stigmatizing attacks. The disease also has become a stigmatizing condition within Africa. In many contexts, as in the United States, stigma and anxiety lead to distancing, to "othering," not only of the afflicted but of those associated with them.

Some of these elements appear in the vignettes presented in the next section. Each woman is from a different ethnic group; each story illustrates a common risk situation in which class differences exist but are not always what might be expected due to the ways that gender is played out (see Robertson & Berger, 1986). In this large city of 3.5 million inhabitants, not all sexually active people are at risk. The sexual culture of any large city is pluralistic. Kinshasa includes an unknown proportion of mutually monogamous couples and celibate single people who live according to traditional or Christian tenets. Nevertheless, polygyny continues to be widespread, and many other types of multiple partner relationships, with varying degrees of social recognition and legitimacy, exist among people of all social classes and ethnic origins. Even socially recognized relationships may be of relatively brief duration, leading, as in the West, to what has been termed "serial polygyny." Some people report that they have changed their life-styles in response to the AIDS danger (Schoepf, 1988a). Monthly condom sales in Kinshasa by a social marketing project rose to 300,000 in June 1988 (Rukarangira & Schoepf, 1989). They were used mainly in casual encounters. Nevertheless, the vignettes illustrate some persistent obstacles to change that an effective prevention program must address. The constraints identified in Kinshasa are common throughout the region (Society for Women and AIDS in Africa [SWAA], 1989).

Women at Risk

Nsanga is 36 and very poor, the mother of a 5-year-old girl and a boy in primary school. Until recently, she contributed to the support of a younger brother in secondary school who lives with an elder brother. A younger sister also lives with Nsanga in a single room with a corrugated iron roof, part of a block surrounding an open courtyard. The yard contains a shared water tap, a roofless bathing stall, and a latrine, but no electricity. In good weather, Nsanga moves her charcoal stove outdoors to cook.

Nsanga wasn't always the head of her household. Village raised, she married a schoolteacher in 1980 and managed—somehow—on his skimpy salary, despite galloping inflation of nearly 100% each year. In 1983, the

International Monetary Fund (IMF) instituted a series of "structural adjustment" measures designed to reduce government expenditures so that Zaire, like other Third World nations that had borrowed heavily in the 1970s, could make payments on its international debt. More than 80,000 teachers and health workers were made redundant by this "*assainissement* in 1984."[13] Nsanga's husband was one of those who, lacking a powerful patron to intercede for him, joined the ranks of the unemployed. After six fruitless months of waiting in offices, he began to drink, selling off the household appliances to pay for beer and then *lutuku,* the cheap home-distilled alcohol.

Nsanga tried many things to earn money. Like most poor women in Kinshasa, she has had only a few years of primary schooling. Because she has no powerful friends or relatives either, she was unable to find waged employment. She cooked food for neighborhood men, she sold uncooked rice in small quantities and dried fish when she could obtain supplies cheaply. These efforts brought in only pennies at a time. Her husband left and Nsanga does not know where he is. The children ate into her stocks and she went into debt for the rent. She asked her elder brother for a loan, but he refused, pleading poverty. Although he has a steady job as a laborer on the docks, he has two wives and nine children.

Without new start-up capital, exchanging sex for subsistence seemed the obvious solution. The first year Nsanga became a *"deuxième bureau,"* "occupied" by a lover who made regular support payments. She also had a few "spare tires" to help out. Then she got pregnant and the "occupant" left. His salary couldn't stretch that far, he told her. So Nsanga had to take on more partners—a fairly typical downward slide. The neighborhood rate was 50 cents per brief encounter in 1987, and Nsanga says that if she is lucky she can get two or three partners per working day, for a total of $30 a month (at most). Many men now avoid sex workers because the mass media have identified "prostitutes" as a source of infection.

Nsanga's baby was sickly and died before her second birthday, following prolonged fever, diarrhea, and skin eruptions. Nsanga believes it was because semen from so many men spoiled her milk. Nsanga reports that she has had a few bouts of gonorrhea, for which she took some tetracycline pills on advice from the drugstore clerk. About a year ago, she had abdominal pains for several months but no money to consult a doctor. She says that the European nuns at the dispensary in her neighborhood do not treat such diseases. Diagnosis at the nearby university clinic costs the equivalent of 30 encounters, so none of the women she knows can afford quality care.

Asked about condoms, Nsanga said that she has heard of but never actually seen one. She has heard that men use them to prevent disease when they have sex with prostitutes. Nsanga rejects this morally stigmatizing label and, if a lover were to propose using a condom, she would be angry: "It would mean that he doesn't trust me." In her own eyes, Nsanga is not a prostitute because she is not a "bad woman." On the contrary, as a mother who has fallen on hard times through no fault of her own, she is trying her best, "breaking stones" (kobeta libanga), to meet family obligations. In the presence of HIV, Nsanga's survival strategy has been transformed into a death strategy.[14]

Nsanga has become very thin and believes that people are whispering about her. In fact, her neighbors are sure Nsanga has AIDS. But then, Nsanga reasons, "People say this about everyone who loses weight, even when it is just from hunger and worry. All these people who are dying nowadays, are they really all dying from AIDS?" Her defensiveness is shared by numerous women in similar circumstances, for whom denial is a stratagem for coping with a situation they cannot change.

Tango is a college graduate, aged 40. She has worked for 14 years in a gender-typed formal sector job. Her work demands considerable technical and public relations skills. Unmarried, with a slim figure and wearing stylish European clothes, she has had a succession of lovers over the past 25 years. These have included fellow students and wealthy older men from both the African and expatriate elites. Four years ago, she became pregnant and decided to keep the child rather than going to a doctor in her network for an illegal abortion. Although formerly her ethnic tradition strongly discouraged premarital pregnancy and imposed heavy sanctions on unwed mothers, Tango's parents were delighted with her decision.[15] They reasoned that she is not likely to marry and will not have many more opportunities to bear a child.

The infant was robust, healthy, and much loved. When he was 1 year old, Tango was hospitalized for pneumonia, a disease one type of which is frequently associated with AIDS. The sickness dragged on and she lost weight; tongues began to wag. Tango became frightened. Then she reassured herself: "My child is not sick; therefore I am not infected." After six months, her health improved and Tango was further reassured. Nevertheless, her long sickness and the deaths of a former lover and numerous acquaintances from AIDS have made her prudent. Because she has read that condoms are not 100% sure protection, Tango now prefers to forgo sex: "I have my child to think of. My parents are too old to raise him properly."

Tango remains unmarried by choice. She has refused to place herself in the subordinate status and in what she feels are the uncomfortable situations that marriage imposes on women—in her culture and in the West. Friends say that she could have married an American lover who was ready to divorce his wife for her. In the pre-AIDS era, Tango believed that she had the best possible sort of life for a woman without wealthy parents. She has a moderate-paying job that she enjoys, health insurance, vacation travel, a low-rent apartment in the center of town, many friends and relations in the city, and the moral support of her parents living in a distant city. In addition, Tango enjoyed the fun of having lovers, with dinner dates, dancing, and gifts. She suffered none of the heartbreak that comes from emotional involvement with one (she believes, inevitably) unfaithful man; no jealousy of rivals or the galling burden of having to support and care for children while their father divides his resources among several women.

Tango's apartment is old, with unreliable plumbing and indestructible cockroaches, but relatively cheap and very convenient. Tango walks to work and to shops, saving on fares and on waiting time for the collective taxis that supplement the overcrowded bus system. She owns numerous furnishings, accumulated from her salary and gifts. To these blessings—and the pitfalls avoided—Tango has added the joy of a child of her own, a boy named after her father.

Because of AIDS, Tango has given up lovers. She misses both sexual satisfaction and luxuries that her wages cannot provide. Trade might be an option, but her private sector job is demanding and, unlike many people in government employment, Tango cannot take off time from work to conduct a business on the side. "Besides, everyone is selling something these days and nobody has money to buy." Tango voices a common complaint. Whether she will remain celibate is unknown. But, because she is single and can manage on her salary, the choice is hers to make. Moreover, if she decides to take a lover, she can insist on regular condom use. Tango might follow the example of her friend Zola, who is divorced, self-employed, and apparently well off.

In 1985, Zola, Tango, and their friends dismissed the news of this mysterious new disease as an "Imaginary Syndrome Invented to Discourage Lovers."[16] "Which lovers were being discouraged? Africans, of course. By whom? Europeans of course. Why? Because they believe that Africans have too much sex. Really, they are jealous." This denial served as a cultural defense. Then there were too many cases reported by physician-friends working at the three major hospitals in Kinshasa. By 1987, people in their relatively privileged circle acknowledged that AIDS is real, fatal, and sexually transmitted. In 1988, some began to use condoms. Fear of AIDS caused Zola to remain celibate for about six months. Then she took a very young lover to meet her "hygiene needs."[17] She initiated him into adult sexuality and believes that she can count on his manifest attachment (and her gifts) to keep him faithful.

Tango and Zola are unusual. Because of their relative economic independence, they can control their sexuality and negotiate condom use. Since learning about AIDS, they have significantly reduced their level of risk. Not all employed single women are so fortunate. Most women who are employed receive very low wages and, sexual clientship is a condition of employment for many.

Vumba is a nurse, aged 25, who in 1987 earned $35 per month. She grew up in Kinshasa and is single, without children. She lives with her widowed mother and two younger sisters, still in school. The rent for two rooms in a courtyard very much like the one where Nsanga lives is $11. However, Vumba's courtyard has electricity and she splits the bill with the neighbors. She pays $5 per month to run her two electric lights, a two-coil hot plate, a radio, a fan, and an old refrigerator. (The first woman described had lost these things connoting lower-middle-class status.) Vumba's mother sells beer in the courtyard, "but with everybody selling something there is very little profit." She is looking around for something else to sell that would make more money. Meanwhile, Vumba is the family's mainstay.

She has a lover, a clerical worker who earns less than she. Although they have been together for nearly five years, he seems in no hurry to get married. Vumba reasons that he probably sees no advantage to marrying, because she would still have to use her salary to support mother and sisters. She talked to him about using condoms but he refused: "Because they aren't natural." He believes that condoms would interfere with his pleasure. He has never tried one, but friends who have complain of reduced sensation: "They say 'it's like eating a banana with the skin on.' "[18] Her lover already has children with another woman and has no objection to Vumba taking the pill. In her experience, this is unusual and is one more indication that he is not serious, because "children are the seal of a marriage."

In 1986, hospital workers were screened for HIV. Nearly 9% were infected. Vumba was among those found seropositive but was not told at the time. "Maybe they thought I would commit suicide?"[19] When she learned of her test results, Vumba was devastated but thus far there have been no signs of disease. Has she told her lover? "No, of course not. I proposed to use condoms. But since he refused, the consequences are his lookout! Where do you think I got it, anyway?" she asks.

Vumba's defensiveness arises from a situation of relative powerlessness. She believes that, if she were to tell her lover of her serostatus, he would disappear. This assessment is shared by many women and has been borne out in practice. Because HIV-infected persons may be shunned by friends and even by some family members, Vumba's behavior is self-protective. She believes that the pleasure she experiences with her lover is essential to her health and that, if she were to worry about her HIV status, the disease would come on right away.

Actually Vumba *has* had a few other partners (she says she doesn't remember how many). She began having sex in nursing school at age 17. Because she did not experience satisfaction in those days, she has put them out of her mind. Vumba likes to dress well. A six-yard length of locally made wax print fabric and tailoring for an ensemble (blouse and two *pagnes*) cost two months' salary. These days, AIDS is called *Salaire Insuffisant Depuis des Années*.[20] Moreover, Vumba says, "The doctors at the clinic are demanding; they can cause endless complications for a nurse who refuses their advances." She heard that several doctors are infected too. Quite a few are no longer at the hospital, and two are said to have died of AIDS. "Others just don't want to be around so many infected people!"

Vumba was frightened too. Although the nurses were told that AIDS is hard to catch, she would have liked to find another job where she would feel less exposed. "Maybe, after all, one could get infected from a patient?" But now, she asks: "What's the use?" Vumba is afraid of the pain and the wasting. Without children, she will never become an ancestor. She fears that she will die "an insignificant person" and that her name will be forgotten, because she will have no children to name their children after her.

Vumba has other worries: "What will become of my younger sisters?" With men now looking for younger and younger partners whom they believe less likely to be infected, the temptations for girls from poor families are very strong. The deepening crisis leaves less money to pay school fees, buy clothes, and bribe poorly paid teachers to give them passing grades. Do her sisters know about condoms? Vumba isn't sure. She hasn't told them, because she doesn't want them to think she is encouraging them to have sex. Perhaps they learned about condom protection from Franco's song?[21] Vumba sighs:

> Even if they know about *les Prudences* [this social marketing brand name has become a popular euphemism for condoms], what's the use? Men won't use the things and the girls can't make them. Anyway, a young girl would be ashamed to ask her friend to use a condom. He would think she was a prostitute! It's the same as with birth control pills.

Avoidance, denial, and notions of propriety combine with gender inequality to increase young women's vulnerability. Although at least half the adolescents in Kinshasa are sexually active by age 17, many adults do not consider their desires legitimate and avoid the subject.

Mbeya is a stylish, carefully groomed woman in her late forties. She wore heavy gold jewelry, ensembles of imported Dutch wax print fabric, expensive handbags and matching shoes. She often drove an elderly Mercedes herself, although there was a chauffeur to run errands and drive her youngest child to school. Two elder children were studying in Europe and one in the United States.

Mbeya's husband was for many years an important figure in the ruling party's inner circle. For such men, the company of stylish young women is a prerequisite of the job, a routine part of the socializing integral to politics. Mistresses are also part of the intelligence-gathering networks that no man in high politics can do without. The government's ideology of "authenticity," promulgated partly to undermine the influence of the Catholic church, has made polygyny respectable. As in the slaving period prior to this century, access to numerous women is a symbol of power and wealth. Mbeya says that she was not too jealous because her husband "always respected me as the first wife, mother of his children [*Mama ya Bana*], and kept his other women away from the house." There was plenty of money and she never felt done out of her rights as has been the case with many of her friends whose husbands are unfaithful.

Mbeya had a friend who couldn't abide her husband's outside wives and lovers. "She harangued him about this so much that finally he left. She divorced him, but he got back at her. He forbade their children to visit their mother when they came home from school in Europe." Her friend died of asthma and Mbeya is sure that her condition was aggravated by her chagrin. Mbeya muses: "Everyone is wondering why *that* man hasn't succumbed to AIDS!" The fact that some notorious *coureurs* have remained healthy, and that some people get sick while their spouses do not, causes confusion. AIDS's apparent arbitrariness reinforces beliefs that implicate fate, luck, ancestral spirits, and sorcery in disease causation and contributes to denial of sexual risk.

A wealthy physician-businessman living on Mbeya's street, and two of his wives, died from AIDS. Neighbors blamed the first wife because she traded on her own account, traveling to Nigeria to purchase household appliances on commission for friends and acquaintances. Mbeya reflects:

It could just as well have been the husband who gave *her* AIDS! Who knows what younger wives do when their husband is away? And did he only sleep with his wives? After all, a doctor has many opportunities! Men are always quick to blame women, especially when women earn their own money!

AIDS has entered the complex terrain of gender struggles and competing moral discourses. Mbeya and her friends wonder where AIDS came from. They reject the "monkey's blood" hypothesis as one more racist slur (see Schoepf, 1988c). Several "traditional" healers claim that AIDS is an old disease that has become epidemic because women no longer observe the old sexual customs (Schoepf, in press-b). However, in Mbeya's ethnic group, as in many others, high-status women controlled their own sexuality. Tradition has been reinvented in aid of controlling women (Schoepf, in press-d). Some clergymen claim that AIDS is a divine punishment and that sinners will be struck down while the innocent are safe. They apply the term *sinner* to women who fail to conform to their prescriptions of morality: premarital chastity and marital fidelity. Rejecting these moralistic constructions in favor of a biomedical explanation, Mbeya and her friends say that most women cannot remain with only one partner throughout their lifetime. Moreover, they wonder if it is true that, as they have heard, the virus came to Africa from America.

In May 1987, Mbeya's husband brought home an official notice about AIDS and left it on her bedside table. She laughed: "He just left it here, without saying anything." Concerned, she was afraid to broach the subject of condom protection. Then, late in 1988, Mbeya became aware that her husband was sick and not getting any better. She began to suspect that it might be AIDS and told him that she wanted to use condoms. Her husband refused. So she said that they should stop sexual relations. Her husband's family was outraged and he refused this too. They threatened to throw her out and keep her youngest daughter. Mbeya acquiesced. Following her husband's death, her in-laws accused her of infecting her husband, despite the logic of the situation: Mbeya protests that she married as a young virgin straight from a convent school and that all through the years she was a faithful wife.

Recently widowed, Mbeya soon will have to leave her husband's luxurious villa and all the furnishings. These now belong to the husband's family, who have already taken possession of the cars and the businesses and rental properties her husband had acquired. Formerly, her husband's younger brother might have allowed her to live in the house with his family, even if he did not become her actual husband. Mbeya believes that her affines' accusations are motivated by their self-interest. "The property is too valuable!" The house will be sold and the money shared among her husband's brothers. Turned out of her home, bereaved, and fearing that she is infected, Mbeya will go to her brother's, where she will become his dependent.

Mbeya's story illustrates the ephemeral nature of women's class position when based upon a husband's ownership of resources. Formerly the manager of an extended family household with 22 people to feed, clothe, and care for, Mbeya said that she had no energy or time to start a business for herself. Now she envies women who trade and earn money. "I never dreamt I would need to do that myself!" Now that she does, Mbeya has plans. She belongs to a *musiki,* a rotating credit association of women of her class and ethnic group living in her neighborhood. Like her, they are first wives of senior officials and professors, many of whom circulate between the two roles. "It is a long time since the kitty has come my way, so I'm sure the women will let me have it to start up in trade." What will she do? She is exploring the possibilities:

> First, I thought of trading to Nigeria or to Brussels. But I do not want to be away from my daughter so much. I'm thinking about selling wheat flour in *demi-gros.* I can get a quota from MIDEMA [the mill of Continental Grain Co., which has a monopoly on wheat imports to Zaire and receives cheap PL480 wheat] through a friend of my husband.

Actually, very little money can be made this way (Schoepf & Walu, 1991). Women without valuable connections often exchange sex for facilitating favors by officials to obtain and move goods and to reduce or avoid customs duties and taxes (MacGaffey, 1986; Schoepf, 1978). A devout Catholic, Mbeya would find this stratagem repugnant. Well-connected, she may not be obliged to do so.

Mbeya has not gotten very far with her planning. Emotionally, she is still reeling from her husband's unpleasant death and is in no shape to face the future. Why hasn't Mbeya gone to be tested? Although her husband was treated with drugs that doctors said prolonged his life, Mbeya knows nobody who has recovered from AIDS. She does not believe that the indigenous medicine about which the local press has waxed enthusiastic actually provides a cure: "Even the doctor who is trying it does not claim success." Intellectually, she knows that AIDS is fatal and that, if infected, she will die eventually. However, Mbeya would rather not think about that just yet. "If I am seropositive, then worrying would bring on the disease." Many people use this construction to avoid learning their serostatus.

Gisèle is a European woman with a professional degree whose husband was seconded to Zaire as a member of a technical assistance mission in 1975. She lives a fairly luxurious life, which, although it does not match that enjoyed by Mbeya while her husband was alive, is of a higher standard than she would have attained in her own country. Some years ago, Gisèle suspended her professional career to devote her energies to child rearing. Now that her fourth child is nearly 4, she is thinking about returning to Europe and resuming her career. Fear of AIDS is also a motivating factor.

Gisèle is aware that her husband has taken advantage of the numerous opportunities for sexual adventures that his position affords. One liaison actually seemed serious enough to threaten her marriage, when her husband rented and furnished an apartment for a university student. However, the affair ended when this woman had a baby with another of her partners.[22] Gisèle believes she has reason to fear HIV infection. Although she was tested and found negative, her husband refused the test. When last interviewed, Gisèle had not yet decided what to do.

Although the Catholic Archdiocese of Kinshasa has pronounced in favor of protection (see Schoepf, Rukarangira, et al., 1988), Gisèle's religious convictions preclude asking her husband to use condoms. She was thinking of presenting her husband with two alternatives: testing and fidelity (assuming an HIV negative result) or abstinence, to be enforced by her departure for Europe with the children. In the latter event, Gisèle hopes that she can get a job, but she recognizes that the economic slump in her own country renders this problematic. She may have to take a position at lower level than that which she left. She hopes that her husband will help with support payments for their children. Then again, she reasons, maybe that will not be necessary. Like many African women in Kinshasa, Gisèle prays that risk of AIDS will convince her husband of the advantages of mutually faithful monogamy.

Structure and Agency

The vignettes lend texture to epidemiological data. They confirm the fact that HIV is spreading not because of exotic cultural practices but because of many people's normal responses to situations of everyday life. Commercial sex workers are at very high risk because risk increases with the number of partners (Mann et al., 1988). However, as the women whose stories have been presented here are aware, the majority of those at risk are not engaged in commercial sex work.

The vignettes show how some women have been able to change their behavior to reduce their risk of AIDS. They also indicate some of the obstacles many other women face even when they are relatively well informed about AIDS transmission and safer sex practices. The obstacles to behavior change are social, emotional, and material. Most women are at risk because their relative powerlessness in the overall organization of Zairian society and their subordinate position with respect to men circumscribe their options. Few are able to practice safer sex. Some do not feel able to open dialogue with sexual partners on the subject. Others who have attempted to do so have experienced rejection and retaliation. Those who have reduced their risk are women with decision-making autonomy based on their capacity to support themselves and their dependents without resorting to sex within or outside of marriage. Although the poorest are at highest risk, the experience of married women dependent on wealthy husbands confirms the thesis that women do not automatically share their husbands' class position (Robertson & Berger, 1986).

While, at some levels, gender relations are subject to negotiation, women's struggles to improve their condition take place in circumstances not of their own making (Schoepf, 1988a; Schoepf & Walu, 1991). Incomes have not kept pace with inflation, particularly in the cost of food, rent, health care, and transport. Many who were scraping by in 1987 have fallen into extreme poverty. Although no statistics exist, our observations suggest that multiple-partner situations, particularly those involving various forms of sexual patron-client relationships, appear to be increasing as a result of the deepening economic crisis. The health consequences of multiple-partner strategies, often serious for women and children in the past (Schoepf, 1978, 1981; Schoepf & Schoepf, 1981), have become much more so during the past decade with the spread of HIV.

Primary prevention of AIDS cannot be effected simply by targeting commercial sex workers. Like Nsanga and Vumba, many women who have multiple partners do not think of themselves as prostitutes. They are not professionals sharing a career, an identity, and a mutually supportive organization. Struggling to support their families in a period of economic crisis, they resort to sexual "survival strategies" at a time when these have turned into their opposite, becoming strategies of death.

It is the fact of multiple partners, rather than the type of relationship, however socially categorized and labeled, that puts people at risk. At the same time, faithful monogamous women like Mbeya and Gisèle are at risk if *their* steady partners have had, or continue to have, multiple partners. As AIDS deaths multiply, these women are becoming frightened, and with cause. In areas where between 5% and 30% of sexually active adults already are infected, prevention involves convincing many among the general population to alter behaviors that are widely considered to be normal, "natural," and highly valued.

Popular and biomedical sentiment considers prostitutes to be the major reservoir of AIDS as well as other STDs in Africa as in the West. Viewed from a different perspective, however, the poor sex workers are at much higher risk than their clients. The women serve between 250 and 1,000 men annually, whereas the latter use these services just a few times per month. Condoms are commonly perceived as offering protection for men against women. This stigmatizing gendered perception is involved in many women's refusal of condoms, as we discovered from interviews in several different settings. Men's disparagement of condoms as well as the sex workers' need for cash increase the women's risk. It also underscores the need for activities that can effectively increase women's financial independence and their sense of self-worth and lead to social empowerment over the long term.

Studies made throughout the world show that mass media campaigns increase knowledge of AIDS but seldom lead to change in risky behavior. Nor can they change the situations that place people at risk. Because communication systems are social systems, the reception of information and the ability to act on information received are differentially distributed in hierarchical systems. Differential social power needs to be considered when designing prevention strategies. This point will be elaborated in the concluding section. For these reasons, CONNAISSIDA has emphasized the search for culturally appropriate community-based change strategies. These include experiments with a variety of risk reduction workshops grounded in ethnography and using participatory, experiential learning techniques. Taking advantage of existing social groups and presenting AIDS prevention as a political choice, we found that such workshops can assist people in many social milieus to make informed decisions.[23] The workshops provide a context for people to discuss wider issues related to health, household economics, and social relationships. They can be adapted readily for insertion into programs of existing community development organizations, informal voluntary associations such as the popular *musiki* (a form of revolving credit association), clan gatherings, sports clubs, and local government-sponsored bodies, such as trade unions, youth groups, and market women's associations. The method is effective in raising questions and helping people to pose the problem of AIDS in their own and their families' lives. It does not alter the power relationships that are determined by the structure of social relations in the wider society.

Culturally appropriate empowering education is one necessary but not sufficient part of AIDS prevention or of any health and development strategy. Without widespread implementation of community-based prevention strategies, we can expect differences in the incidence of new HIV infection to follow existing differences in socioeconomic power and access to information. At the same time, the socioeconomic constraints to behavior change that introduced this chapter cannot be ignored, for they continue to limit the possibilities of even highly motivated individuals to alter their behavior.

The most pressing need identified by all the women's groups that invited us was for income-generating activities. Women's incomes need to enable those who cannot depend upon a single male partner to support them and their children without resort to providing sexual services to multiple partners (Schoepf & Walu, 1991). Both sex workers and churchwomen reported having tried numerous other ways to enlarge family resources. Most have had scant success. Two groups drew up lists of needs and possibilities without arriving at a realistic plan of cooperative action that might be sustainable in the medium or long term, even with initial support from a funding agency (Schoepf, Walu, Rukarangira, et al., 1991). The effects of deepening crisis, declining incomes, and rampant inflation are too pervasive to be resolved at the level of local communities (Schoepf, Walu, Russell, & Schoepf, 1991).

In addition to their value to the participants, the workshops afforded the researchers opportunities to gather data on the cultural construction and impact of AIDS. Emotional responses to role-plays suggested areas of high anxiety and resistance to change. Discussions indicated areas of misinformation that need to be addressed and provided ideas about how to convey information. Participants collaborated in problem solving and were able to give information in a general way without exposing their own behavior if they so wished. Perceived as a useful service, the relaxed yet structured informality of the training method generated an atmosphere of confidence between people of markedly different social status. Ethnographers usually work for months to gain entry into communities and to develop relatively open relationships with key informants. The workshop sessions also provided capacity-building field apprenticeship in process training for the research team (Schoepf, Walu, et al., in press-a).

Combined with ethnography, the practice methodology can become a powerful tool for in-depth research. As such, the structured training groups are to be distinguished from the focus group discussion technique, derived from advertising research, as well as from group interviews used in rapid assessments. Both of these are methods that yield mainly normative information rather than in-depth insights. They have their place not as shortcuts to qualitative data-gathering but simply as an introduction to research questions. In a more auspicious setting than Zaire, which is currently in political crisis, the workshop methodology could be used to generate and sustain participatory action research (see Hope, Timmel, & Hodzi, 1984; Schoepf, in press-a, in press-b).

Elsewhere, CONNAISSIDA has suggested that experiential training is a type of health-by-the-people approach, which, if successful in AIDS risk reduction, might serve as a model for other types of health promotion (Schoepf, 1986a, 1986b; Schoepf, Rukarangira, et al., 1988). It could be used not only by community groups but also to train health workers at various levels, including physicians. Budget constraints imposed by structural adjustment programs have reinforced the tendency of planners to equate local-level initiatives and popular participation with reliance on local financial resources (Schoepf, Walu, Russell, & Schoepf, 1991). However, "health on the cheap" will not stop AIDS. On the other hand, successful AIDS prevention based on social and self-empowerment techniques such as the method presented here could strengthen primary health care delivery systems as well as other special (or vertical) programs. Most urban health care programs of either type still fail to incorporate vigorous community participation.

Conclusion

Like many other pandemics, the spread of HIV infection is facilitated by socioeconomic and political conditions. The virus is a biological event the effects of which have been magnified by the conditions of urbanization in African societies, distorted development, and the current world economic crisis. Linking macro-level political economy to micro-level ethnography shows how women's survival strategies have turned into death strategies. Change to safer sexual practices involves much more than the adoption of an unpopular imported technology; it involves redefinition of the gendered social roles and change in the socioeconomic conditions that have contributed to the rapid spread of AIDS in the region.

Most public health research on AIDS has consisted of epidemiological studies and surveys of knowledge, attitudes, and practices. This narrowed gaze results from a restricted definition of disease. Physicians and policymakers in the Belgian Congo were aware that socioeconomic conditions spread preventable diseases among the African population. However, better living conditions would have lowered the profits that were the colony's chief reason for being.[24] Instead of promoting general public health through sanitation, protected water supplies, and better food, the physicians devised a medieval-style measure. They created no-man's lands, planted with eucalyptus trees, around the European central cities to keep the Africans and their pollution at bay. The fragrant leaves, believed to contain medicinal properties, conferred only symbolic protection from contagion. Yet, although streams of Africans crossed into the European cities every day to work, the green belts' material presence bolstered a reassuring myth: that misfortune comes from without. Ethnographic studies of AIDS offer no such reassurance. They do, however, offer more realistic grounds on which to base prevention.

Knowledge of Zaire's history, political economy, and culture is pertinent to controlling the spread of HIV disease as it also is to understanding the potential future social impact of AIDS. The methodological approach of this research is related to advances made in the study of continuity and change in African societies over the past two decades. The first is the need to understand how the macro-level political economy affects sociocultural dynamics at the micro level—including the spread of disease and the social response to epidemics. Life history materials illustrate ways in which the condition of women, culturally constructed gender roles, and concepts of personhood are related to these processes. Although this chapter has only touched upon this aspect, gender relations are emblematic of the process of capital accumulation, which drains resources away from the villages, and upward from the urban poor to national ruling classes, and outward to world markets.[25]

Analysis of texts and discourse about AIDS in the international arena provides a window on the contextual framing of historical and contemporary relations between Africa and the West. Sexual aspects of cultural politics continue to contribute ideological justification for inequality. Both the noise and the silences they create influence the spread of HIV.

Another area of interest is countercurrents of resistance to dominant ideologies and structures. Neither gender roles nor sexual relationships are static. Recent scholarship has brought to light many examples of women's struggles to change their condition. Using a methodological framework linking political economy and culture, studies of response to the AIDS pandemic can illuminate interrelationships between social structures and human agency. Such linkages are essential to understanding processes of sociocultural change and the political ecology of disease and its prevention. The practice methodology affords opportunities to study ongoing social action and perhaps to influence its course. Working in collaboration with people at risk, anthropologists have an opportunity to interrogate the discipline about its objectives: anthropology for what and for whom?

Notes

1. A World Bank team estimated that new infection in Kinshasa could be reduced 75% by "eliminating prostitution" (Bulato & Bos, 1988). They do not indicate how "prostitutes" are to be defined and identified. Neither are they concerned with other multiple partner relationships.

2. Even in the United States, the "health belief model" on which this strategy is based predicts only about 10% of response to AIDS (Hingson et al., 1990).

3. These include broad in-depth study by means of participant observation, interviews, and action research conducted with individuals and small groups as well as surveys on selected topics.

4. More than 32,000 people in Kinshasa are estimated to have become infected annually in 1985 and 1986 (N'Galy et al., 1988).

5. The practice methodology of CONNAISSIDA's action research is described in several papers (Schoepf, Walu, Rukarangira, et al., 1991, in press-a, in press-b; Schoepf, in press-a, in press-b).

6. While this elementary Virchowian postulate has been rejected by biomedical reviewers of my articles, an anthropologist reviewer considered it too trivial to mention.

7. I wish to express my gratitude to colleagues of the core team composed of Professor Payanzo Ntsomo, sociologist; Dr. Rukarangira wa Nkera, public health specialist; Ms. Walu Engundu, anthropologist; and Claude Schoepf, development economist. None is responsible for the work presented here. My own work has spanned these fields.

8. In fact, studies of the lives of African women suffered less from these aberrations than did other areas of investigation (Hay, 1988; Schoepf, in press-b).

9. A book presenting the narrative texts is in preparation.

10. A period of growth between 1968 and 1973 increased dependency on copper and other mineral exports that had dominated the colonial economy from the 1920s. Capital-intensive public investments made from foreign loans created relatively few new jobs, while a dearth of investment in peasant production and transport infrastructure fueled the exodus to cities already crowded with unemployed. In 1973, oil prices rose steeply. To these liabilities were added redistribution of internal economic resources from foreign owners to Zairians linked to the inner circle of political power. Many of these windfalls were plundered by their new owners. In 1974, declining international copper prices sent government revenues plummeting while debt service payments came due. A cumulative negative growth rate of 18% occurred over the next decade, and prices rose 6,580%.

11. Transfusions are fairly common among poor African women with access to biomedical services. Chronic nutritional anemias are aggravated by malaria, pregnancy, intestinal parasites, and blood loss from menstruation, childbirth, and botched abortions.

12. Shilts (1987, pp. 5-6) intimates that the surgeon was a lesbian, with "blond hair worn short in a cut that some delicately called mannish" and "a longtime female companion." This would reduce the likelihood of sexual transmission. He is among the promoters of *Heart of Darkness* stereotypes of Africa as a fetid breeding ground of disease, unbridled sexuality, and cultural exotica.

13. The term *assainissement* is ironic; it means "cleaning up" and, by extension, making healthy. Bringing health to the budget, this housecleaning has brought malnutrition and ill health to hundreds of thousands, including low-paid government employees, their families, and those whom they formerly served. Many no longer have access to even minimal health care or education.

14. Leaders of a churchwomen's club pointed to abandonment, divorce, and widowhood as circumstances forcing women without other resources into commercial sex work. Professor Ngondo of UNIKIN stresses that, even in ethnic groups that stigmatize prostitution, many women are forced by lack of other resources to rely on sex with multiple partners (Schoepf, 1978).

15. Some cultures encouraged young women to bear one or two children for their fathers' patrilineage prior to marriage.

16. SIDA (Syndrome Imaginaire pour Décourager les Amoureux) is the French acronym for AIDS. Dismissal was a cultural defense against Western attribution of the disease to Africa and Africans with accompanying stigmatization (see Schoepf, 1988c, in press-a).

17. Sexual intercourse, with deposition of semen, was considered necessary to the physical and mental health of women in most cultures in the region. Although some people focus on sex rather than semen, the idea that sex is natural and necessary, and abstinence unnatural, for adults persists.

18. In Anglophone countries, the similes are "eating a sweet with a wrapper on" and "taking a shower in a raincoat."

19. Notification of test results without counseling can be counterproductive (see Schoepf, 1988c). Issues of partner notification are complex (see WHO, 1989).

20. In English, "Acquired *Income* Deficiency Syndrome."

21. The late "Franco" (Luambo Makiadi), a renowned popular musician, issued a record of advice on AIDS prevention in May 1987. Set to music, his *SIDA* provides detailed information on transmission and prevention in accessible form and has been played in bars and taxi-buses throughout the city (Schoepf, Rukarangira, et al., 1988).

22. Student argot has identified a triumvirate of male partners, known as "chic, chèque, choc." The *chic* friend is one who helps with study assignments, the *chèque* is an older lover who pays the bills, the *choc* is a young lover who provides sexual satisfaction and to whom the young woman may be emotionally attached.

23. The action research is described in Schoepf, Walu, Rukarangira, et al. (1991, in press-a, in press-b).

24. During this period, Belgian firms operating in the Congo earned an average of 25% annually on investments, while firms in Belgium earned half that rate (Mandel, 1970).

25. However, see Schoepf (1989, in press-a), Schoepf and Schoepf (1981, 1987, 1991), Schoepf and Walu (1991), and Schoepf, Walu, Russell, and Schoepf (1991) for more extensive treatment.

References

Bernard, G. (1972). Conjugalité et role de la femme à Kinshasa. *Canadian Journal of African Studies, 6*(2), 261-274.

Bulato, A., & Bos, A. (1988). *Cost-benefit analysis of AIDS interventions in Kinshasa, Zaire.* Washington, DC: World Bank.

Bygbjerg, I. C. (1983). AIDS in a Danish surgeon (Zaire 1976) [Letter]. *The Lancet, 1,* 925.

Chirimuuta, R. C., & Chirimuuta, R. J. (1987). *AIDS, Africa and racism.* London: Free Association.

Comhaire-Sylvain, S. (1968). *Femmes de Kinshasa hier et aujourd'hui.* Paris: Mouton.

Davison, J. (1989). *Voices from Mutira: Seven Kikuyu women.* Boulder, CO: Lynne Reiner.

Feierman, S. (1985). Struggles for control: The social roots of health and healing in modern Africa. *African Studies Review, 28*(2/3), 73-147.

Geiger, S. (1986). Women's life histories: Method and content. *Signs, 11*(2), 334-351.

Gladwin, C. (Ed.). (1991). *Structural adjustment and African women farmers.* Gainesville: University of Florida Press.

Hartwig, G. W., & Patterson, D. K. (Eds.). (1978). *Disease in African history: An introductory survey and case studies.* Durham, NC: Duke University Press.

Hay, M. J. (1988). Queens, prostitutes, and peasants: Historical perspectives on African women, 1971-1986. *Canadian Journal of African Studies, 22*(3), 431-447.

Hingson, R. W., Strunin, L., et al. (1990). Beliefs about AIDS, use of alcohol and drugs, and unprotected sex among Massachusetts adolescents. *American Journal of Public Health, 80*(3), 295-299.

Houyoux, J., Kinyavwidi, N., & Okita, O. (1986). *Budgets ménagers à Kinshasa, Zaire.* Kinshasa: Département du Plan.

Hope, A., Timmel, S., & Hodzi, P. (1984). *Training for transformation: A handbook for community development workers.* Gweru, Zimbabwe: Mambo.

Hughes, C. C., & Hunter, J. M. (1970). Disease and "development" in tropical Africa. *Social Science and Medicine, 3,* 443-493.

Huizer, G., & Mannheim, B. (Eds.). (1979). *The politics of anthropology.* The Hague, the Netherlands: Mouton.

Kluckhohn, C. (1945). The personal document in anthropological science. In L. Gottschalk, C. Kluckhohn, & R. Angell (Eds.), *The use of personal documents in history, anthropology and sociology* (Bulletin 53, pp. 77-173). New York: Social Science Research Council.

Konotey-Ahulu, F. I. D. (1989). *What is AIDS?* Watford, United Kingdom: Tetteh-A'domeno.

LaFontaine, J. (1974). Free women of Kinshasa: Prostitution in a city of Zaire. In J. Davis (Ed.), *Choice and change: Studies in honor of Audrey I. Richards* (pp. 89-113). Atlantic Highlands, NJ: Humanities.

MacGaffey, J. (1986). Women and class formation in a dependent economy. In C. Robertson & I. Berger (Eds.), *Women and class in Africa* (pp. 161-177). New York: Africana.

Mandel, E. (1970). *Marxist economic theory* (2 vols.). New York: Monthly Review.

Mann, J. M., Nzila, N., Piot, P., N'Galy, B., et al. (1988). HIV infection and associated risk factors in female prostitutes in Kinshasa, Zaire. *AIDS, 2,* 249-254.

Marks, S. (1987). *Not either an experimental doll: The separate worlds of three South African women.* Bloomington: University of Indiana Press.

Marks, S. (1989). The contexts of personal narrative: Reflections on *Not either an experimental doll.* In Personal Narratives Group (Eds.), *Interpreting women's lives: Feminist theory and personal narrative* (pp. 39-58). Bloomington: Indiana University Press.

Mbilinyi, M. (1989). "I'd have been a man": Politics and the labor process in producing personal narratives. In Personal Narratives Group (Eds.), *Interpreting women's lives: Feminist theory and personal narrative* (pp. 39-58). Bloomington: Indiana University Press.

Miller, N., & Rockwell, R. (Eds.). (1988). *AIDS in Africa: Social and policy impact.* Lewiston, NY: Edwin Mellen.

Mizra, S., & Strobel, M. (Eds.). (1989). *Three Swahili women: Life histories from Mombasa, Kenya.* Bloomington: Indiana University Press.

N'Galy, B., Ryder, R. W., & Bila, K. (1988). Human immunodeficiency virus infection among employees in an African hospital. *New England Journal of Medicine, 319*(17), 1123-1127.

N'Galy, B., Ryder, R. W., & Quinn, T. C. (1989). [Letter]. *New England Journal of Medicine, 320*(24), 1625.

Nzila, N., et al. (1988). Prevalence of infection with human immunodeficiency virus over a 10-year period in rural Zaire. *New England Journal of Medicine, 318*(5), 276-279.

Personal Narratives Group. (Eds.). (1989). *Interpreting women's lives: Feminist theory and personal narrative.* Bloomington: Indiana University Press.

Prewitt, K. (1988). AIDS in Africa: The triple disaster [Foreword]. In N. Miller & R. Rockwell (Eds.), *AIDS in Africa: Social and policy impact* (pp. ix-xii). Lewiston, NY: Edwin Mellen.

Robertson, C., & Berger, I. (Eds.). (1986). *Women and class in Africa.* New York: Africana.

Romero, P. W. (1988). Introduction. In P. W. Romero (Ed.), *Life histories of African women* (pp. 1-6). London: Ashfield.

Rukarangira, W., & Schoepf, B. G. (1989). Social marketing of condoms in Zaire. *AIDS Health Promotion Exchange, 3,* 2-4.

Rukarangira, W., & Schoepf, B. G. (1991). Unrecorded trade in Shaba and across Zaire's southern borders. In J. MacGaffey (Ed.), *The real economy in Zaire.* London: James Currey.

Ryder, R. W., Wato, N., Hassig, S., et al. (1989). Perinatal transmission of the HIV-I to infants of seropositive women in Zaire. *New England Journal of Medicine, 320*(25), 1637-1642.

Schoepf, B. G. (1969). *Doctor-patient communication and the medical social system.* Unpublished doctoral dissertation, Columbia University, Department of Anthropology.

Schoepf, B. G. (1975). Human relations versus social relations in medical care. In S. R. Ingman & A. E. Thomas (Eds.), *Topias and utopias in health: Policy studies* (pp. 99-120). The Hague, the Netherlands: Mouton.

Schoepf, B. G. (1978, December). *Women in the informal economy of Lubumbashi.* Paper prepared for the 10th World Congress, International Union of Anthropological and Ethnological Sciences, Delhi, India. (French version presented at the Fourth International Congress of African Studies, Kinshasa)

Schoepf, B. G. (1979). Breaking through the looking glass: The view from below. In G. Huizer & B. Mannheim (Eds.), *The politics of anthropology* (pp. 325-342). The Hague, the Netherlands: Mouton.

Schoepf, B. G. (1981, October). *Women and class formation in Zaire.* Paper presented at the annual meeting of the U.S. African Studies Association, Bloomington, IN.

Schoepf, B. G. (1986a, February). *Out of Africa? Sociocultural aspects of international AIDS research* (Colloquium). New Brunswick, NJ: Rutgers University, Department of Urban Studies, Public Health Program.

Schoepf, B. G. (1986b, November). *CONNAISSIDA: AIDS control research and interventions in Zaire.* Proposal submitted to the Rockefeller Foundation.

Schoepf, B. G. (1988a). Women, AIDS and economic crisis in Zaire. *Canadian Journal of African Studies, 22*(3), 625-644.

Schoepf, B. G. (1988b, July). *Political economy, culture and AIDS control.* Paper presented at International Union of Anthropological and Ethnological Sciences, Zagreb.

Schoepf, B. G. (1988c, December). *Methodology, ethics and politics: AIDS research in Africa for whom?* Paper presented at the 87th Annual Meeting of the American Anthropological Association invited symposium, Ethical Issues in Anthropological Research on AIDS.

Schoepf, B. G. (1989, July). *The social production of heterosexual AIDS in Africa* (Lecture, Science and Moral Values). Woods Hole, MA: Marine Biological Laboratory.

Schoepf, B. G. (1990a). AIDS in Eriaz. *Anthropology Today, 6*(3), 13-14.

Schoepf, B. G. (1990b, November 19-22). *Sex, gender and society in Zaire.* Paper prepared for IUSSP Seminar, Anthropological Studies Relevant to the Sexual Transmission of HIV, Sonderborg, Denmark.

Schoepf, B. G. (in press-a). "That ethereal light . . .": Epistemology and the invention of Marx in Africa. *Public Culture.*

Schoepf, B. G. (in press-b). AIDS, sex and condoms: "Traditional" healers and community-based AIDS prevention in Zaire. *Medical Anthropology.* (Originally paper presented at the 88th Annual Meeting of the American Anthropological Association, November 1989)

Schoepf, B (in press-c). Ethical, methodological and political issues of AIDS research in Central Africa. *Social Science and Medicine.*

Schoepf, B. G. (in press-d). Knowledge of women, women's knowledge: Texts of "tradition" and "modernity" in Zaire. In B. Jewsiewicki (Ed.), *The transfer of knowledge from Europe to Africa.*

Schoepf, B. G. (in preparation). *Women, sex and power: Zaire in the AIDS era.*

Schoepf, B. G., Payanzo, N., Rukarangira, W., Schoepf, C., & Walu, E. (1988). AIDS, women and society in Central Africa. In R. Kulstad (Ed.), *AIDS 1988: AAAS Symposium papers* (pp. 175-181). Washington, DC: AAAS.

Schoepf, B. G., Rukarangira, W., & Matumona, M. M. (1986, August). *Étude des réactions à une nouvelle maladie transmissible (SIDA) et des possibilités de démarrage d'un programme d'education populaire.* Research Proposal to Government of Zaire and USAID.

Schoepf, B. G., Rukarangira, W., Schoepf, C., Walu, E., & Payanzo, N. (1988). AIDS and society in Central Africa: A view from Zaire. In N. Miller & R. Rockwell (Eds.), *AIDS in Africa: Social and policy impact* (pp. 211-235). Lewiston, NY: Edwin Mellen. (Reprinted in D. Koch-Weser & H. Vanderschmidt, Eds., *The heterosexual transmission of AIDS in Africa*; pp. 265-280. Boston: Abt)

Schoepf, B. G., & Schoepf, C. (1981). Zaire's rural development in perspective. In B. G. Schoepf (Ed.), *The role of U.S. universities in international agricultural and rural development* (pp. 243-257). Tuskegee Institute, AL: Center for Rural Development.

Schoepf, B. G., & Schoepf, C. (1987). Food crisis and agrarian change in the Eastern Highlands of Zaire. *Urban Anthropology, 16*(1), 5-37.

Schoepf, B. G., & Schoepf, C. (1991). Gender, land and hunger in Eastern Zaire. In R. Huss-Ashmore & S. Katz (Eds.), *African food systems in crisis: Contending with change* (pp. 75-106). New York: Gordon and Breach.

Schoepf, B. G., & Walu, E. (1991). Women's trade and contribution to household budgets in Kinshasa. In J. MacGaffey (Ed.), *The real economy in Zaire.* London: James Currey; Philadelphia: University of Pennsylvania Press.

Schoepf, B. G., Walu, E., Rukarangira, W., Payanzo, N., & Schoepf, C. (1991). Gender, power and risk of AIDS in Central Africa. In M. Turshen (Ed.), *Women and health in Africa* (pp. 187-203). Trenton, NJ: Africa World.

Schoepf, B. G., Walu, E., Rukarangira, W., Payanzo, N., & Schoepf, C. (in press-a). Community-based risk reduction support in Zaire. In R. Berkvens (Ed.), *AIDS prevention through health promotion: Changing behaviour.* Geneva: WHO.

Schoepf, B. G., Walu, E., Rukarangira, W., Payanzo, N., & Schoepf, C. (in press-b). Action-research on AIDS with women in Kinshasa. *Social Science and Medicine.*

Schoepf, B. G., Walu, E., Russell, D., & Schoepf, C. (1991). Women and structural adjustment in Zaire. In C. Gladwin (Ed.), *Structural adjustment and African women farmers* (pp. 151-168). Gainesville: University of Florida Press.

Shilts, R. (1987). *And the band played on: Politics, people and the AIDS epidemic.* New York: St. Martin's.

Smith, M. F. (1981). *Baba of Karo: A woman of the Muslim Housa.* New Haven, CT: Yale University Press. (Original work published 1954)

Society for Women and AIDS in Africa (SWAA). (1989, May 10-12). First International Workshop on Women and AIDS in Africa, Harare [Report].

Turshen, M. (1984). *The political ecology of disease in Tanzania.* New Brunswick, NJ: Rutgers University Press.

U.N. Children's Emergency Fund (UNICEF). (1989). *The state of the world's children, 1989.* Oxford: Oxford University Press.

U.N. Economic Commission for Africa (UNECA). (1989). *An African alternative to structural adjustment programmes: A framework for transformation and recovery.* Addis Ababa: Author.

Waite, G. (1988). The politics of disease: The AIDS virus and Africa. In N. Miller & R. Rockwell (Eds.), *AIDS in Africa: Social and policy impact* (pp. 145-169). Lewiston, NY: Edwin Mellen.

Walu, E. (1987, June). *La Contribution des Femmes aux Budgets M130nagers à Kinshasa* (Research report). Washington, DC: World Bank.

Watney, S. (1989). Missionary positions: AIDS, "Africa" and race. *Differences: A Journal of Feminist Cultural Studies, 1*(1), 83-100.

World Bank. (1989). *Sub-Saharan Africa: From crisis to sustainable growth.* Washington, DC: World Bank.

World Health Organization (WHO). (1989, February 18). Consensus statements on HIV transmission. *The Lancet,* p. 396.

13

New Disorder, Old Dilemmas: AIDS and Anthropology in Haiti

PAUL FARMER

The emergence of a collective representation of AIDS in a village in rural Haiti is traced in the first section of this chapter. Investigation of evolving understandings of AIDS calls attention to the problems inherent in studying cultural meaning while it is taking shape. The utility of "rapid ethnographic assessments" is called into question by this research. In addition to theoretical and methodological challenges are the ethical dilemmas arising in the study of a new affliction for which there is only limited therapeutic recourse. Research regarding HIV and its biological and social effects forcefully poses questions that turn about several old, but often overlooked, issues: confidentiality in fieldwork and writing; anthropologists' obligations to informants and others; threats from government or agency sponsorship to independent and morally sound research. These issues are considered while raising the question: How might anthropologists best contribute to efforts to prevent transmission of HIV?

AUTHOR'S NOTE. Formal thanks to the MacArthur Foundation, which supported this research, and also to the Wenner-Gren Foundation for Anthropological Research, which supported the conference in which it was presented. In Haiti, I was helped by Marie-Flore Chipps, Lerneus Joseph, Francois Jean, Fritz Lafontant, and Yolande Lafontant. Stateside steering was afforded by Allan Brandt, Mary-Jo Good, Byron Good, Jim Kim, Arthur Kleinman, and Haun Saussy.

The Advent of AIDS

What happens when an altogether new malady appears in a setting of widespread sickness and almost universal poverty? Such a question was posed in contemplating the advent of AIDS in Do Kay, a small village stretching along an unpaved road cutting through Haiti's central plateau. Consisting, in 1990, of close to 1,000 persons, Do Kay is composed substantially of the families of peasant farmers displaced over 30 years ago by Haiti's largest dam. The village of Kay was once situated in a fertile valley, near the banks of the Riviere Artibonite. For generations, these families farmed the broad and gently sloping banks of the river, selling rice, bananas, millet, corn, and sugarcane in regional markets. Harvests were, by all reports, bountiful; life there is now recalled as idyllic. In 1956, progress intervened in the form of a huge dam. When the valley was flooded, the majority of the local population was forced up into the hills on either side of the new reservoir. The village of Kay became divided into *Do* (those who settled on the stony backs of the hills) and *Ba* (those who remained down near the new waterline). By all the standard measures, both parts of Kay are now very poor; its older inhabitants often blame their poverty on the massive buttress dam a few miles away and bitterly note that it brought them neither electricity nor water. The sole improvements in their lives, they observe, have been the construction of a school, a clinic, and other amenities built and operated by a Haitian priest who has been working in the area for over 35 years.

When AIDS appeared in their midst, the water refugees were already bent under the burden of unremitting poverty. The poverty of the region is by no means remarkable in Haiti, a country in which 50% of all deaths are among children under 5, and 75% of these are caused by or associated with malnutrition.[1] The advent of AIDS promises to further immiserate Haitians: The country is among those most gravely affected by HIV. As of March 20, 1990, Haiti has reported 2,331 cases of AIDS to the Pan-American Health Organization, making Haiti one of the world's 20 most affected nations.

In 1983, when this research was initiated, rural Haiti seemed stalled in a well-balanced mixture of fear, apathy, and preoccupation with day-to-day survival. The word *sida,* the Creole gloss for AIDS, was just beginning to work its way into the rural Haitian lexicon. In Do Kay, illnesses are usually the topic of much discussion. Sida was not. Between May 1983 and April 1984, any conversation I may have had about sida was prompted by my questioning. Some villagers had never heard of the disorder already held to be responsible for the ruin of the once important urban tourist industry;

others had only vague ideas about causation or typical clinical presentation. For example, in interviews conducted in 1983 and 1984, only 1 of 20 adult informants mentioned sida as a possible cause of diarrhea. When questioned, 16 of the 20 had heard of sida, but only 13 of them could offer "clinical" characteristics of the disorder, and many of these attributes were not commonly seen in Haitians with AIDS.

If villagers were aware of but uninterested in sida in 1984, interest in the illness was almost universal less than three years later. By then, one of the villagers was dying from AIDS, and another was gravely afflicted. Further, ideas about the disorder and its origin had changed drastically. This was only to be expected. If no collective representation of sida existed in 1983, when the subject elicited little interest and no passion, it is not surprising that some sort of consensus began to emerge in subsequent years, as members of this small community fell ill with the disorder. When what was at stake was nothing less than the life or death of a fellow villager, there resulted a profusion of illness stories; active debate as to what constituted the key features of sida, its course, and its causes was suddenly the order of the day. These narratives substantially shaped the contours of a shared representation of sida and helped to place a new disorder in the context of much older understandings of sickness and misfortune.

From the outset, then, it had become clear that the study of AIDS in rural Haiti would be a study of change. The need for a more processual approach to the study of illness representations is nowhere more dramatically illustrated than when one is witness to the advent of a new disorder or one previously unknown to one's host community. Some of the steps in this process of growing awareness are easily intuited. Before the arrival of the new malady, there exists, of course, no collective representation of the disorder. Then comes a period of exposure, if not to the illness then to rumor of it. With time and experience, low interinformant agreement may give way to a cultural model shared by the majority of a community. What determines whether or not consensus is reached? In studies of illness representations, anthropologists have usually asked, "What does the model mean?" or "To what degree is the model shared?" But when studying a truly novel disorder, a new set of questions pertains. How does cultural consensus emerge? How do illness representations, and the realities they organize and constitute, come into being? How are new representations related to existing structures? How does the suffering of particular human beings contribute to collective understandings, and how much of individual experience is not captured in cultural meaning?

The data presented here speak directly to these questions and raise others regarding the many dilemmas that will be faced by ethnographers who choose to "study AIDS." And so this chapter is divided into two complementary components. The first is primarily an ethnographic exercise and describes the evolving representations of sida in Do Kay. The second component poses critical questions that arose in this work. Some of these, clearly, are posed in the context of a certain place at a certain time; others may be inherent to anthropological studies of AIDS.

AIDS and the Study of Cultural Meaning

Anthropology has become increasingly concerned with questions of process. Although studies have often attempted to depict cultures as self-replicating, culture in formation and transformation is increasingly the subject of current ethnographic inquiry. The advent of a new and deadly disorder, one that does not show any promise of going away, must trigger the elaboration of new illness representations if it is indeed to be perceived as novel. In Haiti, as in much of the world, AIDS was such a sickness. In the Kay area, as noted, some villagers had never heard of sida in 1983. Several had heard of the disorder on the radio or during trips to the capital, and it was clear that sida was popularly associated with urban life. One 36-year-old market woman in early 1984 offered the following commentary, which recalls that of several of her covillagers:

> Sida is a sickness they have in Port-au-Prince and in the United States. It gives you a diarrhea that starts very slowly, but never stops until you're completely dry. There's no water left in your body. . . . Sida is a sickness that you see in men who sleep with other men.

She had little else to say about the syndrome. There was considerable disagreement as to what the characteristics of sida might be. In our 1983-1984 discussions, 7 out of 20 informants mentioned three aspects of sida: the novelty of the disorder, its relation to diarrhea, and its association with homosexuality. The majority mentioned one or two of these attributes. Only five noted that sida was lethal. Three thought that it was originally a disease of pigs; three others were of the opinion that, despite the contrary claims of the foreign press, sida had been brought to Haiti by North Americans. Two of these interviewed asserted that "sida is the same thing as tuberculosis." Several added, often somewhat apologetically, that sida was a sickness that "doesn't concern us, and so we don't know much about it." Before 1984, one would have been hard-pressed to delineate a collective representation of AIDS in the Kay area. Despite several individual's elaborate explanatory models, the lack of natural discourse regarding sida and the low interinformant agreement regarding its core characteristics suggest that, before 1984, no cultural model of AIDS existed in this part of rural Haiti.

If villagers thought of themselves as uninformed about and uninterested in sida in 1984, interest in the syndrome was almost universal less than three years later. Narratives about it were easily triggered, and it was clear that a consensus, albeit tenuous, had emerged. Interviews conducted since 1987 revealed that the semantic network in which sida was embedded had changed substantially. The syndrome was then mentioned by over half of those asked to cite possible causes of diarrhea in an adult. A majority also associated sida with tuberculosis. Further, there was clearly a much more widely shared idea of the way in which it became manifest in the afflicted. The extent of these changes is indicated by the observations of a young schoolteacher, himself a native of Do Kay. He was interviewed several times between 1983 and the present. In a 1984 interview, he noted: "Yes, of course I've heard of [sida]. It's caused by living in the city. It gives you diarrhea and can kill you. . . . We've never had any [sida] here. It's a city sickness."

It was clear from a long exchange recorded late in 1987 that the man's understanding of the syndrome had changed substantially. He also held forth at great length about sida. A chief factor seems to have been that he was now able to refer to the death from sida of his fellow schoolteacher, Manno Surpris:

> It was sida that killed him: that's what I'm trying to tell you. But they say it was a death sent to him. They sent a sida death to him. . . . Sida is caused by a tiny microbe. But not just anybody will catch the microbe that can cause sida.

To assess the rate of change in local understandings of sida, and to gauge the significance to these understandings of intercurrent events, the same 20 villagers were interviewed regarding sida at least once during the years between 1983 and 1989.[2] The interviews have been open-ended and most often focused on specific "illness stories" but have always included discussion of the following topics: causes of the illness, its perceived course, appropriate therapeutic interventions, relation to other sicknesses common in the area, and questions of risk and vulnerability. Manno's illness and death made a lasting contribution to the cultural model of sida that took shape during this period. As shall be shown below, this contribution was not substantially lessened by the subsequent deaths from AIDS of two other villagers.

Manno moved to Do Kay in 1982, when he became a teacher at the large new school established there by a Haitian priest. Manno was then 25 years old. An enthusiastic and hardworking man, he came to be held in high esteem by the school administrators. He was entrusted with a number of public— and renumerative—tasks, including taking care of the village's new water pump as well as the community pig project, both of which were administered by the priest who ran the school. That an outsider would be granted such favors was resented by some of the villagers, as became clear after Manno fell ill.

Beginning in early 1986, Manno had been plagued by intermittent diarrhea. Superficial skin infections recrudesced throughout the summer. By the close of the year, his decline was drastic, and he began to cough. In January 1987, a Port-au-Prince physician referred Manno to the public clinic that could perform the test necessary to diagnose HIV infection. In the first week of February, while waiting for the test results, Manno revealed his own fear about his sickness:

> Most of all, I hope, it's not tuberculosis. But I'm afraid that's what it is. I'm coughing, I've lost weight. . . . I'm afraid I have tuberculosis, and that I'll never get better, never be able to work again. . . . People don't want to be near you if you have tuberculosis.

Manno did indeed have tuberculosis, a disease much feared in Haiti, and he initially responded well to the appropriate treatment. But he also had antibodies to HIV, which suggested to his physicians that immune deficiency caused by the virus was at the root of his health problems.

In a sense, these suspicions were shared by Manno's covillagers, for many of them believed that the sick man's tuberculosis was "not simple." His illness had "another cause." A rumor had circulated around Do Kay, and it was not dampened by Manno's clinical improvement: He was the victim, it was whispered, of sorcery. His illness had been "sent" by some angry or jealous rival. Manno's wife was among those interviewed in 1984. She had then offered the opinion that sida was "a form of diarrhea seen in homosexuals." Informed in February 1987 by Manno's physician that her husband was infected with HIV, she accepted this as true. But she and her husband also knew Manno to be the victim of sorcery: "They did this to him because they were jealous that he had three jobs—teaching, the pigsty, and the water pump."

Because treatment of a "sent sickness" requires that the perpetrators be identified, Manno and his family were increasingly obsessed not with the course of the disease but with its utmost origin. They consulted a voodoo priest, who revealed through divination the authors of the crime. One of those accused of killing Manno was his wife's cousin; another, a schoolteacher, was more distantly related to his wife. The third, "the master of the affair," was also a coworker of Manno's. But divination and the indicated treatment could not save Manno, who succumbed in mid-September. His sida death was the chief topic of "semiprivate" conversation for months.

Less than one year later, a young woman named Anita Joseph seemed to endure an illness strikingly dissimilar from that of Manno: Not only was her illness clinically different, but Anita was extremely poor and locally perceived as the victim of great misfortune. She was also a native of Do Kay, as her parents had been inhabitants of the valley flooded in 1956. Anita's mother died of tuberculosis when Anita was an adolescent. It was very nearly the coup de grace for her father, who became depressed and abusive. Anita, the oldest of five children, bore the brunt of his spleen. "One day, I'd just had it with his yelling. I took what money I could find, about $2, and left for the city. I didn't know where to go." Anita had the good fortune to find a family in need of a maid. The two women in the household had jobs in a U.S.-owned assembly plant; the husband of one ran a snack concession out of the house. Anita received a meal a day, a bit of dry floor to sleep on, and $10 per month for what sounded like incessant labor. She was not unhappy with the arrangement, which lasted until both women were fired for participating in "political meetings." Unable to make ends meet, the family made plans to emigrate to the job market in the United States.

Anita wandered about for two days, until she happened upon a kinswoman selling gum and candies near a downtown theater. She was, Anita related, "a sort of aunt." Anita could come and stay with her, the aunt said, as long as she could help pay the rent. And so Anita moved into Cite Simone, the sprawling slum on the northern fringes of the capital.[3] It was through the offices of her aunt that she met Vincent, one of the few men in the neighborhood with anything resembling a job: "He unloaded the whites' luggage at the airport." Vincent made a living from tourists' tips. In 1982, the year before Haiti became associated, in the North American press, with AIDS, the city of Port-au-Prince counted tourism as its chief industry.

In the setting of an unemployment rate of greater than 60%, Vincent could command considerable respect. He turned his attentions to Anita. "What could I do, really? He had a good job. My aunt thought I should go with him." Anita was not yet 15 when she entered her first and only sexual union. Her lover set her up in a shack in the same neighborhood. Anita cooked and washed and waited for him. When Vincent fell ill, Anita again became a nurse. It began insidiously, she recalled: night sweats, loss of appetite, swollen lymph nodes. Then came months of unpredictable and debilitating diarrhea. "We tried everything—doctors, charlatans, herbal remedies, injections, prayers." After a year of decline, she took Vincent to his hometown in the south of Haiti. There it was revealed that Vincent's illness was the result of malign magic: "It was one of the men at the airport who did this to him. The man wanted Vincent's job. He sent an AIDS death to him."

The voodoo priest who heard their story and deciphered the signs was straightforward. He told Anita and Vincent's family that the sick man's chances were slim, even with the appropriate interventions. There were, however, steps to be taken. He outlined them, they were followed by the family, but still Vincent succumbed. "When he died," recalled Anita, "I felt spent. I couldn't get out of bed. I thought that his family would try to help me to get better, but they didn't. I knew I needed to go home."

She made it as far as Croix-des-Bouquets, a large market town at least two hours from Kay. There she collapsed, feverish and coughing, and was taken in by a woman who lived near the market. She stayed for a month, unable to walk, until her father came to take her back home. Five years had elapsed since she'd last seen him. Anita's father was by then a friendly but broken-down man with a leaking roof over his one-room, dirt-floor hut. It was no place for a sick woman, the villagers said, and Anita's godmother, honoring 20-year-old vows, made room in her overcrowded but dry house.

Anita was promptly diagnosed as having tuberculosis, and she responded rapidly to antituberculosis therapy. But six months after the initiation of treatment, her health again declined precipitously. Convinced that she was indeed taking her medications, those treating her were concerned about AIDS, especially upon hearing of the death of her lover. Anita's father was poised to sell his last bit of land to "buy more nourishing food for the child." It was imperative that the underlying cause of Anita's poor response to treatment be found. A laboratory test confirmed her doctors' suspicions.

Anita's father and godmother alone were apprised of the test results. It was clear from serial interviews with regular informants that few in Do Kay believed Anita to have been a victim of sida. Two persons who had explained to me the nature of Manno's illness queried rhetorically, referring to Anita, "Who would send a sida death on this poor unfortunate child?" Because the sole case of sida registered in the Kay area was already known to have been caused by sorcery, it stood to follow, some thought initially, that Anita could not have sida. Few believed her to be the victim of malign magic, and her father's lack of success in the quest for therapy was seen not as an indication of the power of her enemies but of the virulence of her "natural" illness. Gradually, however, villagers came to agree that she did indeed have sida but that it could also be caused "naturally." As one of Anita's aunts put it, "we don't know whether or not they sent a sida death to [her lover], but we do know that she did not have a death sent to her. She had it in her blood. She caught it from him." Despite the disparities vis-à-vis Manno's illness, Anita's experience did not serve to weaken the slowly emerging cultural model.

Dieudonne was the third villager to fall ill with sida. Somewhat older than Anita, Dieudonne shared her origins: He was the child of refugees from the rising waters. He dropped out of elementary school because his family became too poor to pay his tuition and began to work with his father, a carpenter living in Do Kay. But Do Kay was "too small a place for Dieudonne," as his mother noted. "He wanted to be somewhere where there were roads and cars, somewhere where the streets make corners." Sometime during 1983, Dieudonne left for Port-au-Prince. Through a relative from Do Kay, he had found a position as the "yard boy" for a bourgeois family. He spent the next two years opening gates, fetching heavy things from the car, and tending flowers in the cool heights of one of the city's ostentatious suburbs. The head of the household was a "businessman," but Dieudonne was not sure what his business was. The young man was paid $20 per month for his round-the-clock (excepting only Saturday afternoons) work. Boss Yonel recounts that his son was "well situated" in Port-au-Prince, although he did not manage to send home any money. It was enough that Dieudonne was "responsible for himself." Dieudonne returned to Kay, according to Yonel, when he was fired by the family for whom he worked. This came to pass because the young man had fallen ill "and was no longer any use to them."

Dieudonne had a great deal to say about sickness in Haiti. His analysis recalled elements of both of those who had died before him. Like Manno, he was a victim of sorcery. Like Anita, he tended to cast things in sociological terms. Dieudonne also voiced what have been termed "conspiracy theories" regarding the origins of AIDS. On more than one occasion, he "wondered whether sida might not have been sent to Haiti by the United States. That's why they were so quick to say that Haitians gave [the world] sida." When asked why the United States would wish such a pestilence on Haitians, Dieudonne had a ready answer: "They say there are too many Haitians over there now. They needed us to work for them, but now there are too many over there." The significance of conspiracy theories, especially those linking AIDS to the machinations of racist "America," has yet to decline. Although such expressions emanated from Port-au-Prince, it is possible that in some areas they have had a greater effect on the elaboration of rural illness realities than has the virus itself. Many areas of rural Haiti have to date registered no local cases of sida; inhabitants of these regions are nonetheless familiar with many of these expressions.

The term *sida,* unknown in rural Haiti before 1983, became a prominent part of everyday discourse about misfortune. Sida was the topic of several popular songs, all of which tended to affirm associations that were important to an emerging cultural model of AIDS. For the inhabitants of Do Kay, the advent of a new and fatal disease was, in the words of one of those who lives there, "the last thing." The last thing, that is, in a long series of trials that have afflicted the rural poor of Haiti. When people from Do Kay speak of sida, it is quite often in the same breath as the other afflictions, past and present, that have rendered life in rural Haiti a precarious enterprise. For many in Do Kay, observations about a new and deadly disorder are worked into stories that relate the ways in which misfortune is manifest in the lives of individuals, communities, and even a nation.

The illnesses of Manno, Anita, and Dieudonne helped to sculpt the collective representation of sida that was taking shape over the years. Serial interviews with the same 20 adults served as one means of following this process. Their commentaries, over the years, were the web in which were enmeshed new ideas, tentative suggestions, timid conclusions, and, finally, growing consensus. As an illness caused by sorcery, sida came to stand for local, rather than "large-scale," conflicts. Several villagers, including Dieudonne, referred to sida as a "jealousy sickness"—an illness sent to one poor person by another, even poorer person. Attending closely to their rhetoric of complaint leads one to an analysis that takes seriously the many large-scale interconnections revealed in these illness stories. Based upon the serial interviews with the cohort of 20 villagers, based upon the illness stories sketched above, the following points summarize the shared under-standing of AIDS in the Kay area at the close of 1989:

(1) Sida is a new disease. It is not of Haitian origin.

(2) Sida is strongly associated with "skin infections," "drying up," "diarrhea," and, especially, "tuberculosis."

(3) Sida may occur both "naturally" (*maladi bondje,* "God's illness") and "unnat-urally." Natural sida is caused by sexual contact with someone who "carries the germ." In the latter case, the illness is "sent" by someone who willfully inflicts death upon the afflicted. The mechanism of malice is through "expe-dition of the dead" in the same manner that tuberculosis may be sent.

(4) Whether God's illness or sent, sida may be held to be caused by a "microbe."

(5) Sida may be contracted through contact with contaminated or "dirty" blood, but earlier associations with homosexuality and transfusion are less frequently cited.

(6) The term *sida* reverberates with associations, drawn from the larger political-economic context, of North American imperialism, a lack of class solidarity among the poor, and the corruption of Port-au-Prince and of the ruling Haitian elite.

Although the current meanings will be contested and changed, the above points summarize a *cultural* model, in that high interinformant agreement regarding the nature of the illness has emerged. And although there is significant "surface variation" in models that may be elicited from individuals, even these discrepant versions seem to be generated by schema comprising the above points. It may be the case that it is this model that will have enduring significance in the area around Kay. It remains nonetheless true that only long-term ethnographic research could have delineated the model, its emergence, and the forces that helped to shape it.

In at least one small village in rural Haiti, then, it was possible to document first the lack of a cultural model of AIDS and then the evolution of a representation of sida that seemed to be widely shared. A number of steps important in this process have been underlined in the preceding sections: Direct exposure to the illness was almost requisite, as sida needed a high enough ranking in the hierarchy of perceived stress to warrant sustained communitywide attention. Look at the "background noise" of life in poverty-stricken Do Kay: Diarrheal disease in infants, neonatal tetanus, typhoid, cerebral malaria, government-sponsored violence, hunger, and coups d'etat were standard fare in my years in rural Haiti. Once a "critical mass" of both local interest and interested parties was achieved, the generation of illness stories seemed to follow naturally. It was in these narratives that nascent representations were anchored. As time passed, these narratives came to be much more similarly structured; slowly waning interinformant discrepancy entered a phase of rapid decline as Manno's illness triggered a great deal of natural discourse about the new sickness. People began to recount the "same story," and the illness of which they spoke came to have characteristics and features that varied less and less from informant to informant. This consensus was cobbled together toward the end of 1987, and subsequent events tended to shape the nascent model of sida rather than remake it. Anita's illness, though strikingly different than Manno's, served largely to reinforce features of a model put into circulation by stories relating the details of Manno's illness. It was for this reason that his experience was termed "prototypical."

The research reviewed here also speaks to the anthropological study of illness representations. In a recent review of such studies, it was argued that a number of factors were almost always relevant to the study of illness representations: intracultural variation in the representation of illness, the relation of such representations to the structured narratives in which they are so frequently embedded, the effect on representation of the rhetorical exigencies of such narratives, the effects of social setting on representations (e.g., performative considerations), and the politics of representation. It was further suggested that each of these considerations may be expected to change over time (Farmer & Good, 1990).

In Haiti, each of these considerations was shown to be significant to the investigation of sida. The study of emerging cultural consensus was in many ways that of decreasing intracultural variation in representations of the new disorder. Yet, important variation remained even after a genuine cultural model of sida came into being. The relation of representation to illness stories was paramount in Do Kay, as *stories were the matrix in which representations took form.* In fact, before the advent of natural discourse about sida, there was simply no consensus as to what sida was, what caused it, what might prevent it, and how it came to be manifest in the bodies of individuals. The embeddedness of representations in narratives meant that rhetorical exigencies and performative factors could be shown to have determinant effects upon the shaping of the cultural models. None of this is surprising to those who have long argued that illness meanings emerge in situated discourse (Good, 1986).

The politics of representation changed during the study period, demonstrating the significance to such representations of political exigencies. When Jean-Claude Duvalier's ambassador wrote to the *New England Journal of Medicine* to complain that "we, as black nation, well understand the pains of world discrimination," one suspects that representations of AIDS are being willfully manipulated, especially when translations of this letter are read on national media. Duvalier himself joined in the AIDS fray. In the same interview in which he predicted that "democracy could be very catastrophic for Haiti," the dictator deplored the fact that "health officials in America did not consider all the facts" when they classed all Haitians as a "high-risk group."[4] The collapse of the Duvalier regime had a palpable effect on the way in which AIDS-related accusation was marshaled and used, further emphasizing the effects on illness representations of performative factors. One noted a shift from recrimination focusing on racist North America, a rhetoric encouraged by the regime, to one suggesting the ill will of the Haitian rulers. "Conspiracy theories" abounded: Some suggested that the

Duvalier clique had caused AIDS; others elaborated conspiracy theories that pegged the blame on the United States.

In Do Kay, representations of sida were changed even more dramatically by the illnesses of villagers. Suddenly, much more was at stake. It was bad enough that Manno's illness proved that the new disorder had reached Kay. It was downright disastrous that sida would strike Anita, long-suffering child of a long-suffering people. Interviews with the "cohort of 20" began to reveal a mounting sentiment of personal vulnerability. Sida, previously remote, a sickness of others, had insinuated itself into the intimate drama of survival in Do Kay. The new disorder had also insinuated itself into an illness paradigm of great importance in rural Haiti, that in which are embedded understandings of tuberculosis.

Juggling all of these "confounding factors" renders the study of a cultural model of AIDS a difficult venture. That each of these factors is of changing significance led me, at times, to question the relevance of such fine-grained analyses. And yet failure to take these shifts into account would seriously distort not only our understanding of sida but also that of the constitution of a new illness representation: Research conducted in 1983 would have yielded no cultural model of AIDS in the Kay area and, in 1985, would have revealed a model quite different than that which took shape in the course of 1987. What is needed, clearly, is a processual ethnography that can

> show how local events and local commentary on them can be linked to a variety of processes unfolding simultaneously on *very different scales of time and place,* and to note the difference between what might be called the "foreground preoccupation" of the actors or commentators on these events, and the "background conditions" informing their situation that figure much more prominently in the preoccupations of the historically minded ethnographer. (Moore, 1987, p. 731; emphasis added)

Processual ethnography helps to bring into relief changes in what was important to the people of Do Kay. How do these ethnographic data, which are described in greater detail elsewhere, speak to current debates about "social science" research on AIDS? For example, what relevance might the Haitian material have to the "rapid ethnographic surveys" that are now incorporated in so many federally funded studies of AIDS?

In no small number of scientific congresses, grand claims are made for the relevance of anthropology to efforts to "combat AIDS." It is argued that "local knowledge" such as that presented above does much to explain health-seeking behavior and other social responses to AIDS. Epidemiologists, demographers, and health providers have objected that ethnographic data are too cumbersome to be of use in this eminently pragmatic struggle. One response to this critique has been to proffer "rapid ethnographic assessments" of settings in which HIV transmission is thought to occur. Such assessments employ crude representations of anthropological methods: Often, the time frame proposed for such research is a mere four to eight weeks.[5] Many large epidemiological surveys now contain an "ethnographic component" patterned along these lines, although the research is often conducted by nonanthropologists.

The data gathered in rural Haiti should at least give pause to those who perform their ethnographic assessments too rapidly. The researcher in quest of "local knowledge" of AIDS would have discovered different knowledge at different times. The relevance of some of this "knowledge"—especially that which proved to be of no enduring significance—to the villagers' responses to sida is not demonstrable. It is only through careful elicitation of narratives over time that an emerging model is discerned. It is only through old-fashioned ethnography that this model's relation to preexisting paradigms may be appreciated and that the relationship of all of this to human agency may be suggested.

But Haitian readings of AIDS have much more to teach us, particularly when we attend closely to the lived experience of the afflicted. Their world is intimately linked to other worlds. Their commentaries, and those of their families, force us to lift our eyes from the local dramas of a small village. Anita, for example, has exposed for us the mechanisms by which she and others like her have been "put at risk" for exposure to HIV. Others have explicitly linked contemporary travails to the oppression and struggle that have long been the heritage of the Haitian poor. In an interview shortly before his death, Dieudonne observed that "sida is a jealousy sickness." When asked to explain more fully what he intended by his observation, Dieudonne replied,

> What I see is that poor people catch it more easily. They say the rich get sida; I don't see that. But what I do see is that one poor person sends it to another poor person. It's like the army: brothers shooting brothers.

Dieudonne's story, like that of Manno, casts sida as a "jealousy sickness" and a disorder of the poor. Anita reminds us that certain events, such as the flooding of a valley, help to make people poor and jealous. Neither the dam nor the AIDS epidemic would have been as they are if Haiti had not been caught up in a network of relations that are economic as well as sexual. That these conditions have been important in the lineaments of the U.S. epidemics is suggested by comparing Haiti with a neighboring island. In 1986, in Cuba, only 0.01% of 1,000,000 persons tested were found to have antibodies to HIV (Liautaud, Pape, & Pamphile, 1988, p. 690). Had the pandemic began a few decades earlier, the epidemiology of HIV infection in the Caribbean might well be different. Havana might have been as much an epicenter of the pandemic as Carrefour, the nexus of Haitian domestic and international prostitution.

The net is cast wide, taking us to Port-au-Prince, to the United States, and far back in time. Indeed, those who study AIDS in such "exotic" places as Haiti are most often entrapped in the very same net. Or, to put it more honestly, those who study the exotic are often a part of those cultures that have long cast nets. It is an acknowledgment of these connections that brings us to the second half of this chapter.

AIDS, Ethics, Anthropology

Given that, with AIDS, the stakes are always high, it is not surprising that anthropological research regarding AIDS poses difficult ethical questions. Some of these dilemmas seem native to our discipline, and perhaps inevitable, but others are clearly a result of the rush to perform "rapid ethnographic assessments" for the federal bureaucracies that direct most AIDS research in North America and Europe.

How well do our current guidelines address these dilemmas? In its "Principles of Professional Responsibility," the American Anthropological Association reminds its constituents of their responsibilities to those studied, to the public, to the discipline, to students, to sponsors, to the anthropologists' governments, and to host governments. Acknowledging that the anthropologist cannot please everybody, the statement's authors allow that the "paramount responsibility is to those [the anthropologist] studies. When there is a conflict of interest, these individuals must come first." It is easy enough to say that one's paramount responsibility is to "those studied." But most contemporary anthropologists must at least acknowledge that their informants are linked to larger networks of domination and power. These may be masked in certain settings, but even those working in a village as small as Do Kay have several "sets" or "classes" of informants. Not all of them may have equal claim to the allegiance of the anthropologist. In the Kay area, "those studied" included Manno, a young schoolteacher with AIDS, his wife and other family members, his employer, his physician, and even those accused of causing, through sorcery, his illness. And the village was small enough that Manno's employer was also the ethnographer's host and the person most committed to assuring the continuity of the sick man's medical care. My research assistant was a former student of Manno's and a distant relative of his wife. Manno's wife worked in the same school; one of those accused of killing Manno was her father's brother's daughter and the sister of one of my coworkers and informants; another was more distantly related to the wife but was for me a trusted friend with whom I had worked for years.

For the afflicted and his family, the quest for therapy and healing involved knowing who "ensorcelled" Manno. The accused, equally my informants, sought public affirmation of their innocence—and one of them, under considerable pressure as a result of the accusation, asked me to publicly deny the possibility of sorcery-induced AIDS. For Manno's employer, a priest, community healing required renunciation of "false and divisive beliefs" about sorcery. The staff of the village clinic wanted the names of Manno's sexual contacts and knew that I had elicited a sexual history. Each of these persons had impeccable reasons for seeking the allegiance of someone they knew to be committed to the study of this new and frightening disease. Again, the problem is not specific to Haiti: One easily imagines analogous situations in a North American hospital.

The point here is not that our Principles of Professional Responsibility are no longer useful, but they may well prove inadequate as guides to ethically sound anthropological research on AIDS. These shortcomings suggest that those engaged in such research bring our most critical thinking to bear on our work and elaborate a series of sharp questions that may serve as corollaries to our existing framework; that critical thinking should take seriously problems that arise in one setting and anticipate their possible emergence in another. The exercise should also consider likely Third World critiques of our involvement in efforts to "control AIDS." What follows is a series of questions that I have endeavored to ask myself during fieldwork both in rural Haiti and in the United States. This thinking could itself be guided by a central question: What are the threats—political, methodological, epistemological—to ethically sound anthropological research on AIDS?

Question 1. How was the research funded? In most meetings of anthropologists and other social scientists who study or wish to study AIDS, one inevitable subject is money. How will we fund our research? But experience suggests that time should also be allotted the obverse question: How will we *not* fund our research? Our professional code states that the anthropologist "faces the obligation, prior to entering any commitment for research, to reflect sincerely upon the purposes of his sponsors in terms of their past behavior." In one of several considerations of this thorny issue, Berreman (1981, pp. 60-61) observes,

> There are those who say that sources of funds are irrelevant to scholarship—that it is the nature and motives of research alone which define its legitimacy. Many cite freedom to accept funds from any source as a fundamental aspect of academic freedom. There are those who cannot or do not distinguish between funding from one governmental agency and from another—from the Department of Defense, for example, and from the Department of Health, Education and Welfare—or who see no difference between a corporate foundation which is known to monitor CIA funds and one which is thought not to. These viewpoints indicate remarkable blindness to the political and social realities of international scholarship in today's world.

Social science has not and will not be able to define any hard-and-fast rules regarding funding. It should be noted at the outset that the majority of AIDS research, both at home and abroad, is funded by state agencies. Many anthropologists engaged in AIDS research are paid by a federal government, often through the intermediary of a university, and some of them have been contracted to provide the "ethnographic components" of larger studies. Most important, it is important to acknowledge that AIDS is a problem of such proportions that it demands, in most countries, centrally coordinated intervention. But let us equally acknowledge the fact that sponsored research carries its own inherent risk, to which anthropology seems particularly vulnerable.

One aspect of this risk might be termed "epistemological." Called by some the "uncomfortable science," anthropology demands of its practitioners a certain alienation, often more cognitive than geographic, from their cultures—and classes—of origin. It is for precisely this reason that Hazel Weidman has cautioned against an applied anthropology that leaves unexamined the ways in which the anthropologist's intellectual integrity may be subtly undermined by allegiance to the "system" sponsoring the research. In her view, "the basic 'alienated' stance must be maintained if we are to be truly successful in our applications" (Weidman, 1976). This essentially epistemological problem is not infrequently linked to less subtle ones. Blumer (1967, p. 157), a sociologist, discerns three major threats to the integrity of social science from agency-directed research: "(1) the restraints imposed on the scientific pursuit of truth, (2) a disrespect of the rights of the human beings being studied, and (3) an unwitting corruption of scholars engaging in agency-directed research." Similarly, Berreman (1981, p. 70) has deplored "free enterprise scholarship," which he describes as "scholarship which uses whatever resources are available by whomever has access to them." Indiscriminant fund-raising has led to our involvement in a number of morally questionable projects, such as those funded by the Department of Defense, and to a great deal of bitterness between anthropologist and host community, anthropologist and host government, and anthropologist and anthropologist. Twenty years ago, the American Anthropological Association was divided into hostile factions over many of these same issues.

These tensions are sure to surface in AIDS research, which has served as a lightning rod for the attentions of various groups, many of whom are clearly at cross-purposes with each other. Why, for example, might an anthropologist wish to know the same information as the representatives of an insurance company, the Immigration and Naturalization Service, and the police? AIDS research among Haitians in both Boston and Miami was stalled for precisely these reasons. In one large, federally funded study, those administering questionnaires sought histories of a number of venereal diseases that Haitian entrants knew to be reasons for exclusion from the United States. And where were these data to be sent? To a U.S. government agency! At the height of this research, investigators were embarrassed by a front-page headline, "Haitian AIDS Victim Battles to Stay in U.S."[6]

Question 2. What steps were taken to ensure that the informants are willing to participate in the research? A more honest way of putting this might be as follows: What steps were taken to *lessen* the coercion of the research? For, in many settings, imbalances of power ensure that "force" will be on the side of the investigator. It is well known that anthropology is a discipline that has "studied down," taking advantage, wittingly or unwittingly, of these same imbalances to facilitate our own agendas. I refer not only to the crude disparities that separate First World ethnographers from Third World peasants but to the inequality inherent in all encounters between the well and the sick. If there is any truth at all to the saw that severe illness often engenders feelings of extreme helplessness, then there inevitably exists a "power gap" between the healthy researcher and the sick informant.[7]

Even if these forms of inequity are rarely exploited in medical anthropology, the moral challenge is to diminish the *relative* significance of such forces in the conduct of our investigations. In the United States, "informed consent" is now required in much social research in biomedical settings. Consent forms may be indicated in some field settings. The approbation of a human studies committee might be useful in others—if the committees are altered to include persons with AIDS (PWAs) and the representatives of communities afflicted by HIV or its stigma. In still other settings, local input might be sought to devise true "community research initiatives" that reflect from the outset the needs and desires of both the researchers and the community (Farmer & Kim, 1991). Such safeguards are clearly the product of certain cultural preoccupations more native to the United States than to rural Haiti—but the same might also be said for anthropological research on AIDS.

Subtle coercion is intimately linked to the symbolic affiliation of the ethnographer. Anthropological research on AIDS usually entails symbolic attachment to institutions (hospitals, federal bureaucracies, churches, community agencies) or larger groups of people (physicians and other clinicians, missionaries, PWAs). Just as it was once possible to use the cloak of colonial authority and still maintain a definition of self as opposed to that authority, so too is it possible for self-defined reformers of biomedicine to gain access to informants through recourse to "therapeutic authority." One of the best ways of avoiding abuse of the symbolic authority is being honest about the nature of the anthropological project. Social scientists have often been accused of promising, through naïveté or guile, much more than can ever be offered. Although our Principles of Professional Responsibility remind us that "the aims of the investigation should be communicated as well as possible to the informant," Chen and Murray (1976) have qualified "arousing false hopes" as one of the most commonly applied means of inducing Third World people to divulge information: "If the researcher talks about the possible benefits that might come from [a] research project, the respondents may get the impression that the researcher's immediate purpose is to *help* the community, rather than *study* it, as is in fact more often the case." Anthropologists are not currently in a position to argue that their research might help prolong the lives of those already exposed to the virus; neither are we sure that such investigations will help to limit the spread of HIV.

The question of incentives is closely related to that of benefit to informants, an issue treated more fully at the end of this chapter. Regarding lessening the coercion of research, however, it should be noted that, in some settings, reimbursing informants will be the morally sound thing to do. In others, remuneration will smack more of bribery, itself a form of coercion. But dismissing such transactions as crass by no means addresses the problem of coercion, which is built into any situation in which there exist differentials of wealth and of health.

Question 3. To whom were the results of the HIV antibody test given? How did the anthropologist come by this knowledge? Issues of confidentiality so central to contemporary biomedicine are not substantially different for the anthropologist. If anything, the responsibility to protect confidentiality is further heightened when the setting for the exchange of protected knowledge is the home or small village and not the culturally and physically distant setting of the hospital or office. Research that involves persons already exposed to HIV relies on knowledge of laboratory data. In most places in which anthropologists work, legislation protecting the rights of those with HIV infection—including the right to confidentiality—is ineffective or does not exist. The very fact that we are able to conduct social science research bespeaks a certain laxity in standards of protection of such rights. How might anthropologists avoid taking advantage of easy access to potentially damaging data? How might we avoid contributing to the diffusion of information that has been, in settings throughout the world, particularly destructive?

A related question is this: Who participated in the research? Many anthropologists rely on the help of paid assistants; virtually all of us rely on dependable friends ("key informants") who are to be counted on when we attempt to unravel a confusing event or interview. If the material collected was recorded on magnetic tape, who helped to transcribe the interviews? Who was privy to the ethnographer's notes? In my years of research in village Haiti, I have come to rely heavily on Saul Joseph—not just as a key informant but as someone who has helped me to transcribe taped interviews, and someone who has himself conducted interviews. But Saul was also a former student of Manno Surpris. For months, I said nothing to Saul about my research, preferring to let my untranscribed tapes accumulate: I had not yet convinced myself that it was "right" to conduct such sensitive research with one of Manno's covillagers. I later discovered that Saul knew of the AIDS diagnosis and sorcery accusations from the start. Although there are a number of interviews that he has not seen, we have resumed our work together. These are decisions that I would have made more comfortably if I could have referred to the published opinions of colleagues working in similar circumstances.

More recent discussions with anthropologists working in North America suggest that these dilemmas are not substantially different in cultures in which there is loud insistence on the sacredness of human rights. In the United States, for example, anthropologists are employed by the federal bureaucracies charged with addressing the use of illicit drugs. They are, therefore, the employees of a government that has decreed such practices felonies and must work over the background noise of the punitive rhetoric of a largely rhetorical "war on drugs." Again, many of the anthropologists employed by such bureaucracies have signed contracts to provide "the ethnographic component" of much larger research surveys. And although the candor of colloquia is seldom reproduced in the scholarly literature—the chapter by Kane and Mason (this volume) being a notable exception—it is clear that such a role has strained the integrity of several field-workers. The question of allegiance is so problematic in such settings that the National Association of Practicing Anthropologists has elaborated its own "ethical guidelines for practicing anthropologists." To cite from an unpublished draft of these guidelines that circulated at the 1987 meeting of the American Anthropological Association:

> At the outset of a relationship or contract . . . we should also discuss with our employer or client the intended use of the data or materials to be generated by our work and clarify the extent to which information developed during our activities can be made available to the public. Issues surrounding the protection of subject confidentiality and disclosure of information or findings should be thoroughly reviewed with the potential employer or client.

But anthropologists employed by large bureaucracies are seldom consulted regarding the disposition of information, and they are certainly not privy to top-level discussions regarding major decisions. Even the U.S. Centers for Disease Control, which prides itself on its ability to protect confidentiality, has engaged in activities that must have compromised the integrity of field-workers who have had no hand in disclosing private information. It was recently reported that "the CDC denies it has released confidential information to nonhealth agencies but does concede that on at least three occasions it has released lists of names of AIDS victims to local health agencies not affiliated with the federal government" (Marwick, 1983, p. 1945).

In parts of the United States, laws have been enacted to protect the right of those tested to determine who shall have access to the results. The vast majority of legislation, however, has been proposed in order to erode the rights of PWAs and others with HIV infection—this against the background of the long-standing "antisodomy" statutes that exist in many states in that country. In several states and cities, legislation is being elaborated that would make notification of sexual contacts obligatory once a person is determined to be seropositive. If these are enacted as law, what will be the roles, real and imagined, of anthropologists employed by the federal agencies attempting to enforce such laws?

Question 4. With whom was the anthropologist's "special knowledge" shared? What should become of the "finished products" of ethnographic research on AIDS? Although most of the dilemmas discussed above have been the subject of extensive debate, this question has usually been regarded as unproblematic. The association's guidelines note only that the anthropologist "should not communicate his findings secretly to some and withhold them from others." Because we are unaccustomed to having our work taken seriously by those outside of the discipline, we are in danger of being overly casual regarding the diffusion of our work. The debate surrounding Haiti's role in the U.S. AIDS pandemic is a case in point. Haitian community leaders, many of them physicians, objected to the results of the North American research that led to the inclusion of "Haitian" as a "risk group." This designation reflected, they asserted, the North Americans' inability to define risk groups within the group of Haitians with AIDS. Many Haitian observers felt that the Haitian informants were concealing information about same-sex contacts. They referred to a brisk business in male prostitution, which catered to gay North Americans visiting Port-au-Prince. One Haitian researcher and community activist insisted that "there is no way a study [of lifestyles] could be done by an American doctor."[8] To whom would he turn instead to elicit such knowledge? He proposed that Haitian physicians would be better able to extract information about sexual practices from reluctant informants. The University of Miami's foremost AIDS researcher termed these conditions "unacceptable." "Haitians are too close to the AIDS issue to conduct the questioning," she said. To whom would she turn to elicit such knowledge? She "would prefer an anthropologist fluent in Creole who has worked in Haiti."[9]

Those debating the question in North American could agree on only a couple of points. One of these was that the answer to the epidemiological mystery might be found in urban Haiti: What were the patterns of transmission there? Another was that proper investigation of such a question would require knowledge of Haitian language and culture. Let us suppose that, in 1983, an anthropologist decides to participate in state-funded AIDS research in Haiti. The proposal called for a "brief ethnographic component" to "flesh in the settings of presumed HIV transmission." The ethnographer is aware of the discrimination engendered by the recent inclusion of Haitians on the CDC's risk group list and has reason to believe that there is nothing about Haitianness per se that makes citizens of that nation particularly vulnerable to HIV infection. Let us assume that, through rapid ethnographic assessment procedures, the anthropologist soon demonstrates that a number of male AIDS victims from the area have had sexual contact with both men and women, a fact they had been reluctant to share with the doctors at the public clinic nearby. Some of these contacts have been with North American tourists in a couple of hotels catering to such exchanges. The anthropologist makes these findings available to Haitian health officials, confident that this collaboration will help to curb the spread of the virus.

The research scenario was hypothetical; the results it might have led to were not. In August 1983, the government of Jean-Claude Duvalier initiated repressive measures against gays in Port-au-Prince. "We have found that most people with AIDS are homosexuals, and that's why we moved against homosexuals," said a government spokesman. The regime was "planning a general fight against homosexuality." Another official predicted that "arrested homosexuals can look forward to three to six months in jail and then 'will be sent somewhere to reform them.' No lawyers will defend them."[10] Clubs and hotels were also forcibly closed; scores of "homosexuals" were arrested and beaten; a few foreigners were deported.

Later it was to be the turn of the prostitutes, and here the scenario is even more troubling, as force was used in the name of science itself. In 1987, one Port-au-Prince sex worker related the following story to a North American reporter: "One day the police came here. Believe me, they are worse than the *tonton macoutes* [Duvalierist militia] with their submachine guns. They rounded up 105 of us and they took our blood. That was a year ago."[11] Such was the climate of AIDS research when I began working in Duvalier's Haiti, and agency-sponsored and university-backed research continued smoothly during these operations. The academic community remained silent.

A very different possibility might be offered by "intervention ethnography." One example of such work is to be found in settings in which informants can themselves use the conclusions of ethnographic research to protect their health and that of their significant others. A group of social scientists in Seattle, Washington, claims that they

> are not just obtaining information related to the transmission of AIDS, but providing it. Given the speed with which the AIDS virus [sic] can move through a population of IV drug users, providing study participants with ways to reduce their risk was considered an ethical necessity. (Jacobs et al., 1988, p. 5)

Such interventions have not proceeded without snarls, however, and this may be due to some of the forces mentioned above. The authors of the Seattle study complain that

> the number of individuals who expressed willingness to be interviewed was considerably less than expected, some of those who agreed to be interviewed did not keep their appointments, and those who were interviewed did not prove to be good sources of referrals to other IV drug users. (Jacobs et al., 1988, p. 8)

Although they attribute this poor response to their research strategy, perhaps they underestimate the effects of other forces. The scholars are affiliated with a state university, and their work is funded by the federal government through county authorities. And it is to the local authorities that the project director submits a quarterly report. Acknowledging that "IV drug use is an illegal behavior," a number of research risks are cited. Research design reflects these tensions: "because agreements with the Seattle and other King County police have not been finalized, all three researchers have been instructed to restrict their observations and interviews to public places or to private locations only where drugs are not in evidence" (Jacobs et al., 1988, p. 5).

The study refers primarily to the risks run by researchers, not informants. We read on page 7 that, according to "the deputy prosecutor whose job it is to review the King County AIDS Prevention Project's contracts with outside agencies," an ethnographer in "an illegal setting . . . might find him or herself charged with and possibly convicted of obstructing an officer or other, more serious charges." But would such a charge harm or facilitate fieldwork in the context of informant reluctance? In settings of significant social inequality, the success of the ethnographic project may depend on perceived opposition—which reflects, presumably, genuine opposition—to local authorities.[12] We may be sure of our own good intentions, but we will certainly have to struggle to prove them in many of the communities at greatest risk of exposure to HIV. The author of an essay regarding "the wall" that has greeted those attempting to respond to AIDS in the African American community puts it starkly: "No matter how pure your motives, we will question why you are in our midst. No matter how deep your commitment, we will wonder what you are getting out of it" (Dalton, 1989, p. 223). These suspicions will only be enhanced by anthropologists overeager to find a role in turning out "ethnographic components" of large-scale, state-directed research.

Question 5. How will informants benefit from anthropological research? I have reserved a place of honor for a question that many anthropologists seem reluctant to ask: How will "those studied" benefit from our research? It is not, sadly, a question that arose early in the history of our professional debates but one that disgruntled informants or their postcolonial governments have forced us to consider. Tambiah (1985, p. 350) has neatly summarized the resulting anthropological angst that turns about the following issues:

> the question of whether it is possible to study other people without asserting a power over them, whether too many anthropologists take knowledge away to

advance their careers abroad rather than share their skills with those they study, whether this appropriated knowledge and heritage when deposited and concretized in museums and authoritative texts become enduring emblems and repositories of "looting" without reciprocity.

Some will consider the question of benefit for informants to be crassly utilitarian, but, as one Africanist noted years ago, "the beautiful faith that unfettered, unmolested scholarship automatically contributed to the welfare of the species is dying, even if there are among us those who would refuse to recognize the symptoms" (Burke, 1969, pp. 8-9).

The American Anthropological Association's Principles of Professional Responsibility answers this question with a rather vague injunction: "Fair return should be given [informants] for all services." Does "fair return" mean appropriate reciprocity as locally defined? Some sort of cash reimbursement or gift? A share of research monies or royalties? To the accusation that remuneration commercializes and thus cheapens social research, Chen and Murray—writing of research in Haiti—retort,

> Not so; it merely helps to remove one of its most exploitative aspects. The humanitarian motives which so easily bubble forth in introductory explanations and justification to the respondents tend to obscure the equally strong academic and career interests of the social scientist. Though the investigator may believe that his research activities will help improve the situation of the people studied, the prime beneficiary is probably the researcher himself. (Chen & Murray, 1976, p. 257)

For most, "fair return" means much more than on-the-spot payment. Some anthropologists investigating AIDS feel that their research is itself just recompense for privileged access to extremely private information. As noted above, "intervention ethnography"—conducted to bring to light the means by which HIV is spread in a specific population—has been conceived in such a manner. But such research may have little to no effect on rates of spread. One is so far rather underwhelmed by the secrets brought to light by ethnographic research on HIV. Throughout the world, the virus is transmitted in very few ways, and our task may be less to expose new ways of transmission and more to show the ways in which the virus is *not* spread. Such is surely the case with regard to Haiti, because members of the international scientific community speculated that the disease might be transmitted there by voodoo rites, the ingestion of sacrificial animal blood, the eating of cats, ritualized homosexuality, and so on—a rich panoply of exotica. Further, we have yet to demonstrate that decreased transmission is the necessary sequela of sound knowledge of the nature of spread. Research in several North American cities has shown that the majority of intravenous drug users who share works are well aware that dirty needles transmit HIV.

It is thus a series of key demands—that we make our research and its application useful, that we remain accountable to "the right people," and also that we find more satisfying responses to a pandemic that will not be slowed by research alone—that brings me to a closing challenge, one that should transcend theoretical and political boundaries.

Immanuel Wallerstein's (1974) suggestion that many of our far-flung and exotic stomping grounds have long been part of a single worldwide economic system received a predictably mixed reception in anthropology.[13] Most Marxists applauded him; many particularists objected to such sweeping generality; and some structural-functionalists dismissed his arguments as irrelevant to the key tasks of anthropology. But, regardless of partisan response, it must be noted that his formulation stimulated a heightened awareness of the interconnections that do indeed characterize our world. There may be many systems, rather than one, and some only tangentially related to the industrialized Western countries. There are also culturally distinctive responses to these systems and thus their nature is by no means determined solely in centers of power such as Washington and Moscow.

HIV is yet another reminder, a biological one, of these social networks, which are sexual as well as economic. The virus and the speed of its spread speak eloquently to the intimacy of the connections. And yet, despite the relatively unhindered movement of HIV, responses to it have been predictably inequitable. The harvest of the last decade of clinical and basic research has been spread among the wealthy developed nations. In fact, if HIV did not affect these nations, experience with the major tropical disorders suggests it is highly likely that the pandemic would have attracted more newsprint than money. Due to the lack of funds for screening, transfusion-associated transmission of HIV continues apace in many of the countries hit hardest by AIDS—this when the majority of those infected with the virus are thought to live in the Third World. In poor countries like Haiti, drugs like AZT—to date the sole agent with clinically proven efficacy against HIV—are simply not available. To quote one of the Haitian doctors with whom I work, the network in which Haitians now find themselves is divided by "a semi-permeable barrier through which we share the diseases, but not the treatments."

North American and European academics, perhaps especially anthropologists, are caught up in these systems. The challenge, then, is that each of us engaged in AIDS research acknowledge and reflect on *the anthropologist as link:* What are the mechanisms by which we come to represent very real links, often between wealthy countries and poor ones, between rich universities and impoverished villages, between empowered and disempowered people, between the admired and the stigmatized, and even between the well and the sick? What are the mechanisms by which we wittingly or unwittingly mask these ties? What responsibility might these connections entail?

Such a challenge, laden with the history of our discipline, brings us back to our guiding question: What are the threats—political, methodological, epistemological—to ethically sound anthropological research on AIDS? The answer may be summed up in few words: They are many.

What Is to Be Done?

How, then, might anthropologists and other social scientists bring their insights to bear on a world pandemic that shows few signs of abating, especially among the poor? In some settings, the surest path will be through "community research initiatives" that tie investigations to locally determined needs, many of which are linked as much to alleviation of existing suffering as to the prevention of future cases. But there are many other opportunities for humane involvement in efforts to counter HIV.

Several of these efforts would seem to require the tools of the trade. The most important of these is exposing the way that AIDS "moves along the fault lines of our society," as Bateson and Goldsby (1988, p. 4) have put it. Anthropologists are uniquely placed to explain why AIDS is fast becoming an illness of the disadvantaged. Why, for example, is the incidence of AIDS in the United States so heavily skewed in the direction of Blacks and Hispanics? And is it true, as one report would have it, that "while the average lifespan of a white person after diagnosis is two years, the average minority person survives only 19 weeks" (Sabatier, 1988, p. 7)?[14] We need engage in no windy polemics; interpretations alone would be imbued with moral bite.

A second properly anthropological task would be to use ethnology as "cultural critique" (Marcus & Fischer, 1986). Practices in our cultures of origin may be critiqued merely by juxtaposition with more humane responses seen in other settings. For example, we have recently contrasted the high-tech hospital care accorded a North American man with AIDS with the more community-based care given a rural Haitian woman. We did this not to suggest that one would receive better care in Haiti, although this was certainly the case in that comparison. Rather, the exercise afforded the context in which the weaknesses of our current responses, both social and medical, were laid bare. By showing how responses to AIDS are embedded in core cultural constructs, it was possible to deplore "the denial of suffering and death, the impersonal bureaucratization of care, the recourse to techno-logical 'fixes,' and our failure to lighten the degrading burden of stigma" (Farmer & Kleinman, 1989, p. 158).

A third option would be to counter false information, a primary source of what the World Health Organization has termed "the other AIDS epidemic," that of "unnecessary suffering for the general population including the HIV seropositive and people with AIDS caused, not by biological, but by socially determined factors" (Frankenberg, 1988). Much of the stigma and many of the inappropriate and cruel responses to the perceived threat of HIV have been due to misinformation about the nature of the virus. Gilman (1988, p. 88) is correct when he asserts that

> people have been stigmatized (and destroyed) as much by the "idea" of AIDS as by its reality. Since each of us has the potential of stigmatizing and being stigmatized, since the construction of images of disease is a dynamic process to which the sufferers, real and imagined, consistently respond, it is in our best interest to recognize the process.

Some of the false information has been of a distinctly "ethnographic" nature. In her review of the role of prejudice and misinformation in the global pandemic, Renee Sabatier notes the damage done by "armchair anthropology." Haitians and Africans were among the hardest hit by the epidemic of fear, misinformation, and outright racism. Sabatier recounts the effects of such "theories" as the one that "proposed that Haitians may have contracted the virus from monkeys as part of bizarre sexual practices in Haitian broth-els." Another choice example was advanced in 1986 by British authors: "Monkeys are often hunted for food in Africa. Once caught, monkeys are often kept in huts for some time before they are eaten. Dead monkeys are often used as toys by African children" (Sabatier, 1988, pp. 45, 62).

Fourth, anthropologists may also use their skills to document the effects of such misinformation and to join forces with community groups in using such information to develop "cultural-activist" responses not only to the AIDS pandemic but to the epidemic of discrimination that has arisen in the wake of HIV. When the voices of the victims of discrimination "have been unheard because of their triple minority status as black, foreign, and French- and Creole-speaking" (Laguerre, 1984, p. 9), as is the case with Haitians in North America, scholars who speak English as a first language and are well versed in grantsmanship may actually apply these skills on behalf of com-munity-based groups rather than through universities and state bureaucra-cies.[15] Often, academics will be obliged to demonstrate a great deal of good will before their services are asked for, as the assumption is that "they're in it for their own advancement."

A fifth anthropological task might be that of witnessing—that is, honoring the memory of persons who have died from AIDS and of communities sorely afflicted by HIV or its stigma. A compelling argument has often been made for such a commemorative role for anthropology, especially on behalf of tribal culture on the wane. Regarding the AIDS pandemic, however, we seem not to have done a stellar job, as one person with the syndrome attests: "Anthropologists of our tristes tropiques have accumulated a considerable store of information and conclusions about our genes and our mores, our mode of socialization and our myths, but in so doing, they've lost sight of our humanity" (Dreuilh, 1988, p. 4). Still others will term such witnessing a "bourgeois luxury" and point to the need for medicines, health personnel, and funds for prevention. There is, it has been impatiently noted, a pandemic going on here.

This impatience brings us up short: We are hard-pressed to think of other morally sure roles for anthropology. But there would seem to be no shortage of tasks for anthropologists wishing to address suffering caused by HIV. It's just that *these are not intrinsically anthropological roles.* The need for community involvement is especially acute in countries such as the United States and Haiti, where there are no national health insurance plans. In Haiti, one works with villagers who have run out of medication for their active tuberculosis, a disease known to respond to treatment even among AIDS patients. These individuals simply lack the funds and transportation necessary to fill a prescription. And yet who among us, even in the field, cannot drum up some money and a ride? In the United States, one meets PWAs who are dying quickly, simply because their resources are exhausted and they have nothing to eat. It is difficult to imagine interviewing someone in such circumstances. These scenarios, inevitably moral dilemmas, are inescapable in anthropological research on AIDS and may simply point to the fact that research is very often an inappropriate response to suffering. In such instances, we may find that personal integrity *and* professional interests are best served by putting aside tape recorders and notebooks.

Notes

1. These figures come from a 1980 report compiled by Feilden et al. For the most up-to-date national data, see UNICEF (1987); for a politically astute consideration of what these numbers mean, see the brief monograph by Prince (1985).

2. At this writing, two of these persons have died, and another has left Do Kay. See Farmer (1990a) for a more thorough presentation and discussion of these data.

3. The slum, one of the worst in the hemisphere, had been named after Francois Duvalier's wife. It was rebaptized "Cite Soleil" after the February 1986 departure of Jean-Claude Duvalier. Some felt that poetic justice would have been better served by leaving the name as it was.

4. From an interview published in *U.S. News and World Report, 95*(18), 44 (October 31, 1983).

5. It is clear that many such proposals are patterned on the "Rapid Assessment Procedures" advanced by Scrimshaw for nutrition and primary health care programs: "RAP provides health workers, researchers and social scientists in fields other than anthropology, and anthropologists with guidelines for assessments of health-seeking behaviour, behaviour involved in maintaining health and overcoming illness, including the use of both traditional and modern health services" (Scrimshaw & Hurtado, 1987, p. 1).

6. From the *Miami News* (November 1, 1986). The man, who was being held in the INS detention center in South Dade, was to be deported on charges of drug trafficking. When I attempted to delineate the difference between the public hospital in which I worked and the INS, one of the Haitians who refused to participate in a program sponsored by the former countered *leta se leta*: "the state is the state."

7. This may be less true among gay North American men with AIDS. As Gorman (1986, p. 167) has put it, "Perhaps at no time in medical history has a group of afflicted people so rejected the role of being the sick and helpless victim."

8. Dr. Jean Claude Desgranges, cited in the *Miami News* (May 24, 1983, p. 2A).

9. Dr. Margaret Fischl, cited in the *Miami Herald* (August 31, 1983, p. 3D).

10. From the *Miami News* (August 10, 1983, p. 1).

11. Reported in *Life* (August 1987).

12. In anthropology, the classic example of this means of gaining entrée is Clifford Geertz's (1973) celebrated account of being busted at an illegal Balinese cockfight.

13. I have attempted to refine Wallerstein's theory as regards Haiti in a recent review (Farmer, 1988) and have also examined the role of such large-scale trends in the shaping of the AIDS-HIV pandemic (Farmer, 1990b).

14. Sabatier (1988) offers the following statistics: "Among white adults in the United States, the incidence of AIDS cases is 189 per million population; for blacks it is 578 per million; and for Hispanics it is 564 per million."

15. For example, see the essay by Farmer and Kim (1991), which describes a community-based project that allows Haitian American teenagers to play an important role in combating both AIDS and racism.

References

Bateson, C., & Goldsby, R. (1988). *Thinking AIDS: The social response to the biological threat.* Reading, MA: Addison-Wesley.

Berreman, G. (1981). *The politics of truth: Essays in critical anthropology.* New Delhi: South Asian.

Blumer, H. (1967). Threats from agency-determined research: The case of Camelot. In I. Horowitz (Ed.), *The rise and fall of Project Camelot.* Cambridge: MIT Press.

Chaze, W. (1983). In Haiti, a view of life at the bottom. *US News and World Report, 95*(18), 41-42.

Chen, Kwan-Hwa, & Murray, G. (1976). Truths and untruths in village Haiti: An experiment in Third World survey research. In J. Marshall & S. Polgar (Eds.), *Culture, natality, and family planning.* Chapel Hill: University of North Carolina Press.

Collaborative Study Group of AIDS in Haitian-Americans. (1987). Risk factors for AIDS among Haitians residing in the United States: Evidence of heterosexual transmission. *Journal of the American Medical Association, 257*(5), 635-639.

Crimp, D. (1988). How to have promiscuity in an epidemic. In D. Crimp (Ed.), *AIDS: Cultural analysis/cultural activism.* Cambridge: MIT Press.

Dalton, H. (1989). AIDS in blackface. *Daedalus, 118*(3), 205-228.

Dreuilh, E. (1988). *Mortal embrace: Living with AIDS.* New York: Hill & Wang.

Farmer, P. (1988). Blood, sweat, and baseballs: Haiti in the West Atlantic system. *Dialectical Anthropology, 13,* 83-99.

Farmer, P. (1990a). Sending sickness: Sorcery, politics, and changing concepts of AIDS in rural Haiti. *Medical Anthropology Quarterly, 4*(1), 6-27.

Farmer, P. (1990b). The exotic and the mundane: Human immunodeficiency virus in Haiti. *Human Nature, 1*(4), 415-446.

Farmer, P., & Kim, J. (1991). Anthropology, accountability, and the prevention of AIDS. *Journal of Sex Research, 28*(2).

Farmer, P., & Kleinman, A. (1989). AIDS as human suffering. *Daedalus, 118*(2), 135-160.

Frankenberg, R. (1988). AIDS and anthropologists. *Anthropology Today, 4*(2), 14-19.

Geertz, C. (1973). Notes on a Balinese cockfight: *The Interpretation of Cultures.* Epidemiological and Anthropological Perspectives. In Janes, C., Stall, R., & Gifford, S. (Eds.), *Anthropology and Epidemiology.* Dordrecht: Reidel.

Jacobs, S., Kleyn, J., Osborne, O., Clay, C., & Charles, F. (1988, April 20-23). *Intervention ethnography in two communities at high risk for AIDS.* Paper presented at the Society for Applied Anthropology, Tampa, FL.

Laguerre, M. (1984). *American odyssey: Haitians in New York.* Ithaca, NY: Cornell University Press.

Landesman, S. (1983). The Haitian connection. In K. Cahill (Ed.), *The AIDS epidemic.* New York: St. Martin's.

Liautaud, B., Pape, J., & Pamphile, M. (1988, December). Le Sida dans les Caraibes. *Medecine et Maladies Infectieuses,* pp. 687-697.

Marcus, G., & Fischer, M. (1986). *Anthropology as cultural critique: An experimental moment in the human sciences.* Chicago: University of Chicago Press.

Marwick, C. (1983). "Confidentiality" issues may cloud epidemiological studies of AIDS. *Journal of the American Medical Association, 250*(15), 1945-1946.

Moore, S. (1987). Explaining the present: Theoretical dilemmas in processual ethnography. *American Ethnologist, 14*(4), 123-132.

Prince, R. (1985). *Haiti: Family business.* London: Latin America Bureau.

Sabatier, R. (1988). *Blaming others: Prejudice, race and worldwide AIDS.* Philadelphia: New Society.

Scrimshaw, S., & Hurtado, E. (1987). *Rapid assessment procedures for nutrition and primary health care.* Los Angeles: University of California, Latin American Center.

Tambiah, S. (1985). *Culture, thought, and social action: An anthropological perspective.* Cambridge, MA: Harvard University Press.

UNICEF. (1987). *The state of the world's children*. New York: Author.

Wallerstein, I. (1974). *The modern world-system: Capitalist agriculture and the origins of the European world-economy in the sixteenth century*. San Diego, CA: Academic Press.

Weidman, H. (1976). In praise of the double bind inherent in anthropological application. In M. Agrosino (Ed.), *Do applied anthropologists apply anthropology?* Athens, GA: Southern Anthropological Society.

14

Knowledge and Action in the
Shadow of AIDS

SHIRLEY LINDENBAUM

The influenza epidemic of 1918, which killed more than 21 million people in a very short span of time, left little imprint on historical consciousness. Absent from war histories, college texts, and most novels of the period, the pandemic may have passed too rapidly to have more than an ephemeral effect on the economy, its demographic effects apparently concealed by the war (Crosby, 1989).

The epidemic of AIDS differs from the influenza epidemic in many respects. Unlike influenza, HIV disease is a chronic condition, and one that appears to be uniformly fatal. While the greatest ravages of influenza occurred in a little less than a year, the AIDS pandemic is now in its second decade. In addition, AIDS seized the U.S., if not international, imagination when Rock Hudson died of the disease, whereas influenza is said to have bypassed famous national or world figures and those in positions of authority and thus had no comparable effect (Crosby, 1989, p. 322). The influenza epidemic also left little imprint in the public record. AIDS, by way of contrast, is leaving its mark in popular and high culture—in newspapers, magazines, television, plays, novels, and street theater.

The epidemics are alike, however, in that both appear to have had little impact on the structures or procedures of our major cultural or governmental institutions, with the exception of those of medical science. The influenza epidemic is said to have spurred great activity among medical scientists and their institutions (Crosby, 1989, p. 323), and AIDS has similarly provided increased funding and prestige to some medical specialties (such as infectious disease) and has changed or at least perhaps hastened changes already under way in some areas of research. For example, AIDS activists have increased public awareness concerning drug development and the structure and purpose of clinical trials, resulting in changes in both areas. However, it is too early to conclude that the changes are permanent.

Although AIDS may be creating little institutional or structural change, it has affected the way those in the medical and human sciences think about, produce, and acquire knowledge. The participants in this conference were thus asked to consider the impact of AIDS especially on anthropological theory, method, and practice. For those who had already lost friends, lovers, a way of life, and a community, this was more than an intellectual exercise. Using the disciplinary tools at their disposal, and modifying them as they confronted the existential reality of the disease, they attempted to make sense out of a frightening phenomenon. As Martin Levine observes, the recent focus on subjective experience and a constructionist approach to social analysis revealed the limits of earlier epidemiological and psychological research on the epidemic among gay men.

As the conference discussant, I was asked to comment on the themes that emerged during our days of animated conversation. In the chapter that follows, I have selected and elaborated on five topics that I hope convey the sense of intellectual challenge and involvement that AIDS elicits from those experiencing the epidemic at its center as well as from those at a safer distance. Drawing upon our current understanding of the nature of the epidemic, we examined the following issues: the crossing of disciplinary boundaries; culture, history, and the study of disease; the relationship of social theory to social life; the creation of scientific knowledge; and the call for both knowledge and practice.

The Crossing of Disciplinary Boundaries

As the chapters in this volume attest, scholarly research on AIDS crosses many boundaries—in this case, anthropology, sociology, psychology, linguistics, history, and medicine. We also live and write at a moment when the trespass is considered a healthy, if not unavoidable, procedure and in which we assume that the merger of partial accounts may provide the best possible answers.[1]

Although boundary crossings have been a feature of research in agriculture and in family planning for the past several decades, AIDS research brings into sharp focus the question of what we mean by *interdisciplinary research.* Is there a body of shared theory underlying our joint analyses? Is there sufficient precision in our use of key terms? And is real interdisciplinary research and practice possible, especially when the boundaries cross the so-called social, natural, and physical sciences?

As Rosenfield (1989) indicates, collaboration across disciplinary boundaries may mean different things in different contexts. *Multidisciplinary* research, for example, involves little more than bringing together investigators from different disciplines to work on various aspects of a broad problem. Here, each disciplinary representative works independently, and the results are brought together at the end. The publication is usually organized as a set of separate chapters with an introduction or conclusion by the principal investigator, who summarizes the findings. Multidisciplinary research may shed light on problems that call for immediate solution but rarely provides path-breaking information. This is not a model to seduce the participants at this conference.

Interdisciplinary research invites investigators from different disciplines to use their techniques and skills to address a common problem. New insights may result from the research, but in large projects, the issues are dealt with on a discipline-specific basis. The final analysis is prepared by the principal investigator. Many of us at the conference had been involved in and had struggled with the problems posed by this research procedure.

The rarest form of investigation, *transdisciplinary* research, requires that members of each discipline attempt to transcend their own conceptual, theoretical, and methodological orientations and attempt to develop a common approach or a common conceptual framework. The papers by Carrier, Frankenberg, and Schoepf perhaps best illustrate this more radical approach, and much of our discussion dealt with the issues raised by the possibility of undertaking transdisciplinary work.

The choice of procedure is not to be taken lightly. The three approaches require different training as well as career paths (Rosenfield, 1989), and the participants agreed that little prestige accrues to those who work with other disciplines and submerge their own. Employment and tenure decisions are based on single-authored pieces in one's own disciplinary journals, and rewards are given to those who focus on contemporary issues in their own field. Nevertheless, it was apparent that the classical ethnographic method of a lone investigator undertaking "participant observation" was not possible for many aspects of AIDS research. The barriers to undertaking transdisciplinary research were also fully appreciated. For example, medicine and social science have different notions of causality (the former searching, in general, for a single, necessary cause; the latter focusing on multicausality), and epidemiology is a method rather than a discipline based in social theory, whereas the anthropological perspective is based on theory, and research methods are selected according to context.

Because most of the participants had undertaken collaborative research and recognized the problems of joint investigation, the search for remedies was particularly fruitful. We appear to have moved beyond an earlier phase in medical anthropology when it seemed that our main assignment was to call attention to the way in which the language and concepts of biology and culture are socially constructed and historically situated. Our discussions indicated that this notion was now taken for granted. We spoke less of the need to fuse static objects of study (body and mind, matter and symbol) and more about ways to conceive of and to undertake the process of sociomedical analysis. The "risk groups" of epidemiology, a concept that separates people from context, gave way to a more dynamic language concerning behaviors in historical contexts, specific locations, and individual conception. Kane, for example, proposed the concept of "social interfaces" for situations in which people come together as a result of such political and economic forces as tourism, migration, or a military presence that create new sites of social interaction. Treichler's notion of "discordant identities" attempted to capture the way people articulate multiple identities in concrete situations. Frankenberg avoided speaking about "subcultures," favoring instead the notions of "embedded cultures" and "mindful bodies."

Our discussions indicated that we had journeyed to Colorado venerating a wide array of sacred texts. Our most hallowed ancestors seemed to include Malinowski, Marx, Weber, Mills, Freud, and Rousseau and, among more recent ascensions, Mintz, Wolf, Raymond Williams, E. P. Thompson, Geertz, Bourdieu, Foucault, Gramsci, and Freire. As a result, we did not all share the same definition of culture but agreed with Treichler that culture was not everything left over when you have identified what might be called "science." Despite our different points of departure, we spoke of culture in more interactional terms as both process and product.

Culture, History, and the Study of Disease

Democratic and Undemocratic Diseases

Some of our most fruitful discussions followed Virginia Berridge's suggestion that we distinguish several kinds of history; in particular, long history

(history as background or lesson) and contemporary history, which focuses on the immediate pre-AIDS period, borrows concepts and methods from other disciplines, and makes an alliance with policy studies. Contemporary history thus closely resembles contemporary medical anthropology in its interests and approach, underscoring our sense of affinity between the two disciplines. It seems an irony, however, that, as historians look to contemporary events, anthropologists and other human scientists have recently adopted the "long history" approach in investigating epidemics and illness (Comaroff, in press; Gilman, 1988; Gussow, 1989).

For anthropologists, the long view provides a basic for resisting the "naturalizations" and inappropriate generalizations we encounter in the language and concepts of science. It also reminds us of the ways in which the AIDS epidemic and HIV disease are both like and unlike past epidemics and disease states. As the opening segment of this chapter indicates, the AIDS epidemic differs in many ways from that of influenza. Consideration of current and past epidemics and historical contexts reveals instructive similarities as well as differences.

An overriding theme of our commentaries, as well as much of the AIDS literature, for example, refers to the stigma, discrimination, and inequalities of the current epidemic, as Herdt's introduction indicates. At its outset, HIV disease settled upon socially disvalued groups and, as the epidemic progresses, AIDS becomes increasingly an affliction of marginal and socially disempowered groups. In the United States, for example, HIV disease is located predominantly in large urban centers and, within those centers, it afflicts the residents of the least favored neighborhoods. Within New York City, for instance, AIDS cases are concentrated in zones of urban poverty, where drug addiction, homelessness, poor health care, and the spread of other epidemic diseases simultaneously imperil the lives of minority populations. However, the penchant for drawing parallels between the stigma of AIDS and the stigma associated with earlier diseases and social groups tends to mask the fact that the AIDS epidemic differs from earlier epidemics of infectious disease in significant ways. AIDS is an undemocratic affliction.

In "democratic epidemics" (Arras, 1988), communicable illnesses cut across class, racial, and ethnic lines and threaten the community at large. Faced with such diseases—for example, smallpox—a community's sense of mutual vulnerability prevents it from stigmatizing and making outcasts of those who fall ill. AIDS does not similarly threaten the community at large. Moreover, inequalities in mortality and life expectancy are a relatively recent phenomenon. Social class differences in life expectancy emerged for the first time in Europe during the 18th century (Kunitz, 1983, p. 363). Prior to that time, much of the mortality was caused by epidemics against which wealth was no protection. During the 18th century, social and biological conditions changed. Plague and typhus diminished as a result of changes in military organization (a shift to naval warfare and improvements in military hygiene) and from the increasing effectiveness of quarantine. With population growth and the integration of national economies, the crowd diseases (measles and smallpox) became more benign, childhood afflictions. It is at this time that we see a divergence in the life expectancy of aristocrats and commoners in England and probably throughout northwest Europe. By the mid-18th century, differences in mortality and life expectancy by region and social class can be attributed to a marked reduction in pandemics (although they tended to affect everyone equally) and to the better living conditions, dietary practices, nursing care, and nutritional status of the peerage. These latter conditions provided better protection against the most important remaining causes of illness and death—the infectious diseases of childhood and the pneumonia-diarrhea complex. Infant mortality among the aristocracy declined more rapidly than it did among the general population, and the life expectancy of the aristocracy increased beyond that of the rest of the population for the first time (Kunitz, 1983, p. 355, 1987). The narrowing of differences in life expectancy has occurred since the late 19th century.

As this account suggests, inequalities in morbidity and mortality are part biological and part social phenomena. An explanation for the unequal concentration of AIDS in certain regions and among certain populations results again from a convergence of biological, ecological, and social factors (see Grmek, 1990). The undemocratic nature of the AIDS epidemic is not the inevitable result of an encounter with infectious disease.

Understanding and Intervention

The problematic, if productive, relationship of anthropology and epidemiology was a recurrent theme. Would anthropologists, like historians in other contexts, become the "great toadies of power" (Berridge, this volume)? Do the "risk groups" of epidemiology, particularly in infectious disease epidemiology, still carry an echo of their origin, tied to protecting the bourgeoisie from disease? How should we best frame the epidemic? By helping to refine and improve the categories and language of epidemiology or by searching for causes at the level of the political economy?

The "lesson of history" approach again helps to refine the question. The campaigns to eradicate hookworm and pellagra in the cotton mill villages of the U.S. South during the 1920s, for example, illustrate the degree to which the values and ideology of the investigator determine the approach to understanding the cause, cure, and prevention of disease (Kunitz, 1988). Investigators studying pellagra held to a model of causation in which "society" was the independent variable. Thus poverty and the availability of food were said to explain the differences in the incidence of pellagra among the villages. The hookworm campaign, on the other hand, which assimilated the germ theory to a religious conception of individual sin and redemption, called for little institutional or social change and much personal transformation (Kunitz, 1988, p. 143).

The intellectual basis of this latter campaign (extended later to other infectious diseases, such as malaria and yellow fever) is based on the belief that particular diseases are the same everywhere. Local culture and socioeconomic structures are considered largely irrelevant. The irony is that pellagra disappeared from the United States when niacin was put in bread. Hookworm, on the other hand, proved intractable, requiring social changes that allowed people to build better houses, wear shoes, and improve sanitation. That is, in contrast to the ideological presuppositions of the investigators, pellagra was amenable to a technical intervention; the diminution of hookworm depended on social and economic changes (Kunitz, 1988, p. 146).

There is a lesson here for a fuller understanding of the etiology, cure, and prevention of HIV disease. Just as the prevention and treatment of pellagra and hookworm required intimate knowledge of particular peoples and settings, the AIDS epidemic should also be examined in particular contexts. Even within the United States, the epidemic is concentrated in certain regions; within those regions, in certain urban centers; and within those centers, in particular localities. Without wishing to be misunderstood, one could say that pellagra provides the model for understanding HIV disease among hemophiliacs and gay men: A simple intervention—a change in blood bank procedures and new ways to express love and affection (adopted voluntarily by many gay men)—can interrupt transmission of the virus. To understand and prevent continuation of the epidemic among intravenous drug users and their sexual partners, however, hookworm provides the better model. Here, the behaviors to be modified require vast social and economic change. Drug use, sex for drugs, and the spread of HIV disease to the sexual partners of drug users occur in zones of urban poverty, poor health care, social disintegration, and the epidemic spread of other diseases, including diseases that interact with HIV and facilitate its spread. That is, the epidemic of HIV disease is not the same phenomenon everywhere but is a series of superimposed epidemics in different subpopulations (see Grmek, 1990) requiring different approaches to prevention and treatment. Moreover, the relevance of "local knowledge" for prevention and treatment may differ from the need to understand its ecology.

Disease as Metaphor

Sander Gilman's conference paper led us to reflect on the ways in which some diseases are interpreted through existing cultural categories. Myth making about disease in German literature, for example, differs from myth making elsewhere. Moreover, different genres have a life of their own. This latter feature of representation is well understood by gay activists who are divided about whether the press should be given access to photographic images of the dying.

As Gilman's paper further suggested, certain diseases acquire an iconic status. Particular diseases fade in and out of consciousness, become metaphor, myth, disappear and reappear. If the magic bullet were found for HIV disease, we wondered, would our myth making and stereotypical views about the disease and its victims come to a halt? Historical material again reveals the conditions in which diseases taken on a heavy social load as they become intertwined with the political, economic, and religious issues of the day. Leprosy and silicosis provide two illuminating examples.

Contrary to popular understanding, leprosy has not had a history of constant stigma. During the Middle Ages, leprosy disappeared from Europe and declined as a salient theological concept. By the 19th century, however, it had reappeared. Neither was leprosy universally stigmatized in the societies in which it occurred. Its reappearance in European consciousness during the 19th century coincided with the discovery that leprosy was hyperendemic in parts of the world that Western nations were then annexing and colonizing. Seen as the disease of "inferior" peoples and a danger to the civilized world, leprosy again became a salient, stigmatizing condition: By the turn of the century, Western nations had become leprophobic. Images of leprosy incorporated stereotypical European perceptions of "coolies" and "hindoos." (This is the era of the "yellow peril.") U.S. immigration restrictions date from this period with its exaggerated fears of introduced disease.

A second influence on the mythic image of leprosy came from linking the fears and representations of contagious disease with biblical and medieval images of taint. Late-19th-century imperialism and a religious revival in England led to intensified mission activities. From 1870 on, missionary travels abroad systematically focused on work among lepers, associating the condition with biblical images of leprosy (which may or may not have been the same disease). Lepers were segregated in special colonies, and, where prejudice did not exist, Christian preachers constructed it anew. Thus a Christian image of leprosy as the "disease of the soul," an image that had died out in the Middle Ages, was reinvigorated by 19th-century notions of contagion, inferiority, and the racism of colonial expansion, a stigmatizing image that remains with us today (Gussow, 1989).

Silicosis, a chronic lung disease, similarly moves in and out of historical focus, masked and unmasked by social and political events and not by the presence or absence of the disease. Professional groups, government officials, insurance executives, and labor representatives all contribute to shaping disability policies as well as the definition of this industrial disease. Like leprosy, silicosis depends on historical context for its particular social importance (Markowitz & Rosner, 1989). As AIDS in the United States becomes increasingly a disease of poor minorities, we may witness again the conditions under which another fatal disease ceases to be a salient issue for society in general. It is an irony of the racism in U.S. culture, as Quimby observes, that many African Americans have already chosen the path of denial and avoidance, fearing association with a disease depicted as associated mainly with gays and addicts.

On the Relation of Social Theory to Social Life

John Gagnon's presentation drew attention to the contemporary sense of epistemological doubt in some quarters of interpretive social science. "Genre merging" in method and reporting, the rise of a strong antipositivist position in all of the social sciences, the tendency for some investigators to treat all science as entirely social, and the critique of science by political and religious groups, among other things, challenge the notion of the "authoritative voice" in science and provide evidence for doubt about the "science" in the human sciences.

A recent tide of anthropological literature has been devoted also to analyzing the rhetoric of ethnographic writing, questioning the discipline's objectifying authority (Clifford & Marcus, 1986; Marcus & Fischer, 1986). Avoiding the nihilistic impulses of much of this literature, and acknowledging that anthropologists might become more sensitive to their own role in the construction of ethnographic facts, Mintz (1989, p. 793) points to a change in the way the anthropological ego is now managed: "Forty years ago there seem to have been more scientists; now there appear to be more selves."

A similar reassessment has occurred in other fields as well. For adherents of Process Theology, the image of an omnipotent God has been supplanted by that of a supreme being having persuasive power (E. Shelp, 1990, personal communication). The authoritative posture of the psychoanalyst is also said to have changed as psychoanalytic theory has moved from a view of the therapist as a "blank screen" against which the patient's fantasies were projected to a notion of psychoanalyst and patient as collaborators who share the construction of a coherent narrative.

As Gagnon notes, the contemporary crisis of meaning and action in the human sciences predates the advent of HIV disease. Nevertheless, we questioned how we might speak about AIDS in the absence of any master theories of society or the logic of history. We agreed that a "deconstructive" postmodern stance, which asserts that the material world is imaginary, does not provide the appropriate forum. Death is not a constructed event. Moreover, deconstruction's focus on the "unreliability" of language and the "indeterminacy" of texts concentrates on language to the exclusion of the world. Although the content of the postmodern critique calls for questioning *textually* constituted authority, the endeavor is a play for *socially* created power and authority (see Sangren, 1988).

As Sangren observes, attention to the locus of authority in ethnographic writing and cultural studies in general has had a salutary effect. Worthwhile questions are raised about the ways in which knowledge, power, and authority are socially and culturally reproduced in ways that may be opaque to the actors. However, the analysis of the authority of ethnography must specify the conditions of ethnography's production and reproduction in society, especially in academic institutions, not just in texts. The current popularity of postmodern ethnography should be viewed not as a consequence of the failure of preceding "paradigms" but as a bid for the professional advantages postmodernism confers upon those who advocate it in particular institutions.

It should be noted also that postmodern critics also confuse science as critical judgment with science as revealed authority. The rejection of science as a legitimating value further creates and legitimates the eclectic humanism proposed by postmodernists (Sangren, 1988, pp. 48-50), reproducing the symmetrical contrast between the humanities and the sciences that much recent scholarship in medical anthropology has been at pains to reveal and dissolve.

In addition, a postmodern anthropology that asserts that the material world is imaginary, and the imaginary world of pastiche is real, does not contribute to the task of social analysis, which is to comprehend the unity and diversity of historical processes. How do we think about the unfolding AIDS epidemic? And what is the relation of social theory to social life?

In regard to the latter, Gagnon offered the view that social scientists often appear at moments of crisis to explain, record, and perhaps adjust to the crisis. Erikson's notion of the life course, for example, arrived just as the notion of the life course was taken for granted and began to fall apart; the current focus on the self occurs as an earlier sense of self begins to disintegrate. This mode of analysis, which locates intellectual movements in terms of particular political, economic, and social histories, can be applied also to recent trends in anthropological theory.

As Polier and Roseberry (1989) note, the postwar decades from about 1945 to 1970 were characterized by U.S. world hegemony, for which modernization theory was its most confident expression. The past 15 years have been characterized by deepening crisis and restructuring. World systems theory and postmodern thought, both of which began as critiques of modernization theory, can be seen as intellectual expressions of that crisis. Extreme versions of world systems theory (in Latin American dependency thought) had the effect of denying the possibility of movement in the system at the moment when movement became possible. Similarly, extreme versions of postmodern thought have the effect of denying a world of politics and economics as both become more threatening. Postmodernism and world systems theory can thus be seen as responses inimical to history and to any philosophy of action.

The conference participants called for a theoretical approach that would examine the social circumstances that have produced a world that appears to be without history and structure (see Polier & Roseberry, 1989) but that, as Quimby's presentation underscored, is a world of differential empowerment. Several of the authors, especially Farmer and Schoepf, have adopted Gramsci's (1971) suggestion that we locate objectivity in processes of historical construction and locate that construction in fields of power, that is, in the "specific relations between cultural complexes" (Polier & Roseberry, 1989). The ethnographic "facts" in Haiti, for example, are composed of what the peasants tell us about their lives and those of their neighbors. These "facts" are then placed in the context of other "facts" about health histories and economic transactions, and these are placed in the context of the "region" in which the events take place, which, as Farmer indicates, reaches as far afield as Washington.

As Mintz observes, anthropology must be humanistic in its orientation, but scientific too. "That not every fact may be equal in status to every other fact does not prove that there is no objective reality."

> There appear to be no facts, not because facts do not exist, but because facts exist only in relationship to each other. Hence, the specification of relationships means an interpretation of reality, not a long list of facts; and interpretation of human behavior by humans means only that a certain kind of science is not feasible. (Mintz, 1989, p. 794)

A full rendering of the AIDS epidemic in a particular location thus places it in local, regional, and national contexts and, in some cases, the geopolitics of competing international communities (see Bond & Vincent, in press).

On the Creation of Scientific Knowledge

On the first day of our meeting, we were asked to provide each other with short autobiographies. There were similarities in several of the stories. Richard Parker, Ernest Quimby, and Paul Farmer, for instance, all spoke of their experience with the epidemic at home and abroad. In 1983, Parker left the vortex of concern in San Francisco only to find a complete absence of discussion about the disease in Brazil. Returning to New York from Granada in 1985, Quimby had the reverse experience, hearing little about the disease in Granada but finding at home a community in the midst of crisis. Farmer shuttled between Boston and Haiti: AIDS information filled the newspapers and engaged the medical communities in both places.

A second set of related experiences emerged from Berridge's comment that her research had focused on the developmental progression in AIDS debates as they related to policy development. Treichler's interest in the social construction of the notion of the virus in the United States, and Farmer's documentation of its changing construction in Haiti, seemed to form another related set.

Taken together, all the stories provided evidence of alternate meanings and understandings of the epidemic in different locations. This simultaneous reading of the epidemic in both core and margin, present also in the essays by Carrier, Gilman, Levine, and Schoepf, begins to describe the way in which biomedical knowledge and local knowledge may be produced and interdigitate in transnational settings.

If science is the primary symbolic code, technical practice, and dominant form of ritual in the 20th century, our documentation of the creation of scientific knowledge in these international contexts provides a window on the construction of a world culture (Bastos, n.d.), a construction in the making. How and to what degree will dominant forms of scientific knowledge be reproduced in peripheral areas by an international research-based culture? Will Haitian, Brazilian, or Granadian constructions enter into the final scientific product?

Contemporary doubt about the legitimacy of science may leave space for peripheral and marginal contributions to scientific knowledge. There is some evidence that this has already occurred. As Indyk and Rier (1991) note, AIDS has narrowed the gap between the producers and consumers of knowledge. In some cases, the roles have been reversed. Frustrated with the pace of mainstream research, gay men gathered and distributed information on new treatments and cures, aided by new rapid-dissemination tools, such as PCs and CD-ROM and on-line data bases (Indyk & Rier, 1991, p. 2).

In addition to seeking out and sharing knowledge, people with AIDS created information themselves. As Levine commented, gay men created alternate, "folk" models of risk, provoked to do so by the ambiguities of biomedicine and epidemiology. Researchers, clinicians, and patients thus often confronted new data almost simultaneously. Grass-roots groups continue to interact with academic researchers and administrators in large government or tertiary-center programs, sending knowledge gained in the community back to the center (Indyk & Rier, 1991).

The appearance of a host of new publications read by academic researchers as well as by PWAs helped to reshape the perception of the disease from that of an automatic sentence of death to that of a chronic, treatable affliction. As these activities continue (and as lay intervention brings about change in the conduct of clinical trials), it becomes apparent that scientific knowledge is created and communicated outside scientific communities and professional journals (see Indyk & Rier, 1991). Berridge's chapter reminds us, however, that the contribution of nonprofessionals to both scientific knowledge and policymaking in Britain was true for only the earliest phase of the epidemic.

Knowledge and Practice

An activist stance in anthropology moves the anthropologist into the production and dissemination of knowledge. Schoepf's method of collaborative research in Zaire commits its findings to advance cultural survival and justice. Her data are designed for ready adoption into WHO schedules. Similarly, Carrier presents his information about Mexican and Mexican

American sexuality in a format that can be readily used in educational intervention programs. The knowledge Frankenberg acquires in Italy is applied at the site of its joint construction by epidemiologist, anthropologist, and patient. A method of inquiry based on a view of culture as process and product, not of culture as text, makes interpretive anthropology a natural companion for an anthropology of action. The theories we adopt are important because they have a demonstrable pragmatic outcome. In several cases (Abramson and Bolton), the methods of data collection are tied to the development of a science of sexual behavior.

The relationship of knowledge and practice was a topic central to all our endeavors, because knowledge gained in the midst of an epidemic is knowledge of a particularly urgent sort. Moreover, AIDS transports its investigators into marginal terrain, a journey begun prior to the epidemic. In the late 1960s, for example, historians turned away from the lives of great doctors toward a history of common people and populations: patients, minorities, and women. Research on the medical "fringe" is now said to lie at the heart of contemporary interest in history (Rogers, 1989).

AIDS research finds many anthropologists aligned also with marginal groups, although it might be said that anthropologists have a leaning toward the location of subversive knowledge. The vulnerability of these communities, however, and the fact that many investigators themselves come from the affected groups, results in a commitment to action rarely present in recent times.

As a consequence, perhaps, many of our concerns were ethical. Quimby, for example, portrayed the recognizable dilemma for investigators who acquire information that can be misused, further stigmatizing neighborhoods in need of government resources. Kane asked us to consider our responsibility to those who yielded sensitive information. Should revelations about sexual intimacies, necessary for epidemiology, be disclosed to the outside world? The power of funding agencies to influence research results was noted by Farmer, who limits such problems in his own case by working for a cooperative of Haitian peasants. Levine pulled us back to the center of the enterprise, reminding us of our obligation to "bear witness," to find a method to convey the experience of those suffering from the disease in word and image or in material objects such as the quilt. This volume is our first response to his request.

Note

1. From several telling confessions, it became apparent that few participants felt that they stayed within the boundaries of a single discipline. for example, Berridge: "I am a mongrel historian"; Abramson (psychology): "I am not a representative of my discipline"; Gagnon (sociology): "I work with problems and cross disciplinary boundaries all the time"; and Treichler: "As a linguist, I am a person without a field."

References

Arras, J. (1988). The fragile web of responsibility: AIDS and the duty to treat. *Hastings Center Report, 18*(2), 10-20.

Bastos, C. (n.d.). *AIDS and the contemporary world culture.* Unpublished manuscript.

Bond, G. C., & Vincent, J. (in press). Living on the edge: Structural adjustment in the context of AIDS. In H. Hansen & M. Twaddle (Eds.), *Uganda: Structural adjustment and change.* London: James Currey.

Clifford, J., & Marcus, G. (Eds.). (1986). *Writing culture.* Berkeley: University of California Press.

Comaroff, J. (in press). The diseased heart of Africa: Medicine, colonialism and the Black body. In S. Lindenbaum & M. Lock (Eds.), *Situated knowledge: Theory, analysis, and practice in medical anthropology.* Berkeley: University of California Press.

Crosby, A. W. (1989). *America's forgotten pandemic: The influenza of 1918.* Cambridge: Cambridge University Press.

Gilman, S. L. (1988). *Disease and representation: Images of illness from madness to AIDS.* Ithaca, NY: Cornell University Press.

Gramsci, A. (1971). Critical notes on an attempt at popular sociology. In Q. Hoare & G. Nowell Smith (Eds.), *Selections from the prison notebooks* (pp. 419-472). New York: International.

Grmek, M. D. (1990). *History of AIDS: Emergence and origin of a modern pandemic.* Princeton, NJ: Princeton University Press.

Gussow, Z. (1989). *Leprosy, racism, and public health: Social policy in chronic disease control.* Boulder, CO: Westview.

Indyk, D., & Rier, D. (1991). *Grassroots AIDS groups: 1. Marginal innovators?* Conference paper, American Sociological Association, Cincinnati, OH.

Kunitz, S. J. (1983). Speculations on the European mortality decline. *Economic History Review, 36*(3), 349-364.

Kunitz, S. J. (1987). Making a long story short: A note on men's height and mortality in England from the first through the nineteenth centuries. *Medical History, 31,* 269-280.

Kunitz, S. J. (1988). Hookworm and pellagra: Exemplary diseases in the New South. *Journal of Health and Social Behavior, 29,* 139-148.

Marcus, G., & Fischer, M. (1986). *Anthropology as cultural critique.* Chicago: University of Chicago Press.

Markowitz, G., & Rosner, D. (1989). The illusion of medical certainty: Silicosis and the politics of industrial disability, 1930-1960. *Milbank Quarterly, 67*(Suppl. 2, Pt. 1), 1-26.

Mintz, S. (1989). The sensation of moving, while standing still. *American Ethnologist, 16*(4), 786-796.

Polier, N., & Roseberry, W. (1989). "Tristes Tropes." *Economy and Society, 18*, 246-264.

Rogers, P. (1989, October 20-26). Review of R. Porter, *Health for sale: Quackery in England, 1660-1850. Times Literary Supplement,* p. 1146.

Rosenfield, P. L. (1989). *Achieving sustainability in interdisciplinary research linking health and social scientists.* Conference paper, American Anthropological Association, Washington, DC.

Sangren, S. (1988). Rhetoric and the authority of ethnography: "Postmodernism" and the social reproduction of texts. *Current Anthropology, 29*(3), 1-87.

Acknowledgments

This work is based upon the following papers presented at the 1990 Wenner-Gren Foundation Conference:

GILBERT HERDT
Introduction: Social Analysis in the Time of AIDS

PAUL R. ABRAMSON
Sex, Lies and Ethnography

VIRGINIA BERRIDGE
AIDS: History and Contemporary History

RALPH BOLTON
Mapping Terra Incognita: Sex Research for AIDS Prevention, an Urgent Agenda for the Nineties

JOSEPH M. CARRIER
Use of Ethnosexual Data on Men of Mexican Origin for HIV/AIDS Prevention Programs

PAUL FARMER
New Disorder, Old Dilemmas: AIDS and Anthropology in Haiti

RONALD FRANKENBERG
Radical approaches to risk and culture in British community epidemiology: Targets, relative risk, and "candidates" amd the impact of HIV/AIDS.

JOHN H. GAGNON
Epidemics and Researchers: AIDS and the Practice of Social Studies

335

SANDER L. GILMAN
Plague in Germany, 1939/1989: Cultural Images of Race, Space and Disease

STEPHANIE KANE and THERESA MASON
"IV Drug Users" and "Sex Partners": The Limits of Epidemiological Categories and the Ethnography of Risk

MARTIN P. LEVINE
The Implications of Constructionist Theory for Social Research on the AIDS Epidemic Among Gay Men

SHIRLEY LINDENBAUM
Knowledge and Action in the Shadow of AIDS

RICHARD G. PARKER
Sexual Diversity, Cultural Analysis, and AIDS Education in Brazil

ERNEST QUIMBY
Anthropological Witnessing for African Americans: Power, Responsibility and Choice in the Age of AIDS

BROOKE GRUNDFEST SCHOEPF
Women at Risk: Case Studies from Zaire

PAULA A. TREICHLER
AIDS, HIV, and the Cultural Construction of Reality

About the Authors

Paul R. Abramson is Professor of Psychology at the University of California, Los Angeles. He is the current editor of the *Journal of Sex Research* and has been a technical adviser for the World Health Organization's Global Program on AIDS. His publications cover a wide range of research on human sexual behavior, including methodological issues, psychophysiological assessment, cross-cultural differences, and measurement construction. His most current books include *Sarah: A Sexual Biography* (1984) and *A Case for Case Studies: An Immigrant's Journal* (1992).

Virginia Berridge is Senior Lecturer in History at the London School of Hygiene and Tropical Medicine, University of London, and Deputy Director of the AIDS Social History Programme there. Her research has focused on the social history of medicine and health policy, on media history, drug and alcohol policy, and, more recently, on the history of U.K. AIDS policies. Her publications include *Opium and the People: Opiate Use in 19th Century England* (1987), *Drugs Research and Policy in Britain: A Review of the 1980's* (1990, editor), and "Health and Medicine 1750-1950" in *The Cambridge Social History of Britain.*

Ralph Bolton, Professor of Anthropology at Pomona College in Claremont, California, teaches courses primarily in the areas of human sexuality and medical anthropology. His research has on two occasions won the Stirling Award. Author of more than 60 publications based on fieldwork in Peru, Norway, and Belgium, supported in each country by Fulbright Senior

Scholar grants, he has recently edited two volumes: *The Content of Culture: Constants and Variants* (1989) and *The AIDS Pandemic: A Global Emergency* (1989). He has served as president of the Association for Political and Legal Anthropology and is currently chair of the AIDS and Anthropology Research Group and president of the Society for Cross-Cultural Research. His major research interests include societal responses to the AIDS pandemic, the sexual behavior and cognition of gay men, and the anthropology of anthropology.

Joseph M. Carrier received his Ph.D. in social science at the University of California, Irvine. His research on the sexual behavior of Mexican and Mexican American men in northwestern Mexico and southern California has been ongoing since 1969. In recent years, in response to the AIDS epidemic, he has also done research on the relationship between male sexual behavior, HIV infection, and the spread of AIDS. He is currently a consultant to the AIDS Community Education Project, Orange County Health Care Agency, California, and is a reserve member of the Mental Health AIDS Research Review Committee, National Institute of Mental Health. Some recent publications are "Mexican Male Bisexuality" in *Journal of Homosexuality* (1985); "Sexual Behavior and Spread of AIDS in Mexico" in *Medical Anthropology* (1989); "Gay Liberation and Coming Out in Mexico" in *Gay and Lesbian Youth* (Gilbert Herdt, editor, 1989); and "Miguel: Sexual Life History of a Gay Mexican American" in *The Culture of Gay Men* (Gilbert Herdt, editor, in press).

Paul Farmer, a physician-anthropologist, is Instructor in the Department of Social Medicine, Harvard Medical School. For the past several years, he has conducted research on AIDS and tuberculosis in rural Haiti and has participated in community-based responses to these disorders. His publications include *AIDS and Accusation: Haiti and the Geography of Blame* (forthcoming).

John H. Gagnon is Professor of Sociology and Psychology at the State University of New York at Stony Brook. An internationally known authority on sex and gender, he is a member of the NRC/CBASSE Committe on AIDS Research in the Social Behavioral and Statistical Sciences. He is the author of numerous books and papers, including *Human Sexualities.*

Gilbert Herdt is Chairman of the Committee on Human Development and Professor of Human Development, Psychology, at the University of Chicago. Graduate training was completed at the University of Washington and Australian National University, from which he received the Ph.D. in anthropology for fieldwork on initiation rites and masculinity among the Sambia of Papua New Guinea. Some of his books include *Guardians of the Flutes* (1981), *Ritualized Homosexuality in Melanesia* (1984, editor), *The Sambia: Ritual and Gender in New Guinea* (1987), *Intimate Communication: Erotics and the Study of Culture* (1990, with Robert J. Stoller), and *Gay and Lesbian Youth* (1989). Recently, he completed a study of gay and lesbian youth in Chicago, including their AIDS risk awareness, and he is currently a member of the American Anthropological Association Task Force on AIDS.

Stephanie Kane is an independent scholar with a master's degree in zoology and a doctorate in social anthropology from the University of Texas at Austin. She has done ethnographic fieldwork in Panama, the United States, and Belize. Her research on the social dimension of heterosexual HIV transmission has been published in the *Journal of Sex Research* and *Social Science and Medicine*.

Martin P. Levine is Associate Professor of Sociology at Florida Atlantic University and a Research Associate at Memorial Sloan-Kettering Cancer Center. He helped found and lead both the Sociologists AIDS Network and the Lesbian and Gay Caucus and has served as an adviser to the Presidential Commission on the Human Immunodeficiency Virus Epidemic and the National Academy of Sciences' Panel on Monitoring the Social Impact of the AIDS Epidemic. He edited the anthology *Gay Men: The Sociology of Male Homosexuality* and has published widely on the sociology of AIDS, sexuality, and homosexuality. In addition, he has volunteered at the Body Positive of New York and Gay Men's Health Crisis.

Shirley Lindenbaum is Professor of Anthropology at the Graduate Center, City University of New York. Fieldwork in Papua New Guinea (on kuru) and in Bangladesh (on cholera) were a prelude to her current study of AIDS in New York City. Her publications include *Kuru Sorcery: Disease and Danger in the New Guinea Highlands* (1979) and various segments in *AIDS, Sexual Behavior and Intravenous Drug Use* (1989) and *AIDS: The Second Decade* (1990).

J. Raúl Magaña received his Ph.D. in social sciences at the University of California, Irvine, and was a Harvard Fellow at the Harvard Graduate School of Education. He has conducted research on reproductive career decisions in Mexico and sexual behavior in California. He is a member of the AMFAR

Board of Advisors for educational and behavioral programs and is a consultant for the American Red Cross, the National Institute of Drug Abuse, and the Centers for Disease Control campaign "America Responds to AIDS." He is currently vice president of BuenaCare and the research division of AltaMed Health Services Corporation and was formerly director of the AIDS Community Education Project, Orange County Health Care Agency. Some recent publications are "Sex, Drugs, and HIV: An Ethnographic Approach" in *Social Science and Medicine* (in press); "Pedagogy for Health: AIDS Education and Empowerment" in *NIDA Research Monographs* (1990); "Pediatric AIDS: American Latino Children" in an American Psychiatric Association publication (1990); and, with Joe Carrier, "Mexican and Mexican American Male Sexual Behavior and Spread of AIDS in California" in *Journal of Sex Research* (in press).

Theresa Mason received a Ph.D. in social anthropology from the University of Texas, Austin. She has engaged in policy-related research on AIDS prevention, drug use, drug treatment, and applied social analysis of inequality in a variety of settings in the United States. She is currently a staff member of Abt Associates, Inc., in Cambridge, Massachusetts.

Richard G. Parker is Professor of Anthropology in the Institute of Social Medicine at the State University of Rio de Janeiro. His extensive field research in Brazil has focused primarily on the social and cultural construction of gender and sexuality and, more recently, on the social dimensions of AIDS. His publications include *Bodies, Pleasures, and Passions: Sexual Culture in Contemporary Brazil* (1991), and, in collaboration with the Brazilian writer and AIDS activist, Herbert Daniel, *AIDS: A Terceira Epidemia* [AIDS: The Third Epidemic] (1991).

Ernest Quimby (Ph.D.) is Assistant Graduate Professor of Sociology and Criminal Justice in the Department of Sociology and Anthropology at Howard University. He has had broad experience in teaching and studying the dynamics of development in the Caribbean and the United States. His ongoing extensive research on AIDS and drug mobilization issues began when he was a National Institute on Drug Abuse Post-Doctoral Research Fellow in the late 1980s. He is also a coprincipal investigator of a new study of homeless people in Washington, D.C., who are dually diagnosed with substance abuse and mental health illnesses. His publications include "Dynamics of Black Mobilization Against AIDS in New York City" (with Samuel Friedman) in *Social Problems* (1989), "Precarious Dilemmas: Mobilizing Blacks Against AIDS" in *Problems of Drug Dependence* (1989), and "African American Perspectives on Mobilizing Organizational Responses to Drugs" (forthcoming).

Brooke Grundfest Schoepf is an economic and medical anthropologist, with a Ph.D. from Columbia University (1969). She has taught and researched development issues in Africa since 1974, when she joined the Rockefeller Foundation's field staff at the Université Nationale du Zaire in Lubumbashi. From 1985 to 1990, she led the collaborative CONNAISSIDA project, conducting participatory action research on AIDS prevention in Kinshasa. She edited *The Role of US Universities in Rural and Agricultural Development* (1981) and has published more than 50 articles in journals and collections. She was a Fellow of the Bunting Institute, Radcliffe College, in 1989-1990. A book, *Women, Sex and Power: Zaire in the AIDS Era,* is in preparation. She chairs the U.S. African Studies Association's 1990s Task Force Working Group on Gender Relations and Development.

Paula A. Treichler teaches on the faculty of the University of Illinois at Urbana-Champaign, in the College of Medicine, the Institute of Communications Research, and the Women's Studies Program. She is coauthor of *A Feminist Dictionary* (1985) and *Language, Gender, and Professional Writing: Theoretical Approaches and Guidelines for Nonsexist Usage* (1989) and coeditor of *For Alma Mater: Theory and Practice in Feminist Scholarship* (1985) and *Cultural Studies* (1992). She has published widely on feminist theory, medical discourse, and the AIDS epidemic. Her Ph.D. is in linguistics.